Text and Ritual in Early China

Text and Ritual
in Early China

Edited by
MARTIN KERN

UNIVERSITY OF WASHINGTON PRESS
Seattle and London

Publication of *Text and Ritual in Early China* was supported in part by the Commitee on Research in the Humanities and Social Sciences, Princeton University. Additional support was provided by the East Asian Studies Program, Princeton University.

© 2005 by the University of Washington Press
Design and composition by Martin Kern
Printed in the United States of America
12 11 10 09 08 07 06 05   5 4 3 2 1

University of Washington Press
P.O. Box 50096, Seattle, WA 98145
www.washington.edu/uwpress

Library of Congress Cataloging-in-Publication Data

Text and ritual in early China / Edited by Martin Kern.
     p.   cm.
Includes bibliographical references index.
ISBN 0-295-98562-3 (hardback : alk. paper)
1. Chinese classics—Criticism, Textual. 2. Religion in literature.
I. Kern, Martin.
PL2461.Z6T49 2005
895.1'09382—dc22   2005015812

The paper used in this publication is acid-free and 90 percent recycled from at least 50 percent post-consumer waste. It meets the minimum requirements of American National Standard for Information Sciences— Permanence of Paper for Printed Library Materials, ANSI Z39.48-1984.

Contents

Introduction
The Ritual Texture of Early China

Martin Kern

The study of early China has been pushed into hitherto-uncharted territory both by archaeology and by the increasing awareness that scholars of ancient China are facing issues not entirely specific to their domain but long recognized—and struggled with—in other fields, such as Classics (with all its subfields), Religion, Biblical studies, Near Eastern studies, or European medieval literature, to name just some of the obvious. The combination of newly discovered materials with newly discovered approaches holds particularly strong potential for fresh insights into the culture of early China, as the present volume will help to show. Its double focus on "text" and "ritual," and especially on their manifestations in one another, tries to capture two central aspects of early Chinese cultural history—if not indeed *the* two central aspects of it—and put each of them into a new perspective by relating it to the other. There are, of course, numerous studies devoted to either Chinese texts or various forms of Chinese ritual. What distinguishes the present volume is its consistent focus on the interaction between "text" and "ritual" by looking at the ritual structures of textual composition and textual circulation on the one hand and at the textuality of ritual practices on the other. Meanwhile, as will become clear from each of the following chapters, "text" and "ritual"—especially in their interaction—are among the topics where students of the Chinese tradition can profit greatly from the admirable work done in other fields of the humanities.

For the longer time of Chinese studies, and partly following choices by the Chinese tradition in reflecting upon itself, much of the culture of the Zhou dynasty and the early empire has been discussed in terms of intellectual history. The center of this reception is marked by a slim body of received texts from which cultural constructs like the rise of "Confucianism" and "philosophical Daoism," the struggle of the "Confucians" with the

"Mohists" and the "Legalists," or "Han philosophical syncretism" have been created. Yet it has become abundantly clear that even within the limited social group of ancient practitioners of textual knowledge, the particular circle that Western scholarship usually calls the "philosophers" was a rather small minority.[1] However, beginning in the early empire—notably through measures of canonization and censorship, and supported by the classification of writings after 26 B.C.E.[2]—it was their texts, as a carefully guarded selection, around which the imperial tradition organized itself.

Recent scholarship has moved other aspects into the foreground of what anglophone Sinology now refers to as "early China":[3] the broad spectrum of ancient religious (or, in a more general term: ritual) practice, the *Fachprosa* of various disciplines, the material culture, and, finally, reflections upon the very nature of early Chinese texts from bronze inscriptions to the ancient *Odes* (Shi 詩), from the Five Canons (Wu jing 五經; also Five Classics) to historiography, from the composition of excavated manuscripts to that of the elaborate literary works of the Han *fu* 賦. The scholarship on these topics in Chinese, Japanese, and the European languages is far too extensive to even begin listing here. Much of it has been inspired and continuously fueled by the unprecedented surge of archaeological finds over the last few decades, which have brought to light hundreds of thousands of artifacts. Among these, there are several hundred thousand pieces of oracle bone and plastron inscriptions dating from the Late Shang (ca. 1200–ca. 1045 B.C.E.) period, thousands of inscribed bronze vessels mainly from the Western (ca. 1045–771 B.C.E.) and Eastern (770–256 B.C.E.) Zhou periods, some 15,000 fragments of early–fifth-century B.C.E. covenant texts on stone and jade tablets, thousands of Warring States and early imperial administrative and economic records, and several hundred manuscripts, dating from the fourth century B.C.E. onward, that encompass the broadest variety of subjects.[4]

The Chinese tradition of the last two millennia, and with it the modern scholarly exploration of Chinese antiquity, has always privileged text—and especially those written texts guarded and preserved by the tradition—as the primary medium of early Chinese cultural self-expression and self-representation. Emerging only gradually in late Western (202 B.C.E.–9 C.E.) and then through Eastern Han (25–220 C.E.) times, the imperial discourse on the written text went so far as to use the same word (*wen* 文) for both "culture" and "writing," symbolically collapsing the former into the latter, or making the latter the emblem of the former.[5] Indeed, the amount of recent Chinese, Japanese, and Western scholarship devoted to a very limited number of newly excavated texts vastly exceeds publications on nontextual artifacts, although these artifacts by far outnumber the texts and are decidedly more stunning in what they reveal about hitherto-unimagined technological and aesthetic accomplishments of the ancient Chinese.[6] The additional fact that most of the work now done on excavated texts is limited to only a small fragment of this newly available corpus, namely, writings that can be related to the received philosophical framework, testifies even more profoundly to the enduring ability of the Chinese tradition to control so much of our imagination. Yet while the tradition has certainly exaggerated the case of the text by envisioning it as the single defining phenomenon in the formation and expression of early Chinese culture, texts of course did enjoy a strong presence in this culture. The earliest bibliography of China, compiled by Liu Xiang 劉向 (79–8 B.C.E.) and preserved in abbreviated form in the "Monograph on Arts and Letters" (Yiwen zhi 藝文志) of Ban Gu's 班固 (32–92) *Hanshu* 漢書, contained thousands of entries—and yet was far from complete, as we now realize through numerous excavated texts that find no counterpart there.

No doubt, the newly available manuscripts confirm the presence and (however undefined) prestige of texts in early China; yet at the same time, they allow us to ask some fundamental questions about the ancient textual culture that have barely been considered: What exactly is a text in early China? What are its boundaries? How do different versions of the same text relate to one another? What is textual authority, and in what does it rest? How were texts composed, preserved, transmitted, and received? How and why do texts change? What is the early canon? What are the specific functions of the written text? How should we imagine the relation and balance between oral and written textual practices? What are the social contexts of texts? Such questions do not replace or reject traditional intellectual history centered on the contents of transmitted (and now also excavated) texts, but they alert us to a host of problematic assumptions about the material and intellectual integrity of what has mostly been taken for granted as a more or less secure corpus of writings and ideas. The manuscripts confirm the early authenticity and relative reliability of certain texts known to the tradition, and they enrich the tradition by an additional body of writings that can be related to the received one. Yet at the same time, if considered with respect to the questions just mentioned, the manuscripts also embody a formidable potential to destabilize at its foundations the all-too-neat construction of early Chinese textuality and intellectual history adopted by the tradition. So far, very little work has been done to explore this problematic aspect of our new materials.

It has, however, not gone unnoticed that oracle bone and plastron inscriptions, bronze inscriptions, covenant texts, and inscribed curses, as well as a substantial number of *Fachprosa* manuscripts in areas like astrology, hemerology, medicine, divination, and exorcism, were created to be used in a broad range of ritual practices. The same is true for early transmitted poetry, from parts of the *Chu ci* 楚辭 to the Qin stele inscriptions and the Western Han state sacrificial hymns. Yet most importantly, the entire body of the Five Canons and the Six Arts (Liu yi 六藝),[7] together with the works immediately attached to them, is in one way or another defined and shaped by the ideal of ritual order (*li* 禮). The notion of *li* 禮 is at the center of three works that at different stages entered the traditional canon: *Zhou li* 周禮, *Yili* 儀禮, and *Liji* 禮記, with the *Yili* (in Han times designated *Shili* 士禮) being already canonized under the Western Han. The hymnic songs from the *Odes* as well as the speeches from the *Documents* (Shu 書) not only epitomize the ideal of ritual order but also on occasion provide elaborate descriptions of ritual acts. The *Changes* (Yi 易) originated as a divination manual, that is, a manual of ritual practice. The *Spring and Autumn Annals* (Chunqiu 春秋) have been—to my mind, persuasively—analyzed as ritual messages communicated to the ancestral spirits and thus are to some extent similar in nature and function to the early bronze inscriptions.[8] Their catechistic explanations in *Gongyang zhuan* 公羊傳 and *Guliang zhuan* 穀梁傳 are organized in a highly formalized "ritual hermeneutic,"[9] while the great historiography of the *Zuo zhuan* 左傳, which toward the end of the Western Han received imperial recognition as another "tradition" (*zhuan* 傳) of the *Spring and Autumn Annals*, is organized around the principle of appropriate ritual order.[10] Finally, the *Music* canon—whatever text or group of texts it may originally have denoted—was devoted to ritual music.

I would not wish to go so far as to suggest that Chinese writing itself emerged for ritual purposes; indeed, there is more than enough circumstantial evidence for other purposes, and probably the origin, of early Chinese writing.[11] But it remains an irreducible fact that of all its manifestations of writing during the Western Zhou period, the Chinese tradition has chosen to preserve only a very limited body of strictly ritualistic texts. Moreover, for their writings, the Late Shang and Western Zhou elites themselves restricted the use of the precious, nonperishable material of bone and bronze to texts concerned with divination and the ancestral sacrifice—a fact that speaks eloquently to the original significance of writing as ritual display.[12] Thus, while one should not exaggerate the centrality of texts from ritual contexts solely on the basis that ritual has left stronger material traces than other expressions of early Chinese civilization, we also would not wish to undervalue this civilization's extraordinary material expenses and deliberate choices of transmission to lend longevity to ritual texts.

It is therefore not inappropriate to assume that, especially in its display form, the early development of the writing system went hand in hand with its use for ritual purposes. It seems indeed more difficult to argue for a purely bureaucratic or archival nature of the oracle bone and plastron inscriptions or for a primarily documentary and historically oriented function of the bronze texts. After all, the oracle records were carved next to the divination cracks that literally embodied the response from the spirits, and the bronze texts were cast into objects used in religious ceremonies. Such writing materials were both cumbersome and costly; for practical purposes, they were inferior to other surfaces and formats, while their appearance added nothing to the informational substance of the texts. Even if one wanted to preserve certain texts in a nonperishable material like bronze, it would have been easy to design better solutions than inscribing the inside of ritual vessels or running the text in various directions around the outside ornament of bells. Yet no doubt, the bones, plastrons, and bronze paraphernalia were indexical of sheer power (in terms of control over resources, labor, technology, and the cultural tradition), and their use in religious practices documented, before anything else, successful communication with the spirits. Whatever other forms of writing on perishable materials may have existed, the production of divination records and bronze inscriptions in enormous quantities cannot be dissociated from particular ritual functions specific to their media.

The inscriptions do contain—and presumably were meant to help to preserve—historical knowledge. This fact is not diminished by their ritual environment, nor does it erase this environment. We need to avoid positing false alternatives: the question is, not whether bronze inscriptions are historical or religious documents, but how the two functions were mutually related. To the ancient Chinese, historical memory—including what may sometimes look like tedious bureaucratic accounting—was a significant dimension of political identity and expression; yet it also was shaped according to the ritual context. Nothing suggests that we should artificially isolate one from the other. As has been independently observed in both divination and bronze inscriptions, their records were highly tendentious, expressing authority and tight control over historical memory rather than offering an objective account of the bare facts: over the some 150 years of their documented history, Late Shang oracle records became overwhelmingly optimistic and affirmative, [13] while all known Western Zhou bronze inscriptions related to military matters were exclusively devoted to victories. [14] Thus, in making the best use of the historical information found in bronze inscriptions, one needs to take seriously that they were claims for authority that were expressed in religious and political rituals and were consciously formed and purposefully manipulated by these specific functions and contexts. Would bronze inscriptions, with their highly formalized structure and self-referential gestures toward the donor's merits and purposes, exist at all if not within and because of these circumstances? [15]

Apart from the immediate ritual contexts of early textual practice, there is what one may call a secondary ritual context to texts, namely, the locale where writings were finally placed. Almost all our manuscripts of *Fachprosa* and philosophical orientation have been found in the ritual space of tombs, buried alongside other funerary items. Given that the preservation of texts on perishable materials like bamboo, silk, and wood was largely a matter of accidental environmental happenstance, the archaeological record does not accurately tell us how widespread the practice of placing texts in tombs was, and how it compared to the prevalence of written texts aboveground, in storage pits, or in the ruins of abandoned buildings. All we may be able to say is that certain tombs (mostly in the southern region of the old state of Chu 楚) provided a particularly favorable and protective environment. On the other hand, such a qualified account does nothing to downplay the actual existence of texts in tombs, that is, in a specific social and representational space devoted to the rituals for the dead, and perhaps even to the rituals performed by the dead in the afterlife. [16] Funerary objects enter tombs not by accident but on somebody's purpose; and perhaps more often than not, the purpose was not the disposal but, in a curious sense, the preservation of an object, however far removed from the realm of the living.

Instead of the perspective of the text, one can also choose that of ritual to describe the nexus between the two as a symbiotic relationship: just as texts infused ritual acts with meaning, performances formalized and sacralized texts. Indeed, parallel to the privileging of text, the other prominent discourse in the representation of early Chinese culture is that of ritual. This discourse is not limited to the three early *li* canons; it pervades early Chinese texts in their quest for social, political, and cosmological order, extending from the core of the original canon to the sayings of Confucius, the discussions of Mencius, the *Canon of Filial Piety* (Xiaojing

孝經), the systematic exposition of the principles and functions of ritual in the *Xunzi* 荀子, the encyclopedic syncretism of the *Lüshi chunqiu* 呂氏春秋, and a range of early historiographical and anecdotal works. Not surprisingly, it also is reflected in a string of excavated manuscripts, most prominently in those from Guodian 郭店.[17] And even more than the textual record, it is the archaeological one that brings to light the full extent of ritual practice in early China. Even when considering that the vast majority of buried manuscripts must have perished over the span of two millennia, their presence as tomb-furnishing objects was incomparably surpassed by that of ritual paraphernalia like vessels, bells, weapons, lacquer tableware and coffins, jade implements, earthenware, textiles, and numerous other utensils produced in astounding quantities. Such artifacts certainly enjoyed pragmatic use among the living, but their often elaborate splendor betrays not only exceptional expenditure but also a conscious effort toward aesthetic representation that points beyond the mere functionality of things. It directs us to a sphere of "public display" (to use Michael Nylan's felicitous phrase developed in this volume) that was to some extent governed by sumptuary rules and intended to express the ideal of ritual order and at the same to enforce its regime. Judging from the enormous number of artifacts whose forceful aesthetic expression seems to relegate their basic functionality to a concern of secondary order, ritual was omnipresent in a profound sense texts perhaps never were.

Ritual was often interpreted by early texts, including its own textual voices of hymns, prayers, and inscriptions, yet it decidedly also encompassed large parts of the textual sphere. Deep into early imperial times, the capacious ideal of *wen* 文 was primarily one of ritual order; it could embrace texts, but it was not restricted to them.[18] The canonical text that elaborates by far most extensively on terms like *wen* and *wenzhang* 文章 ("patterned brilliance," a term that only in late Western Han times began to refer to textual compositions) is, unsurprisingly, the *Liji* (Records of ritual), in particular in its essay on music, the "Yueji" 樂記 (Records of music). The dimension of *wen* in early texts included "patterned phrasing" (*wenci* 文辭, an Eastern Zhou term known, for example, from *Zuo zhuan*), yet it also seems to have extended to a visual dimension. Already among the Late Shang oracle bone and plastron inscriptions, we find what David N. Keightley has labeled "display inscriptions," executed in large script that clearly emphasizes the visual appearance of these records; in other cases, they were carefully pigmented or created in series of identical texts.[19] Along with other Western Zhou inscriptions, the famous water basin of Scribe

Qiang 墙, dating from around 900 B.C.E., has its inscribed text arranged in two beautifully symmetric columns. The bells from the tomb of Marquis Yi of Zeng 曾侯乙 carry inscriptions inlaid with gold (as do the bronze tallies discussed by Lothar von Falkenhausen in the present volume). The calligraphy of the Guodian and Shanghai Museum bamboo manuscripts is marked by marvelous clarity and regularity. The Chu silk manuscript displays its writing in a mandala-like format, accompanied by colorful drawings, to reflect its cosmological contents. Textual *wen* cannot be reduced to such features, but it is clear that these added a dimension of expression beyond the propositional information of the words.

Altogether, it is not difficult to show how in early China the aesthetic manifestations of literature and calligraphy emerged directly out of contexts of ritual performances where verbal expression and the display of writing were part of a larger synesthetic whole.[20] The cultural artifact that can be regarded as the emblem of the process through which the discourse of (poetic) text emerged gradually out of the earlier one of music is the "Great Preface" (Daxu 大序) to the *Odes*.[21] Yet the overall shift from ritual to textual coherence[22] that in China began in early imperial times (and parallels similar developments in other ancient civilizations) is beyond the scope of the present volume.

The chapters assembled here illuminate the fusion of text and ritual in Eastern Zhou and Han China. Five of them (Falkenhausen, Gentz, Kern, Csikszentmihalyi, Brashier) were originally prepared for an international conference, "Text and Ritual in Early China," that was held at Princeton University in October 2000, and one (Schaberg) was substituted for a paper presented on that occasion. In addition, I have asked two of the conference participants (Nylan and Boltz) not to submit their—indeed excellent—conference contributions but to present us instead with two anchor chapters that provide the foundation for the other six: Nylan on cultural history, Boltz on philolological method. In what strikes me as a particularly fine example of the mutual support and collaboration that can happen among scholars who are also friends, both have graciously responded to my request by writing entirely new and original contributions. Thus, the volume begins with their two chapters, followed by six case studies on different textual genres in their ritual contexts.

In a tour de force spanning the centuries from the Warring States through the late Eastern Han, Michael Nylan opens the discussion with the call for "an increased readiness to acknowledge our confusions." As things stand right now, the field has been more successful in removing old orthodoxies than in replacing them with new ones—which, in fact, should be taken as a good sign. Archaeology has given us new facts and, perhaps even more importantly, has taught us how little we actually know to put them into perspective. Yet being aware of these limitations also allows us to raise some of the more productive questions. They may not yet, and perhaps never, give us a chance at finally "seeing the entire sky" or "fathoming the sea," but they do get us closer. Nylan identifies three aspects of the text and ritual relation for such inquiry: writing's share in ritual; historical shifts in how textual and ritual classicism is represented in the successive biographies of classical masters in Sima Qian's (ca. 145–ca. 86 B.C.E.) *Shiji* 史記, Ban Gu's *Hanshu*, and Fan Ye's 范曄 (398–445) *Hou Hanshu* 後漢書; and the presence of texts and rituals as edifying spectacles of public display. As Nylan points out, in order to understand the classical period better, "we have little choice but to study texts, ritual sites, and ritual objects together," as text and ritual shared fundamental aspects of their raison d'être: they were "always connected with power, with the past, and with memory," and at every social level "operated in tandem to enhance authority." Furthermore, they both were seen as decreed by some higher authority; they were used in the same ceremonies; they were composite and formulaic in a way that generated cultural stability and fostered a "classical style"; they were not plain images of reality but highly compressed and intensified representations; they were constrained by a limited code of expression; their creation required expert techniques; and their possession was controlled in the service of political and spiritual force.

In her account of the biographies of classical masters, Nylan discusses in detail the changing attitudes and ideals they embodied over time. Her close comparison of the three major sources reveals how over the course of half a millennium, the image of the Ru 儒 scholars developed from exemplary teachers and ritual specialists to masters of written works and their written exegesis. While "the *Shiji* states unequivocally that the best classical masters did not write down their teachings, that they had no use for fine phrasing, and that they were in a few cases not all that adept at explicating written texts, as opposed to transmitting a powerful, suasive example," the fifth-century *Hou Hanshu* "regularly lists the writings composed by its biographical subjects, casting their compositions as a form of patrimony attached at the ends of the biographies proper." It was this new self-representation of the tradition that retrospectively exaggerated the social status of Han canonical learning just as it exaggerated the purported collapse of learning under the Qin and its all the more glorious resurrection under the Han.

In the final section of chapter 1, Nylan offers a strikingly new and original perspective on the interplay of text and ritual by locating both at the core of a system of public display. This system was drawn up in Warring States texts like *Xunzi*, after which it granted relative social stability to the early empire before finally, at the end of the Eastern Han, collapsing under its own weight. The culture of public display was one where gratification and obligation were shared and reciprocated, reinforcing authority, solidarity, and a stable hierarchy of roles. It embraced the human desire for pleasure and social participation by distributing—in manifestly staggering amounts—goods and rewards according to a ritual norm of sumptuary rules, and it sustained the authority of an emperor who governed the world "as the embodiment of all the collectivities operating within the public display culture" by representing the ideal of rulership through codes of text and ritual, the emblems of legitimate pleasure and good order.

In chapter 2, through a meticulous analysis of passages from both excavated and transmitted texts, William G. Boltz raises the fundamental questions of textual authorship, textual boundaries, and modes of textual composition in early China. In a first step, he shows how excavated manuscripts tend to differ from their transmitted counterparts not necessarily in their contents and wording but in their internal textual order. The evidence is compelling that early texts were composed of small "building blocks"—discrete, self-contained textual units—that were arranged in wildly different ways, albeit sometimes maintaining certain clusters. As a consequence, we are now compelled to understand that, in their particular form, the received versions of the classical corpus are likely to represent not so much the integrity of a single authorial composition but the final result of editorial interpretation and rearrangement. The texts we have are fundamentally "composite" in nature, and we are no longer in the position to routinely equate any received text with a particular authorial hand (not to mention the biographical circumstances of an author, which often, in a perfectly circular fashion, have been reconstructed only from the text identified with the person). As Boltz notes, "all of this suggests that lengthy, literary or essay-like texts, authored by a single writer, in the way we typically think of a text in the modern world, do not reflect the norm for early China but were, at best, the exception." Boltz's observation tallies nicely with Nylan's conclusion that in pre-imperial China textual lineages were much less coherent than is assumed in the usual constructs of intellectual history; a received text, especially one that bears the name of a particular "master," is to be recognized as the final product of an editorial

—and very likely also doctrinal—process that easily spanned several generations not merely of disciples but also of the type of editor we find in the figure of Liu Xiang. In Boltz's words, "particular doctrines, philosophies, precepts, belief systems, and so forth that we have come to associate with specific texts we now must recognize might only be properly associated with the *transmitted, received* versions of those texts, and not necessarily with manuscripts that include portions, even large portions, of those same texts."[23]

The significance of this finding extends beyond a new understanding of the composite *structure* of virtually all our texts, excavated and transmitted. As Boltz points out, this structure is the immediate result of a particular mode of composition—one that was not confined to a single moment but one that shows texts in "a performative or *practicum* kind of role." In a very literal sense, the ancient texts were alive; they were not simply handed down from master to disciple but existed within "a framework for maintaining social norms for the performance of ceremonial and religious rites, funeral and ancestral worship practices and customs," where a text "was more than a passive and static record." The continuous recomposing of the text, which could involve both the rearrangement of existing "building blocks" and the introduction of additional material, was as much an act of authorship as any original composition; moreover, "the reordering and revising may easily have been an orally accomplished process, finding its written form only after the fact, if at all." In short, the composition of the ancient texts was not a closed act but one that took shape through acts of intellectual exchange and textual performance (teaching, memorization): "The broader we envision this circulation to have been, the likelier it was to have been oral and associated with practices, rather than written and reflective of scholasticism." Such a conclusion, one might wish to add, seems to apply to the traditional canon, whose presence is documented across vast geographical regions and long periods of time, at least as forcefully as to any other, more locally confined, text.

In chapter 3, in his account of five bronze tallies from Chu that are dated to 323 B.C.E. and probably belonged to a larger set, Lothar von Falkenhausen examines written documents of a seemingly utterly profane function: a group of inscribed texts used to exempt merchants from being taxed when transporting goods along their trading routes. These documents, which Falkenhausen presents in a careful, fully annotated translation, are first of all important witnesses of late–fourth/early–third-century B.C.E. economic history—yet they are also far more than just that. "Tokens of official authority" intended for display, their outer appearance alone betrays a significance that reaches far beyond the practical use of a document created for plain economic purposes. Their extremely careful calligraphy, cast in bronze (the religiously charged and most prestigious of materials), their golden inlay, and their balanced visual distribution along a fixed number of vertical columns all must have intensified their efficacy by marking the tallies as icons of ritual kingship and indeed religious authority. Likewise, their self-referential naming as "bronze tallies" (*jinjie* 金節), their ritualistic, restricted code of expression, their tripartite textual structure, their reference to the Chu king's calendar and his capital, and the use of the quasi-religious term *wangming* 王命 ("kingly decree") all were explicit references to the hallowed ritual order exemplified in Zhou bronze inscriptions and even Late Shang divination records. In both their linguistic and their aesthetic appearance, the tallies were securely placed into the larger ritual system that governed the exchange with the spirits as well as the distribution of goods as far as the king's authority could be felt (especially including territories only recently acquired). As inscribed bronze vessels were used in ancestral sacrifices to extend the ruler's communication to the realm of the ancestors, the bronze tallies—sharing the aesthetics of the religious paraphernalia— advanced his reach to the outer geography of his realm. Moreover, it is clear that both the ancestral sacrifice and the trade sanctified by the king's authority were part of the same system of *do ut des*, or—in Michael Nylan's concept of public display—the controlled exchange not merely of goods but of obligations, rewards, and the gratification of pleasures. In more than one sense, and again on both the linguistic and the material level, the tallies embodied and exposed a profoundly cosmological ideal of kingship. Needless to say, economic trade was *also*, and in pragmatic terms perhaps primarily, a thoroughly mundane activity. Yet as Falkenhausen's study lucidly shows, in order to understand even the pragmatic nature of economic transactions correctly, one must not reduce the function of the tallies to purely economic terms or ignore their rich display of ritual capital and "awesome, mana-like force." The question is simple: why such expensive display (another economic aspect of the tallies) of ritual prerogative if some plain document, perhaps written on bamboo, would have sufficed? Why inlays of gold in bronze to authorize a tax exemption?

In chapter 4, Joachim Gentz unveils how the text of the *Gongyang zhuan*, in its deep structure, is constructed according to the same principles that guide nontextual ritual practice. Texts themselves were perceived as ritual performances; in the same way as ritual functions as the "outer formal expression of an invisible ideal order" (and also expresses the realization of that order), the *Gongyang zhuan* operates on the assumption that the text of the *Chunqiu* is based on a strict system of formal rules of how to mimetically represent historical events. In the logic of the *Gongyang zhuan*, wherever Confucius (the purported author of the *Chunqiu*) encountered historical events that deviated from the ritual standards, his historiography was designed to expose them through subtle deviation in linguistic expression. Thus, the *Gongyang zhuan*'s exegetic strategy makes explicit Confucius's ideal of linguistic form together with his choices of deviation from that ideal, serving as a mirror both to the ideal order of history and to the cases where events fail to match it. It shows the *Chunqiu* as a text that through its linguistic choices performs the ideal ritual order even where it criticizes the lack of it in historical reality—indeed, it represents the resurrection of ritual in historiography vis-à-vis its collapse in history.[24] According to the *Gongyang zhuan*, Confucius's composition of the *Chunqiu* "is a ritually correct behavior in its own right because it produces an adequate formal correspondence to every historical situation"; the text, as it "attempts to express an ideal order in which everything has its adequate position and expression, . . . becomes the expression and the textual remains of a ritual act undertaken by Confucius."

If Falkenhausen's study is original and important for bringing economic documents into the realm of ritual, Gentz's is so for doing the same with historiographical writing, another sphere of early textuality whose pervasive ritual framework has only recently begun to become visible. What makes Gentz's structural reading particularly compelling is the fact that it reveals that the *Gongyang zhuan*'s formal reading strategy of the *Chunqiu* is perfectly parallel to other ritual practices. Specifically, the interpretation of linguistic signs as deviations from an implied ideal order is precisely what early astrologers did when "reading" the natural world and interpreting deviations from the natural course as signs of imminent disaster. Thus, from the *Gongyang zhuan* perspective we find that Confucius "expresses himself just as Heaven does in the cosmos." In other words, the exegetical strategy manifest in the *Gongyang zhuan* may well have originated from the principles of astrology, a suggestion that becomes even more attractive when we consider (as Gentz does) that in institutional terms, the office of the historian and that of the astrologer—both *shi* 史—were one and the same.

In chapter 5, I offer a comprehensive account of the appearance of *Odes* fragments and quotations in the six excavated manuscripts from late Warring States and early Western Han times that include substantial traces of the ancient anthology of songs.[25] Here, the systematic examination of textual variants—which make up 30–40 % of the characters, compared among the manuscripts as well as to the received recension of the *Mao Shi* 毛詩—leads to suggestions concerning the early status of the *Odes* as written versus orally circulating texts as well as to considerations on the performative aspects of the *Odes* in Eastern Zhou and early imperial times. Like Michael Nylan, I hold that the Qin proscription of texts has been much exaggerated and that, in fact, the manuscripts provide clear evidence that the written text of the *Odes* was just "as unstable before the bibliocaust as it was immediately thereafter." In fact, it appears that no two of the six manuscripts under discussion that contain lines from the *Odes* adhere to a common written tradition of these texts, that is, a textual lineage based on the copying and recopying from one manuscript to the next. This conclusion gains strength from the fact that in their overwhelming majority, the textual variants in excavated *Odes* lines are merely graphic, that is, representing the same sound (and word) with a different—graphically unrelated—character. Such an overall situation cannot be explained through a model of copying an existing written text into a new one; instead, it is plain evidence of the interference of oral transmission, where written versions were produced independently from one another, that is, according to a text that was memorized by or recited to a scribe. In the case of the early manuscripts, neither the *Odes* texts proper nor the texts in which their quotations are embedded—for example, the two "Wu xing" 五行 (Five conducts) manuscripts and the two "Zi yi" 緇衣 (Black robes) manuscripts and their counterparts in the received *Liji*—are graphically related in the way that a process of direct copying would manifest itself.

While traditional scholarship has imagined the relatively minor traces of orthographic differences between the four known Western Han exegetical lineages of the *Odes* as an expression of a period of oral transmission following the Qin proscription, I argue that only the manuscripts show us the true extent to which probably *all* early written versions of the *Odes* differed. Moreover, the evidence from the manuscripts suggests that the entire tradition, wherever it includes citations from the *Odes*, is retrospectively normalized to adhere with very little variation to the Mao recension that became dominant only from late Eastern Han times onward. Such observations are in accord with the nature of the early teaching lineages: while written texts certainly played a role in some auxiliary sense, the omnipresence of graphic variants must have rendered the surface of the written texts largely opaque to any uninitiated reader; to correctly identify the words behind the graphs, one already had to know the text. In other words, written texts were very unlikely to have traveled on their own or to have been studied in quiet isolation. Instead, written versions of traditional texts must have been transmitted in a larger framework of oral teaching and performance. The authoritative text was not any idiosyncratic graphic representation; it was, in a double sense, the *mastered* text, "internalized through memorization and externalized in performance," through which the textual heritage maintained its stability. Thus, "for the late pre-imperial and early imperial period, we witness the double phenomenon of a canonical text that is as stable in its wording as it is unstable in its writing."

In chapter 6, on indirect remonstrance, David Schaberg brings to our attention an early textual genre that is presented as fundamentally theatrical and ritualized in nature. However fictional and anachronistic the early imperial anecdotes surrounding indirect remonstrance may be, as they appear in historiography and in separate anecdote collections, they testify to a dimension of Han court culture that the tradition knows about only in subdued terms: a performative practice of verbal art that continuously oscillated between entertainment and moral admonition. None of our sources tells us how to imagine their verbal presentations, but there is little doubt about the fact that moral admonition as well as court panegyrics were ostentatiously staged. [26] This element is still preserved in the later genre designation of *shelun* 設論—variously translated as "hypothetical discourse" or "staged debate"—that according to the tradition begins with Dongfang Shuo's "Responding to a Guest's Objections" (Da ke nan 答客難), in which Dongfang "used [his disquisition] as an illustration of how he consoled himself about his low position." [27] As Schaberg notes, the later tradition's "association of acting with high-minded critique, by which true theatrical representation was linked to the early historiographical tradition, was an important step in the conceptual preparation for Chinese theater and helped to bolster the status of entertainers in later ages."

What is more, the remonstrant "poses a riddle, sings an obscure song, or wordlessly—as with a sigh or a gesture—defies expectations of court behavior" and thus "performs an act that in one way or another engages the ruler in a game of decoding." To employ Gentz's analysis of the *Gongyang zhuan* exegetical strategy, the remonstrant presents a deviation from the implied ritual code which serves as a mirror to the ruler's own failures. The jester's performance is a ritual act in two senses: it represents a perfect match (just as Confucius did according to the *Gongyang* reading of the *Chunqiu*) of the historical situation, and by doing so, it exerts a transformative force upon the addressee, who then changes his behavior back to the ritual standards. In Schaberg's words, "through an uplifting anamnesis, the king shakes off his wooziness and dissolution and becomes mindful again of propriety." Thus, to fully appreciate the nature and workings of indirect remonstration, as when "the jester uses all the accoutrements of theater to remind the king of his debts," we must take its engaging performative—and entertaining—nature seriously. Finally, Schaberg points to another important detail in the early imperial records of indirect remonstrance: its reliance not only on coded speech and behavior but also on song, that is, a mode of patterned speech that formally intensifies the crucial message. While anecdotes appear in markedly different versions, their poetic core is usually preserved in all of them. Very likely, the performative nature of song helped to carry the anecdote through its various early channels of oral (and even performative?) transmission; yet it also served the historiographic function of marking the importance of the moment.[28]

In his exploration of the legendary "four faces" of the Yellow Emperor in chapter 7, Mark Csikszentmihalyi suggests that the Mawangdui 馬王堆 silk text "Liming" 立命 (Establishing the mandate)—part of the so-called *Sixteen Classics* (Shiliu jing 十六經) preceding version B of the Mawang-dui *Laozi* on the same sheet of silk—was an inscription-style text "composed to evoke a vessel that literally depicted the Yellow Emperor as having four faces." According to late Warring States and Qin–Han sources, various inscribed objects of daily life were created to admonish their owners, to remind them of their duties, or to urge them to take warning. Inscribed figurines were believed to possess magical, especially apotropaic, power. The *Hanshu* "Monograph on Arts and Letters" notes a number of didactic texts that are titled "inscriptions" (i.e., texts purportedly inscribed on actual objects), including a set of "inscriptions" associated with the Yellow Emperor. As Csikszentmihalyi points out, the title "inscription" may often have been rhetorical rather than real. Not every didactic "inscription" mentioned in the *Hanshu* or preserved in transmitted sources was originally inscribed; but as literary texts, they could have mimicked the established compositional patterns of actual inscriptions.

Discussing such "literary inscriptions" that appear in different Han sources, Csikszentmihaly shows how one of them—the "Bronze Man Inscription" (Jinren ming 金人銘) included in Liu Xiang's *Shuiyuan* 説苑 (or *Shuoyuan*) and purportedly originally inscribed on a bronze figurine—is connected to Han perceptions of the Yellow Emperor and may well have been part of the *Yellow Emperor Inscriptions*, which we otherwise know only by title from the *Hanshu*. Moreover, Csikszentmihalyi argues, the silk text "Liming," which speaks in the voice of the Yellow Emperor, appears to represent just such an inscriptional composition originally placed on a four-faced image of his, or imagined as such. While the literary tradition has preserved the notion of a "four-faced" Yellow Emperor, since Han times this tradition has always interpreted it in mere symbolic terms as referring to the emperor's four ministers sent out to govern the four directions. Yet as Csikszentmihalyi points out, parts of the "Liming" adhere closely to literary conventions (like the intense use of first-person pronouns) characteristic of inscribed admonitions (like the "Bronze Man Inscription") as we know them from literary sources. Specifically, the contents of the "Liming"—and its likely underlying literary or actual inscription—can be related to a set of cosmological images of the four directions that in Han times was both frequently depicted and associated with the Yellow Emperor. Thus, the manuscript allows us to tentatively restore the original ritual medium and context of part of the "Liming" silk text and to reimagine the Yellow Emperor's four faces not only symbolically but in terms of a tangible ritual object bearing specific cosmological imagery. Even if taken as a literary inscription, the respective parts of the "Liming," like other texts of the genre, "lay claim to some aspect of the formal connection to inscriptions on ritual objects found in culturally significant sites (e.g., in the lineage temples from the Zhou period), and in this sense they may be read as attempts to borrow the authority of the ancient."

The composite nature of the "Liming," with a literary or actual inscription likely involved, allows Csikszentmihalyi to extend his analysis to the—in the Mawangdui silk manuscript physically adjacent— *Laozi*. It appears that the *Laozi*, another composite text (as discussed in chapter 2), contains passages reminiscent of the language of the "Bronze Man Inscription." It is thus possible that parts of the *Laozi* "once were connected to an authorizing medium" just like the passages from literary inscriptions, "with which they share some formal similarities." In other words, certain passages from the *Laozi* may well have originated in specific ritual objects and religious contexts, or at least in the mental conception of such objects and contexts, before becoming radically decontextualized, and recontextualized, in the form that is now familiar to us.

Concluding the present volume, K. E. Brashier's chapter on stele inscriptions describes the Eastern Han memorial culture, the core of which was defined by the memorization and recitation of texts. This fact is repeatedly stated in contemporaneous sources; even stele inscriptions themselves exhort their readers to memorize and recite the inscribed words. Thus, inscriptions include specific mnemonic devices: set formulae and clichés; exaggeration; the construction of "memory places" where facts and names are organized around well-known models; and versification, ranging "from rhymed medical knowledge . . . to rhymed primers that sorted out general knowledge." As Brashier quotes from Rosalind Thomas, whatever had to be remembered "would be better remembered if it was in verse." The model text of Han memorial culture—and indeed of Chinese cultural memory in general—is the anthology of the *Odes*, on which, accordingly, numerous Eastern Han stele inscriptions draw directly. As Brashier shows, not only do the inscriptions present themselves as a new version of the ancient *Odes*, but their authors also identify themselves as followers of those—very few—named figures that are traditionally seen behind the composition of certain *Odes*. The inscription authors, when imitating those of the *Odes*, thus "had a surprisingly specific image of the textual role they were reenacting." Their texts remembered the person praised in the inscription and at the same time also the earlier model of remembering; and in this vein, they ultimately commended themselves to the memory of later generations of readers and authors of commemorative texts (a topos of self-reference that is explicitly expressed in the *Liji* account concerning the inscription of tripods).[29]

The stele inscriptions' relation to the ancient *Odes*, however, goes much beyond citing their texts or referring to their purported authors. Here, Brashier is able to overturn several traditional assumptions at once: first, although carved into stone, stele inscriptions were meant to be memorized and recited, that is, ritually enacted in oral performance (one inscription even carries an explicit reference to the musical accompaniment of its own text). Second, there is compelling evidence that the rhymed portion at the end of a stele inscription was not some kind of decorative appendix to the historical-biographical record but was itself the core of the inscription, embodying the essence of what was to be remembered in poetic—that is, ritualized—form. And third, tetrasyllabic stele inscriptions were composed by the major scholars and writers of the time and considered monuments of public display—a fact that offers quite a different picture of Eastern Han literary history than does the traditional emphasis on anonymous ballads or pentasyllabic poetry.

Stone inscriptions, as recognized already by Eastern Han times, are the late descendants of bronze inscriptions. Here, Brashier points to a fascinating detail about the stelae: a hole, "regularly positioned roughly one and a half meters above the base," that remained an enigma to earlier scholars. Marshaling an array of sources, Brashier suggests that these holes were used to suspend food offerings to the ancestors—thus making the stelae even more akin in nature to the earlier bronze vessels. Astoundingly, the hole was sometimes added to an already-inscribed stele, destroying parts of its text and suggesting that the ritual performance even overrode the written word (which, ideally, was memorized anyway). Thus, although the inscribed text was itself entirely ritualized, it was not the entire ritual.

Stele inscriptions are monuments of both closure and continuous memory—and the ideal texts to end a volume on "text and ritual." Its introduction shall conclude with a note, less duty than pleasure, of profound gratitude: to the participants of the original conference for their excellent papers and discussions; to the contributors to this volume for their responsiveness, patience, and fine essays; to the Chiang Ching-kuo Foundation for International Scholarly Exchange as the main sponsor of the conference; to Princeton University's East Asian Studies Program and its director, Professor Martin C. Collcutt, for additional support toward both the conference and the preparation of the present volume; to the Princeton University Commitee on Research in the Humanities and Social Sciences for a substantial publication subsidy; to Richard J. Chafey, Manager of Princeton's East Asian Studies Program, and Michael A. Reeve, now Publications Manager for the *Cambridge History of China* Project at Princeton, for their competent and graceful assistance in organizing and helping to manage the conference; to Alexei K. Ditter, Brigitta A. Lee, and Esther Sunkyung Park, all Ph.D. candidates in the university's Department of East Asian Studies, for their meticulous editorial help with the volume; and to the University of Washington Press editors Pamela J. Bruton, Lorri Hagman, Mary C. Ribesky, and Marilyn Trueblood for their exceptionally timely and attentive work in getting the text to our readers!

NOTES

1. Lewis, *Writing and Authority in Early China*, 96. "Philosophers" is the common—and misleading—translation of *zhuzi* 諸子, which refers to a range of intellectual lineages that organized their wisdom retrospectively around the name and selected words of a master. Lewis, who calls the *zhuzi* "schoolmen," has argued (58–59) that the actual "master" (*zi* 子) of such a lineage was not the author of its texts, but on the contrary, his particular stature and image were largely created through these texts that accumulated over generations of

disciples. One may note that from this perspective, textual transmission appears much akin to ancestor worship, ubiquitous in early China, where the descendants turned their forebear into a model (formally designated by a posthumous temple name, *shi* 諡), perpetuated that model's accomplishments, and derived from it their own authority and name (*ming* 名).

2. In 26 B.C.E. Emperor Cheng 成 (r. 33–7 B.C.E.) issued an edict to collect the writings from all over the empire and had Liu Xiang organize them in the catalogue of the imperial library; see *Hanshu* 10.310 and 30.1701.

3. "Early China" is also the name of the journal of record for this field, founded in 1976. "Early China" is a vague and somewhat problematic term, as it is used to denote not only the ancient Chinese tradition but also all civilizational remnants from the earliest times, as long as they have been found within the geographical boundaries of the modern Chinese state. In the present volume, the term is used to refer to the Chinese tradition only, and specifically to the periods of the Warring States and the Qin and Han empires.

4. There are no hard figures for any of these groups of texts, partly because new materials continue to be found. The account given in Shaughnessy, *New Sources of Early Chinese History*, published in 1997, is already dated; see Giele, "Early Chinese Manuscripts." A valuable survey of excavated manuscripts, though also in need of further updates, is Giele, *Database of Early Chinese Manuscripts*.

5. It is, however, anachronistic to project such identity into pre-imperial times; see Kern, "Ritual, Text, and the Formation of the Canon."

6. To illustrate this point, one only needs to compare the incredible artifacts unearthed in 1977 from the mid–fifth-century B.C.E. tomb of Marquis Yi of Zeng 曾侯乙, which number more than 15,000, with the handful of short manuscripts from ca. 300 B.C.E. discovered in Guodian 郭店 tomb 1 in 1993. While some of the earlier artifacts—especially the magnificent set of chime bells—have received due scholarly attention, only the later manuscripts, published in 1998, have by now generated more than 3,000 publications.

7. In Han times, an unknown *Canon of Music* (Yue 樂) was already lost (if it had ever existed as a discrete, self-contained text), leaving the core of five textual canons to be sponsored by the imperial state: the *Yi*, the *Shi*, the *Shu*, the *Li* 禮 (Ritual), and the *Chunqiu* 春秋. The term *Wu jing* itself may be a late Western Han coinage, as argued by Fukui, "Rikukei; rikugei to gokei," "Shin Kan jidai ni okeru hakase seido no tenkai," and "Tō Chūjo no taisaku no kisoteki kenkyū." The manuscripts from Guodian show that by 300 B.C.E. the earlier canon of the Six Arts was already in place. Strips 24–25 of the "Liu de" 六德 manuscript mention all six terms together, while strips 15–16 of the "Xing zi ming chu" 性自命出 manuscript list the *Shi*, *Shu*, *Li*, and *Yue*, and strips 36–41 of the first "Yu cong" 語叢 manuscript discuss the *Yi*, *Shi*, and *Chunqiu*; see Jingmen shi bowuguan, *Guodian Chu mu zhujian*, 179, 188, 194–195.

8. Pines, "Intellectual Change in the Chunqiu Period," 80–86; see also Pines, *Foundations of Confucian Thought*, 17–18, 250 nn. 8–9, for further references.

9. Gentz, *Das Gongyang zhuan*; see also chapter 4 in the present volume.

10. Lewis, *Writing and Authority in Early China*, 132–139; and esp.

Schaberg, *A Patterned Past.*

11. See Bagley, "Anyang Writing and the Origin of the Chinese Writing System."

12. See Kern, "The Performance of Writing in Western Zhou China."

13. Keightley, *Sources of Shang History*, 42–44, 117–119.

14. Shaughnessy, *Sources of Western Zhou History*, 176–177.

15. See Falkenhausen, "Issues in Western Zhou Studies," 145–171; Kern, *The Stele Inscriptions of Ch'in Shih huang*, 140–154; Kern, "*Shi jing* Songs as Performance Texts," 58–66.

16. For this hypothesis, see Hayashi, "Concerning the Inscription 'May Sons and Grandsons Eternally Use This [Vessel].'"

17. The ritual discourse also appears prominently in the corpus of bamboo manuscripts now in the possession of the Shanghai Museum. These texts may or may not come from a site closely related to that of Guodian; see Ma Chengyuan, *Shanghai bowuguan cang Zhanguo Chu zhushu (yi)*, 2.

18. Kern, "Ritual, Text, and the Formation of the Canon"; Nylan, "Calligraphy, the Sacred Text and Test of Culture."

19. For these and other aspects of the display character of some of the Shang divination records, see Keightley, *Sources of Shang History*, 46, 54, 56, 76–77, 83–84, 89.

20. Falkenhausen, "Ritual Music in Bronze Age China," 693; Kern, "*Shi jing* Songs as Performance Texts."

21. Van Zoeren, *Poetry and Personality*, 17–115; Owen, *Readings in Chinese Literary Thought*, 37–56.

22. This phrase is borrowed from Assmann, *Das kulturelle Gedächtnis*, 87–89.

23. This matches precisely the observation originally made by Xing Wen, "Chu jian 'Wu xing' shi lun," and also found in Pang, *Zhu bo "Wu xing" pian jiaozhu ji yanjiu*, 92, that the different internal order of the two "Wu xing" manuscripts from Guodian and Mawangdui 馬王堆 reflects different philosophical arguments.

24. In this as well as in other points, Gentz's analysis elegantly dovetails with the one developed by Schaberg in *A Patterned Past* for early narrative historiography (most notably in *Zuo zhuan*).

25. My study includes the manuscripts published in the first volume (2001) of the Shanghai Museum corpus but not those in subsequent volumes. The small number of *Odes* quotations there does not affect the conclusions reached in chapter 5.

26. For an extensive discussion, see Kern, "Western Han Aesthetics and the Genesis of the *Fu*."

27. *Hanshu* 65.2864.

28. See Schaberg, "Song and the Historical Imagination in Early China"; Kern, "The Poetry of Han Historiography."

29. See *Liji zhengyi* 49.378c–379a.

Text and Ritual
in Early China

Chapter 1

Toward an Archaeology of Writing
Text, Ritual, and the Culture of Public Display in the Classical Period (475 B.C.E.–220 C.E.)

Michael Nylan

Over the last fifty years, archaeological evidence, poststructuralist theories, and comparative studies have fairly well battered the traditional accounts of antiquity in China that posited from time immemorial a slow but steady evolution toward a single, coherent, and recognizably "Chinese" culture. The excavations have no doubt yielded the merest fraction of the materials originally available, only a small percentage of finds have been reported, and the large proportion of items acquired through salvage archaeology or looting continues to frustrate efforts in systematic sorting.[1] Nonetheless, the finds, in supplying the inadvertently durable alongside the intentionally monumental, represent previously unimaginable riches to modern researchers. With respect to writing, the sheer magnitude of the finds is stunning, as can be seen from the estimates given for two sites: the Western Han dynasty Weiyang Palace 未央宮 complex, which produced 57,000 inscribed ox-bone tags for weapons and 115 wooden strips citing medical recipes or brief histories, and the Han frontier outpost of Juyan 居延 (present-day Inner Mongolia), where some 32,000 bamboo strips and wooden tablets dating from 119 B.C.E. to 167 C.E. have been recovered.[2]

If the received texts largely consist of canons, polemics, poems, and histories in the service of the reigning political ideologies, the newly discovered writings have just as often provided much-needed evidence about other aspects of classical life, since they include (1) detailed inscriptions of quality control and accounting produced during the course of the state administration (e.g., those from Yinwan 尹灣, Juyan, and Dunhuang 敦煌) and others compiled as inventories of tomb furnishings (*qiance* 遣冊); (2) sections of the penal codes attesting to the same preoccupations with precise accountability and with finely graded rank; (3) inscriptions, seals, labels, and tallies naming objects for inventory or ritual purposes and assigning value or authority to status items; (4) letters, essays, and school exercises; (5) calendars, historical annals, and almanacs listing auspicious and inauspicious days; (6) maps and charts with accompanying text (e.g., the Chu 楚 silk manuscript; the "Daoyin tu" 導引圖 from Mawangdui 馬王堆); and (7) medical texts. Scholars now confront a vast range of new ritual objects, among them lacquered coffins; serving pieces for sacrifices and banquets; pottery models of watchtowers, fishponds, pigsties, and manors; *liubo* 六博 game boards; *shi* 式 divination boards; pictorial bricks and stones; and funeral silks, to name but a few. A single magnificent tomb may yield many thousands of grave goods, as with the three thousand items found in the Shanxi Taiyuan 太原 tomb (of a high-ranking Jin official?) or the fifteen thousand buried with Marquis Yi of Zeng 曾侯乙 (Zeng Hou Yi). [3] Interpreting this wealth of new material, which has been subject to assorted ethnic and regional claims and shaped by obvious biases in the collection and analysis of materials, [4] has so complicated our current notions of text and ritual in the classical world that many in the field seem ready to jettison the old commonplaces, even if they remain unsure how to proceed. Naturally enough, those dissatisfied with the major propositions that once informed scholarly opinion on the classical period began by formulating a series of negative hypotheses, among them the following:

• No "China" as such existed in the ancient world. Cultural unity was only gradually constructed over long centuries by successive classicisms proposed by theorists ranging from Sima Qian 司馬遷 (ca. 145–ca. 86 B.C.E.), Liu Xiang 劉向 (79–8 B.C.E.), and Yang Xiong 揚雄 (53 B.C.E.–18 C.E.) in the Han to modern masters like Pi Xirui 皮錫瑞 (1850–1908), Qian Mu 錢穆 (1895–1990), and Yü Ying-shih 余英時 (b. 1930). [5]

• No philosophical "schools" or "academies" in the modern sense existed in the classical period, despite earlier talk of the "Confucian school," for instance, or the "Jixia Academy." [6]

• No imperial capital ever served as the sole source of culture within the huge area defined today by the borders of the People's Republic of China; continual exchanges of people, things, and ideas took place between core and periphery and official and unofficial. [7]

• The Weberian model of "rational" rule cannot account for all the activities of the classical courts and their bureaucracies, however organized in certain respects, [8] and no very sharp distinction separated civil and military bureaucrats, in contrast to the later dynasties. [9]

• The famous "unification of script" in Qin 秦 times did not obliterate the new empire's mosaic of distinct local languages, styles, and customs from the era prior to unification, though their significance was recast through a series of new imperial inventions, including cosmographies and dialect dictionaries.[10]

• Classical Chinese in its various forms, spoken and written, is really no better or worse than more inflected languages in its capacities to specify, abstract, or ambiguate concepts.[11]

• The shared outlooks and practices that bound members of the elite to those less privileged are no less important a subject of study than the divisions between "high" literate culture and the vulgar.

• The dividing line between science and superstition does not exist.[12]

• Cultivation was far less "interior" than hitherto thought, with a greater emphasis on performance and embodiment, so the classicists of yore do not really represent the forerunners of modern Chinese intellectuals.[13]

• Women were not uniquely oppressed in China; denied entrance into most ranks of the regular bureaucracy, women nonetheless participated in a range of other productive activities, including moneymaking, reading, writing, and ritual performance, in which activities they appear to have been judged according to much the same standards as contemporary males.[14]

That it has often proven extremely difficult to move beyond such deconstruction to generate positive statements about the classical world is perhaps not surprising. Unfortunately, a narrower focus on smaller slices of the past will not necessarily pave the way for broader insights, if the course of Chu 楚 studies is any indication. Chu seems a logical place to begin discussions of text and ritual, since (a) the majority of excavated texts antedating the mid–Han period come from areas under the sway of the Chu state prior to its conquest by Qin in 223 B.C.E., with Chu finds far exceeding those from Shaanxi and Henan, the locations of the Western Zhou, Qin, and Han capitals;[15] and (b) Chu sites have also given us some of the most spectacular ritual implements, including the Zeng Hou Yi bell set and lacquered coffins. Thus, the excavated materials directly challenge long-standing traditions that ascribe the preservation of ancient texts and rituals mainly, if not exclusively, to the Central States region, especially Qi 齊, Lu 魯, and Song 宋 (present-day Shandong), treating Chu and Qin as "barbarian states" incapable of making major contributions to Central States civilization. For a long time, the field of Chu studies has sought to explain the predominance of Chu in the archaeological records. Some suggest that the comparative stability of the Chu royal line fostered the preservation of traditions bequeathed from Western Zhou; others, that Chu's comparative wealth meant that its subjects could afford more rituals and texts (especially bamboo and silk as Chu products), or that residents of this peripheral area were more inclined, as "outsiders" and as intermediaries between north and far south, to meticulously preserve and transmit the texts and rituals they knew.[16] But Chu's shifting borders during the Zhou, not to mention the extent of Chu trading, so inflate the size of the area under Chu influence as to render such inquiries fruitless. Any attempt to use the number of finds to measure the significance accorded to texts or rituals in a given time and place is a misbegotten endeavor, and it would be a mistake to read too much into the current distribution patterns, as these represent unsystematic samples reflecting the relative intensity of excavation work done in a particular area, which is itself determined by modern geopolitical concerns and by preservation biases. Eventually, early writings and other ritual items may well be found throughout the territories belonging to the Warring States, Qin, and Han states, except where local conditions mitigate against the survival of such materials.

All we can say at this point is that the complex patterns of cultural and material exchange between and within regions, attested by both the literary and the archaeological record, call into question the sharp regional divisions once posited for the classical era. Interstate trade, war, and travel in Warring States, Qin, and early Western Han times facilitated the merging of more localized traditions, accelerating the convergence of repertoires and styles of ritual items across the area. By early Western Han times, the convergence is marked—at least in the very highest ranks of society. The tombs of the early Western Han princes in the east resemble in most respects the roughly contemporaneous tomb of the king of Nanyue 南越, far to the south.[17] As for the texts buried in tombs, recent archaeological finds offer little support to earlier views projecting discrete, regionally based "schools" of thought onto the classical landscape. In the area corresponding to the old states of Qi, Zou 鄒, and Lu (in present-day Shandong), the supposed centers of early Confucian classicism, tombs well into the Han period have yielded *yinyang* 陰陽 treatises and military texts. The Shandong Peninsula may have been the birthplace of Confucius, Mencius, and Xunzi 荀子, but it was also home to the Jixia 稷下 retainers, the reformer Zou Yan 鄒衍, and the two great military theorists Sun Wu 孫武 and Sun Bin 孫臏.[18]

More valuable to scholarly endeavors than any new theory may be a frank willingness to admit that we remain in the dark about a great many aspects of classical text and ritual. We have no idea, for example, why two or more recensions of a single text are found in the same tomb, when the tomb occupant did not specialize in teaching that text, nor do we see why grave furnishings would include a set of predictions achieved through divination that were wrong. For whom was this sort of documentation prepared? An afterworld court that would punish the givers of curses or the inept diviners? Before throwing up our hands in despair at our ignorance, we would do well to recall a pronouncement made in 1977 by Richard Hallock, the eminent scholar of Persian seals, who summed up his long and distinguished career researching a culture of comparable antiquity in this way: "In that time I have made some discoveries about the ways they [the seals] were used, but I am still confused about many things. *It is one of those cases in which if you are not confused you do not understand the problem.*" [19] One of the most welcome developments in the field of classical studies, to my mind, has been an increased readiness to acknowledge our confusions, though the impulse to posit great coherence where none exists is tempting, as the energies expended on the drive to establish the status of Huang Lao 黃老 Daoism attest. As historians of early China we all are in the unenviable position of a person who tries "to see an entire sky looking through a tube or to fathom the sea with a gourd." Therefore, the following discussion offers three sightings which may be of some use to the field.

Writing's Share in Ritual

However substantial they seem, text and ritual are slippery concepts. Both remain, adopting Maurice Freedman's phrase, historical if not functional enigmas: we can never know enough about the range of uses to which they were put by specific people at specific times in specific locations. [20] Needless to say, writing fulfilled many of the same mundane functions in the classical era that we see today; it conveyed information, recorded practices, persuaded readers, and transmitted beliefs. The bureaucratic documents found at Juyan and Dunhuang are proof of this, as is the low status of many who took up the brush. (Some bureaucratic documents were probably filled in by the semi-illiterate, though certain practices—the use of punctuation, the use of single or double horizontal lines to mark paragraphs or repeated characters—bespeak a professionalized corps of scribes and copyists.) Still, a simple list of the main functions of text and ritual in the classical period (e.g., to appease occult forces; to pray for the relief of suffering; to provide suitable outlets for the messy emotions; to reenact important myths and legends in all solemnity; to transmit information; to preserve the family and state hierarchies; and to establish a sense of continuity in this transient world) tells us frustratingly little about the interaction of texts and rituals at the time.

Many of the received traditions point to the ritual contexts for writing, suggesting that writing was not necessarily perceived in the same way when a text was seen, heard, read, interpreted, or internalized.[21] The archaeological records from the classical period also draw our attention to writing's place within the ritual systems—not because of the tomb origin of the excavated texts, since virtually all the archaeological evidence for early China comes from tombs, but because, within the tomb itself, writings often receive special treatment or they are put in a special location that marks them as ritual items. At Mawangdui, for example, the silk manuscripts were found in a lacquer box that also contained flutes, bamboo strips in rolls, oyster shells, and plant branches (the shells and branches presumably used for exorcistic and fumigation rites). In addition, many writings share the same formulae with the inscriptions found on ritual objects (e.g., late Zhou bronzes). Even some of the texts most liable to be straightforward reportage (e.g., maps and population registers) had important symbolic functions as well.[22] For instance, the stone stelae erected by order of the First Emperor of Qin represented proclamations to the gods of the mountains and seas, whose protection was sought.[23] Had writing been seen as separate from the ritual realm, it is doubtful that the classical legends would have depicted Confucius and Laozi 老子, the two archetypal sages, as ritual masters and archivists,[24] nor is it likely that the Han (apparently following the Warring States and Qin courts) would have allowed a single court institution to supervise both the state-sponsored writings and rituals.[25] To understand the classical world better, we have little choice but to study texts, ritual sites, and ritual objects together.[26]

Some preliminary observations can be made about the ways in which texts—especially, but not exclusively, those that Martin Kern dubs "texts with a history"[27]—played a role in classical ritual comparable to that of other ritual items. First, while not every society has chosen to use text and ritual in the same way, text and ritual are always connected with power, with the past, and with memory.[28] It was not only that text and ritual made the absent ones present and the dead come alive.[29] By the late Warring States period, training in the arts associated with the early Zhou aristocrats (including the composing of texts and the performance of select rites) qualified a man to enter at least the lower ranks of public office, from which foothold he and his family might hope to gain greater access to the privileges and pleasures desired by the living and possibly by the dead.[30] At every level of society, text and ritual operated in tandem to enhance authority, so much so that the linkage between such training and the attainment of high status had become proverbial by Han times. In all solemn and extended ritual observances, suasive authority was said to be lodged in four ceremonial aspects: the insignia (badges, seals, tablets, and weapons); the dress (clothing and coiffure); the demeanor (gestures and the degree of poise); and the rhetoric (forms of address and discourse). Texts, written and oral, were as important a component of ceremony as ritual gestures and dress. It was precisely Shusun Tong's 叔孫通 (late third-early second century B.C.E.) ability to craft an impressive liturgy that ensured Liu Bang's 劉邦 (Gaozu 高祖; r. 202–195 B.C.E.) elevation over his old cohorts and brought the Ru 儒 ("classicists") to the attention of the Han court.[31]

Second, the classicists of old traced the ultimate authority of both text and ritual to *ming* 命, "what has been decreed": mandates from the king, the will of Heaven, or the operations of fate. It is not unusual for tomb furnishings in certain burials to include various sorts of conferred *ming* in the form of inscriptions on bronze vessels, bells, seals, and tallies, and as written contracts, decrees, or copies of administrative or legal codes. All such items, insofar as they conveyed the will of the higher powers, were presumed to confer blessings and avert evil, in this life and the next.[32] Chapter 9 of the *Fengsu tongyi* 風俗通義, devoted to the irruption of the spirit world into the human, relates two instances in which the ritual recitation of a single canonical text deflected evil powers attributed, in one case, to a magician, in the other, to a vengeful ghost.[33] The writing brush was endowed with similar powers, for deities and strange creatures depicted and named could be controlled.[34]

Third, with texts, as with other ritual items, meaning accrues over time. In the case of rituals, it is the successive agents and onlookers who assign meanings to the performance, with the result that traditions designed to conserve the past invariably register current preoccupations as well. With texts, the accounts must be fleshed out via the proper formulae and then read against the background of successive interpretive layers (sometimes taking the form of lengthy commentaries) to which the reader/reciter responds. Out of necessity or ignorance, scholars may choose to divorce a particular ritual or a particular text from its performance context, but they do so at their peril, as the Han thinkers knew.[35]

Fourth, texts, like rituals, produce unusually compressed versions of reality that are more vivid and focused than ordinary perceptions. A double compression occurs, as it were, when symbolic formulae are employed within the short duration and confined space of the text or ritual act. At a time when the universe was believed to reflect an infinite and infinitely varied sign system whose decoding would supply the necessary guidelines for human conduct, text and ritual could offer vital clues as to its highly patterned workings. In this way, text and ritual served as "framing devices" within which to interpret the inexplicable changes occurring outside the confines of text and ritual, converting the incoherence and unintelligibility of the mundane and the merely personal into "usable" insights of broader relevance. Then, too, in guiding the imagination along preestablished paths, text and ritual confirmed the very possibility of duration, which was crucial to such highly abstracted concepts as time, cosmic history, the soul, and one's identity. Things and institutions "modeled on the old" (*shigu* 師古) would naturally last longer—or so their advocates insisted. 36 For this reason, even the masters of text and ritual were ultimately held in thrall to the potent visual and verbal vocabulary they adopted.

Fifth, the regular invocation of a few formal patterns in writing and ritual, no less than the choice of subtle variations wrought upon those patterns, defined the self-conscious archaizing mode dubbed the "classical style." Insofar as the style's technical demands, heightened awareness, and inherent artificiality were offset by a strong commitment to the "fundamentals," as constructed by the classical world, even the simplest of substances and the most meager appeals could assume an air of admirable refinement, and it was formal beauty that readily secured the person's assent to everything the style invoked. 37 In this way, the classical style laid claim to a naturalness born of pleasurable ease that was completely at variance with the arduous labors expended in pursuit of it.

Sixth, given the nearly infinite applicability of text and ritual to areas well beyond their original scope, 38 the capacity to write well or perform ritual correctly was identified as a marvelous technique (*shu* 術) likely to catapult the expert above the common run of men. The famous story about Wheelwright Bian in the *Zhuangzi* 莊子 certainly plays with this notion: the duke disdains the lowly artisan, even as he values the fine craftsmanship of his exquisite ritual paraphernalia. The artisan, illiterate but much the wiser, is surprised to find that the duke cannot see the obvious: that the artisan's craft, just as much as writing, "has an art in it somewhere," an art that cannot be transmitted to anyone without the gift. 39 The *Zhuangzi* passage would have us ask how one acquires true superiority and whether the inspiration for the production of a finely wrought piece, be it an essay or a carved wheel, is in any way lodged within the particular piece, from which it can be extracted by later generations. If the inspiration lies in the maker, not the piece, wherein lies the authority of an artful piece, let alone its possessors? The *Zhuangzi*, of course, intends to be provocative. Nearly all the great thinkers of the classical period whose teachings have survived had asserted the reverse, that the essential features of the sages not only inhered in the transmitted rituals and texts but also could be readily extracted from them.

Throughout the classical period, texts, along with other highly worked ritual paraphernalia, were available to very few outside the ranks of the political elite, for considerable expense and trouble were involved in procuring the basic materials. Writing provides a case in point: the cost of silk was high; bamboo strips were complicated to prepare and too cumbersome for casual use; and even in late Eastern Han less expensive paper did not often replace silk or bamboo in writing. But potentially of greater value than any single text or ritual item were the people who could wield them, for they had acquired their proficiency over long years of training. Therefore, powerful rulers, in making their courts repositories of texts and rituals, gathered around them as many experts as possible. "To acquire" (*de* 得) these experts was the very definition of "success" (*de* 得); to lose them, through ignorance, carelessness, or neglect, was to fail.

A fearful corollary was that such artful productions were prone to misconstruction and misuse. The power of text and ritual would surely be diluted if indiscriminately employed by the masses to their own advantage—hence the continual exhortations by leading thinkers that learning is best undertaken under the direction of a true master capable of gauging the pupil's readiness to wield such powerful techniques for constructive ends.[40] Many in high places looked askance at the steady proliferation of texts and rituals, official and unofficial—a proliferation promoted by the significance the state and society attached to them. Would-be reformers proposed again and again to slash the stupendous commentarial traditions attached to the canonical texts and to reduce the number of state sacrifices and ceremonies, citing the benefits of curbing superfluities and excesses.[41] Some of the most powerful written texts and objects were kept from circulation altogether, stored in secret archives and treasure-houses, to be seen and used only by the emperor, his inner circle, and their representatives.[42] When such secrecy attended the transmission of texts and rituals, their publicity gained added allure, as we shall see.

Still, the constant diatribes inveighing against the excessive production of texts and rites resulted in astonishingly few outright acts of state censorship of texts already in circulation. The proscriptions announced by the Qin in ca. 350 and 213 B.C.E. were soon labeled draconian, though entire categories of texts had been exempted.[43] No state, including the Qin, ever sought an absolute monopoly over text and ritual. Instead, as we shall see, reasoned assessments of the benefits to be gained from the judicious use of ritual and text turned on the question of how the ruler could legitimately employ the resources at his command to promote the common good (defined as *gong* 公) above private interests (si 私). For that reason, it may be helpful to turn to the biographies of the classical masters of writing and ritual that are found in the early standard histories to consider three of the most influential assessments relating to Han.

Evidence from the "Rulin" 儒林
Biographical Chapters

The "Rulin zhuan" 儒林傳 chapters in the three standard histories of Han take as their subject the classicists (Ru) as experts in antique rituals and writings. With respect to writings, it was certainly expertise in the Five Classics that qualified a man as a classicist; only those five canons—and not the Confucian *Analects*, the *Classic of Filial Piety*, or the *Mencius*—were deemed sufficiently profound in the classical era.[44] This we learn from the "Rulin" chapters, and more—for the introductory paragraphs, the organization of the chapters, the selection of subjects, and even the chapters' omissions tell us something about the place of the Ru in Han times.

The *Shiji* "Rulin" chapter opens with a sigh. According to the *Shiji* account, the system of "rites and music" collapsed in mid–Zhou, when the lords usurped the imperial prerogatives and "rule proceeded from the strong states" rather than its center in the Zhou capital. Distressed by the collapse of the unitary Kingly Rule of Zhou, Confucius did everything he could at every court he visited to promote the canonical texts and to restore the old rites and music. And when he had finally abandoned all hope of finding suitable employment as advisor to a powerful state, Confucius began to compile the *Spring and Autumn Annals* (Chunqiu 春秋), hoping to provide future generations with an outline of the kingly Way. After his death, Confucius's disciples dispersed to the various courts of the realm, in some cases becoming the "true teachers of kings." But, the *Shiji* further tells us, in the incessant wars that preceded unification, the classicists' Way was shunted aside. Only in Qi and Lu did it survive, thanks in large part to the efforts of Mencius and Xunzi. Under Qin rule, the *Odes* (Shi 詩) and *Documents* (Shu 書) were censored, and some of the most famous classicists suffered persecution. So incensed were the classicists at the First Emperor of Qin's attack on their profession that many classicists from Lu lent their support to the rebel Chen She as soon as he took up arms against Qin.

The *Shiji* goes on to describe how, when the troops of the Han founder came to attack Lu, the besieged Ru, seemingly oblivious to the danger, continued to recite and practice their rites and music as usual. No finer proof of their absolute devotion to the Way could be offered; because the subjects of Qi and Lu had for so long been schooled in the way of the sages, the courage of their convictions had become "second nature" to them. And with Han rule, the classicists promptly set about reviving their traditions, "putting their canons and their arts in order." One of their number, Shusun Tong, was asked to devise the court rituals for the Han, and it was not long before classicists were managing the imperial ceremonies and framing the imperial rhetoric, but so long as parts of the empire remained unsubdued, candidates trained in the military and in the law were bound to receive preferment. When peace finally came to the empire, Emperor Jing 景 (r. 157–141 B.C.E.) and the Dowager Empress Dou 竇 (d. 135 B.C.E.) favored less-interventionist methods of rule than the Ru would have liked. Emperor Wu 武 (r. 141–87 B.C.E.) was to change all that. Three of his ministers convinced him that rites and music were the most effective tools to be employed in leading the people, and so he agreed to set up institutions of learning at court that would measure a man's learning by the quantity of texts he could recite. "From this time on," the *Shiji* concludes, "the best and brightest of the high ministers, counselors, and officers at every level were drawn increasingly from the ranks of those proficient in learning."[45]

However, this brief historical synopsis at the outset of the *Shiji* "Rulin" chapter, praising the progress of learning under the Han, is then to a large degree contradicted by the following biographies of the classicist masters. Most of the masters selected for inclusion in the chapter had achieved fame long before Emperor Wu's time, and the beneficial effects of his new institutions are nowhere evident in the *Shiji* chapter. Instead, the classicists serving Emperor Wu's court are shown to be decidedly inferior to the old masters. The classicists chosen by the emperor could recite as many texts and perform as many rituals. But the old Ru had spoken their minds when remonstration was warranted, and they were ready enough to put their bodies on the line. By contrast, the new Ru tended to look out for themselves; they were either toadies or cranks. Evidently, the new institutions of learning did little to form character, so they failed to turn out exceptional candidates for public office. Perhaps Sima Qian, living in an earlier era more reliant upon oral recitation and collective memory, was less inclined to exaggerate Emperor Wu's achievements because he had never overestimated the degree to which the brief interruptions in textual transmissions had threatened the classical arts.[46] Whatever the case, the *Shiji* "Rulin" chapter sends a contradictory message that may be explained in one of two ways: either Sima Qian expected his readers to reach their own judgment regarding the discrepancies between his rosy preliminary account of Han learning and the implicit criticism registered in the subsequent biographies, or the initial part is an interpolation taken from the *Hanshu*.[47]

By contrast, both the *Hanshu* and *Hou Hanshu* chapters were far more intent upon, and consistent in, stressing the heroic efforts of the Han emperors in restoring order. Indeed, the introductory remarks in the *Hanshu* "Rulin" chapter can be read as rebuttal to the biographical accounts in the *Shiji*. The *Hanshu* replaces the *Shiji*'s sigh with a confident assertion: the Ru of antiquity were broadly learned in the canonical texts, and it is these very texts which encapsulate the Kingly Teachings and manifest the collective wisdom of the sages. It was true, of course, that the system of rites and music fell into decline with the collapse of Zhou power, and that Confucius, though able to "perfect a unitary Kingly Rule," was frustrated in his attempts to restore the old imperial order. The *Shiji* account of the early Western Han was accurate as well. But while matching nearly verbatim the *Shiji*'s description of the circumstances surrounding Emperor Wu's momentous decision to institute the Imperial Academy, the *Hanshu* then launches into a series of triumphal statistics: under Emperor Wu's successors, significantly more students entered the Imperial Academy, just at the time when new institutions of learning were being established throughout the provinces, so that the imperial administration was well stocked with those trained in the classics and the rites. The sanguine tone of the *Hanshu* introduction correlating the rise of enlightened rulership with a steep rise in professionally qualified men is reinforced in the closing remarks of the chapter, which portray the court as a passionate advocate of classical learning. The century after Emperor Wu witnessed a dramatic rise in the number of classicists on the government payroll; this overall rise was mirrored in the number of Academicians at court. Never mind that some of these increases came under Wang Mang's 王莽 (45 B.C.E.–23 C.E.) watch.

By these measures, "all omissions and mistakes were caught; everything was preserved and given its proper place at the center." Unity and coherence, so the *Hanshu* tells us, were thus assured.[48]

But if ample provision for classical scholarship were sufficient guarantee of the health of the body politic, how is it that the Liu clan had forfeited the throne, not once but twice? The *Hou Hanshu* chapter devoted to the classicists had to explain the usurpation of the throne by Wang Mang, that ardent sponsor of the old learning, as well as the demise of Eastern Han, with its long-standing allegiance to the uncrowned king. The problem of Wang Mang was neatly elided in the opening line of the chapter: "Long ago," under Wang Mang and the Gengshi 更始 Emperor (r. 23–25 C.E.), the empire was in chaos, and so the system of rites and music collapsed.[49] Succeeding paragraphs described the efforts of the Eastern Han founder, Emperor Guangwu 光武 (r. 25–57), and his successor, Emperor Ming 明 (r. 57–75), to reassure the classicists of their place in the new regime. The Eastern Han founder was so anxious to promote classical learning that "even before he descended from his carriage," he made it a priority to visit the classicists and have them institute a search for the missing texts, "so that the losses might be made good."[50] Emperor Guangwu himself purportedly brought some two thousand carts full of books to the capital and threw himself into the task of supervising the restoration work. Emperor Ming, not content to watch, insisted on carrying out the most solemn imperial rites in person in ceremonies calculated to produce the maximum effect. He built several new ceremonial halls, where he entertained the aged, received the members of his nobility, and communicated with Heaven. He held archery contests and banquets in the old style. Bowing to the nominal authority of the Academicians, he allowed them to test him on his erudition, and thousands of his officers attended his lectures on the classics. He dispensed copies of the classics, giving each of the palace guards the *Classic of Filial Piety* (presumably to ensure their loyalty). And in all of these cases, the vast numbers of people involved as witnesses is explicitly described or implied by the narrative. According to the *Hou Hanshu*, so exemplary were Emperor Guangwu and his successor that the Xiongnu 匈奴 sent their sons to be enrolled in the institutions of learning at the capital.

Many of the later Eastern Han emperors were equally strong advocates of classicism. "No distance was too great" when they sought students of the classics for appointment to the court.[51] They convened academic conferences; they increased the numbers of classically trained students registered at the Imperial Academy, who then received appointments in both the capital and provincial bureaucracies; and they built a number of libraries in the capital. Imperial patronage produced immediate results: "So many were the learned in the Eastern Capital that it would be hard to calculate their numbers." But one can have too much of a good thing—especially when it is mandated by a woman. The downfall of Eastern Han is traced, curiously enough, to an edict issued in 146 C.E. in which the Empress Dowager Liang 梁 decreed that all the sons of the higher-ranking bureaucrats take up the study of the classical arts. From this time on, "study away from home" became the fashion, and the so-called experts, now openly competing for students, produced commentaries that were ever longer and more far-fetched. Once the proscriptions had denied a meaningful profession to the most serious among the scholar-officials,[52] the rest of the classicists began quarreling over the various interpretations. At that point, nothing could stop the rapid slide into ignorance, barbarism, and crass commercialism, symbolized by the pieces of silk that were looted from the imperial libraries and made into tents and pouches. The *Hou Hanshu* reports that of the thousands of carts of books that had been gathered in the Eastern Han capital, a mere seventy remained at the very end, and half of those were destroyed in the attempt to save them from further depredation.

The three short introductions provided by the "Rulin" chapters agree only that it was crucial for the state to gather into its service as many good advisors as feasible. Men trained in the classics could be expected to have the discipline, the erudition, and the morality needed for public service. They would know the precedents, they could provide the sorts of literary flourishes that were needed for court documents, and they could inject the proper style into court rituals. The unitary Way of Confucius would be brought into the service of a unified empire. If the biographies can be trusted (and this is a fairly large "if"), all ranks in Han society recognized the innate worth of the scholar. The emperor himself "honored his teachers and tutors,"[53] conferring lavish gifts upon them in their lifetimes and posthumous titles after their deaths. The imperial princes and the *waiqi* 外戚 (imperial relatives by marriage) followed suit, going out of their way to attract good scholars to their entourages; even the dregs of society—the robbers, bandits, and rebels—might refuse upon occasion to do the true scholar any harm.[54]

Still, those men selected for inclusion in the three "Rulin" chapters were generally not officials of the highest rank, as the *Hou Hanshu* confesses, but simply those not important enough to merit a separate biography on their own.[55] By a rough count, about 69 out of 189 men (nearly 28 %) appearing in the *Hanshu* "Rulin" chapters are otherwise unknown, and the majority of the masters received notices so perfunctory that it is impossible to ascertain when they lived or even what version of a canonical text they had studied.[56] Of Heng Hu 衡胡, for instance, it is merely reported that "he used his [expertise in the] *Changes* to get high office."[57] Nearly all of the men taught at one time or another, however, and not a few eventually served as tutors to the nobility or the imperial household.[58] The problem was, as Yang Xiong had observed, "To practice the Way is best; to speak of it is second best; and to teach it to others, [a distant?] third."[59] "All the Ru" basked in reflected glory when one of their group, the scholar Fu Gong 伏恭, was appointed to one of the three highest ministerial posts in the government. Not to participate in the administration of the realm was to waste the long years spent in painfully acquiring knowledge. But ideally, the post of Academician, earning some 600 bushels of grain in annual salary, would be parlayed into a higher-ranking post in the provinces. Even the fairly low-ranking post of local prefect was considered a promotion, and those who continued to teach after receiving a nonacademic appointment were the exceptions rather than the rule, despite the higher fees and greater numbers of "students" (a term denoting clients and retainers as well) that teacher-administrators could command.[60]

It was assumed that those who followed the "family business" (*jia ye* 家業) would perform more admirably in their professions. To not a few biographies, especially in the fifth-century *Hou Hanshu*, a brief notice is appended to the effect that one or more sons had specialized in the same interpretive line as the father. (In only one recorded case did a son train in a different tradition.)[61] Of Zhen Yu's 甄宇 grandson, it was said, for example, "The Ru thought that it was a fine thing for three generations to carry on the family business, so everyone honored him."[62] The Kongs 孔 in Confucius's line, the Dais 戴 as *Rites* teachers, and the Xiahous 夏侯 and Ouyangs 歐陽 as *Documents* teachers enjoyed extraordinary prestige as families who had specialized in the same texts over eight generations or more. Of course, it was almost ludicrous to apply the model of Confucius and his disciples to the very different teaching conditions prevailing in the Han, when a student could go for three years without ever catching a glimpse of his "teacher."[63] The sheer numbers of students registered per teacher in Eastern Han—often greater by a factor of ten than the numbers of students reported for the Western Han masters—precluded regular face-to-face encounters between teacher and pupils. That may explain why a standard entry reports that a given master trained others in one or more traditions, and that those students went on to take up the same line of work. [64] It is the rare biography that even alludes to a master's contributions to academic discourse by the briefest of citations. [65] The Ru appear in these chapters, then, not as the intellectual or moral lights of the empire but as bureaucrats of middling stature, who were often enough caught in highly unethical practices, as was true of Ouyang Xi 歐陽歙, the eighth-generation teacher of the *Documents*.

The "Rulin" chapters allow us to trace the typical career trajectories of the successful classical scholar. The vast majority seem to have entered office through the *ren* 任 privilege on account of their fathers' high rank, through local recommendations as "filial and incorrupt" (*xiaolian* 孝廉), "knowledgeable in the classics" (*mingjing* 明經), or "canonical scholars" (*wenxue* 文學), or through the "family business" (*jia ye*). As local recommendations were usually in the hands of the local elites, it is not at all clear that study of the classics represented an important avenue for social mobility, as is sometimes alleged. Only a handful of scholars are described as "poor," [66] and many of the classical masters could afford to refuse invitations to take up public office, waiting in "reclusion" until better offers came their way. Of course, this was a time when teachers who had a thousand or more students on their rolls were still considered "recluses" if they were not holding public office. [67] Only a handful of classical masters made a career of refusing office, usually in the most dangerous times of dynastic change.

About a third of the Eastern Han subjects in the *Hou Hanshu* wrote abridged versions of one of the classics or more advanced textbooks delving into the more abstruse connections between two or more of the Five Classics. [68] Comparison of the three "Rulin" chapters suggests that such writings may have become more central to the definition of the Ru scholar over the course of the Han. The *Shiji* states unequivocally that the best classical masters did not write down their teachings, that they had no use for fine phrasing, and that they were in a few cases not all that adept at explicating written texts, as opposed to transmitting a powerful, suasive example. [69] The early masters' legacy, according to the *Shiji*, was the disciples they had trained for public office, not the texts they had written down. [70] (One of the few Ru masters explicitly praised for his writing skills, Ni Kuan 兒寬, is portrayed as a moral waffler and a poor administrator.) [71] The *Hou Hanshu* regularly lists the writings composed by its biographical subjects, casting their compositions as a form of patrimony in notices attached at the ends of the biographies proper. The *Hanshu* (compiled ca.

100 C.E), occupies the middle ground among the three "Rulin" chapters, as we might expect. Its biography of Xu Shang 許商 (fl. early first century) gives the title of one of the two calendrical studies attributed to Xu, but it quickly moves on to expound upon the real source of his fame: Xu held one of the nine ministerial posts, and two of his four main disciples went on to become ministers and two became Academicians.[72] Perhaps the most telling anecdotes to illustrate the overall shift in the classicists' practice and perception concern two moments of crisis and empire building. As the *Shiji* describes it, during the civil war after the collapse of the Qin, when the classicists from Confucius's home state of Lu went to offer their services to one contender for the imperial throne, they carried the ritual vessels of Confucius's family in their arms to express allegiance; in one version of the story in the *Shiji*, they were even carrying Confucius's own vessels.[73] When a very similar situation occurred two hundred years later, in the civil war following Wang Mang's short-lived rule, the sources mention the early Eastern Han Ru scholars "carrying off on their backs their charts and written texts" when they defected to the future Eastern Han founder—showing a clear and dramatic shift from ritual practice to text-based learning.[74]

Conventionally "good" careers usually required (1) access to the emperor, his regents, or members of the royal family, (2) an ability to impress others in formal contests in rhetoric and recitation, (3) prognostic powers, or (4) an ability to efficiently conduct high-profile treason cases. As the importance of good connections is fairly obvious, let us turn to some of the evidence regarding the many competitions that were required of the up-and-coming scholar. One of the longer anecdotes included in the *Hou Hanshu* describes the behavior of one student attending what was bound to be his first imperial conference on the classics at the tender age of sixteen. At the opening ceremonies, Dai Feng 戴豐 was the only conferee who refused to assume his assigned place. When asked the reason for his peculiar behavior, Dai replied that his mat had been wrongly placed among those of the lower ranks, since his interpretations of the classics could easily trump those of the more established classical masters. Asked to verify the truth of his assertions, Dai Feng proceeded to challenge all those in attendance to a display of erudition. When he had finally outtalked the best of the assembly, the emperor "approved him" and granted him a promotion.[75]

That this anecdote hardly represents a veiled attack on the judgment of the emperor in question is shown by a second anecdote, in which two scholars, in response to an academician's call for disciples,

hitched up their robes and ascended the steps of the hall. In intoning
hymns and performing rituals, they were exceedingly reverent; in
chanting and explicating [the canonical texts], they demonstrated their
method. . . . Astonished [at the degree of savoir faire they displayed],
the court Academicians asked to know the identity of their teacher, and
they responded, "We serve Wang Shi." Wang Shi was then recom-
mended for a post by all the Academicians.[76]

Often it is enough to say of a particular scholar that the other masters
"were unable to stump him" or that he had participated in a scholarly
conference where lively debates were held.[77] The outcome of such
disputations would determine the good students' course of study and
teachers.[78] Even the best of them seemed determined not only to surpass
their masters but to boast of having done so.[79]

Other classical masters made their names predicting the future and
accounting for prodigies.[80] The biography of Liangqiu He 梁丘賀 gives a
fairly typical account: it was customary to offer sacrifices by night in the
ancestral temple of Emperor Zhao 昭 (97–74 B.C.E.), but the advance guards
for the emperor encountered several difficulties on the road, at which point
Liangqiu was summoned so that he might divine the reason. He predicted a
plot against the emperor, at which point the emperor returned to the palace
and ordered an underling to conduct the sacrifices on his behalf. As soon as
the representatives of the imperial family arrived at the temple, it was clear
that armed guards had been placed there by members of the rebellious Huo
霍 clan to await the emperor's arrival. The plot was soon revealed, and the
imperial sacrifices were henceforth conducted in broad daylight.[81] It was the
swift prosecution of just this sort of treason case that caused Emperor Wu to
favor the Ru. But omen predictions and judicial proceedings in major court
cases were both risky ventures, and this may go a long way toward
explaining why so many of the subjects of the three "Rulin" chapters land
in jail. At any rate, this much is clear: by mid– to late Western Han, the
traditions associated with the Five Classics—once seen as separate traditions
yielding logically separable, if equally noble, insights—had merged in such
a way that the *Gongyang* no longer enjoyed a near monopoly on the
adjudication of treason cases, nor the *Changes* on prognostication and
wonder-working.[82]

The "Rulin" biographies give us some idea what Han society looked
for in a classical scholar, with the anecdotes following predictable
patterns.[83] An act of extreme self-sacrifice could catapult an otherwise

obscure scholar to sudden fame, especially if the case involved a celebrity. Li Zhen's 李震 reputation was made, for example, when he offered to be executed in place of Ouyang Xi, the *Documents* teacher then in prison on corruption charges. [84] In a similar case, Yang Zheng 楊政 was promoted after his submission of a strongly worded defense of his teacher Master Fan 范生, who was due to be cashiered for his serial divorces. [85] Exemplary behavior when mourning a friend, a teacher, or the emperor himself was always gratifying to society. Zhou Ze 周澤, in his capacity as master of ceremonies for the ancestral sacrifices of the Liu ruling clan, was always fasting, despite his very poor health. Once, when he had been away from home for a particularly long period, his wife was so worried that she ventured to inquire about his health. Zhou Ze, furious at his wife for violating his fast, impeached himself, and though many judged him to be overscrupulous (and expressed their views in satirical verse), he was, if possible, even more honored after the incident. [86] Yang Lun 楊倫, who had steadfastly refused a position at the court under Emperor An, won praise for his public mourning for the same emperor; Ren Mo 任末, was hailed for pulling the funeral hearse of his beloved friend to the grave site rather than using an ox. And when several thousand students took part in Lou Wang's 樓望 funeral, "the Ru thought it reflected very well on them." [87] Courage set the real Ru apart from the bookworm, and so the biographer hastens to inform the reader that it was the scholar Yang Ren 楊仁 who barred the way into the palace to the emperor's own relatives by marriage and the scholar Yin Min 殷敏 who told the emperor to his face that his beloved apocrypha were latter-day forgeries riddled with errors. [88]

Still, there are some surprises in the "Rulin" chapters, chief among them the disparagement of the so-called masters specializing in the transmission of the *Rites* in early to mid–Western Han. The name of Confucius may have been synonymous with "rule by ritual" and Lu the center of classical learning, but these rites teachers, all of whom hailed from Lu, were manifestly incapable of advising the court on ritual matters. The *Shiji* concedes that one of the nine mentioned was "somewhat capable, if hardly good"; another could explain one canonical text. [89] Mostly these masters worked on their demeanors (*rong* 容), and it was presumably because they made a good showing that they were eventually rewarded with provincial posts. In passing, the "Rulin" chapters also reveal the underhandedness of the Ru, who, finding themselves at a loss in court debates, were apt to whine feebly that their rivals had abandoned "the old way"! [90] (Two of the more capable masters were held back by reports that their teachings were more innovative than was the norm.) [91] Some of the classical masters were less than ardent in their devotion to their work. One ritual master calculated the precise degree of difficulty required for each of the classics so that he could advise his son to settle on an easier classic. [92] And while the chapters show that a fair proportion of the foremost experts enjoyed a reputation for honesty, neither malfeasance in office nor plagiarism necessarily ended a scholar's career. [93] It was only the very wisest of the Ru who urged his children not to accept any "gifts" from his former subordinates after his death, knowing that ostentatious self-abnegation would so impress the emperor that he would shower the family with all the more largesse. [94]

What the "Rulin" chapters do not openly discuss is one issue implicitly raised by Sima Qian's account: How is the ruling house to distinguish the ethical classicist from the opportunist using his classical training to attain higher office? How, in other words, is the state to find the sort of men who can make policy and even reform it, if the need arises? That the "Rulin" chapters do not address the issue is not because the classicists were unconcerned. Yang Xiong devoted several long dialogues in his neoclassic, the *Fayan* 法言, to describing the poseur. In one such passage he wrote:

> Let us suppose that there was a man who took the family name of Kong and the style Zhongni [those of Confucius]. Were he to enter the gate [of the temple to Confucius(?)], ascend into the hall, lean on his stool, and don his robes, could such a man rightly be called a Confucius?" "The surface appearance would be right, but the essence would be wrong." "May I ask your thoughts on the question of essence?" "Take a sheep in wolf's clothing. Were the animal to see grass, it would be thrilled. But at the sight of a jackal it would tremble with fear, forgetting that it wears the wolfskin. . . . To like books but to fail to make Confucius the real target of study—that's a waste of books. To enjoy rhetoric but to fail to put Confucius at the center—that is to emit only the faintest tinkling sound. The right way may be transmitted and then gradually be perverted, but if what is passed on is skewed to begin with, it will never correct itself little by little. [95]

From the very beginning, the ranks of the Ru included the most disparate sorts of people: invocators and legal experts, those drawn to the classics because of their appeal as literature and those committed to cultivation and ethical principles.[96] By some process never fully explained in the standard histories, the classicists—whose trappings were once so utterly distinctive—had become virtually indistinguishable from the ordinary run of men filling office.[97] Evidently, "clothing oneself in the sage's teachings and reciting and intoning their works day and night" did not automatically mean that a person "assumed the virtues of the sage."[98] Xu Gan 徐幹 (170–217), writing two centuries after Yang, was still excoriating the seeker after fame: "He may not count himself among Confucius's disciples. . . . He may imitate the former kings in declaiming the *Odes* and the *Documents*, but it is to no avail. He has merely acquired a method to poison the people, with the result that all of them reject the fundamental and race to what is less essential."[99] For this reason, as Wang Chong 王充 put it, "All the world faults the Ru and even the students of classical learning are apt to belittle themselves."[100] Certainly, four centuries of classical learning had done little to advance the ethical and political program of the sage, perhaps because no one of the Ru "carved out his moral power [with the same determination that he brought to] seeing that ornate patterns were carved on the central column of his home."[101] That trenchant observation leads us to a third topic: the place of public display in the classical period.

Texts and Rituals as Edifying Spectacles

Perhaps the most striking change in ritual practices over the course of the classical period is the growing emphasis on its publicity. Circumscribed rituals once conducted for very limited audiences yield to increasingly public displays intended for ever wider audiences, and the judicious use of magnificence and monumentality required to establish "awesome authority" (*wei yi* 威儀) became unprecedentedly "public" (*gong* 公) in this one specific sense: those commanding sufficient resources regularly sought to demonstrate their power before large audiences, and where only a select group witnessed the actual display, as many as possible were meant to hear of it. The displays of wealth and power took many forms: the First Emperor's solemn progresses through the newly conquered Qin territories; the frequent banquets held in the Changle 長樂 Palace, whose thousands of guests were invited to partake of multicourse dinners before taking home the sumptuously appointed lacquer serving dishes; the annual processions in which a deceased emperor's remains were paraded as they were conveyed from gravesite to temple; or a dramatic expansion in the number of stone stelae memorializing the dead and addressed to "all onlookers." [102] The stated intention behind such displays was to convert mere munificence into a quality more glorious still. By the prevailing rationale, the gracious condescension of a superior sharing objects and experiences through public spectacles revealed that laudable self-abnegation, freedom from selfishness, and political transparency that alone could sustain, to the mutual benefit of all, an equitable, stable sociopolitical order. In many contexts, an aversion to publicity was conversely associated with behavior that was supremely selfish and self-defeating, as when the tyrannical Qin rulers of popular fiction sought to conceal their own movements within the palace precincts.

This link between edifying display, the sharing of pleasures, and the search for lasting security was forged in response to a new set of political problems that had arisen in the Warring States period. It was supported by Warring States polemics on the human condition that came to inform nearly all the official and semiofficial writings known from Qin and Han. And until late Eastern Han, the capacity of this display culture to conflate public service with private gratifications propped many a ruling house. How did this phenomenon arise at a specific time, in the Warring States? Farsighted leaders of the states in that period, intent upon rapid expansion and centralization, confronted an urgent new dilemma: how best to distribute rewards and punishments in order to enforce power and solidarity over vast new populations not inclined either by hereditary ties or by local custom to uphold the relatively small kin, surrogate-kin, and cult groups associated with the old courts. The formal *ming* 命, or writ, recorded on Western Zhou bronzes could extend the ruler's power beyond his immediate circle to a few allied families, and the Chunqiu blood covenants (*meng* 盟) involved still greater numbers in binding agreements. But by the Warring States, any state set upon conquest needed to sponsor and direct much larger (even overlapping) networks in the social, political, military, and economic spheres, networks capable of persuading influential figures to contribute to its service their best efforts and those of their men.

Responding to this dilemma, the Warring States thinkers soon devised the theoretical foundations of the public display culture. According to fourth- and third-century B.C.E. thinkers, who reached near consensus on this one issue, it is the human condition (a) to desire social ties with other human beings; (b) to crave spectacle, safety, and pleasure, in addition to material goods; and (c) to experience mimetic desires (i.e., desires prompted by the realization that someone else has in his or her possession an object of desire).[103] While the desire for companionship generally leads men and women to act in socially responsible ways, compulsions to attain the other desires are apt to provoke destructive competition between persons and between groups, in view of the natural limit on available resources. Even where competitors have been fended off temporarily, the insecurities engendered by the prospect of competition can prevent true enjoyment. Pleasure loses much of its savor when it can so easily be wrested away. Ideally, the worthy man will see the wisdom in learning to reduce or refine his desires, but even the stupidest blockhead can be persuaded to secure his pleasures by sharing them with others, if he sees that gifts and benefactions forestall the envy and malice of others. (The ruler's pleasure-taking is only stupid and wrong, as Mencius says, when it is obviously "selfish," in that it breaks community through its extravagant use of scarce resources or its demotion of human beings to the status of commodities or providers.)

This is where the ideal state intervenes, for its ruler and officials, armed with the knowledge of human contradictions and cravings, can easily motivate entire populations to act in conformity with the ruler's dictates, identified as the "common good," by making the rewards and punishments—material and immaterial—predictable and proportionate. As the theory goes, when "those below" see an obvious advantage to denying themselves and acting in accordance with the ruler's will, they will happily undertake to attain their desires for wealth and status through the adoption of the state-sponsored social virtues, if only because that path spells safety rather than danger. In effect, in the short run they willingly forgo the chance to act upon present appetites in order to achieve in the long run their highest goals, identified in the relevant texts with such goods as psychic and physical survival and a fine reputation. Those who accustom themselves to this complex negotiation of desire have the capacity to develop a "second nature" more reliable and discriminating than the first, a second nature that will, not coincidentally, exhibit the serene and eloquent affability that was so admired in classical cultivation.

Therefore Xunzi's "Enrich the State" (Fu guo 富國) chapter, to take but one elegant exposition based on such ideas, envisions the state as the primary distributor of status items, including texts. For Xunzi, regular ritual dispersals of high-quality material goods (many of them inscribed) represent the carrot to the penal code's stick. Of the two means at his disposal, the carrot and the stick, the wise ruler knows that it is primarily the carrot by which the ruler motivates subjects to follow his lead, generating good order throughout the realm. Thus, the wise ruler is eager to garner (through taxation and tribute) wealth in the form of grain and finished goods—not so that he can hoard this wealth but so that he can disperse a portion of it among his subjects, making their homes in effect his own storehouses. However great the expense entailed by gifts and awards, the regular dispersal of boons is cheap at any price, for it binds the ruler's subjects to him. According to Xunzi, the stark alternatives are rebellion and regicide, so the old Mohist arguments in favor of ritual frugality must be condemned as "exaggerated reckoning," a counterproductive concentration on the fiscal bottom line that fails to take into account the undeniable fact that material goods represent one of the best incentives at the ruler's disposal.

It was important to this theory, it need hardly be said, that the ruler be seen as a model of open-handedness, for in public display culture, "making a standard of virtue" (in both senses)[104] simultaneously accomplishes three tasks vital to the preservation of the state and society. It identifies to "those below" the mandated "general," "public," or "common" interests; it advertises the material utility of actively promoting those interests (though it provides no mechanism by which to distinguish apparent conformity from real commitment); and it gratifies those inclined by custom or by aspirations to identify with the prevailing hierarchies. The thought was to generate in as many people as possible the pleasurable sensation that great honor had been conferred upon them as onlookers in an *edifying* public spectacle, even if they, as witnesses, were excluded from the more obvious satisfactions to be had from direct participation and representation in exchanges and spectacles. Thus, the archaeological record left by the display culture bears witness to something very like Veblen's "conspicuous consumption," with one important difference: the culture sought not to dramatize the gaps between classes or estates, but to foster a belief in the underlying fabric weaving disparate groups together in such a way that "each found his proper place" in a coherent and unified whole.

The ruler in particular was to present himself as the embodiment of all the collectivities operating within the public display culture. Through spectacle and exchange, he was "the one man" who could most effectively make visible the normally invisible ties binding persons and elevate those public ties as prior to (and more exalted than) any private claims that his subjects might put forward. For the emperor resided at center, the natural focus of all attention, and it was the stability of the center, illustrated and enhanced by the regular resort to display mechanisms, that guaranteed the physical security of the other social units—the security that must be established if pleasure-seeking was to result in pleasure-taking at any level.

With the king's person serving as the emblem par excellence, the court could allow, even encourage, public figures at lower levels to imitate the lavish displays of the court. The representatives of the court, as stand-ins for the throne, would naturally appear to their contemporaries to be more deserving of general esteem than those who lacked comparable publicity. In one voice, then, high theory and local mores exhorted "those below" to follow the worthy example of their superiors, so that their desires might be at once satisfied and regulated throughout the realm. Through the circle of gifting and receiving, display culture could, in theory, successfully convert the inherent disorderliness of human impulses into a factor for social stability and cohesiveness. The mimetic desires inhering in the human makeup would cause people to emulate their superiors, especially when their highest pretensions and aspirations were accounted a major credit to the family.

No abstract theory of display could have been imposed on society unless it admirably met contemporary conditions. And no theoretical solution devised to resolve inequities in distribution and offset the disaffection of subjects could have succeeded unless it addressed the ruling elite's desires to preserve their prerogatives and pleasures. The talk of sharing pleasures accomplished this, for it allowed the members of the ruling elite to assert their authority in a gentile fashion through the regular donation of scarce resources, in the belief that this could convert patterns of lavish consumption into public pleasures that could conceivably sustain their persons, their families, and the body politic. As I see it, throughout the classical period, in order to feel properly protected, those at every rank in society sought as best they could to place themselves firmly within a web of mutual obligations (*do ut des*) woven by regular formalized exchanges in the forms of gift, tribute, and sacrifice. [105] Such ritualized exchanges—rendered more visible at specified intervals and locations by modifications in the *form* of the exchanges—demonstrated, to potential friends and allies no less than to oneself, the reliable nature of the protection afforded those in the exchange circle by their fellow participants. [106] As the fully ritualized person by definition reaffirmed his exemplary perfection through public acts, those outside the web were put on notice that it would be foolhardy to harm members of a public display circle, since those within the circle could call upon the collective strength of a group ready to tender its services. Of course, when honor and "glory" (*rong* 榮) somehow depended as much on the presence of the people before whom they were displayed as on the agent's demeanor, they could be denied at any moment by these witnesses swiftly and absolutely (as Sima Qian is wont to remind us). Hence, the

philosophical texts of the period continually reiterate that others constitute a
person's chief security[107] and that the empire is not the possession of a
single person—reiterations which may have moderated the impulse toward
tyranny, at least for a while.

It would be hard to overestimate for the classical period the pervasiveness of the webs formed through public display within and beyond polite
society, webs that bound not only the living and the dead but also—what
often proves harder—people of quite different economic status. Display
culture was thought to be ideally suited to the task of conveying two very
difficult messages: that socially constructive behavior would benefit
everyone in the community and that the prevailing hierarchies exemplified a
deeper order unshakable and just. Once learned, these lessons were not so
easily confused or forgotten—hence, the enormous potential credited to
ceremonial display to construct enduring relationships of political
dominance as fundamentally voluntarist and reciprocal.[108] For anyone who
aspired to or wished to maintain his elite status, all acts in this life,
beginning with the announcement of birth and ending with the funeral
procession itself, were calculated to impress upon other viewers the status of
the family to which the person belonged. (Gender construction was merely a
subplot in the many elaborate public status performances required of all
members of the elite.)[109]

One local display event having the expected political and psychological
impacts was the funeral of Chen Shi 陳寔, whose death at the age of eighty-
four *sui* in 187 C.E. reportedly attracted over 30,000 men, with hundreds
wearing the deepest grade of mourning for the great man.[110] Many
self-identified members of the mourning public at Chen Shi's time, it
should be noted, were low-ranking office holders, clerks and aides, or those
who held no official rank at all, as we discover from late Han stelae.
(Presumably, when such men needed more capital to maintain a public
presence, their neighbors, friends, and relatives offered financial assistance,
knowing that aid rendered upon such occasions would only heighten the
sense of obligation in the future.)[111] And while the literary evidence culled
from the standard histories, from stelae, and from tombs has thrust the
memorializing aspects of this culture on our attention, the works of the
period, pictorial as well as literary, portray life and death as the public
setting for the round of activities—funeral processions, parades, hunts,
communal banquets, and public award ceremonies—designated to assure the
family and state (and the individual through them) of continued protection
and material prosperity.

Numerous passages in the received literature suggest the extraordinary scale that public display could take at the imperial level. Two descriptions of the regular Lunar New Year imperial audiences, when taken together, sketch the cycle of gift-and-tribute for this single occasion, lauding emperor and court for making visible the ties binding the royal family, bureaucracy, and select dependents in mutual cooperation, ties analogous to those that bound the dead to the living through sacrificial offerings. The first passage, from the *Hou Hanshu* "Treatise on Ritual," shows the emperor receiving, shortly before dawn, congratulations and gifts. From each of the Three Lords and the marquises came a jade disk; from the officials ranked at two thousand bushels came one lamb each; from those of one thousand bushels and of six hundred bushels came one wild goose each; from those ranked four hundred bushels and below came one pheasant each. The treatise confines itself to a description of the court's receipt of gifts, but another text, a passage from Zhang Heng's 張衡 (78–139) "Rhapsody on the Eastern Capital," lists a huge range of imperial guests, of every rank and ethnic origin, converging upon the capital—not simply so that they may add to the imperial coffers, but also so that they may go away with gifts of equal or greater value. For once he had solemnly acknowledged their gifts, the emperor invited the lords, marquises, ministers, and officials to ascend by way of the eastern steps, inquiring as to their vicissitudes and conferring with them on governmental matters. Then the emperor "opened the great granaries and distributed stored-up wealth, bestowing largesse for all, from great officials down to the humblest servitors." Afterward, the imperial steward provided a great feast, at which he distributed cooked meats and live sacrificial animals to the family dependents of officials. Such bestowals by the emperor aimed to "reinforce at the beginning of each year the ties of loyalty . . . and benevolence between the emperor and his subjects," thereby reaffirming the emperor's position at the very center of the civilized universe and consecrating the alliances among the "one man," his subjects, and the celestial powers. [112] In Han times, the ruler could become "the standard for the empire" (*tianxia zhi biao* 天下之表) because it was he "who distributes largesse according to ritual." [113]

The foregoing descriptions might be taken as hyperbole were it not for recent archaeological evidence, such as the ten strips and two dove-staffs found in tomb 18 at Mozuizi 磨嘴子, Gansu. Dating from Eastern Han these burial goods offer a nice illustration of the support of text and ritual in the state-sponsored public display system. The strips carry the text of an edict from 31 B.C.E. that stipulates the public honors to be accorded those who have attained the ripe old age of seventy. The edict decrees, first, that wooden staffs topped by jade carved in the shape of doves shall be bestowed upon these elders in a ceremony; second, that all holders of staffs are entitled by law to certain rights and exemptions; third, that detailed records of bestowals shall be housed in the stone chambers of the Lantai 蘭台 imperial library; and fourth, that the jade staffs shall be repaired at imperial expense as needed. A related document reports a court case in which a local constable was condemned to public execution for maltreating an elderly person entitled to the perquisites associated with the dove-staff. The inclusion of strips and staffs among the burial items found in tomb 18, despite some puzzling features, attests to the magnitude of the Han imperial bestowals and presumably also to the belief that written orders handed down from powerful superiors, like ritual activities, served to protect both the living and the dead from harm. [114]

Some may object that such massive dispersals at the imperial level, let alone the lower levels, were probably carried out only at rare intervals, despite the official histories' passing references to them. After all, historians know full well that other institutions of comparable importance to the body politic were never fully implemented. [115] But in this case, as with others (e.g., the donation of jade suits from the imperial workshop), the archaeological record corroborates pretty well the picture given in the received sources, leaving us to gasp at estimates of the costs incurred by the regular dispersals that were mandated for so many, even when the individual ritual items were not of particularly high quality. [116] Now we see one reason for the meticulous accounting measures featured in the numerous excavated documents from the capital and outlying provinces. The customary outlays, if not anticipated by the most careful budgeting, might at any moment exhaust the resources of state and ruling family. If those in charge really intended to maintain and enlarge their domains, extending their sway in an era expecting regular public displays, they could not afford to lose a single penny that came in, for it would soon be needed for the elaborate gift, tribute, and sacrificial exchanges that were mandated by this form of culture. Reportedly, one-third of the emperor's privy purse was designated for state funerals, one-third for gifts, and one-third for the ceremonies held at the ancestral temple. [117] On a smaller scale, the local manor head made similar preparations for provisioning, mourning, and exchange, as Cui Shi's 崔寔 (second century C.E.) *Simin yueling* 四民月令 shows. [118] Such strictness in accounting, often erroneously identified as a "holdover" from "tyrannical Qin" that survived into "Confucianizing" Han, signal the degree to which the formalities favored in the classical period depleted the surplus of cash and goods generated by the early empires.[119]

To identify public display culture as dominant in the classical period is not to deny that there were voices raised in protest against it. Mozi 墨子 (traditionally 480–390 B.C.E.) was the first identifiable opponent of public display in the period under review. In his strict cost-benefit analysis, he castigated any extractions of wealth from the commoners for ostensibly nonutilitarian purposes as "selfish" rather than "public-minded." The author of the "Moderate Burials" essay included in the *Lüshi chunqiu* 呂氏春秋 (compiled ca. 239 B.C.E.) continues in the vein of the *Mozi*, denouncing the luxurious funeral paraphernalia placed in contemporary tombs on grounds that it incites thievery and ostentation, which undermine the fundamental interests of the "filial son, the loyal subject, the loving parent, and the devoted friend" :

> As states grow larger and families richer, burials become more elaborate, [including] pearls put in the mouth of the corpse, a jade shroud covering the body like overlapping fish scales, bamboo strips bound by silk cords, trinkets and treasures, bronze goblets, tripods, pots, basins, horse-drawn carriages, clothes and coverlets, as well as halberds and swords—and in innumerable quantities.[120]

That excessive display, by confusing reckless expenditure for private self-aggrandizement with public generosity, could actually be inimical to the health of the body politic was a note sounded again two centuries later by Counselor Gong Yu 貢禹 and Chancellor Kuang Heng 匡衡, two famous high officials at the Han court who wished to introduce major economies in the state. In the short-lived religious reform of 31–28 B.C.E., Kuang Heng successfully petitioned the throne to reduce radically, in sixty-eight divisions of the empire and at 176 sites of worship in the capital, the number of state offerings to the imperial ancestors,[121] which had hitherto employed some 12,147 priests, cooks, and musicians, not counting the 25,129 men guarding the sites and tending the sacrificial animals. But Gong Yu, his contemporary, struck still closer to home when he criticized the gifts regularly dispersed by the throne to the high-ranking bureaucrats in its employ:

> Later generations [after Emperor Wen, r. 180–157 B.C.E.][122] have competed with predecessors in excess. . . . The court ministers have

also taken to emulating this model of excess, so that their clothing, footgear, and ornamented arms have become confusingly like those of the emperor. . . . [Here the memorial urges the palace to set an example of austerity.] . . . Your servant . . . once accompanied His Majesty on a trip to the empress's palace. I was presented with gifts of lacquer cups and trays, all of which had painted decoration and gold and silver mounts. These are not appropriate objects to give to a subject to sup upon.[123]

That public display could undercut the twin bases of harmonious civilized life—sedentary agriculture and ritual distinction—was the premise of similar tirades reported in sources as various as chapter 29 of the *Yantie lun* 鹽鐵論 and chapter 12 of the *Qianfu lun* 潛夫論; the propensity to "go beyond the ritual" (*guo li* 過禮) in order to create ever-more-memorable displays, rather than binding communities together, would destroy them. Once they caught sight of the luxuries regularly enjoyed by the more privileged, farmers would never be content to till the soil. And the blurring of distinctions that marked many of the public activities, with men and women of every occupation jostling for the front-row places and upstarts usurping attention, would inevitably wreak havoc with the social order.[124] Such critiques notwithstanding, the most incisive of the late Eastern Han writers testify to the remarkable persistence and pervasiveness of this display culture, as when Ying Shao 應邵 (ca.140–before 204), in *Fengsu tongyi* (compiled ca. 203), finds it simply inconceivable that an enlightened emperor like Emperor Wen would ever willfully diminish the throne's authority by refusing to have his audience halls decorated with the most sumptuous materials. Even while Ying bemoans the abuses entailed by "going beyond the rituals," he celebrates the display system as the single best means by which state and family alike may assert and maintain "awesome authority" over succeeding generations. At the imperial level, the emperor needed to uphold his supreme position by the scale and munificence of the setting provided for his activities. On the local level, unless a man found a way to "publicize his virtue locally" and thereby "acquire a powerful patron to support him," his official career would come to a standstill, no matter how great his love of learning or how dignified his private comportment.

For Ying Shao, as for many of his contemporaries, the necessity to uphold the public display system was never at issue. It was only that conflicting loyalties owed to the state, to one's own family, and to one's surrogate family through patronage occasionally made it hard to know where one's first duty lay at a time of crisis, since the multiple display networks in which elites operated were by no means at every point coextensive with those mandated by the state. Hence, in the *Fengsu tongyi* Ying determined to prioritize the tangle of obligations burdening the members of the elite in their public capacity. [125] In one entry, for example, Ying demands that men acknowledge in a public fashion the obligations established through public avowals. [126] Governor Li Zhang 李張 had nominated six men for the prestigious appointment of "Filial and Incorrupt" but he happened to die before the letters of recommendation, already sealed, reached the capital. Yet Ying concludes that the nominees were bound to carry out years of public mourning for their patron, since they had once appeared in public as the governor's protégés. To do less was to allow the entire system of public display to devolve into a matter of personal convenience—an oxymoronic situation portending ritual and political chaos.

Of course, the empire was already sliding into chaos when Ying Shao composed his analysis of contemporary mores, hoping to set some reasonable limits on local forms of participation in public display culture. Unfortunately from the government's standpoint, the same display mechanisms once emanating principally from the ruling house were liable to appropriation, in a refeudalizing era, by every manorial house and local cult, whose displays were held even in defiance of the court. [127] Thus, paradoxically, the more weight put on public display, the greater the likelihood of its collapse. Simply put, the practical problems created by extravagant displays soon outstripped the system's capacity to resolve inequities and secure men in their "proper place."

The great social theorists of Warring States and Western Han times, after all, had sold public display as a way to balance hierarchy with reciprocity. Disseminating meritocratic slogans alongside modified aristocratic models, their theories attracted adherents of starkly opposing views, habits, and goals: those with a flair for politics or for entertainment, for instance, those driven by personal devotion to others or by self-interest. But each display had to be showier than the last if it was to satisfy the public's avid desire for spectacle and imprint itself for long on memories. To meet the ever-spiraling costs of the display system, by Eastern Han times the local elites looked to unfair levies and other forms of corruption to squeeze the very segments of society whose pitiable lot the display culture was supposed to relieve: the poor farmers, tenants, and clients. Meanwhile, the huge estates of Eastern Han had made it possible to seal the enclaves of the rich from the prying eyes of the less fortunate. This only exacerbated perceptions of social and political polarization that led to empire-wide rebellions in 184 C.E. In the end, public display had turned private and selfish, just as its critics had charged it would, and just when the new Buddhist and Daoist religious organizations, contesting older ideas about the state and family, were expanding the traditional venues for display. Cao Cao 曹操 (155–220) in 206 showed his usual canniness when he expressly forbade the construction of two of the most visible signs of public display—funeral mounds and gravesite stelae—by parties outside the court.[128]

Still, as we have seen, for nearly all but the last few decades of the period under review, the dominant rhetoric of text and ritual upheld the conflation of public and private interests that lay at the theoretical heart of classical public display. And while it would be foolish to assert that impulses toward public display constituted the whole of ritual and textual activity in the period (talk of public display tells us nothing about tenant farmers' rituals or the conditions experienced by local scribes, to take two obvious examples), it is no exaggeration to say that public display consumed a great deal of many people's time, energy, and wealth.

I have dwelt on what I call the public display culture binding members through text and ritual because this helps to make sense of the archaeological record to date by removing the possibility of viewing ritual as "empty" and by suggesting one reason (probably among several) why we begin, with the late Warring States period, to find what we ordinarily think of as "secular" texts buried in tombs. Not so very long ago, people assumed that the different categories of texts found in tombs, whether bamboo or silk, administrative documents or philosophical essays, would neatly correlate with the political rank, societal status, and gender of the tomb occupants, as would the quality of the ritual items buried with the dead (pottery vs. bronze or lacquer, for example). But the record is muddier. Burial items for local elites of mid-rank include copies of the central government's penal code (as did tomb 11 at Shuihudi 睡虎地), copies of imperial decrees (as did tomb 18 at Mozuizi), and copies of texts that seem to have been addressed to the ruler (as with the "Prohibitions" strip, no. 1407, at Yinqueshan 銀雀山). The grave goods in a woman's tomb sometimes surpass in quality those of her male relatives (as at Mawangdui). The tombs do not assure us that sumptuary regulations were strictly upheld; and certain ritual items denoting the highest authority (e.g., those lacquer bowls inscribed as "fit for imperial use") come from tombs in the outlying areas of local elites or even "barbarians."[129] It is the tombs of mid-ranking officials of local prominence that have yielded many of the most impressive finds of bamboo and wooden strips, not to mention murals and pictorial stone carvings.[130] We need to think about why that might be so.

Let us begin with tomb inventories, since these figure prominently in the archaeological record. The *Yili* describes the public reading of the inventory as an important part of the funeral ritual prior to the procession, and presumably a copy was put in the tomb first for the sake of the afterworld public. Inventories, along with certain other types of documents written on bamboo, wood, or silk (especially seals, tallies, and texts testifying to public officeholding), in company with an older repertoire of ritual items (e.g., vessel sets and jade *bi* 璧) and imitations thereof (the more exalted their reputed provenance, the better), indicated the powerful connections of the deceased and possibly, in the case of males, were thought to guarantee the tomb occupant official rank in the world beyond. An analogy in America might be the nearly obligatory photograph of the mayor in the genial company of a President that most town halls sport, if the mayor has been lucky enough to score such a ritual item. Such a photo betokens the protected status of the town within the larger administration and its ability to call upon the full resources of the state in a crisis. (People have described the inventories, edicts, and statutes placed in the tombs as the "personal libraries" of the tomb occupants and imagined the dead reading these texts in the afterlife, but that particular conceit excises the social context of writing within the ritual system; fails to explain why the texts and inscriptions consigned to tombs were often written in beautiful script full of mistakes; and presumes that the tomb occupants would not have preferred the Han equivalent of light reading.) Eventually, the Han elites came to replace the old Warring States single-occupant shaft tombs with multichambered crypts for joint burials that could accommodate as many as ten family members. These joint burials had the distinct advantage of making available to the relatives, friends, and clients who gathered there to mourn the dead all the contents of the crypt on multiple occasions.[131]

During their lifetimes and after their deaths, the heads of great households, their scions, and even their chief clients commanded a vast repertoire of ritual items, some of which would have ended up in the tombs of their dead and some would have been given to allies and dependents as visible tokens of continuing ties. Having secured the loyalty of so many through public events, especially funerals, donations, and spectacles, members of this elite group could expect their followers to make offerings on their behalf down through the ages. In the tombs built for those of the highest rank, then, it was probably the totality of the rich assemblages, as much as any particular token of authority, be it a seal, a tally, or an administrative document, that testified to the tomb occupant's position and resources in this life and the next. No single item, such as a lacquer bowl marked "fit for imperial use" or a bamboo bundle of inscribed strips, was needed to authenticate a person's exalted rank when all unmistakably did so. Of course, even in the case of the tombs of the nobility, certain items might be included in the tomb for the explicit purpose of verifying the deceased's close relationship with a still more powerful patron. This may explain the inclusion in the tomb of Marquis Yi of Zeng, closed ca. 433 B.C.E., of an inscribed bell attesting close relations between the marquis and King Hui of Chu.[132]

Presumably most of those of mid-ranking wealth or status would have found it more difficult to supply the tomb with a complete set of sumptuous grave furnishings verifying the "protected" status of the tomb occupant. One solution was for them to rely upon writings to establish the status of the deceased; another, to forgo the spectacular assemblages of bronze, jade, and ivory items favored by royalty and devote their funds to two relatively cheaper means of decorating their tombs that promised to yield maximum effect: mural paintings and mass-produced stone carvings.[133] They could also provide cheaper imitations of the ritual assemblages found in the tombs of their superiors or supply fewer spectacular grave goods , as was the case with the wife of a local dignitary buried at Mashan 馬山 (Jiangling 江陵, Hubei). Except for four bronzes (two *ding* 鼎, one *hu* 壺, and a mirror), a dozen or so small lacquer items, and one strange "evil-averting" (*bixie* 辟邪) animal carved in wood, lavish silks (and the bamboo hampers to hold them) constitute nearly the whole of the grave goods at Mashan. The tomb held no writing—not even a tomb inventory—aside from three characters inscribed in black on two robes and two patterns (their legends no longer legible) stamped in red on other items.[134] Presumably, the sheer quantity and superb quality of the silks, as testaments to high status and gender, would suffice to keep the tomb occupant safe from all harm.[135]

It remains for us to perform the basic calculations: how many, how various, how valuable, and in what combinations were the status items (from concubines to bells to seals) typically supplied for different levels of society over the course of the classical period? What were acceptable substitutes in the ritual emplacements, and was a system of sumptuary regulations strictly upheld in either life or death? Archaeologists of the classical Mediterranean cultures have already begun to attend to what is *not* buried in the tombs, understanding the material world of the tombs to be very much governed by scarcity. [136] It will not be easy to come up with confident answers to these basic questions, when so many tombs from the classical era have been looted, and new, unprovenanced materials continue to flood today's market. Still, judicious conjectures about the place of text and ritual cannot be arrived at without further details about their original contexts, for text and ritual have no particular need to tell us about themselves. [137]

* * *

The preceding pages have addressed three aspects of a single topic: writing in relation to ritual in the classical period. This hasty tour of the classical period is doubtlessly oversimplified, but in the manner of the good guide, I have endeavored to direct the reader's attention to a few features of the classical landscape so that others better trained may point out, in the succeeding chapters of the volume, the finer aspects of the prospect that lies before us.

NOTES

I wish first to thank the scholars who have advised me on drafts of this paper: Robert W. Bagley, Christian De Pee, Lothar von Falkenhausen, Martin Kern, Geoffrey Lloyd, Michael Loewe, and Nathan Sivin. Geoffrey Lloyd in particular pointed out extremely useful parallels between the classical worlds in China and in the Mediterranean, but these I could not pursue in a work of this length. Any mistakes in the manuscript are my own, of course.

1. Liu Qing, "Qin Han kaoguxue wushi nian," 807, give a calculation of 30,000 Han excavated tombs.

2. For the Weiyang Palace, see *Han Chang'an cheng Weiyanggong fajue baogao*. For Juyan, see *Juyan Hanjian jiayi bian*; Loewe, *Records of Han Administration*; and Chen Zhi, *Juyan Hanjian yanjiu*. Some 180 photographs and 430 transcriptions of the Weiyang bone labels have been published so far.

3. See Tao et al., *Taiyuan Jin guo Zhaoqing mu*; Hubei sheng bowuguan, *Zeng Hou Yi mu*; Hubei sheng bowuguan and Hubei sheng wenwu kaogu yanjiusuo, *Zhanguo dixia yuegong*.

4. The bias consists of a clear preference for precious materials over nonprecious, for the inscribed over the uninscribed, and for materials that can be made to support the national discourse of Chinese exceptionalism.

5. We have only begun to understand how much of Han classicism was constructed by Yang Xiong and his admirers Huan Tan 桓譚 (ca. 43 B.C.E.–28 C.E.), Wang Chong 王充 (27–ca.100), and Ban Gu 班固 (32–92). See Nylan and Sivin, "The First Neo-Confucianism"; and Kern, "The 'Biography of Sima Xiangru'"; see also Cheng, review of *From Chronicle to Canon*; and Loewe, *The Men Who Governed Han China*, chaps. 13–15, for the role of Dong Zhongshu and Five Phases construction, which tallies with Arbuckle, "The Five Divine Lords."

6. See Sivin, "The Myth of the Naturalists"; Csikszentmihalyi and Nylan, "Constructing Lineages and Inventing Traditions." Because scholars did not organize themselves according to ideological "schools," the sweeping explanations pitting, for example, "Confucian rule by ritual" against "Legalist rule by law" and "Confucian conservatism" against "Legalist innovation" cannot elucidate much. For example, Ban Gu registers his hearty approval of Li Si 李斯, who is often portrayed as the strictest of Legalists, in remarks appended to *Shiji* (hereafter *SJ*) 6.

7. "Core" refers here to "center of population density," though many would equate it with the capital. For core vs. periphery, see, e.g., Bagley, *Ancient Sichuan*.

8. The *Zhou li*'s descriptions of high officials in no way tallies with Weber's emphasis on rational justification for bureaucratic action. As Yates, "Some Notes on Ch'in Law," 245, notes: "religious and 'magical' concepts underpinned the Ch'in bureaucratic system to a greater extent than has previously been acknowledged." See Kalinowski, "Les traités de Shuihuidi et l'hémérologie chinoise à la fin des Royaumes-Combattants."

9. A letter by Kong Rong 孔融 (153–208) plainly states that the best classicists are those that in "both civil and military are of use" (*Hou Hanshu* [hereafter *HHS*] 79B.2584). The three "Rulin zhuan" show that the typical career choice for famous Ru 儒 was assignment to the staffs of generals if the Ru did not themselves become cavalry generals or governors (a position with a definite military component). See *HHS* 79B.2571, 2577–2578, 2581.

10. For the "Six States script," see Qiu, *Chinese Writing*, 78–112. For Shu script, see Bagley, *Ancient Sichuan*, 42–45.

11. Wardy, *Aristotle in China*, dispels the myth of the unique properties of Chinese language. Barr, *The Semantics of Biblical Language*, should be required reading for all Sinologists, as some seem to subscribe to arguments that were discredited long ago in other circles.

12. For further details, see Poo, *In Search of Personal Welfare*; Harper, *Chinese Medical Texts*.

13. On this point, see Zufferey, *To the Origins of Confucianism*, esp. 361.

14. The inscribers of lacquer at the Shu Xigong 蜀西宮 imperial lacquer factory were female as well as male, and one supervisor is known to have been female. See Barbieri-Low, "The Organization of Imperial Workshops," 201, 343. Tomb M2 at Yinwan, the burial of a middle-aged woman, includes a "scholar's knife," though the woman may have been a textile worker. Shuihudi 睡虎地 strips A60 and 875 speak casually of women engaging in textile factory work and in trading. *SJ* 129 and *Hanshu* (hereafter *HS*) 91 describe the wealthy

Widow of Ba (fl. 246–210 B.C.E.), who managed a cinnabar mining operation, as a model to be emulated by women. For women as readers and agents, see Raphals, *Sharing the Light*; for women taking revenge on males, see Wang Sili, "Cong Ju Xian Dongwan Han huaxiang shi zhong di qi nü tushi Wushi ci shuilu gongzhan tu."

15. For the texts, readers may consult three new bibliographies for the classical period: Giele's *Database of Early Chinese Manuscripts*; Gentz's *Bibliographie zu Grabtexten von Joachim Gentz*; and Pian and Duan's *Ben shiji yilai chutu jianbo gaishu*. Li Yunfu, *Chuguo jianbo wenzi gouxing xitong yanjiu*, describes the excavated manuscripts and lists some 400 studies of them. The Qin commandery of Nanjun, the site of the Shuihudi finds, was once part of Chu. In fact, to date, only three Warring States sites that have yielded written texts lie outside the Chu state borders: Henan, Xinyang Changtaiguan 信陽長臺官; Gansu, Tianshuishi 天水市, Fangmatan 放馬灘; and Sichuan, Haojiaping Qingchuan 郝佳坪青川 (Giele serial nos. 005, 028, 037).

16. This last point is essentially the hypothesis advanced by Li Zehou, Connie Cook, John Major, and Li Ling, who see a Chu "high culture . . . deeply rooted in recognizable earlier Zhou and Shang cultural foundations, . . . a synthesis of transmitted high culture and the numerous regional cultures absorbed during its expansion" (Cook and Major, *Defining Chu*, 1); see also Li Zehou, *The Path of Beauty*, esp. chaps. 3–4. This interpretation unwittingly perpetuates the so-called northern bias, the belief that the most sophisticated elements of Chinese civilization came from the Central States in the middle and lower valleys of the Yellow River. Contributors to Cook and Major, particularly Barry Blakely and Susan Weld, portray Chu society as a complex, highly stratified society that valued hierarchy and order and that consequently maintained its consortium of ruling families more successfully over time than many northern states.

17. Rawson, "Western Zhou Archaeology," sees the convergence beginning already in the late Western Zhou; for the Nanyue tombs, see *Lingnan Xi Han wenwu baoku*. Of course, many of the ritual items (e.g., the jade suits and the *bi* disks) at Nanyue are undoubtedly inferior in quality to those of the Han princes.

18. See Sivin, "The Myth of the Naturalists."

19. Hallock, "The Use of Seals on the Persepolis Fortification Tablets," 128 (italics mine).

20. Freedman, *Lineage Organization in Southeastern China*, 2.

21. See DeWoskin, *A Song for One or Two*; Nylan, "Calligraphy." On this issue, I have found very helpful comparative material in Ford, *Homer*.

22. Hence, the transfers of maps, items in the Xianyang 咸陽 libraries, or ritual bronzes to rival forces were significant, as in *HHS* 66.2174, which says that, in 189 C.E., Wang Yun's 王允 intention to rebel was revealed when he "assembled the entire collection of maps and *secret* documents held in the stone chamber of the Lantai 蘭台 and took them with him."

23. For instance, the caches at Houma 侯馬 and Wen Xian 溫縣 may not be archives to be consulted but ritual objects consigned to sacrificial pits. Apparently, the Qin stone inscriptions were placed at their locations so that

announcements to the sacred mountains and seas could be made. (See *HS* 58.2632, where Ni Kuan 兒寬 congratulates Emperor Wu in 110 B.C.E. for announcing the new reign era to Daizong [Mount Tai].) In another early culture, that of Persia, we see kings inscribing rocks for the gods to read: the life of Darius was inscribed on the rock face at Behistun for the sake of Ahura Mazda.

24. For Laozi as Zhou archivist, see *Zhuangzi yinde* 35/13/46; *SJ* 67.2186. See Bi and Ruan, *Shanzuo Jinshizhi*, *juan* 19, for discussions of the popular Han scene that shows Confucius consulting Laozi on ritual and archival matters.

25. Thus, the *taixue* 太學 was placed under the aegis of the minister of rites, the *taichang* 太常, who supervised the training of official candidates in the major state rituals and in the reading, performing, and copying of sponsored texts. Not surprisingly, then, Emperor Shun 順 (r. 125–144) selected an expert in rites and music to head the *taixue* (*HHS* 79A.2557). So akin did text training and ritual performance appear to one Han emperor lauded for his patronage of culture that he considered abolishing the *taixue* after the construction of a new ritual center, the Biyong 辟雍, seemed to render the *taixue* superfluous (*HHS* 48.1606). For the pre–Qin antecedents of such institutions, one may consult Cook and Major, *Defining Chu*, 67–70, on the role of the *shi* 士.

26. Modern theories of text and ritual support their conflation, enumerating a number of functional similarities between them and urging us to see how often texts are ritualized and rituals textualized. See Bell, "Ritualization of Texts and the Textualization of Ritual." Typically texts circulated in much smaller units, and we should begin, wherever feasible, to consider these shorter units as "complete."

27. Kern, "Methodological Reflections."

28. See Pattison, *On Literacy*, viii, which confines the remark to literacy.

29. Nylan, "Sima Qian: A True Historian," relates texts to sacrificial offerings, in that both can make the dead alive and the absent present. See Connerton, *How Societies Remember*, esp. 68–69. See *Xunzi*, chap. 19, for mourning as the quintessential virtuous act that gives "body to the bodiless"; and *Mencius*, chap. 3, for Duke Wen of Teng.

30. Mozi and his followers argued that the dead do not desire the same things as the living. Xunzi believed that the dead are not conscious.

31. *SJ* 99.2722; *HS* 43.2126.

32. Some tombs include texts of edicts (e.g., Mozuizi 磨嘴子 tomb 18).

33. *Fengsu tongyi* 9.73–74. See *HHS* 79B.2570 for another case of biblioexorcism; Harper, "Wang Yen-shou's Nightmare Poem"; Knechtges and Swanson, "Seven Stimuli."

34. See Lian, "Yunmeng Qin jian 'Jie' pian kaoshu." The canonical texts are used in warding off demons in Ying Shao, *Fengsu tongyi*, chap. 9. For one example of the classical master as magician, see *HHS* 79A.2545.

35. Keegan, "The *Huang-ti Nei-ching*," 249–259, asserts that no original text ever existed in the sense of a first recension produced by a single editor or editors. Instead, a text comes into being as a consequence of an ongoing process by which pieces of texts are combined and recombined. Sima Qian's *Shiji* (ca. 100 B.C.E.) is perhaps the first long work to be conceived as a whole. Modern readers intent upon situating texts within their early cultural contexts may also

see the wisdom of breaking the old habit of considering the book to be the basic unit, when texts were more typically known throughout the classical period in much smaller units, those of *juan* 卷 or *pian* 篇.

36. See *SJ* 6.254.

37. This observation comes directly from Bagley, "Meaning and Explanation," 44.

38. On this point, see, e.g., Van Zoeren, *Poetry and Personality*; and Rouzer, *Articulated Ladies*.

39. *Zhuangzi yinde* 36/68–74.

40. See, e.g., *Xunzi*, chaps. 1 and 23; *Xinshu* 7.1a; *Yangzi Fayan*, chap. 1. In a nice example, one expert refused an imperial order to teach a prince his technique on the grounds that an immoral man used his knowledge only to do further harm; cf. *HHS* 75.3167–68. See Harper, *Chinese Medical Texts*, 55–67.

41. See Nylan, *The Five "Confucian" Classics*, chap. 1, for ritual's proliferation; for the proliferation of commentaries, see, e.g., *HS* 30.1704, 1712; *HHS* 79A.2547. Kamiya, "Gokan jidai ni okeru 'karei' o megutte iwaguru 'gokanmatsu fuzoku' saikô no kokomoi toshite," discusses mourning that "goes beyond the ritual prescriptions" as an "unorthodox" remnant of the old un-Confucianized (by which she means "uncivilized" or "unconventional") elements in Han society. On the contrary, public display of all sorts tended toward proliferation, and the most civilized elements in society tended to excess, as the *Fengsu tongyi* makes clear.

42. For the secret imperial archive (*mi shu* 祕書), see, e.g., *HS* 10.310; *HS* 100A.4203. For ritual implements normally reserved only for imperial use, the *mi qi* 祕器, and weapons so reserved, see *HS* 93.3734.

43. Han Fei 韓非 alleges that the same proscriptions occurred under Shang Yang 商鞅 (ca. 350 B.C.E.). But when Li Si advised the First Emperor of Qin in 213 B.C.E. to exempt from proscription texts on medicine, divination, and land use, did he do so not only because such technical books did not bear upon thorny questions of legitimacy but also because many households relied in daily life on having access to such texts (as Han Fei alleges of copies of the penal code)? Certainly, we find these sorts of texts in late Warring States tombs. The best source on Qin is now Kern, *The Stele Inscriptions of Ch'in Shih-huang*, esp. 188–196.

44. Mastery of the *Analects* (and, once, the *Mencius*) is mentioned in both the *HS* and the *HHS* as a source of fame; the *Xiaojing* is never so mentioned (presumably because it was too simple). It is clear, however, from the chapters that expertise in the *Analects* is considered secondary to expertise in other classics, as in *HHS* 79A.2560–2562. For further discussion on four key terms having to do with text and ritual—*wen* 文 (the character routinely translated as "literature" or "writing"), *jia* 家 ("experts" rather than "schools" organized around textual transmission), *shi* 士 ("man of service" rather than "literatus"), and Ru 儒 ("classicist" more often than "Confucian")—see Nylan, "A Problematic Model," and "Calligraphy"; Kern, "Ritual, Text, and the Formation of the Canon."

45. *HS* 88.3596.

46. So while the *SJ* noted threats to the persons of individual Han masters

and spoke of the existence of lacunae within the extant classical traditions (often in order to mock the pretensions of the so-called experts on text and ritual), it also had most of the pre–Qin traditions continuing into Han. Hence, it is likely that the Fu Sheng biography is a later interpolation, as many have suggested before me. In any case, the twenty-nine *pian* supposedly hidden in the walls of Fu Sheng's house may have represented explications or sayings (*shuo* 説), not just the *Documents* text itself. Early traditions, including the *SJ*, barely distinguish between canon and commentaries, explications, and sayings, citing the *Gongyang zhuan* 公羊傳 as *Chunqiu* 春秋 and the "Xici zhuan" 繫辭傳 as the *Changes* (Yi 易).

47. While the first alternative is certainly possible, interpolations from the *HS* have been discussed for a number of *SJ* chapters and amount to a veritable subfield of *SJ* research. The debate, which has generated a series of studies, remains controversial; for the most recent examples, see Csikszentmihalyi and Nylan, "Constructing Lineages"; and Kern, "The 'Biography of Sima Xiangru,'" which also includes further references to the major contributions on the issue so far (303 n.2).

48. *HS* 88.3621, literally "as in a net." This translation is fairly loose, since putting things "at the center" has three layers of meaning: first (and most obviously), to rectify errors; second, to make (such policies) a target (a goal) or a priority; and third, to put (them in effect) at the center (i.e., at court).

49. *HHS* 79A.2545. In the body of the chapter, it is revealed that Wang Mang wanted to monopolize all ritual activities, so he jailed one master, Liu Kun 劉昆 (who was, not coincidentally, a member of the ruling house), because Liu had drawn huge crowds when he carried out the major rituals using the simplest of materials (an implicit reproof of Wang Mang's lavish expenditures). Liu Kun and his relatives were charged with illegal gatherings and with "harboring the intention to usurp the throne." *HHS* 79A.2551 tells us that Wang Mang was jealous of those families which had made teaching the family business for several generations.

50. *HHS* 79A.2545.

51. *HHS* 79B.2588.

52. After Emperor Huan's 桓 (r. 146–167) ascension to the throne in 146, the enmity between the eunuchs of the "inner court" and the regular bureaucrats of the "outer court" escalated. This situation ended twice in proscriptions whereby a group of the court officials, together with their close relatives and clients, were forbidden to serve in office. Some of the background to the proscriptions has been ably reviewed in Li, "Handai haozu daxing de yanjiu huigu."

53. *HS* 88.3605. *HHS* 79A.2570 shows what largesse could be bestowed on such tutors. Bao Xian 包咸 was regularly given precious baubles and silk, and his salary and emoluments surpassed those of all other ministers.

54. See, e.g., *HHS* 79A.2570, 2582, and 2585 (the last shows a good official saying that "he would be loathe to lose a worthy man").

55. *HHS* 79A.2548. In the *HHS* "Rulin," the most important teachers, such as Ma Rong 馬榮 and Zheng Xuan 鄭玄 (127–200), are mentioned only in passing, though they are also credited with the popularity of a particular intepretive line.

56. That is, these men do not appear elsewhere in the *HS* (though the same men may appear in *SJ* 121). The calculation is necessarily approximate, as the identification of some men is somewhat hazy. It is very unlikely that higher number could be attained for figures in the *HHS*.

57. *HS* 88.3599.

58. *HS* 88.3616 makes it very clear, however, that "without the backing of the nobles, a man will not attain the chancellor's post, no matter how high the level of his expertise in the classics."

59. Han Jing, *Fayan zhu* (1/1), 1. Perhaps the ultimate academic honor was to have an Academician's post established within the teacher's lifetime, but we hear of that happening only once, with Xiahou Jian 夏侯建 (*HS* 6.272), so far as I know.

60. *HHS* 79B.2581. Many in Eastern Han reportedly taught several thousand students. See *HHS* 79A.2571, 2578, for examples.

61. The one exception is Meng Xi 孟喜, whose father Meng Qing 孟卿 thought his own specialty, the *Rites* canon, too difficult. See *HS* 88.3599.

62. *HHS* 79B.2580.

63. *HHS* 79A.2571.

64. See, e.g., the *HHS* 79A.2554 biography of Wei Man 魏滿 (fl. mid–Yongping period [58–76]); or the *HHS* 79A.2556 biography of Chen Yuan 陳元 (fl. 133). The record is so paltry presumably because there was as yet little cult of the individual teacher. (If the *HS* and *HHS* had followed the *SJ* model, the biographies would be much fuller, though they would still say little more about the specific content of these men's teachings.)

65. Of course it is also true that contemporary readers would have had better access to the masters' texts than we have today.

66. *SJ* 121.3125; *HHS* 79A.2554. The Zhangjiashan materials seem to imply that the appointments to clerical posts were made on a hereditary basis, subject to satisfactory performances on the tests. See Loewe, *The Men Who Governed Han China*, chap. 4, esp. 117.

67. For the first quotation, see *HHS* 79A.2565, biography of Yang Lun 楊倫 (fl. 133), which has Yang "lecturing in the marshes" to over a thousand students. For the second, see *HHS* 79A.2557, said of Mou Zhang's 牟張 (fl. 26–57) son. See the biography of Zhou Ze 周澤 (fl. 50–70), who is described as a recluse though at any given time he teaches several hundred students and clients (*HHS* 79B.2578). Zhou Fang 周防 had to decline the first offer of an appointment to a post in classical studies on the grounds that he was underage. He was soon given another offer (*HHS* 79A.2559).

68. By my count, fifteen of the forty-two men treated in the *HHS* had written textbooks of some sort.

69. See *SJ* 121.3116 and *HS* 88.3592. It was said of the *Rites* masters Xu Yan 徐延 and Xu Xiang 徐襄 (dates unknown; late second/early first century B.C.E.?) that they could not communicate to others the meaning (*tong* 通) of the *Rites* canon (*SJ* 121.3126). The *SJ* is also quite caustic in its treatment of Dong Zhongshu, a man who "perfected his learning and wrote texts" as his main job (*SJ* 121.3128). But the *HS* ascribes writings to a few more classical masters, as in *HS* 88.3597. A close comparison of the opening passages to the *SJ* and *HS*

shows how much more the Ru tradition is tied to learning the "texts of the Six Canons" in Ban Gu's history. Passages that refer to *practices* in the *SJ* are altered so that they refer to *texts* in the later history, which leaves open the question of what "learning" meant for Ban Gu. Passages that refer to *practices* in the *SJ* are altered so that they refer to *texts* in the later history. For further information, see Csikszentmihalyi and Nylan, "Constructing Lineages." By contrast, the *HHS* accounts (e.g., *HHS* 79A.2545) speak often of scholars with their bamboo bundles (i.e., texts).

70. This is very clear from the *SJ* biographies of Masters Shen 申 (fl. early second century B.C.E.) and Yuangu 轅固 (fl. mid–first century B.C.E.). See *SJ* 121.3122. (But note that *HHS* 79B.2569 says of both masters that they composed or initiated [*zuo* 作] glosses on the *Odes*, which most have taken to mean that they "wrote" the glosses.) Dong Zhongshu's writings, of course, nearly got him killed (*SJ* 121.3128).

71. *SJ* 121.3125.

72. *HS* 88.3605, which remarks that the "Ru all reveled in his glory" (*rong zhi* 榮之). The *HS* compliments Xu Shang by drawing an analogy between Xu's four most famous disciples and those of Confucius (as Yan Shigu's 顏師古 [581–645] note explains). Note that figures as late as Cai Yong 蔡邕 (132–192) assert that "explications of the classics and indirect criticism," let alone the diversions of reading "works of literature," are of little use in "rectifying the state" (*HHS* 60B.1996).

73. *SJ* 121.3115–3116.

74. *HHS* 79A.2515; this account is based on earlier versions dating from Eastern Han times. For further discussion of these anecdotes and their implications, see Nylan, "Calligraphy," 40–41.

75. *HHS* 79A.2553.

76. *HS* 88.3610.

77. *HS* 88.3598–3599 (for an example of each) and 3604.

78. E.g., *HS* 88.3602, 3617.

79. *HS* 64.2106.

80. For *Chunqiu* prognostications, see, e.g., *HS* 88.3615–3618; *HHS* 79B.2479, 2583, which make this fairly plain. For prognostications by the *Odes* and *Rites*, see *HHS* 79B.2575, 79A.2572. That the technical arts are tied to prognostication is made clear in numerous biographies, including *HHS* 79B.2582–2583. *HHS* 79B.2575 shows clearly that those who could not boast of such arts were treated more or less as menials at court. See *HHS* 79A.2550, 79B.2573. *HHS* 79B.2585 remarks that the "men at court valued the Ru arts more" after successful predictions had been made.

81. *HS* 88.3600.

82. For examples where the Five Classics are treated as discrete parts making up a whole, see my introduction to *Five "Confucian" Classics*, section 3.

83. The anecdotes about Bao Xian, Red Eyebrows, and Yellow Turbans are typical. For the *waiqi* search for talent, see *HHS* 79A.2581.

84. *HHS* 79A.2556. Li Zhen was not a student of Ouyang Xi. In another famous case, Yang Lun left his post to mourn Emperor An 安 (r. 106–125)—whose invitations to serve at court Yang had refused—though the law

required that he request permission to leave (*HHS* 79A.2564).

85. *HHS* 79A.2552.

86. *HHS* 79A.2579.

87. *HHS* 79A.2581.

88. *HHS* 79A.2574, 2558.

89. *SJ* 121.3126. This may be why the court in Eastern Han is still working on the rites and music for the ancestral shrines dedicated to the imperial family and drafting the liturgies for the all-important suburban sacrifices (*HHS* 79A.2577).

90. *HS* 88.3599.

91. *HS* 88.3599; *HHS* 79B.2587.

92. *HS* 88.3599.

93. See *HS* 88.3599, 88.3607, for examples. Two students of the *Yijing* were singled out as honest officials (*HS* 88.3598), but it is clear that another student's fame derived from his position as governor of Changshan 常山 (*HS* 88.3598). Evidently, it was rarely the case that an officer "took not the smallest item from anyone else" while in office (*HHS* 79B.2578–2579).

94. *HS* 88.3603.

95. Han Jing, *Fayan zhu* (2/12), 94.

96. On this point, see Lü, *Lü Simian du shi zha ji*, vol. 1, 637–657.

97. For the imperial favor granted those exemplifying such learning, see *HHS* 79A.2545. One is reminded of the modern case of Mao's peasant father, who wanted his son to learn the classics because some well-chosen quotations, produced at the right moment, "could help in winning lawsuits." See Spence, *Mao*, 4.

98. *Lunheng jiaoshi* 21.547, citing the views attributed to *Xunzi*.

99. Translation modified from Makeham, *Balanced Discourses*, 143.

100. *Lunheng jiaoshi* 21.535.

101. Han Jing, *Fayan zhu* (1/15), 14.

102. Chapter 8 of the *Mozi*, "Honoring the Worthy," discusses the popular associations of "wealth and power" and "display." Barbieri-Low, "The Organization of Imperial Workshops," discusses the Changle banquets; Loewe, "The Imperial Tombs of the Former Han Dynasty and Their Shrines," 283, the parade of the emperor's effects. I had already discussed "public display culture" when a colleague, Gary McDonogh, gave me Habermas, *The Structural Transformation of the Public Sphere*, which uses, especially in its informative introduction, the same term and comparable descriptions to explain the eventual creation of the modern public space. (See also the opening chapters of Foucault's *Discipline and Punish*.) Texts as various as the "Hong fan" 鴻範 chapter of the *Documents* and the *Han Feizi* chapter "Two Handles" (Er bing 二柄) consider how to motivate subject populations through their desire for material goods. Xu Anguo's 許安國 stone shrine (dated 157 C.E.) is addressed to "all you onlookers" (*zhu you guan zhe* 諸游觀者), as reported in Jining diqu wenwuzu and Jiaxiang Xian wenguansuo, "Shandong Jiaxiang Songshan 1980 nian chutu de Han huaxiang shi," 63, 69–70.

103. I am careful to speak of "human condition," rather than "human nature," as theorists of the classical period disputed which aspects of the human

condition are due to nature and which to nurture. (The Chinese wrote of *renqing* 人情.) I relate such arguments in my "On the Politics of Pleasure."

104. See the Wu Ban 武班 stele (ca. 148 C.E.), cited in Rong, *Han Wu Liang ci huaxiang lu, kaoshi* section, 5b. A similar phrase used of state representatives is that they should "discern and display for commoners [right conduct]" (*HHS* 39.1307); Han Jing, *Fayan zhu* (6/19), 140.

105. Poo, *In Search of Personal Welfare.*

106. According to *Chunqiu fanlu yizheng* 1.19, the reason for altering the color of vestments, the form of the ritual music used, and so on, is that such changes "make clear . . . and visible" the legitimacy of the authorities.

107. See, e.g., the argumentation of the *Xici* B/4.

108. It is my contention that the slippery rhetoric of *gong* 公 and *si* 私 impeded substantive debate on the nature of authority. Moreover, Kertzer, *Ritual, Politics, and Power*, 1–14, 77–101, has noted that ritual works against certain sorts of critical reflection on its own origins and institutions. According to Bell, *Ritual*, 129, "When ritual is the principal medium by which power relationships are constructed, the power is usually perceived as coming from sources beyond the immediate control of the human community."

109. Sommer, *Sex, Law, and Society in Late Imperial China*, 5, distinguishes status performance from gender performance in this way: with status performance, different status groups are held to distinct standards of familial and sexual morality; with gender performance, a uniform standard of sexual morality and criminal liability is extended across old status boundaries, and all people are expected to conform to gender roles strictly defined in terms of marriage. Only women of high status were asked in Han to parade their chaste widowhood, for example.

110. For the annual parade, see n. 77; for Chen Shi, see *HHS* 62.2067. Note that mourning was defined as the prototypical ritual by the *Xunzi* and by the three *Rites* canons.

111. About 39% of the extant stelae are dedicated to those with high official positions. Some dedicatees were political dissidents, but many held low rank. For example, Zhang Xuan 張玄 was a county clerk, according to Cai Yong, "Junyuanli Zhang Xuan citang beiming 郡掾吏張玄祠堂碑銘," in *Cai zhonglang ji* 6.3a. For financial assistance by neighbors, see *HHS* 68.2233; *Fengsu tongyi* 5.218–219; and Brown, "Men in Mourning," 8.

112. Bodde, *Festivals in Classical China*, 139, 140, 142. Many passages describe the court's formal funeral donations (e.g., *HHS* 10B.442). For Zhang Heng's *fu*, see *Wen xuan* 3.1a–35a; trans. Knechtges, *Wen xuan*, vol. 1, 181–310.

113. For the emperor as standard or banner, see chapter 4 of the *Lienü zhuan* 列女傳; for him as distributor, see *Han Shi waizhuan zhuzi suoyin* 4/11.

114. See Loewe, "The Wooden and Bamboo Strips Found at Mo-chü-tzu." At least four possibilities may account for the staffs' being topped by wooden, rather than jade, doves: (1) jade figured only very minimally in the decoration of the staffs (perhaps as a tag or in the doves' eyes?), since Han references to "gold and silver vessels" sometimes describe vessels with gold and silver only in their mounts; (2) the staffs buried in tombs are only replicas of staffs still held in the

families' possession; (3) as Han rule declined, it could no longer afford to give out jade-topped staffs on the scale required by law; or (4) only officials received the jade doves.

115. For example, the Eastern Han emperor was unable to conduct, as mandated, the accurate cadastral surveys on which taxation was to be based. Similarly, the court was unable to enforce the decreed limitations on landholdings. As for sumptuary laws, to date there have been too few excavations in the capital areas of Xianyang/Chang'an and Luoyang to help us assess the pervasiveness or effectiveness of observance of either the *Yili*'s 儀禮 sumptuary system or that outlined in the standard histories. How far sumptuary regulations prevailed during Han is hotly debated in China; one would expect obedience in proportion to the strength of the enforcer and the proximity to the local seats of government. There may have been sumptuary regulations of which we are ignorant. At this point, we also do not know how the sumptuary system(s) worked with the gift-exchange and tributary systems.

116. If estimates have nearly 10% of the state revenues going to pay for the gifts to tributary states alone, we can only guess how much of the budget was allotted to domestic spectacles of one sort or another. See Ebrey, *The Cambridge Illustrated History of China*, 70. One estimate from the *Jinshu* (given above) may be relevant to Han.

117. See Loewe, "State Funerals of the Han Empire," and "The Imperial Way of Death in Han China."

118. Fragments of Cui Shi's work survive in *Qimin yaoshu* 齊民要術, which is quoted in *Simin yueling jishu*, annotated by Miao Qiyu; see also Ebrey, "Estate and Family Management in the Later Han." See *Fan Shengzhi shu jin shi*, as analyzed by Shi Shenghan. One could also cite the many murals that depict manor activities. In a memorial addressed to the throne in 178 B.C.E. Chao Cuo 晁錯 spoke of quite ordinary families needing funds to "*entertain guests*, bury the dead, visit the sick, care for orphans, and bring up the young" (italics mine).

119. I think here of the slow change in fashions in grave furnishings, whereby an initial emphasis in Western Han on ceremonial ritual vessels (either real vessels themselves or pottery models of them) yields to models and images of moneymaking ventures. So many of the Han graves have been looted, however, that one can only hypothesize on this point.

120. *Lüshi chunqiu*, "Jiesang" 解喪, 98–100, which is the subject of two recent studies: Kawasaki, "*Ryoshi shunjū* 'Setsusō hen' to 'Anshi hen' to ni tsuite"; Riegel, "Do Not Serve the Dead as You Serve the Living."

121. Loewe, *Crisis and Conflict in Han China*, 154–192. The drastic reduction in the number and frequency of imperial offerings (abolishing 475 out of 683 primary and secondary sites for worship) lasted only from 31 to 28 B.C.E.

122. The mythic stature of Emperor Wen 文 (r. 180–157 B.C.E.) as a "frugal emperor" appears to be based on his deathbed edict (*HS* 4.131–133) and his refusal to build an open-air terrace (*SJ* 10.433). For a critique of the myth, see *Fengsu tongyi* 2.13–16. Ying Shao argues that every good emperor must uphold the imperial prerogatives and lavish court rituals. (Ying Shao here adopted the *Xunzi*'s line in "Fu guo.") Complaints about lavish expenditures by Emperor Wen's court were, in fact, registered by Emperor Wen's advisor, Jia Yi 賈誼

(200–168 B.C.E.).

123. *HS* 72.3070, citing *Analects* 16/5. I am indebted to Anthony Barbieri-Low for bringing this passage to my attention. It figures largely in Barbieri-Low, "The Organization of Imperial Workshops."

124. Both these points trouble Yang Xiong, who wrote in his *Fayan* (Han Jing, *Fayan zhu* [9/27], 220): "If there are no constraints imposed by the law [via sumptuary regulations], then commoners will till fields as extensive as those of a lord; live in houses fit for a lord; eat meals fit for a lord; and wear clothes fit for a lord. At the same time, most of the people will not have a sufficiency."

125. Ying Shao gave four simple guidelines: (1) except that to the ruler, no obligation, including that to the teacher, supersedes the obligations owed to a parent; (2) kin and surrogate-kin obligations must never be motivated by gain; (3) men must never feel free to opt out of the obligations laid down by convention in the public sphere; (4) nor may they regard mourning as an obligation essentially private in nature. See *Fengsu tongyi* 3.21–25. With point (4), Ying was arguing against Xun Shuang 荀爽 (128–190), who had opined in a memorial that social relations expressed through mourning ritual transcended all claims made on the person by political institutions, even those by the ruling house.

126. *Fengsu tongyi* 5.37–38.

127. The archaeological record confirms that the Western Han court had greater control over the public display system than the Eastern Han. See Huang, "Handai zhuhou wang mu lunshu." Scholars have debated the main source of elite status in Eastern Han, which I here ascribe, at least in part, to the production and control of display mechanisms that make for "awesome authority." My view supplements those of Niida Noboru 仁井田陞, who saw in court appointments the main source of status and power; of those who, including Mao Han-kuang and Yang Lien-sheng, derived elite status from control over production and virtual autonomy from the central court; and of members of the Kyoto and Tokyo schools (led by Kawakatsu Yoshi 川勝義雄 in the former and Masubuchi Tatsuo 増淵龍夫 in the latter), who all emphasize the importance to Eastern Han elite status of partisanship against the eunuchs. See, e.g., Mao, "The Evolution in the Nature of the Medieval Genteel Family"; Yang Lien-sheng, "Great Families of Eastern Han."

128. Cao Cao prohibited the erection of new stelae and sought to destroy existing ones (*Sanguozhi* 1.27, 51; 2.81). Grave stelae thereafter were to be concealed from public view. Third-century tombs were much smaller and less ornate. See Zhao Chao, *Zhongguo gudai shike gailun*, 91–93; Zhang Jiefu, *Zhongguo sangzangshi*, 119, 137; Steinhardt, "From Koguryo to Gansu and Xinjiang." Note that in the Tang, in contrast to the Han, commoners were forbidden to witness the elaborate ceremonial processions conducted by the emperor, aristocrats, or court eunuchs, though the emperor might be accompanied by "a crowd of 200,000 guards and soldiers." See Heng, *Cities of Aristocrats and Bureaucrats*, 1–10, 45–46.

129. No such lacquer items have been found to date in the rich burial assemblages in the tombs of members of the royal family, even when those

tombs contain numerous lacquer items suitable for ritual use. See Barbieri-Low, "The Organization of Imperial Workshops," chap. 2, on the distribution of thousands of lacquer vessels to provincial officials and barbarians, as well as to members of the court. Of course, bowls said to be "fit for imperial use" were not necessarily made for imperial use; they may have been knock-offs of the imperial models.

130. Jiang Yingju, "Guanyu Han huaxiang shi chansheng beijing yu yishu gongneng de xikao," notes that as yet no excavated tombs of the Eastern Han princes have had painted murals or pictorial carvings on the wall.

131. In the multichambered tombs there is also a clear shift to a focus on the domed audience hall rather than the coffin chamber itself.

132. Hubei sheng bowuguan, *Suixian Zenghou Yi mu*; also Bagley, *Music in the Age of Confucius*.

133. See Jiang Yingju, "Guanyu Han huaxiang shi chansheng beijing yu yishu gongneng de xikao." That these murals and carvings were seen when the Eastern Han tombs were reopened for successive burials goes without saying. Eastern Han tombs contain up to ten separate chambers for the dead. For the history of joint burials in the immediate post–Han period, see Zhu Dawei et al., *Wei Jin nanbeichao shehui kexue shenghuo shi*, 288–292.

134. Hubei sheng Jingzhou diqu bowuguan, *Jiangling Mashan yihao Chu mu*.

135. Of course, we can also imagine that a person might so prize one or two precious status objects (including texts) that he or she would wish to be buried with them.

136. See Morris, *Archaeology as Cultural History*, 27.

137. As others have observed, the first complete site report of a Han or Six Dynasties tomb came in 1991, with Yinan 沂南. Surprisingly few exhaustive reports of Han tombs have followed, though reports on excavations at the Han capital of Chang'an have been exemplary. There is as yet no full excavation report on tombs 2 and 3 at Mawangdui, as pointed out in Harper, *Chinese Medical Texts*, 14.

Chapter 2

The Composite Nature of Early Chinese Texts

William G. Boltz

To gain the clearest and most comprehensive understanding of an early Chinese written text we must take into account the text's structural, and sometimes physical, form and its structural, and sometimes physical, relation to other early texts. Beyond this, ultimately, we must consider its relation to the literate environment in which it was produced. Only when all of these aspects have been fully scrutinized can we be sure that we have laid the best foundation possible on which to achieve an understanding of the text's meaning in all respects: its function and use, its intention and purport, and its status in the cultural setting of which it was a part. Early Chinese texts were, we presume, by and large not composed in isolation, and certainly they did not exist in a vacuum. Some texts may have originated in written form directly among the literate levels of the society; others likely were in origin oral, performative compositions and in such cases are products of an environment where the role or degree of literacy is not at issue. Texts that arose and were transmitted exclusively orally are probably the exception; even if they were common, in the absence of written versions we would know virtually nothing of them. Many texts, perhaps the majority in the pre–Han world, are likely to have partaken of both oral and written devices. In any event texts generally, we may confidently suppose, arose as products of an intellectually, ceremonially, and culturally complex society, and their meaning thus depends in its fullest form on their relation to and role in that society. One of the most concrete, specific expressions of this point in recent sinological literature is spelled out by Lothar von Falkenhausen in a review article discussing the reading and interpretation of bronze inscriptions:

At the outset of any discussion of the Zhou bronze inscriptions, it must be understood that they were inscribed on ritual vessels, implements, and tuned bells, which were placed in lineage temples. The vessels and implements were to be displayed on an altar and used for sacrificing foodstuffs to the ancestors, and ritual music was played on the bells during these sacrifices. In order to understand the full meaning of a bronze inscription, therefore, we must consider it in conjunction with the *use* of the inscribed medium.[1]

To illustrate particularly what he has in mind here, Falkenhausen refers to Xu Zhongshu's 徐中舒 now classic article on the *guci* 嘏辭, "felicitous phrases," component of Western Zhou bronze inscriptions, in which Xu showed that these phrases, which appear regularly as the concluding lines of inscriptions, are in fact written representations of what clearly seem to have been oral, invocational parts of a ceremonial performance, presumably involving the use of the inscribed bronze itself.[2] The central point is that a full understanding of the inscriptions in which the *guci* appear is possible only when this complex relation among the text, the physical text-carrier, and a ceremonial performance context is recognized.[3] While this observation in a generalized form lies in a sense at the center of the thesis explored here, in another sense the scope of its implications and possible ramifications from text to text, genre to genre, and epoch to epoch is so great that it can serve no more specific purpose than to remind us in principle of the need to understand the details of the compositional structure of early Chinese texts and of the nature of authorship *more sinico*. My specific goal here is to try to demonstrate the extent to which we can see how "compositional" early Chinese texts are and to suggest that this composite structure is more of a norm than an exception in the periods before the empire. The implications and interpretations that may present themselves as a consequence of seeing texts in this way I leave for others to explore.

Any investigation into the structure and physical nature of early texts can go only where the evidence allows it to go, and there are really only two kinds of evidence, corresponding to the two general kinds of text documents that we have available: evidence from discovered texts and evidence from transmitted texts.[4] Some questions will perforce be largely unanswerable, for want of direct evidence of any kind: questions, for example, of authorial identity, of the extent of readership and literacy, among others. Clearly, evidence from exclusively written documents will tell us nothing about texts that might have originated and existed only orally. But texts that we know solely from written sources and that we tend to think of somewhat uncritically as having always from the moment of their first composition been written may very well, when carefully scrutinized, reveal vestiges of oral performance, even oral origin and transmission. The evidence we now have from the large quantity of recently discovered manuscripts, taken together with what we can deduce from careful analyses of transmitted texts, allows us to say something about the general nature of early Chinese texts overall that will have the potential, I hope, to throw some light on the deeper question of the meaning and function of these texts in pre-imperial China.

Evidence from Manuscripts

Enno Giele's recently compiled catalogue of reports on nearly all of the early Chinese manuscript finds known and reported in the literature to date identifies each text by site location and type.[5] Among other information, he notes the occurrences of manuscripts that have counterparts among extant, transmitted texts. His catalogue reports on manuscript finds from 149 sites. Of these, 16 have yielded manuscripts with transmitted counterparts, which is very close to 10%. In other words, 90% of sites where manuscripts have been found do not include anything that has any match among transmitted texts that we know of.[6] Of Giele's 149 archaeological sites, the great majority are tombs. Most of the non-tomb sites are ruins in the sands of Central Asia; these total 35, of which 5 have yielded manuscripts with transmitted counterparts. If we eliminate these from the totals, so as to restrict ourselves to tomb texts, we end up with 114 sites where manuscripts have been found, of which 11 include manuscripts that have matches among transmitted texts. Notice that we are still at a 10 % figure, which means that, at least based on this sampling, the ratio of manuscripts with transmitted textual counterparts to those without is about 1 to 10, irrespective of whether the texts come from tombs or not.[7]

Of the tomb texts that have been identified precisely enough to be recognizable as having substantial transmitted counterparts, only three works are recognized or reported to date as occurring more than once: the *Yijing* 易經, the *Laozi* 老子, and the "Zi yi" 緇衣 chapter of the *Liji* 禮記.[8] We might have guessed the first two; but the presence of the "Zi yi" on this list is a bit of a surprise, since it is not generally considered to stand as one of the major literary, philosophical, or religious treatises of the pre-imperial Chinese noetic world.[9]

While the primary text of the Mawangdui 馬王堆 *Yijing* is pretty close to its received counterpart at the level of individual passages, in his study of this manuscript Edward L. Shaughnessy has drawn particular attention to the fact that the order of the hexagrams and their associated texts and the order of passages in the appended texts differ "appreciably from those of the received versions."[10] Shaughnessy gives a table of the correspondences between the Mawangdui manuscript text and the received *Yijing* text from which my table 2.1 has been abstracted.[11]

TABLE 2.1

MWD	R	MWD	R	MWD	R	MWD	R
01	01	17	29	33	02	49	30
02	12	18	05	34	11	50	14
03	33	19	08	35	15	51	35
04	10	20	34	36	19	52	56
05	06	21	60	37	07	53	38
06	13	22	63	38	36	54	64
07	25	23	03	39	24	55	21
08	44	24	48	40	46	56	50
09	52	25	51	41	58	57	57
10	26	26	34	42	43	58	09
11	23	27	16	43	45	59	20
12	41	28	62	44	31	60	53
13	04	29	54	45	47	61	61
14	22	30	40	46	49	62	59
15	27	31	55	47	17	63	37
16	18	32	32	48	28	64	42

Note: MWD = Mawangdui; R = received, i.e., transmitted.

It is clear from the table that there is no systematic or identifiably regular pattern to the set of correspondences. We can only conclude that the order of the parts of each version relative to the order in the other version is random. This does not mean that the internal order of one or the other version is necessarily random in and of itself. Rather, quite to the contrary, it may well be that there is a significance to the order in which the parts occur in a given version; that is to say, the order in which passages such as these are assembled is a meaningful inherent part of textual composition overall.[12] Shaughnessy in fact points out that in regard to the structure of the hexagrams there is in his view more logic to the order of the parts in the Mawangdui manuscript version than to the order found in the received text.[13] Whatever interpretation we may wish to give to the varying order of parts from version to version, the fact of the variation itself is a feature that we will find repeatedly characteristic of the relation between discovered and transmitted texts, and its implications for overall textual structure is what I would like to focus on here.

If we look at the Guodian 郭店 *Laozi*, we will find exactly the same kind of thing; namely, at the level of individual sections and lines the match with the received *Laozi* is pretty close throughout, but the order of the passages varies considerably from the order they take in the received *Laozi*. And, as we shall see, that is also what we find in the case of the Guodian "Zi yi" text. In table 2.2, I have listed in numerical order the Guodian strips for the three separate manuscripts that have passages with matches in the transmitted *Laozi* and have given the numbers of the chapters of the transmitted version with which the text of the strip in question matches.[14]

To the extent that the order of the strips is arbitrary, this is the order fixed by the Chinese editors. Places where I have marked a horizontal line between strip numbers are places where the sequence of strips is not defined or determined by content. But elsewhere the order of the strips is fixed by the text itself, with continuous passages going from the bottom of one strip to the top of the next, determining what strip follows what strip. Clearly, this also defines unambiguously the order of the text in those large sections, and as can be seen from the numbers of the corresponding transmitted *Laozi* chapters, the order of the passages in the Guodian strips is wildly different from that of the received version. Even the overarching division between "Dao jing" 道經 chapters and "De jing" 德經 chapters is not in evidence, suggesting that the Dao 道 – De 德 dichotomy, or complementarity, however it is better viewed, is an alternative, and perhaps later, textual and conceptual imposition, not an originally exclusive or intrinsic one. There

TABLE 2.2

| GD manuscript A | | | |
GD strip	LZ chapter	GD strip	LZ chapter
01	19	21	25
02	19, 66	22	25
03	66	23	25, 05
04	66	24	16
05	66, 46	25	64
06	46, 30	26	64
07	30	27	64, 56
08	30, 15	28	56
09	15	29	56, 57
10	15, 64	30	57
11	64	31	57
12	64	32	57
13	64, 37	33	55
14	37, 63	34	55
15	63, 02	35	55, 44
16	02	36	44
17	02	37	44, 40, 09
18	02, 32	38	09
19	32	39	09
20	32		

Note: GD = Guodian strips; *LZ* = *Laozi*

TABLE 2.2 (*continued*)

GD manuscript B		GD manuscript C	
GD strip	*LZ chapter*	*GD strip*	*LZ chapter*
01-02	59	01	17
03	59, 48	02	17, 18
04	48, 20	03	18
05	20, 13	04-05	35
06-07-08	13	06-07-08-09-10	31
09-10-11-12	41	11-12-13-14	64
13	52		
14	45		
15	45, 54		
16-17-18	54		

Note: GD = Guodian strips; *LZ* = *Laozi*

are only two places where the order of the manuscript passages matches that of the received text: strips 27–32 of manuscript A has a passage that matches *Laozi* chapters 56–57, and in manuscript C strips 01–02–03 contain a passage that matches chapters 17 and 18 of the received text. Apart from those instances, the order is entirely different and seems, relative to the received text, to be random.

Table 2.3 shows the correspondences between the sections of the received "Zi yi" chapter of the *Liji* and the Guodian strip manuscript with the same basic text, but again with a very different order of sections.[15] There are twenty-five sections in the transmitted text and twenty-three in the Guodian manuscript.[16] Sections 1, 16, and 18 of the received text do not find any counterparts in the manuscript, and section 7 of the received text is divided into two separate sections in the manuscript. More important than these slight discrepancies, though, is the fact that the order of the sections is substantially different each from the other. We can see that the order in the

TABLE 2.3

GD section	on GD strips	matches R section	GD section	on GD strips	matches R section
A	1–2	2	M	27–29	13
B	2–3	11	N	29–30	7a
C	3–5	10	O	30–32	7b
D	5–8	12	P	32–34	8
E	8–10	17	Q	34–37	24
F	10–12	6	R	37–40	19
G	12–14	5	S	40–41	23
H	14–16	4	T	41–42	22
I	16–17	9	U	42–43	20
J	17–19	15	V	43–45	21
K	19–23	14	W	45–47	25
L	23–27	3			

Note: GD = Guodian strips; R = received "Zi yi" chapter of the *Liji*

Guodian manuscript is not quite scrambled in a way entirely unrelated to the order of the received text; there is a certain consistent grouping of three or four passages together, even though the precise order within the groups is different between the manuscript and transmitted versions. Notice, for example, that Guodian sections B–C–D match R sections 11–10–12, and Q through W, the last seven sections of the manuscript, match R sections 19 through 25, the last seven sections of the transmitted text, though again the internal order of each of these groupings differs from the other.

On the basis of these few observations about the match between manuscripts and transmitted texts I would like to suggest that in all three cases, that is, for the *Laozi*, the *Yijing*, and the "Zi yi" chapter of the *Liji*, the text is constructed out of an assemblage of individual textual units.[17] These units, as I am going to call them, correspond in size to what we might call "paragraphs" in English, though in the Chinese case they were in their content self-contained and self-standing in a way that we do not normally insist on for a paragraph in the Western sense. And the manuscript and transmitted versions of these text units individually are fairly close in form and content to each other. It is the order in which the units themselves are put together to make larger texts that varies greatly between manuscript and received text. The larger texts are, to phrase it another way, constructed out of these kinds of units serving as textual building blocks. In the case of the *Yijing*, the building block is the text for a single hexagram; in the appended passages it is a single corresponding "paragraph." For the "Zi yi" chapter, a paragraph consists of one of the sections identified in table 2.3, each typically ending with a citation of a few lines from one of the *Shijing* 詩經 odes, often along with a line from the *Shujing* 書經 and occasionally a line from a third text.

For the *Laozi*, a building block corresponds to what in modern terms we call a single "chapter." In traditional Chinese terminology this is the *zhang* 章. The identification of the *zhang* as the basic stylistic unit of the *Laozi* has recently been pointed out by Rudolf Wagner, who shows how the textual unit of the *zhang* as a stylistic and rhetorical feature of what he calls interlocking parallelism might be an aid in establishing a critical history of the text.[18] While I have no particular disagreement with what Wagner suggests for the *Laozi*, I think we can defend a more general comment. I would suggest that the evidence we have just surveyed allows us to say something like this: when we find transmitted texts that have manuscript counterparts, the transmitted texts will typically show themselves to be constructed out of individual textual units of about a "paragraph" in length, and the basis of a correspondence with the manuscript will be that unit, not the overall structure of the larger text. The transmitted text in comparison with its manuscript counterpart will give the impression that the *zhang* is a kind of movable piece, and that the order in which these building blocks come, together with whatever other, nonmatching passages may have been introduced, is a consequence of the vicissitudes of a text's compositional history.[19] I have phrased this deliberately in a very general way because I want to allow for as much variation on this pattern as possible, while still preserving the underlying observation. That observation, or claim, in effect is that early manuscripts—chiefly, but not exclusively, tomb manuscripts—are made up of *zhang*-sized pieces, and the corresponding transmitted texts, by and large, are different assemblages of those pieces, with such subtractions or additions from other sources as an editor might wish to make.[20] This gives, I think, a rather good indication of one of the ways that the scholar-editors of the third century B.C.E., and the early Han, went about their compositional, editorial, and revisionist tasks. And all of this suggests that lengthy, literary or essay-like texts, authored by a single writer, in the way we typically think of a text in the modern world, do not reflect the norm for early China but were, at best, the exception.[21] I am tempted to refer to this phenomenon generally as "the composite nature of early Chinese texts."

There is one clear exception to the picture I have tried to draw here contrasting the structure of manuscripts with that of the transmitted texts: the Mawangdui *Laozi*. There are only three places in the manuscripts where the match in the order of the individual *zhang*, that is, chapters, differs from that of the received text.[22] This is a feature of the Mawangdui *Laozi* specifically, not of the Mawangdui manuscripts as a whole, as can be seen from the evidence of the Mawangdui *Yijing* manuscript, which, as I mentioned earlier, varies in the order of its parts from the received text. The fact of such a close match between the A and B Mawangdui *Laozi* manuscripts on the one hand and the received text on the other shows clearly that, unlike the Guodian manuscripts with *Laozi* matches, these two manuscripts represent the same version that we have in the transmitted text. It is this version *alone* that is known as the *Laozi, Dao de jing*.

The point that has been argued so far is that pre–Han texts tend to be structurally composites. This much I have tried to demonstrate on the basis of the tangible evidence of discovered manuscripts when compared to transmitted, received texts that include matching text passages. If we think of the act of composing texts as in significant part the act of selecting and assembling passages from a reservoir of so-called textual building blocks, this then amounts to an editorial process and presumes a doctrinal or other similarly purposeful motivation. And if we allow ourselves further to call an edited version of a text relative to its sources a "textual lineage" and to equate that with a doctrinal school or practice, however ephemeral and local such might have been in the third century B.C.E., we could then say that the Mawangdui manuscripts represent the same "practitioner lineage" seen in the received text and that, by contrast, the Guodian passages of the same material reflect either a different lineage or no lineage at all—in this latter case constituting instead unedited, "raw" source material. I would go so far as to say, in fact, that the Mawangdui *Laozi* is the *Laozi*, whereas the Guodian material is not properly called the *Laozi* in any meaningful sense but is rather a collection of textual units some of which have subsequently been brought together by unknown editors or compilers to constitute the text that has been transmitted as the *Laozi*.[23]

One implication of this is that we cannot assume automatically that the distinction between manuscript and received text corresponds in a fixed way to the distinction between unedited and edited text. A second implication is that the composition of the text that we know as, and can justifiably call, the *Laozi* is as much an editorial enterprise as it is an authorial one, maybe even more so. This editorial enterprise, devoted to fixing a stable form of the text, may have taken place in the context of the emergence of clearly differentiated and self-aware doctrinal schools, what I referred to above as "practitioner lineages."[24] A *stable* form of a text is then in effect that form of the text deemed *acceptable* by whatever school or lineage happened to predominate, by chance or design, over the text's transmission. By the same token, discovered manuscripts that include portions of known transmitted texts, but ordered differently or not ordered at all, cannot a priori be taken as representative of the same doctrinal or intellectual stance associated with the transmitted counterpart. It follows that neither can such a manuscript be automatically called a "version" of the received text in any meaningful sense. Particular doctrines, philosophies, precepts, belief systems, and so forth that we have come to associate with specific texts we now must recognize might only be properly associated with the *transmitted, received* versions of those texts, and not necessarily with manuscripts that include portions, even large portions, of those same texts.[25]

The suggestion that texts such as the *Laozi* arose and took form out of a fund of preexisting textual materials, what I have been calling textual building blocks, is consistent with the picture that Mark Edward Lewis draws in his recent book *Writing and Authority in Early China*, where, for example, he says:

> Texts were written as collections of quotations because they derived their authority from the supposed wisdom of the master. The master in turn derived his authority from the presence of disciples. A simple exposition in essay form would have been the ungrounded assertions of an isolated individual. What made the words worth listening to was the fact of their having been heeded by others, and that fact was proven only in the re-enunciation of the teaching scene. The authority of the master, in turn, was essential to that of the disciples. To the extent that they could be transmitters of the wisdom of a great sage or teacher,

they could present themselves in turn as teachers, . . . Thus the text, the master, and the disciples were inextricably bound together. Without the text there was no master and no disciples . . . ; without the master there was no authoritative text or no transmitters of the text; without the disciples the text was not written or transmitted, and the master vanished together with his teachings.[26]

The crucial implication of this tripartite "master-text-disciple" phenomenon, which Lewis has identified, is that texts serving as vehicles of teaching practice between masters and disciples have a performative or *practicum* kind of role. When this is understood in the broadest sense, not just as a characterization of the conventional "teacher/master-student/disciple" relation but also as a framework for maintaining social norms for the performance of ceremonial and religious rites, funeral and ancestral worship practices and customs, the transmission of revealed beliefs, and so forth, we can see how the text was more than a passive and static record. It seems likely that texts were composed and recomposed actively as they were used by teachers, masters, students, and disciples in the perpetuation of all of these kinds of practices. And this composition and recomposition could have consisted as much in the (re)assembling and (re)ordering of the building-block passages as in the actual composing of new material. If this took place in conjunction with varying ceremonial practices where the texts had a performative role, the reordering and revising may easily have been an orally accomplished process, finding its written form only after the fact, if at all.

While the *Laozi* materials do not show what Lewis refers to as a "teaching scene" directly, shaped by an explicit master-disciple framework of the kind that the *Lunyu* and the *Mencius*, for example, show, still the text itself is the same kind of collection and assortment of quotations and brief passages that are characteristic of the so-called doctrinal or philosophical texts of the late Warring States period in general. And the fact that these textual units show up frequently in roughly contemporaneous texts such as the *Zhuangzi* 莊子, the *Wenzi* 文子, and the *Han Feizi* 韓非子, and many others, which do typically include substantial parts with a master-disciple structure, confirms the validity of seeing their role or presence in the *Laozi* as quotable, and thus movable, units. In the final analysis, what these manuscripts give us is palpable, firsthand evidence of the textual precursors of many of the received texts we know from the Han dynasty on, and these precursors attest to the essential correctness of the view that sees the received texts as edited composites, which have taken their fixed form as late as the third century B.C.E. (maybe even later), made up in large part of paragraph-size textual building blocks that had been in wide circulation in limited and variable groupings, or even in some cases probably independently as individual pieces, for some time. The broader we envision this circulation to have been, the likelier it was to have been oral and associated with practices, rather than written and reflective of scholasticism. The memories of the minds of practitioners were probably a commoner means of text "storage and retrieval" than wagonloads of bamboo strips pulled around the countryside by draft animals or scholars.

Evidence from Transmitted Texts

Apart from such actual textual variation as may occur, the most obvious difference between a discovered manuscript version of a text and a transmitted, received version of the same text (or a clearly related text) lies in their respective physical forms. Transmitted texts are now with rare exception found printed. Pre–Han manuscripts are found normally on bamboo strips. "Hard" texts such as those inscribed on bones and shells or cast (rarely incised) on bronzes are exceptional, that is, atypical, by virtue both of their physical form and the means of their production (they are not just written but "manufactured") and of their specialized and restricted content and function (their use is, at least in the early periods, limited largely to a ceremonial and religious context). Those written on silk are uncommon in comparison with ones on bamboo, presumably because silk was expensive. Other materials on which texts are sometimes found written, such as jade and stone, are significantly less common than bamboo; and even wood, which is, to be sure, a common medium for writing by the Han, is not so widely found in pre–Han contexts. So we may safely say that the normal or "standard" material for written documents in China before the invention of paper was the bamboo strip. One need only look at the layout of a page of traditional wood-block-printed Chinese text to see a clear and direct reflection of this standard.

In one respect I think the traditional wood-block-printed page reflects a very particular and specialized form of a bamboo-strip manuscript, not generally in evidence in the archaeological record: each column of the printed page conventionally has the same number of characters as the next, and I suspect that the form of pre–Han texts prepared for the Han imperial archives, and perhaps for some of the court archives of pre-imperial states as well, was distinguished by this same feature. At the end of the *Shujing* category of the *Hanshu* 漢書 "Yiwen zhi," 藝文志 Ban Gu 班固 (32–92) writes that Liu Xiang 劉向 (79–8 B.C.E.), in comparing the Ouyang 歐陽, Da Xiahou 大夏侯, and Xiao Xiahou 小夏侯 versions of the "Jiu gao" 酒誥 and "Shao gao" 召誥 sections of this classic, was able to determine how many bamboo strips had become lost in each of these chapters on the basis of an apparent standard that allowed either twenty-two or twenty-five characters per strip. The clear implication of this is that in the imperial archive versions of these texts, each strip of a given version of a text had the same number of characters as the others. That number could vary from text to text and from version to version, presumably, but it seems that Ban Gu is here indicating his belief that for Liu Xiang's archive versions, the variation was, at least for the *Shujing* texts, limited to a choice between twenty-two or twenty-five characters per strip.[27] As Chavannes has suggested, and as we shall see from the empirical evidence, Ban Gu's "twenty-five" should probably be regarded as an error for "twenty-four."[28]

Even the most casual reader of pre-imperial Chinese literature is familiar with the fact that passages, stories, anecdotes, parables, and so on found in one well-known text often crop up, sometimes in slightly different wording, expanded or abbreviated, in other, equally well-known texts. It is not uncommon, for example, to find what is basically the same story or anecdote in the *Zhanguoce* 戰國策, the *Zuo zhuan* 左傳, the *Guoyu* 國語, the *Shiji* 史記, the *Guanzi* 管子, and the *Huainanzi* 淮南子, just to name a few of the best-known possibilities. Slightly less often recognized is the related fact that the same story or account is sometimes found in two (or more) different, but similar, versions in the same text. The cosmic order myth, for example, expressed as ridding the world of flooding waters, excessive vegetation, and harmful beasts, is found twice in the *Mencius*, both times in the "Teng wen gong" 滕文公 section (3A.4 and 3B.9), within a few pages of each other. The likeliest explanation for the presence of two different versions of the same basic story in the received text of the *Mencius* is that the text we have drew on two separate sources and included the same story once from each. A careful reading and analysis of the first of these two accounts will suggest that even the sources that the compiler(s) of the *Mencius* drew on were themselves composite in origin.

Consider the following passage from *Mencius* 3A.4, given here unchanged in wording from the original but with lines divided and numbered in a way that allows for the analysis I shall propose:[29]

(a)   當堯之時

At the time of Yao

(b)$_{22}$ 天下猶未平，洪水橫流，氾濫於天下，草木暢茂，禽獸繁殖；

the subcelestial realm had not yet become settled; flooding waters coursed across their banks, spreading far and wide throughout the subcelestial realm; grasses and trees burgeoned and flourished; birds and beasts proliferated and abounded.

(c)$_{22}$ 五穀不登，禽獸偪人，獸蹄鳥跡之道交於中國，堯獨憂之；

None of the five grain crops could be grown; birds and beasts oppressed the people; paths worn by animal hooves and bird tracks criss-crossed throughout the Central States. Yao alone was concerned about this.

(d)$_{22}$ 舉舜而敷治焉，舜使益掌火，益烈山澤而焚之，禽獸逃匿。

Having promoted Shun, he brought a far-reaching order to all of this. Shun charged Yi with control of the fire; Yi then wrought havoc on the hills and marshes, devastating them, such that the birds and beasts fled into hiding.

(e)$_{21}$ 禹疏九河，瀹濟漯而注諸海；決汝漢，排淮泗，而注之江，

Yu channeled the Nine Rivers, trenched the Ji and the Lei, draining them into the sea; bore open the Ru and the Han, furrowed the Huai and the Si, draining them into the Yangtze.

(f)$_{21}$ 然後中國可得而食也。〔當是時也，〕禹八年於外，三過其門而不入，〔雖欲耕，得乎〕。

After all of this had become so, the Central States came to be livable. [Just at this same time] Yu had been away from home for eight years. Thrice he passed his own gate but never once entered. [Even had he wished to do his own plowing, would this have been possible?]

(g)$_{22}$ 后稷教民稼穡，樹藝五穀，五穀熟而民人育，人之有道也，

Hou Ji instructed the people in agricultural techniques; thus they planted and cultivated the five grain crops. When these five grain crops ripened, the people then were well reared; this was owing to the fact that the people had achieved a proper way.

(h)$_{24}$ 飽食煖衣，逸居而無教，則近於禽獸，聖人有憂之，使契為司徒，

People were well fed and warmly clothed but lived indulgently and were devoid of moral training, and so came close to the status of birds and beasts. The Sagely One showed a concern with this and sent Xie to serve as Educational Overseer.

(i)$_{24}$ 教以人倫，父子有親，君臣有義，夫婦有別，長幼有序，朋友
有信。

He taught them about human relations: that between father and son
there is a proper intimacy, between lord and vassal there are correct
proprieties, between husband and wife there are required discrimina-
tions, between old and young there are hierarchical expectations, and
among colleagues and friends there is a presumed credibility.

After a four-character introductory phrase (a), the passage consists of
three lines of 22 characters each (b, c, d), followed by a 51-character passage
(e, f) that can be divided into a 21-character line and a 30-character line. This
is followed by another 22-character line (g), and the passage then ends with
two 24-character lines (h, i). The content of the passage overall can be seen
to be correlated clearly with these formal, structural features:
- Lines b–d, consisting of three 22-character lines, deal with the untamed
  state of affairs and the efforts of Yao and Shun to put things right for
  human habitation (3 × 22 characters = 66).
- Lines e–f describe Yu's famous role in ridding the land of the deluge (2 ×
  21 characters = 42, + 9 secondary, see below).
- Line g contains the sole mention in this passage of Hou Ji (1 × 22
  characters).
- Lines h–i describe the people's indulgent state of affairs and identifies Xie
  as the figure who is called upon to correct this moral lapse through
  education (2 × 24 characters = 48).

Each of these sections reflects a cosmic order or creation myth different
from and probably independent of the others: (I) the "Yao-Shun" account,
(II) the "Yu controls the deluge" account, (III) the Hou Ji creation myth of
the Zhou, and (IV) the role of Xie in teaching the people to be responsible
citizens. In each case the story or account is independently well known from
other transmitted Warring States or early Han texts. My suggestion is that
most, if not all, of these sections in the *Mencius* reflect different
source-texts, distinguished by both content and strip length from the others.
Lines b–d, making up account I, in other words, come from a source-text we
may call α, written in bamboo strips of 22 characters per strip and
presumably dealing exclusively with the Yao-Shun cosmic order myth. Line
g also comes from a 22-character bamboo-strip source, which may or may
not have been a part of source-text α; we have no way of knowing. [30] Lines
h–i, constituting section IV, come from a source-text written in 24-character
strips, which we may call source-text δ. Recall that strips of 22 inches (*cun*

寸) and 24 inches were among the commonest of the typical lengths that appeared in the sources Chavannes surveyed, and strips with 22 or 24 (emended from 25) characters were the "standards" mentioned in the *Hanshu*, "Yiwen zhi."

Slightly less obviously, lines e–f, constituting section II, come, I would suggest, from a source-text with 21 characters per strip, which we might call source-text β and which seems to have been an account of the "Yu and the Flood" myth. This identification depends on recognizing the two phrases marked here with angle brackets, totaling nine characters altogether, as secondary additions. The second of these two phrases clearly refers back to Mencius's argument against the proposition that every person should do his own plowing, that argument (and Mencius's opposition to it) being the context in which the whole passage is introduced in the first place. This makes the phrase's secondary nature transparent. When these nine characters are excepted, the resulting passage makes a perfectly coherent and natural whole, in two 21-character strips. The insertion of extra phrases such as these two and the opening 4-character phrase (a) is precisely the kind of editorial/compositional work that the "author-compiler" of the *Mencius* would contribute as he integrated passages from the various source-texts on which he was relying into an edited narrative whole. The conclusion of this kind of analysis is that even such a well-known, apparently homogeneous text as the *Mencius* shows itself to be made up, at least in part, of passages that are likely to have been drawn from preexisting textual materials.

As a second example of the same kind of analysis, consider the following passage from the *Zuo zhuan*, Zhuang gong 莊公 32. As with the preceding *Mencius* passage, I have not changed any of the wording or omitted anything but simply split the passage up into two parts with several lines each to allow for an explanation of my proposed analysis: part A includes lines a through d and part B includes lines e and f.

A:

(a)₄₄ 秋七月有神降于莘。惠王問諸內史過曰是何故也。對曰國之將
興明神降之監其德也。將亡神又降之觀其惡也。

In the seventh month of autumn a daemon descended to the locale of Xin [in Guo]. King Hui inquired of Guoh, his Court Scribe, about it: "What is the reason for this?" Guoh replied: "When a state is about to flourish, a luminous daemon will descend to it, to survey its Inner-fortitude. When about to perish, a daemon will in that case too descend to it, to observe its odium."

(b)$_{22}$　故有得神以興亦有以亡。虞夏商周皆有之。王曰若之何。

So, there are cases where the arrival of a daemon heralds a flourishing, and where it heralds a demise. Yu, Xia, Shang, and Zhou in all cases were characterized by this kind of thing. The king asked: "What should we do about it?"

(c)$_{15}$　對曰以其物享焉。其至之日亦其物也。

Guoh responded: "Make a ceremonial festival to it according to its 'creature-nature.' The day of its arrival indicates in such cases its creature-nature."[31]

(d)$_{22}$　王從之。內史過往聞虢請命。反曰虢必亡矣。虐而聽於神。

The king acted accordingly. The Court Scribe, Guoh, went there and heard that the state of Guo had made entreaties ([of the daemon] for its fate. He returned and said: "I now see that the state of Guo will inevitably perish; it behaves wantonly and is beholden to the daemon."

B:

(e)$_{21}$　神居莘六月。虢公使祝應宗區史嚚享焉。神賜之土田。

A daemon dwelt in the locale of Xin [of the state of Guo] for six months. The commonlord of the state of Guo sent his Presbyter Ying, his Ancestral officer Qu, and his Scribe Yin to make ceremonial festivals to it, [willing] the daemon to bestow land and territory on him.

(f)$_{44}$　史嚚曰虢其亡乎。吾聞之國將興聽於民。將亡聽於神。神聰明正直而壹者也。依人而行。虢多涼德。其何土之能得。

The Scribe Yin said: "The state of Guo will surely perish! I have learned that when a state is about to flourish, it is beholden to its people; when it is about to perish, it is beholden to daemons. A daemon is such that, being keen of ear and eye, upright and correct, it will maintain its integrity. It moves about by relying on others. The state of Guo has an increasingly unsuitable Inner-fortitude. What land can it in any way hope to gain?"

While this appears to be a single, continuous narrative passage in the received text of the *Zuo zhuan*, I suspect that it reflects two distinct and separate sources corresponding to parts A and B as I have divided the text here. The content of the part I have called A is essentially repeated in part B. The wording of the two parts, and the details that they give, are obviously different, but to the extent that they both narrate the same event, which is interpreted in a certain way and ends up with a certain infelicitous outcome for the state of Guo, they duplicate each other. This suggests that they might reflect the same account as seen in two different narrative versions and prompts us to look for evidence that they represent two different source-texts.

The way I have laid the lines out here suggests that both parts come from a source-text written in bamboo strips of 22 characters each; lines a, b, and d of A and line f of B all suggest a 22-character-per-line original. In both parts there is a strip of anomalous length. Varying strip length does not itself indicate different sources; nor does uniform length guarantee a single source. We can probe the hypothetical source-text(s) by carrying the analysis one step further and comparing with this *Zuo zhuan* passage the matching *Guoyu* version of the same event. The *Guoyu* version has lines clearly and closely matching those of part A of the *Zuo zhuan*, but nothing matching part B. This in itself is a compelling reason to see the *Zuo zhuan* passage as composed of two distinct and separable parts, one of which has a *Guoyu* counterpart and one of which does not. The *Guoyu* version opens with the following line:

(GYa)$_{22}$ 十五年有神降於莘。王問於內史過曰是何故。固有之乎。

In the fifteenth year there was a daemon that descended to Xin. The king inquired of the Court Scribe, Guoh, asking: "What is the meaning of this? Is there a precedent for it?"

This line has, clearly, 22 characters; the matching *Zuo zhuan* line has 20 (from line a above):

秋七月有神降于莘。惠王問諸內史過曰是何故也。

The textual differences are easily spotted, the most prominent being the occurrence of the 4-character question 固有之乎 "Is there a precedent for it?" at the end of the *Guoyu* line. If we accept the premise that these two lines are too similar to each other not to have a common source, and we then allow ourselves to reconstruct a hypothetical original source-text to account for both the *Zuo zhuan* and the *Guoyu* versions, we might posit a 24-character line (marked with an asterisk as hypothetical) as follows:

(*a)$_{24}$ 秋七月有神降于莘。惠王問諸內史過曰是何故也。固有之乎。

If we now reanalyze the *Zuo zhuan* part A, substituting our reconstructed first line with 24 characters for the first line of the transmitted version, we find the following structure, again changing nothing apart from having allowed for a reconstructed opening line:

(*a')$_{24}$ 秋七月有神降于莘。惠王問諸內史過曰是何故也。固有之乎。
(b')$_{24}$ 對曰國之將興明神降之監其德也。將亡神又降之觀其惡也。
(c')$_{24}$ 故有得神以興亦有以亡。虞夏商周皆有之。王曰若之何。對曰
(d')$_{24}$ 以其物享焉。其至之日亦其物也。王從之。內史過往。聞虢
          請命。
(d")$_{11}$ 反曰虢必亡矣。虐而聽於神。

We now have an account that consists of four 24-character strips, followed by an 11-character "coda" (half of a 22-character strip?). It is possible that this version of the story, except for line d", comes originally from a source-text written in strips of 24 characters each, and that it was rewritten on strips of 22 characters per strip when it was incorporated into the *Zuo zhuan* narrative, perhaps to conform to the 22-character-per-strip source-text for part B. The source-text for the B portion of the narrative seems to have been written originally in strips of 22 characters each, with one minor anomaly in line e, with only 21 characters.[32]

The analytical procedure adumbrated here and the attempt to identify source-texts on the basis of this kind of analysis depend, as I have said earlier, on an assumption that formal, perhaps archival, versions of these texts were required to be written on strips of uniform length and with the same number of characters on each strip. This much is implicit in the *Hanshu* "Yiwen zhi" notes that we have already examined. Beyond this, it can be seen that this procedure and its attendant claim to provide a means for identifying and reconstructing source-texts also assume that the narrative comes to a full (grammatical) stop at the end of either every strip or every several strips. In the *Zuo zhuan* passage, for example, lines b and d are identified as having been originally on strips of 22 characters each because they show a full stop after a 22-character narrative passage; by the same token lines a and f are so identified because of the full stop after a 44-character narrative, in these cases tacitly allowing for the assumption that a full stop ending a two-strip narrative unit is a permissible alternative to the requirement that there be one at the end of every strip. Other analyses, not included here, suggest that the full-stop requirement may allow units of three or four strips, perhaps occasionally even more. The feature common to all of these options is that no strip is ever left with unused space at the end.

Unlike the uniform length and uniform number of characters per strip requirements, which are formal in that they determine the physical form and appearance of the text, the full-stop requirement is clearly a stylistic feature and bears on the actual content and language of the text in a way that the "strip uniformity" requirements do not. Short of a discovery of hard archaeological evidence showing bamboo-strip texts that conform to these posited features, there is no way to prove *sensu stricto* that texts did in fact adhere to such prescripts. For the strip uniformity requirements we have the suggestive, but not definitive, evidence of the *Hanshu* "Yiwen zhi" and related material, which Chavannes has surveyed thoroughly.[33] For the full-stop requirement we have only the evidence of my analyses and the twin observations that first, if there were not such a requirement, then there is a remarkably high number of "coincidences" in the structure of these texts, and second, the requirement is entirely consistent with the implications of the evidence of Ban Gu's "Yiwen zhi" comments. Notice two further points in this regard: in identifying misplaced lines in pre–Han texts Qing philologists often rely on this assumption even when they do not explicitly acknowledge it, and the twin requirements that a strip must have no unused space at the end and that there must be a uniform number of characters per strip make it relatively easy to spot errors when texts are being copied.[34]

Numerous further examples from other Warring States and early Han transmitted texts, analyzable in the same way as these from the *Mencius* and the *Zuo zhuan*, could be adduced, all of which seem in sum to suggest that the practice of compiling texts from a reservoir of preexisting materials, combined with whatever newly composed material was called for, was not just widespread but perhaps the norm. The picture that these analyses of transmitted texts imply for the structure of the received pre–Han and early Han corpus shows itself not to be fundamentally different from the picture that the corpus of archaeologically discovered manuscripts increasingly suggests for that same body of received material. In both cases we can reasonably understand textual compilation often to have been an undertaking where the reliance on and incorporation of preexisting textual "building blocks" were natural parts of the process, and the resultant texts were to this extent composite in their structure and nature.

* * *

The thesis that I have developed here of a composite structure as typical of early Chinese texts, as opposed to an assumption of individual written authorship and integral, structurally homogeneous texts, carries with it one or two not inconsequential problems. Chief among these is the fact that so far none of the large quantity of recently discovered bamboo-strip manuscripts shows any evidence of the kinds of formal structural features that the foregoing analyses presume. I have suggested that this may be a consequence of the fact that what we are able to uncover through analyzing transmitted texts this way reflects *archival* versions of those source-texts, edited to conform to an exact format that demanded these structural features and limited in accessibility to state or court ambits, as opposed to the "everyday" versions that may have been subject to less rigid editorial strictures and that may have circulated *ad libitum*, sometimes ending up buried in tombs. If this is so, those archival versions cannot have been from the Han archives, about which much is known, but must have been earlier, pre-imperial archival versions, which can only be thought of as associated with individual pre–Han states. What is known of such early archives is of course next to nothing in comparison with what is known of the Han archives. Beyond this, the argument that the source-text building blocks themselves are to be taken as archival versions, by virtue of seeming to adhere to those requirements of strip structure and form adumbrated above, implies that they were already edited versions of still earlier source materials.

Second, that we find similar results from the analyses of transmitted texts as diverse as the *Mencius*, the *Zuo zhuan*, and the *Guoyu*, coupled with the evidence of early manuscripts from still other kinds of texts, suggests that the conclusion I have drawn about the role of textual building blocks in the composition of these texts pertains to a wide variety of textual types irrespective of whatever other conclusions or surmises we might wish to propose about the circumstances of a text's compilation or composition. The implications of a thesis of composite structure for the *Zuo zhuan*, for example, does not show itself to be incompatible with the proposals made by Yuri Pines when he says that "the *Zuo* author/compiler had at his disposal abundant written materials from various Chunqiu states."[35] These materials, he goes on to say, likely included the texts of speeches made by various political figures that we find cited in the transmitted *Zuo zhuan*, and the content of those speeches seems not to have been altered in any substantive way by later compilers or editors, according to the analyses that Pines sets out.[36] It is not impossible to assume further that these materials, including texts other than speeches, were the kinds of edited, archival documents that I have postulated as the source-texts for the transmitted version of the *Zuo zhuan*, nor is it impossible to envision a comparable set of circumstances pertaining to the composition of the *Mencius*, the *Guoyu*, or other pre–Han works.

The fact that the thesis I present entails a few as yet unverifiable assumptions or implications about the nature of the composition, form, and transmission of pre–Han texts should not, in my view, be regarded as fatal to its eventual tenability, in whatever revised shape subsequent new understanding may dictate. Speaking strictly hypothetically, it may turn out, for example, that the structural features that reveal themselves in the minute analyses of the transmitted texts are to be explained, not by strip lengths and formal physical criteria of source-texts at all, but reflect instead something about the meter and rhythm of the text as it was orally composed, performed, or recited. Or it may be the combined effect of both of these things. It is hardly surprising that the wealth of new and recent archaeological discoveries would raise as many questions as it might answer, compelling us to search for a new way to understand the pre-imperial Chinese textual world, just as those same discoveries force us to rethink what we thought we knew with some confidence about other aspects of the pre-imperial and early imperial Chinese world. Whatever uncertainties remain, there is always, I think, a value in knowing the depths of what we do not (yet) know.

NOTES

1. Falkenhausen, "Issues in Western Zhou Studies," 146 (italics mine).

2. Xu, "Jinwen guci shili."

3. This same point lies at the core of several of Martin Kern's recent studies; see in particular *The Stele Inscriptions of Ch'in Shih-huang*, 59–65; and "*Shi jing* Songs as Performance Texts." For a further discussion of the importance of the *guci* 嘏辭 see sections 1.1 and 3.4 of this last-mentioned article.

4. Discovered texts can be divided into two general types: (1) those written on "soft" materials, such as bamboo, wood, silk, and eventually paper and (2) those inscribed on "hard" materials, such as shell, bone, bronze, jade, and stone. Here I will be concerned chiefly with texts of the first type, which are conventionally called "manuscripts." It is these that have the closest physical and "evolutionary" relation to transmitted texts. Type (2) texts, most importantly oracle bone inscriptions and bronze inscriptions, which in the first case are almost entirely divinatory and in the second are largely monumental, tend to predominate in earlier, preclassical periods and do not bear directly on the analyses or conclusions to be set out here about the structure of manuscripts

and transmitted texts, though neither are they in any way inconsistent with or contradictory to these conclusions.

5. Giele, *Early Chinese Manuscripts*. Giele calls his catalogue an "abridged version" of a computer database containing basic information on all finds of early Chinese manuscripts that he knows of, either through their publication, published reports, or references. The catalogue attempts to be comprehensive through 1999 for early manuscripts on wood, bamboo, silk, and paper, apparently understanding "early" to mean "through the Han." It also includes entries for post–Han manuscripts, including wooden-strip manuscripts as late as the Tang, though the post–Han materials are not comprehensively registered. The database, updated, is available at Giele's electronic *Database of Early Chinese Manuscripts*.

6. The percentage given reflects titles of texts, not quantity of text. Many of the texts falling within the 10% that are said to have transmitted counterparts are only small portions of the transmitted wholes or conversely may have substantial additional portions of text not found in the transmitted versions. This does not invalidate the 1–to–10 proportion of what we might call "known" texts to "unknown" as a meaningful gauge of what the corpus of recently discovered manuscripts holds overall.

7. The distinction between texts found in tombs and texts found elsewhere, chiefly among archaeological ruins, bears on the important question of *why* texts are preserved. Manuscripts found in tombs are there presumably intentionally, while those found at sites of ruins may well be there by an accident of preservation. One would suspect that this reflects a significant difference between the two types in regard to the attitudes of the people toward the texts in question, yet curiously the proportion of unknown texts to those with known transmitted counterparts is approximately the same for both types.

8. Manuscripts matching the transmitted *Laozi* are found at the Mawangdui (Changsha 長沙, Hunan) and Guodian 郭店 (Jingmen 荊門, Hubei) tomb sites, both in the area of the ancient state of Chu. The Mawangdui tomb dates from the middle of the second century B.C.E.; the Guodian tomb, from the late fourth century B.C.E. One of the manuscripts matching the *Yijing* comes from the same Mawangdui tomb as the *Laozi*, the second comes from the Shuanggudui tomb 1 雙古堆 (Fuyang 阜陽, Anhui), from which the well-known so-called Fuyang *Shijing* manuscript fragments also come. This last-mentioned site is contemporaneous with the Mawangdui tomb. One of the two manuscripts corresponding to the transmitted "Zi yi" chapter of the *Liji* comes from the Guodian tomb; the other is a part of the mass of bamboo strips in the Shanghai Museum and reputed to have been acquired from antiquarian dealers, therefore of uncertain provenance. (These materials were published too late to be taken into account here.)

9. If we include the non-tomb finds, there are a few more transmitted, received texts that would have to be included by name on the list of those with matching manuscript fragments occurring more than once: the *Lunyu* 論語, the *Cang jie pian* 蒼頡篇, the *Sanguo zhi* 三國志, and the *Zuo zhuan*. These cases differ from the *Laozi*, *Yijing*, and "Zi yi" in that the *same passages* do not occur more than once; rather, it is simply that different sites have turned up different

passages from what is known as the same text in the (usually later) received
tradition. Beyond this, these fragments are in content meager in comparison to
the ones studied here, generally no more than a few lines each; by size, certainly,
it is the *Liji* "Zi yi," the *Laozi,* and the *Yijing* that dominate the list and that give
us a sizable body of material for a comparative analysis.

10. Shaughnessy, *I Ching*, 16. See also Xing, *Boshu Zhou yi yanjiu*,
34–41. For the Fuyang *Zhou Yi* 周易 bamboo-strip manuscripts, see Hu
Pingsheng, "Fuyang Hanjian 'Zhou yi' gai shu." From the description of the
fragmentary state of the manuscripts that Hu gives, it seems apparent that
nothing can be said one way or the other about the internal order of the parts.
The very fact that there is apparently no one strip that contains portions of more
than a single section, or "paragraph," of the text suggests, but of course does not
prove, that the sections were treated textually as separable units. I am grateful to
Edward L. Shaughnessy for providing me with a copy of Hu's article.

11. Shaughnessy, *I Ching*, 28–29.

12. Joachim Gentz raised the possibility *viva voce* that differing orders of
passages such as this may in effect be an intentional kind of commentary, or at
least a meaningful aspect of the editing of the text, and he cautioned against
jumping to the conclusion that the order of passages in a manuscript is "random"
in any absolute sense of the term just because it does not conform to the order
with which we are familiar in a counterpart received text (Münster Sinological
Workshop, July 14, 2000).

13. Shaughnessy, *I Ching*, 17.

14. Table 2.2 also appears in Boltz, "The Fourth Century B.C. Guodiann
Manuscripts from Chuu," 593.

15. Table 2.3 also appears in Boltz, "*Liijih* 'Tzy i' and the Guodiann
Manuscript Matches."

16. The received text of this *Liji* chapter consists clearly of twenty-five
distinct sections, self-evident on the basis of content, and has been traditionally
so divided. Apart from the traditional, but unverifiable, account given in *Suishu*
隋書 32, the "Jingji zhi" 經籍志, the early textual history of the transmitted *Liji*
itself, not to mention the "Zi yi" chapter, is unknown. The earliest "hard textual
evidence" is Zheng Xuan's 鄭玄 (127–200) second-century C.E. *Liji zhu* 禮記注.
There is no good reason not to assume that that version of the *Liji* is the same as
the received text now transmitted under Zheng Xuan's name, which divides the
"Zi yi" chapter into twenty-five sections. For reasons not entirely clear, though
in some measure surely due to the fact that section 18 appears incomplete, Kong
Yingda's 孔穎達 seventh-century *Liji zhengyi* 禮記正義 combines section 18
and what elsewhere is 19 into one, making a total of twenty-four, rather than
twenty-five, sections. For a further discussion of this aspect of the comparison
between the Guodian and transmitted versions of the "Zi yi" chapter, see
Shaughnessy, "The 'Zi Yi.'"

17. The same thing can be said for the *Shijing* on the basis of the bamboo-
strip manuscripts found in Shuanggudui tomb 1 at Fuyang. Those manuscripts,
fragmentary as they are, still show no evidence that there was ever more than a
single ode written on one bamboo strip; in fact, there was never more than a
single *zhang* (in this case, corresponding to English "stanza") written on one

strip. Thus, the manuscript, if it had remained extant *in toto* and intact would have likely shown a text of many of the odes that we know from the received version that allowed for the rearrangement of the order of both the odes themselves and the stanzas within the odes through simple manipulation of the order of the strips. That portion of the Fuyang strips that corresponds to *guofeng* 國風 odes in the received text does show that the *guofeng* categories known from the transmitted version were also recognized as groupings in the version represented here, but beyond this there seems to be nothing in the manuscript fragments that suggests a fixed order of the odes, or even of the stanzas, though this latter aspect especially we should not assume was arbitrary, of course.

18. See Wagner, "The Impact of Conceptions of Rhetoric and Style." Wagner shows how this structural unit, which he identifies and calls by its traditional Chinese name *zhang*, is related to the more intricate structural feature that he has called interlocking parallel style. At the same time he suggests a contrast between the *zhang* and what he calls "proverbial snippet(s)." It is not quite clear what he means by "snippet," but no one would dispute his identification of the *zhang* as the proper "building-block" unit of the *Laozi*.

The evidence of these versions of the "Zi yi" text only confirms the correctness of this identification and shows that the notion of a *zhang*-size passage seen as a movable textual building block extends also to texts well outside the scope of the *Laozi* itself. Among other pre–Han transmitted texts, the one that has been subjected most radically to such scrutiny in recent years is the *Lun yu* as it has been analyzed and translated by Bruce and Taeko Brooks. See their *Original Analects* and the review article by John Makeham, where it is shown that one can subscribe to the compositional or, as the Brookses call it, accretional structure of the text without necessarily accepting all of their sometimes highly speculative proposals about the dates of the various sections and the internal relation that may obtain among them.

19. Martin Kern has noticed a similar phenomenon in his study of the Qin stele inscription on Mount Yi 嶧. This is the only one of the seven Qin monumental inscriptions that does not have a transmitted counterpart in the *Shiji*, but only in later sources. A comparison of the stele text with its later transmitted version shows that, while the overall text is clearly the same, the two versions differ from each other in the internal order of their parts. See Kern, *The Stele Inscriptions of Ch'in Shih-huang*, 132–143. In the published work presenting his studies of Chinese *Versatzstücke*, which he calls "modules" in English, Lothar Ledderose has, significantly, begun with a discussion and analysis of the Chinese "system of script" (*Ten Thousand Things*, 9–23). He then proceeds to discuss mass production and modular building blocks in connection with bronze casting, terra-cotta armies, factory art (e.g., ceramics, lacquer ware, porcelain), building construction, printing, iconographic representation (of, e.g., hell), and finally, coming full circle, in connection with brush calligraphy. The implications of the analyses of early manuscripts and transmitted texts that I am exploring here suggest that an additional chapter, on the "modular" structure of early Chinese texts, might not have been entirely out of place in Ledderose's scheme.

20. There is no reason to assume a priori that the tomb manuscript versions

of texts are not also editorially selected and motivated assemblages of the textual building blocks. In this connection see the discussion of the Mawangdui *Laozi* manuscripts below.

21. It is only in the Han that we are able to identify a particular literary text (as opposed to "philosophical" works such as, e.g., the *Xunzi* 荀子) with an individual author in any meaningful, if still more traditional and ostensible than factual, way, for example, the traditional identification of Qu Yuan 屈原 as the author of the "Li sao" 離騷.

22. There is also, of course, the matter of the order of the two halves, which, as is well known, is reversed in these manuscripts relative to the order of the halves in the received text, but that is something different from what I am talking about, although it conforms to the sense of "movability" of pieces of text that underlies the structure I am trying to elucidate.

23. In fact we overgeneralize when we speak of the three separate and physically distinct Guodian manuscripts that include passages corresponding to the received *Laozi* as a homogeneous collection. One of the three, called the *bing* 丙 manuscript by the modern editors, consists of six textually and physically discrete parts, four of which are passages with *Laozi* counterparts (chaps. 17 and 18 as a single textual unit, and chaps. 31, 35, and 64 as three separate units), and two of which are heretofore unknown passages ("Taiyi sheng shui" 太一生水 and "Tian dao" 天道; see Boltz, "The Fourth Century B.C. Guodiann Manuscripts from Chuu," esp. 595–596). This six-part manuscript may well represent an edited text; that is, it may be that these six passages have been consciously selected and assembled in this one manuscript for a doctrinal or didactic purpose that is as yet unclear to us. The other two Guodian "Laozi" manuscripts do not suggest this editorial possibility quite as strongly simply because they do not contain any non-*Laozi* passages.

24. In "Constructing Lineages and Inventing Traditions," Csikszentmihalyi and Nylan have recently shown that in the early Han, in particular for Sima Qian and the *Shiji*, "lineage" means the transmission not of intact texts but of practices. Doctrines are associated with practitioners, not with fixed and immutable texts.

25. The account I am proposing here leaves unanswered the question of where, ultimately, these textual building-block pieces come from. My assumption is that they, like similar religious and philosophical texts of all kinds in many cultures, arose as compositions (perhaps as original works, perhaps as devolved from earlier but different contexts, either oral or written, or a mixture of both) in connection with belief systems, ceremonial performances, and teaching practices. Nothing specific or concrete can be said about origins at present for want of tangible data or direct evidence.

26. Lewis, *Writing and Authority in Early China*, 58.

27. See Chavannes, "Les livres chinois avant l'invention du papier," 36–38.

28. Chavannes (ibid., 18–20) shows that the normal (prescribed?) length of a bamboo strip for the classics, including the *Shu* 書, was, according to Zheng Xuan's preface to the *Lunyu*, twenty-four *cun* 寸 ("inches"). He also shows (30) that this standard was observed as late as the year 87 in the Eastern Han for a

version of Shusun Tong's 叔孫通 early Western Han ritual texts that was presented to the throne by Ban Gu. While twenty-four inches seems to have been the predominant length, Chavannes shows (passim) that there were also strips of eight, twelve, twenty-two, and thirty inches. At the same time, he shows that the early texts and commentaries indicate that the number of characters written on a single strip varied among eight, twenty-two, twenty-five, and thirty (38). As we saw above, according to the *Hanshu* "Yiwen zhi," twenty-two characters per strip was the recognized alternative to Ban Gu's ostensible twenty-five.

If we compare what these texts and commentaries that Chavannes has surveyed say about the various possible strip lengths in inches with what they say about the number of characters per strip, we get three perfect matches: (1) eight inches/eight characters per strip, (2) twenty-two inches/twenty-two characters, and (3) thirty inches/thirty characters. And we get an odd match of twelve- and twenty-four-inch strips against Ban Gu's reported strips with twenty-five characters. All of the data given for both lengths of strips and characters per strip come from multiple sources except the number twenty-five, which comes only from Ban Gu. If this number is emended to twenty-four, we would have a number that makes a perfect match with both twelve- and twenty-four-inch strip lengths. We could then surmise that a twenty-two-inch strip normally had twenty-two characters on it, and a twenty-four-inch strip normally had twenty-four characters, or in some cases would be the equivalent to two strips of twelve characters each. This is in fact what my independent analyses of many passages suggest. For these reasons it seems likely that Ban Gu's "twenty-five" here is an error for "twenty-four."

29. Translation here and in subsequent passages is given just for convenience of reference and to provide a general understanding of the content overall, when necessary. The translation itself is not the focus of attention, and I have therefore refrained from giving translation notes to draw attention to ambiguous and uncertain phrases or to explain or justify my understanding. Those places where the understanding bears on the structural analysis of the text with which I am concerned are mentioned at the appropriate points in the main discussion here.

30. Given that the transmitted corpus overall shows the Hou Ji creation myth of the Zhou to be in origin entirely separate from and unrelated to the Yao-Shun cosmic order myth, we would suppose this to have been a separate source-text, written in the twenty-two-character-per-strip "standard."

31. What exactly the word *wu* 物 in this line (twice) means or refers to is anything but clear.

32. As with many *Zuo zhuan* and *Guoyu* passages, this story also appears in Liu Xiang's *Shuiyuan* 説苑. The version now found there is closer overall to the *Guoyu* version than to the *Zuo zhuan* version, though different in some respects from both of these. While a full textual analysis of the whole of this account would have to take the *Shuiyuan* version into consideration, that version does not have any effect on the conclusions regarding the lines examined here.

33. See above, notes 27 and 28.

34. I owe this last-mentioned observation to Mr. Wojciech Simson, of the University of Zurich, who so commented at a workshop in July 2000 at the

University of Munich.

35. Pines, "Intellectual Change in the Chunqiu Period," 121.
36. Ibid., 122.

Chapter 3

The E Jun Qi Metal Tallies
Inscribed Texts and Ritual Contexts

Lothar von Falkenhausen

Five inscribed bronze tallies from the Middle Warring States period (figure 3.1) were collected in 1957 and 1960 in the vicinity of Shou Xian 壽縣 (Anhui). [1] They formed part of two distinct sets of "boat tallies" and "wagon tallies." Issued at the royal capital and apparently intended to be shown to local administrators, such tallies exempted merchants from road tolls or excise along certain explicitly defined trading routes within the Chu 楚 kingdom. Even though these five tallies are the only surviving objects of their kind, and we do not know how widely such tallies were used, they are important documents of economic history. I will here attempt to reconstruct the usage of these tallies and discuss the commercial activity described in their inscribed texts (which are translated in the appendix) as an aspect of territorial, fiscal, military, and ritual administration. This study is intended as an initial step in a multifaceted, archaeologically focused inquiry into the economic aspects of interregional cultural dynamics during the formative phase of Chinese civilization (some general notions on this topic are spelled out below in section VIII).

I

During the Eastern Zhou period, the area along the middle course of the Huai River in present-day central Anhui twice for brief periods became an important political center: first from 493 to 447 B.C.E., when the seat of the Cai 蔡 polity was located at Zhoulai 州來, adjacent to present-day Shou Xian; and again from 241 to 223 B.C.E., when nearby Shouchun 壽春 served as the final capital of the once-mighty kingdom of Chu. Plentiful

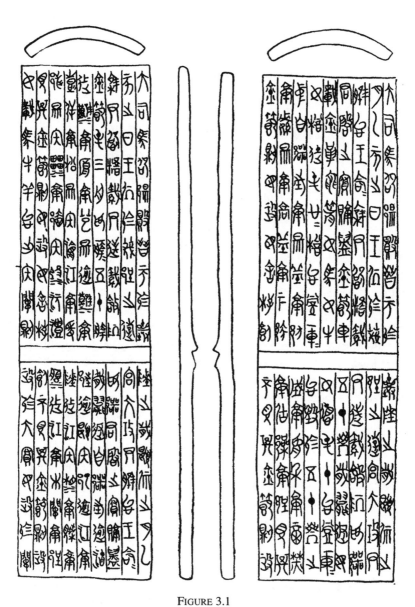

FIGURE 3.1

The E Jun Qi tallies. After Yin and Luo, "Shou Xian chutu de 'E Jun Qi jinjie,'" 9.

archaeological discoveries from both periods have been made in this area since the 1920s.[2] The E Jun Qi 鄂君啟 (Lord E of Qi) metal tallies were collected from farmers in the course of archaeological surveys in 1957 and 1960.[3] Their purported site of discovery, Qiujiahuayuan 丘家花園, is in the north-central portion of the large walled site of the Shouchun capital.[4] Finds of various precious Late Warring States objects inscribed with the characters "Dafu" 大府 (Great Treasury)[5] tantalizingly suggest the existence of major administrative buildings in the immediate vicinity, but this still needs to be verified by excavation.

Since the tallies are precisely dated to a year corresponding to 323 B.C.E., they predate the removal of the Chu capital to this region by almost a century. At that time, the state of Cai had already ceased to exist, and the Shou Xian area had come under direct Chu administration. One wonders why the tallies ended up here rather than being carried back to the Chu capital in south-central Hubei as their inscriptions stipulate. If they entered the archaeological record within a few years after their original issuance, their discovery would attest to the activity of Chu merchants in this region in a period when Shouchun was still at the periphery of the Chu realm. Perhaps more likely, however, they remained in circulation for decades, were revalidated every year at the Chu capital of the moment, and were finally withdrawn from circulation in the late third century when the government had relocated to Shouchun.[6]

II

The two boat tallies and three wagon tallies now known probably came from two distinct sets of five. Their vaulted shape with a "node" in the center mimics that of bamboo tablets. Five tallies, when joined together, would have formed a complete cylinder (figure 3.2). While their length (boat tallies: 31 cm; wagon tallies: 29.6 cm) is determined by that of the inscribed text, all tallies are equal in width (7.3 cm). The cast inscriptions, inlaid in gold, form nine vertical lines. The texts, which are exactly identical in each member of a set, are read starting in the upper right, ignoring the "node." The elegantly written characters exemplify the Chu script of the Warring States period. Even though some characters may reflect Chu scribal idiosyncracies or render Chu dialect words, they present few serious problems of decipherment. Commentators do, however, differ in many details of interpretation.

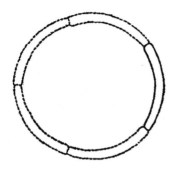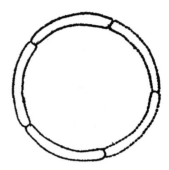

FIGURE 3.2

Section drawing of the E Jun Qi tallies, reconstructing the original arrangement of five. After Yin and Luo, "Shou Xian chutu de 'E Jun Qi jinjie,'" 9.

The inscriptions name these objects as *jinjie* 金節, "metal tallies." The first character implies a distinction vis-à-vis *jie*-tallies made of other kinds of materials. With a base meaning of "a section [or joint] of bamboo," the word *jie* 節 designates a contractual document that was normally inscribed on bamboo. The shape of the E Jun Qi tallies is reminiscent of such an origin, and similar documents made for less-high-ranking persons were undoubtedly written on bamboo during the Warring States period.[7] The *Shuowen* 説文 definition of *jie* as *zhuyue* 竹約 can be translated both as "bamboo [pieces] tied together" and as "bamboo contract." Duan Yucai's 段 玉裁 commentary adds: "The character *yue* 約 [which also means 'contract'] means to tie and fasten together; it refers to the condition of bamboo tallies tied and fastened together."[8] This suggests that, in the case of the E Jun Qi tallies, it was not a single inscription-bearing bronze piece that was considered a *jie*, but the complete five-part set, assembled into a cylinder and bound together, with the groove in the "node" serving to hold the fastening rope in place.

III

One among several different terms for tallies mentioned in the transmitted texts, *jie* were, or could be, tokens of official authority. The *locus classicus*, in the *Zuo zhuan* 左傳, relates how an official "died holding his *jie*-tally; hence [his death] was recorded using his official designation." Du Yu's 杜預 commentary explains: "*Jie*-tallies are tokens of the credibility of the state.

By holding on to it when he died, he showed that he was not abandoning his commission."[9] In the same *Zuo zhuan* episode, another official, when fleeing into exile, handed his *jie* to his accountant (*furen* 府人) in a gesture of loyalty to the state's institutions.

Jie is the term for "tally" used in the *Zhou li* 周禮, which mentions them in a number of contexts and even has a special office in charge of them in its idealized system of administration. The "job description" of the "Managers of the Tallies" (*zhangjie* 掌節) runs as follows:[10]

> The Managers of the Tallies are in charge of guarding the state's tallies (*jie*) and of differentiating their uses, so as to assist the king's commands. Those who protect the state use jade tallies (*yujie* 玉節). Those who protect the outlying domains use horn tallies (*jiaojie* 角節).
>
> Whenever the state sends [an emissary equipped with] a tally, for mountainous territories, one uses a tiger tally (*hujie* 虎節); for soil-rich territories, one uses a human tally (*renjie* 人節); and for marshy territories, one uses a dragon tally (*longjie* 龍節). They are all made of metal and provided with an ornate box.
>
> For gates and passes, one uses matching tallies (*fujie* 符節). For monetary transactions, one uses seal tallies (*xijie* 璽節). For roads and highways, one uses banner tallies (*jingjie* 旌節). All of these have a fixed term of validity, [at the end of which] one is to return the tallies.
>
> All those who circulate and communicate within the Realm under Heaven must have a tally, which is provided through a [bureaucratic] procedure.
>
> Those who do not have a tally undergo questioning and do not proceed to their destination.

This much-commented-on passage is typical for the *Zhou li* in that it attempts to construct a coherent whole by linking isolated bits of information about ancient practices through speculation that seemed reasonable to the text's learned compilers. Anyone wishing to use it as a historical source must therefore exercise critical judgment. Nevertheless, the notion that tallies had a fixed term of validity seems to be borne out by the inscriptions on the E Jun Qi bronze tallies. While there is little support for a binary division of jade and horn tallies or for the association of tallies of certain shapes with territories with specific geographic features, archaeological evidence does confirm that tallies were made from different materials and in different shapes (including those of tigers and dragons).

Another *Zhou li* locus, part of the description of the duties of an official charged with overseeing the movements of visitors from afar, rearranges some of the same information to present a different systematization featuring a binary division of bronze and bamboo tallies:

> He communicates the six kinds of tallies to the Realm under Heaven. For mountainous territories, one uses a tiger tally; for soil-rich territories, one uses a human tally; for marshy territories, one uses a dragon tally. They are all made of metal. For roads and highways, one uses banner tallies; for gates and passes, one uses matching tallies; for outlying domains, one uses tubular tallies (*guanjie* 管節). They are all made of bamboo. [11]

The reference to "tubular tallies" made of bamboo and used in the context of travel to outlying domains is of great interest in connection with the bamboo-shaped "metal tallies" of E Jun Qi, whose text indicates a comparable function.

The rule that all those who traveled had to carry tallies is echoed in many places in the *Zhou li*, [12] although with respect to the ordinary rural population, such regulations were probably meant to be enforced mainly during states of emergency. [13] Then, at least, those caught roaming about without a tally were subject to imprisonment. [14] Ordinarily, the need to present tallies may have applied chiefly to those who traveled in an official capacity and—as was still the case in times I remember well—to foreign guests.

The *Zhou li* also assigns a role to tallies in the traffic of commercial goods, [15] though it curiously never mentions them in direct, explicit connection with merchants. Occasionally, tallies appear as signs of official authority, as tokens of grace, and as signs of a specific privilege. [16] Unfortunately, the early sources neither describe nor depict such objects, and they do not indicate what inscriptions, if any, they bore or how they were used.

IV

Many authors assume that tallies, in order to be activated, had to be matched with a pendant. Ōba Osamu, for instance, has suggested—implausibly, in my opinion—that E Jun Qi's bronze tallies were meant to be broken in half and matched at each toll station. [17] First and foremost, tallies were tokens to be displayed and shown; how far away from the notion of "matching" the usage of tallies was evolving is illustrated by the fact that, by Han times, the term *jie* had come to designate "a tasselled staff given to an imperial messenger to show his authorization." [18] Matching pairs of tallies did exist in Warring States and early imperial China, but these seem to have constituted only a minority among the many different kinds of tallies in use.

Early sources refer to matching tallies as *fu* 符, written, like *jie*, with the bamboo radical but made, also like *jie*, in a number of different materials and shapes. [19] Their function was primarily a military one. In Western Han times, perhaps in deliberate reference to one of the *Zhou li* categorizations of *jie*, a distinction was drawn between bronze tiger *fu* issued to the imperially appointed administrators of the commanderies and princely states, and bamboo *fu* given to emissaries. [20] According to one Han commentator, "by these tallies one replaced the jade tablets (*gui* 圭) and scepters (*zhang* 璋) of old, following [the principle of] simplification." [21] A late instance of jade usage in creating matching tallies is recounted in the *Lüshi chunqiu* 呂氏春秋:

> A prefect in the school of Mozi 墨子 named Meng Sheng 孟勝 was on good terms with the Lord of Yangcheng 陽城君 in Jing 荊 [= Chu]. The Lord of Yangcheng commissioned him to guard his territory [in his absence]. He broke a tiger-shaped piece of jade (*hu*) to serve as a tally (*fu*) and contracted (*yue*) [with Meng Sheng]: "When [your] tally is matched, then obey [the messenger bringing the matching tally]." [22]

The text goes on to narrate how, when the Lord of Yangcheng was later forced to flee the state of Chu and he was dispossessed of his territory, Meng Sheng committed suicide with all his followers. In spite of its evident futility, such action was necessitated as a consequence of the insolubility of the contract concluded by means of a tally. Justifying himself to his followers, Meng Sheng declared:

> I took possession of someone else's territory, and a tally was involved in the transaction. Now the [matching] tally has not been presented, and our strength is insufficient to prevent [the takeover]. There is nothing to be done but to die. [23]

Only if the matching tally had been returned with an order from the Lord of Yangcheng relieving Meng Sheng of his commission could his death have been prevented. Disregarding the philosophical context in which the story is told, it transpires from this account that tallies in and of themselves did not need to bear any writing: they lent credibility to a separate message that might be transmitted either orally or, conceivably, by means of a separate written document.

The importance of matching tallies in controlling the military is also highlighted in an episode from the *Zhanguo ce* 戰國策:

> The envoys of Marquis Rang 穰侯 have arrogated the king's influence. They make and break alliances among the lords and their military tallies (*fu*) are found all over the empire. Everyone must obey when they order this enemy attacked or that country invaded.[24]

Rulers or military commanders at the capital placed one-half of a pair of matching tallies with the military administration of a locality, retaining the other half; once the time had come for action, they would send their half to the locality, which was obliged to obey their command if the two halves of the tally matched.

From the Warring States through the Eastern Han and beyond, tiger-shaped tallies (*hufu* 虎符) were used in such a way.[25] Bronze specimens with gold-inlaid inscriptions seem to have been, at first, a specialty of the state of Qin 秦; several are preserved (figure 3.3).[26] The inscription on the Xinqi-*hufu* 新郪虎符, for instance, reads:

> Tally (*fu*) for armor and weapons. The right [half] is with the king; the left [half] is [kept] at Xinqi. Whenever one is to levy troops and equip them with armor, if more than fifty soldiers are used, one must match the king's tally; only then shall one dare to undertake it. Affairs [communicated by means of] signal-fire stations are to be undertaken even though no matching of tallies has taken place.[27]

When matched, this tally presumably obliged the Qin military administration at Xinqi 新郪 (in present-day northwestern Anhui) to levy troops from the local population and to retrieve armor for them from its armory. That it was intended for repeated use is clear from the formulation of the text (which uses the legally charged term *fan* 凡, "whenever"), the provision for conditions overriding the necessity of matching the tally, and the fact that the tally was made from a permanent material, bronze, and expensively inlaid with gold.[28]

FIGURE 3.3
Tiger-shaped tally (Du-*hufu*) excavated at Beichencun, Xi'an (Shaanxi) in 1973.
After Hei Guang, "Xi'an shijiao faxian Qin guo Du *hufu*," pl. 8.1.

Not all tiger-shaped tallies were matching tallies, however. The gold-inlaid tiger tally (which the archaeological report refers to as *hujie*, using the *Zhou li* term) from the Western Han tomb of King Zhao Mo 趙眜 of Nanyue 南越 (figure 3.4), for instance, was cast as a single piece.[1] Inscribed "Royally appointed chariot dispatch," its intended usage seems to have been as a token identifying its bearer as a government functionary. A similar function may be assumed for various Warring States period tallies in the shape of horses, bears, and wild geese, which bear short and usually quite enigmatic inscriptions.[2] Some of them identify themselves as *jie*, none as *fu*. The Chuanlin 傳賃 (or Wangling 王令) tallies (figure 3.5), one of which was unearthed at Changsha (Hunan) 湖南長沙 in 1946,[3] are from the state of Chu and contemporaneous with the E Jun Qi tallies. Ornamented with a dragon, they identify their bearers as royally appointed officials and stipulate that they are to be lodged and fed while on the road on official business, presumably at official guesthouses or waystations.[4] Such tallies apparently did not need to be matched.

Ōba Osamu 大庭脩 has suggested that the Han period five-part sets of bamboo *fu* tallies issued to official emissaries were derived from an earlier Warring States precedent exemplified by the E Jun Qi bronze tallies.[5] Yan Shigu's 顏師古 commentary on the *Hanshu* 漢書 describes the Han specimens as follows:[6]

> Bamboo emissaries' tallies (*shifu* 使符) all consist of five rectangular strips (*jian* 簡) of bamboo. They measure five *cun* 寸 [11.5 cm accor-

FIGURE 3.4
Tiger-shaped tally (Wangling-*hujie*) excavated in 1983 from the western lateral
chamber of the tomb of the King of Nanyue at Xianggangshan, Guangzhou
(Guangdong). After Guangzhou, *Xi Han Nanyue Wang mu*, vol. 1, 89, fig. 59.

ding to the Han system] in length. On them one engraves seal script writing [numbering them] from 1 to 5.

Yan Shigu does not spell out the reason why Han bamboo tallies were made in five-part sets or exactly how they were put to use. If their designation as *fu* indicates that they were made to be matched, this was presumably done by assembling them into a cylinder, analogous to, but much shorter than, the cylinders into which the E Jun Qi metal tallies could be assembled.[35] On the narrow sides of the latter, there are marks resembling numbers that may relate to the numbering custom mentioned by Yan Shigu.[36] To understand how and when these tallies may have been matched, we must understand their overall context of usage.

V

The trading expeditions of E Jun Qi's merchants moved along waterways and overland roads that were evidently controlled and maintained by the Chu state, which collected tariffs at toll stations (*guan* 關) along the way. The inscriptions do not specify the goods transported,[37] though the boat expeditions, at least, seem to have involved livestock, which would not have been practical to transport on the wagons. On the wagon expeditions, items of potential military use were, moreover, explicitly excluded; transporting these by boat may have been permissible, however. Each tally was good for fifty conveyance units per year; standard-size "boats" or "wagons" could be replaced, respectively, by clearly specified equivalents of smaller boats or animal or human carriers.[38] Liu Hehui 劉和惠 has estimated the loads transported at 18 metric tons per boat unit and 1.5 tons per wagon unit, which would result in an annual volume of up to 900 tons for the boat trade and 75 tons for the wagon trade;[39] though for the wagon trade, one would probably do better to follow Li Jiahao's calculations, which yield a total figure of 270 hectoliters.[40] The staggering discrepancy between boat loads and wagon loads is realistic under conditions of premodern transport.

It is unclear whether each inscribed piece was valid for fifty conveyance units or whether that number referred to the total covered by a five-part set of tallies. Speaking for the latter alternative is the fact that ensembles of ten boats or wagons, when moving together, would have been more manageable than flotillas of fifty boats (or one hundred and fifty small boats) or convoys

FIGURE 3.5
Dragon-ornamented tally (Chuanlin-*jie*) allegedly excavated at Changsha in
1946. After Liu Huo, "Tong *longjie*," 81.

of fifty wagons.[41] That they did have to travel together is indicated by the
stipulation that the tallies had to be physically presented to toll-station
officials, who were apparently in possession of a document identical or
similar to that inscribed on the metal tally. Presumably, this document
would have been sent down to them from the Chu capital by way of
administrative correspondence. The formula "if they do not show their metal
tallies, they will be assessed tariff" suggests that a situation could occur in
which the local officials controlling a passing shipment were able to refer to
(and act upon!) this text when the merchants for whatever reason did not
have their inscribed tallies on hand.

As elsewhere in Chinese epigraphy, we realize that the texts now
preserved in the tally inscriptions are not, strictly speaking, the "original"
versions[42] but merely copies (indeed, in this case, *images*) of the original
texts, translated into a more durable medium. The true originals—the
now-lost documents from which the tally inscriptions were copied—were
kept at the Chu capital in the archives of the Grand Intendant of Public
Works, whose office had issued the tallies.[43] It seems plausible that the use
of the costly and difficult-to-manufacture metal tallies by the merchants was
a measure to prevent forgery.[44] All other versions in circulation—at least a
dozen for the wagon tallies; twice that number or more for the boat
tallies[45]—were presumably written on bamboo. Their production must have
kept the clerical staff of the Grand Intendant of Public Works occupied for
some time.

The E Jun Qi metal tallies seem to have differed at least somewhat
from any other tallies now preserved or mentioned in the literature. Unlike
what is suggested in the *Zhou li* in connection with tallies carried by
voyagers, their primary function does not seem to have been that of a
laissez-passer: their inscriptions give no information on the persons carrying
them, and it appears that, even without a tally present, the goods could still
have been moved—the merchants would merely have had to pay the local
tariff along the way. If regulations like those stipulated in the *Zhou li* were
enforced in Warring States Chu, the merchants may well have had to carry
additional identification documents for themselves. While the cargo was
evidently subject to inspection—if only to enforce the prohibition, on the
wagon tallies, against transporting materials liable to be put to military
use—there is no indication that other documents (such as a "bill of lading")
were needed for it.

By comparison with the Warring States Qin tiger-shaped matching *fu*
tallies, E Jun Qi's metal tallies are notable for carrying on themselves a

version of the legitimating documents rather than validating extraneous written or oral communications. While matching was crucial, in principle, to activating a *hufu*, E Jun Qi's metal tallies resembled the Chuanlin tallies and the tiger-shaped tally from the tomb of the king of Nanyue in that they were primarily tokens of privilege, to be recognized as one would recognize a picture. Since their contents were already known to those inspecting them, and it is not at all certain that the merchants who carried them were literate,[46] it is unlikely that anyone would have read the inscribed texts for their information content. Checking the tallies was, in a very real sense, a formality.

At the same time, the physical shape of the E Jun Qi tallies does suggest that the five constituent pieces of each set were meant to be reassembled ("matched") at certain times. This was probably not, however, what took place whenever they were inspected in the course of the trading expeditions.[47] It seems more likely that the five components of a set circulated separately, and that they were matched only when all the participating ships or wagons had brought their loads to the Chu capital at the end of a year's trading season—perhaps at the Great Treasury (Dafu), mentioned in the inscriptions. At that point, presumably, accounts were settled and outstanding payments were made; for while the tallies exempted the merchants from tariff along the way, tariffs may still have had to be paid at the final destination (the boat tallies specifically state this to be the case for livestock).[48] The tallies could then be reissued (or, perhaps, repurchased) for another year.

VI

The person for whose benefit these tallies were issued, E Jun Qi (Lord E of Qi), was not himself a merchant. The title *jun* 君 (Lord) indicated royally appointed satraps governing territories annexed by Chu or newly brought under central administration. Whether their position was hereditary is unclear. Only one Warring States Lord of E, by the name of E Jun Zi Xi 鄂君子晰, is mentioned in transmitted textual records;[49] the fact that he was a full brother of the Chu king suggests that E was an important place.[50] Where it was located is controversial; while the majority of modern scholars place it near modern-day Wuchang 武昌—opposite the confluence of the Yangzi with the Han 漢水 River[51]—a location further to the north, near Deng Xian in southwestern Henan, appears more likely.[52]

The tallies record the royal privilege of conducting official trading activities administered by E Jun Qi. Their origin at the royal capital and the high status of the awardee no doubt account to some extent for their luxurious execution, which matches the generosity of the privilege extended. E was the point of departure, but by no means the final destination of the trading expeditions, which ended at the Chu capital of Ying 郢, near present-day Jiangling 江陵 (Hubei). While the goods taken along for exchange and the financing of the expeditions presumably came from the public coffers of E, the items obtained (perhaps at a profit) in the course of the journey and transported tariff-exempt across the vast Chu territory were to be brought directly to the royal capital. Rather than being intended to enrich either E Jun Qi or his merchants, or to supply E, these trading expeditions in all probability constituted part of E Jun Qi's official duties.

It is perhaps characteristic of the nature of these documents that they mention only bureaucrats concerned with trade but make no direct reference to the merchants themselves; they do not even give a term for "merchant." Hence it is unclear whether the latter were themselves officials working in E Jun Qi's treasury or private individuals who conducted their business under some arrangement with E Jun Qi's administration. In any case, the tally inscriptions explicitly state that (presumably in contrast to traveling administrators such as the holders of the Chuanlin tallies) the traders were not to be lodged and fed at government expense.

Merchants working on behalf of the government are mentioned with some frequency in the transmitted sources. Their treatment in the *Zhou li* seems relevant here because of that text's administrative concern. The *Zhou li* uses two terms, *shang* 商 and *gu* 賈, which may be subtly different in their connotations though they overlap semantically.[53] Combined into a binome, they form the sixth of the nine population groups enumerated in the description of the official tasks of the Taizai 大宰 officials: peasants, park wardens, mountain guardians, marsh intendants, craftsmen, merchants, wives and consorts, servants and concubines, and idle folk.[54] Varying numbers of *gu* merchants appear in the *Zhou li* staff lists,[55] attached to various offices in order to buy supplies and to sell the products of the palace.[56] They were allegedly not themselves ranked officials but staff members comparable to the accountants, scribes, menials, and runners that were attached to each office. The scope of their activity was closely circumscribed, and none are associated with wide-ranging trading expeditions. If indeed they existed, such officially employed merchants must have been a small minority among Eastern Zhou merchants. Whether the merchants who conducted trade under the administrative auspices of E Jun Qi belonged to this group is not certain. Far from being "free commercial agents," at any rate, they operated in a ritually and politically regimented network of exchanges.

VII

The overland wagon trek of E Jun Qi's merchants proceeded from E northward to the Nanyang 南陽 basin (southwestern Henan) and from there eastward down the Huai 淮 River valley into northern Anhui, before turning west and reaching the Chu capital by some unspecified route.[57] Simultaneously, the boats traveled all over the Middle Yangzi basin. A northwesterly route took them up the Han River and across central Hubei into southern Shaanxi. An easterly route then led them down the Yangzi, past Lake Poyang 鄱陽湖, and to Jiangxi and southern Anhui. A southern route went up the Xiang River deep into the interior of Hunan. Finally, they proceeded up the Yangzi to the Chu capital. It is unclear whether all boats went to all the places mentioned, or whether different groups of boats separately traveled these several routes.[58] Moreover, as Chen Wei 陳偉 has remarked, the itineraries must have touched a number of other places—some important cities among them—which, curiously, are not mentioned in the inscriptions; Chen suggests that E Jun Qi's merchants' tariff-exemption privileges were specifically limited to a certain number of carefully listed places and river courses, not all of them at all prominent, where the Chu central government wanted to develop the local economy.[59]

The trade routes for both boats and wagons led E Jun Qi's merchants to the farthest regions of the Chu state before converging on the capital. Conducted as they were under government auspices, the trading exhibitions may well have had the character of inspection tours.[60] In this respect, they resemble the royal hunting tours of earlier periods, which, by "showing the flag" and bringing home some of the characteristic products (particularly, animals) of the areas visited, asserted the king's sovereignty.[61] Even if they were not officials themselves, E Jun Qi's merchants may have acted, in effect, as extensions of the Chu central government, and the trading items they carried back with them to the center may have had a prestige value that exceeded their mere market appeal.

One purpose of the trading expeditions may have been to supply the royal court with products from the Chu borderlands, as well as, possibly, from areas beyond.[62] By the same token, they served to bring the border regions reached by E Jun Qi's merchants into the Chu economic sphere. The northerly areas visited by the wagons had been conquered at various times by Chu since the early seventh century B.C.E. and had been the scene of many a famous battle.[63] Perhaps because these areas remained contested territory, the wagon tallies prohibit the merchants from bringing in materials of potential military utility. (In the mostly southerly areas visited by E Jun Qi's merchants' boats, by contrast, an acute threat of insurrection did not exist—hence, presumably, the absence of a similar prohibition on the boat tallies.)[64] In discussing the highly distinctive Chu coinage, Ke Peng has recently argued that Chu was intent on setting up a closed-circulation market system distinct from the open markets of the northern states.[65] By directing the flow of goods from the border areas into the center—especially goods from areas bordering on Chu's northern neighbors—E Jun Qi's merchants may have played a part in this process.

In the south, the boats of E Jun Qi's merchants ventured into areas where Chu had only recently begun to penetrate. Archaeological finds from the Xiang River valley in Hunan show that the area's occupation by Chu dates to no earlier than the fourth century B.C.E.,[66] confirming the Qing dynasty historian Gu Donggao's 顧棟高 (1679–1757) contention that "during the Springs and Autumns period, the territory of Chu did not reach as far as Hunan."[67] The inscription mentions five rivers in the vicinity of Lake Dongting without giving names of settlements, possibly indicating that no Chu administrative centers or official markets had yet been set up here. Instead, access to those areas may have been controlled by official Chu river inspectors. E Jun Qi's merchants were presumably engaging in barter trade with the aboriginal tribes, as well as with recent Chu settlers in these areas. Participation in trade with the Chu core must have played a significant role in acculturating the populations of the kingdom's southern peripheries to the lifeways of the Zhou culture sphere.[68]

VIII

During the Warring States period, political centralization, population size, and volume of industrial production all increased in tandem. In this context, long-distance trade—both government sponsored and private—assumed a new importance. As the Warring States kingdoms developed from nuclear polities to territorial states,[69] major attempts were made to bring the proverbial "mountains and marshes" into the fold of the administrative structure and to extract revenue through the control of resource extraction in those formerly marginal areas. In some cases, (e.g., in Qin), they became part of the personal domain of the ruler, strengthening his power vis-à-vis the traditional aristocratic society and enhancing political centralization. [70] In Chu, the detailed arrangements are not known, but here, as well, the royal government steadily strengthened its control over outlying areas. E Jun Qi's metal tallies and their inscriptions have great significance in connection with these wider trends in Warring States period economic history.

The inscribed texts reflect an eminently concentric conceptualization, with the royal capital as the pivot of all economic activity. In ancient China, the principal means by which the flow of goods was directed to the center was not trade but taxation, by which a state exacted the surplus from the agricultural core of its territory. Goods from outlying areas, made by people who were regarded as different from the state's core population, were acquired, in principle, by way of state-sponsored exchange under the guise of tribute. (As is well known, such "tribute" was often no more than a fiction readily acceded to by the tribute-bringing parties for the sake of obtaining terms of trade that were favorable to themselves; on the tribute-receiving side, the profit motive was definitely secondary to a concern with the symbolic expression of power.) Both taxation and tribute were administered by bureaucrats. The E Jun Qi bronze tallies are a fine example of how commercial exchange, when conducted under government auspices, shadowed and supplemented these two activities. On the one hand, such trade established additional economic and psychological links between the center and the inhabitants of outlying areas, especially populations that were incompletely integrated into the territorial administration, or yet insufficiently organized to act as partners in the tributary system; on the other, it could keep the center supplied with goods that were either out of stock or not covered by existing taxation or tributary arrangements.

In certain respects, the relationship between the political centers of early Chinese polities and their trading (or tributary) partners bore an uncanny resemblance to the dynamics between developed and developing countries today. Throughout the Shang and Zhou periods, craft production took place at workshops attached to the ruling houses, which also monopolized the circulation of the manufactured goods;[71] but much of the raw material needed—metal and jade in particular—came from areas that, to judge from the distribution of archaeological relics, appear to have been outside the scope of direct Shang and Zhou political control. The extensive copper resources south of the Yangzi,[72] for instance, seem to have been exploited neither by the far-away Shang and Zhou courts nor, later on, by the Chu state, but by aboriginal tribal populations.[73] These locals mined and smelted the copper and traded it in the form of ingots; in exchange, they received manufactured commodities that appear to have included bronze vessels manufactured from the very metal originally exported by them.[74] Although they refrained from imposing their presence on the places of extraction, the Shang and Zhou (and, during much of the Zhou period, the Chu) maintained trading posts nearby—Panlongcheng 盤龍城 in Huangpi 黃陂 (Hubei) may have been one during Middle Shang[75]—to ensure the supply of the metal they needed. Likewise, in connection with the hypothesis that the frequent removals of the Shang administrative capitals were motivated by concern about access to metal resources,[76] one should emphasize that it was not necessarily the Shang state that engaged in the mining; it merely acted as the principal—perhaps indeed the only—customer of neighboring non-Shang mining populations. In spite of the increased degree of administrative centralization, a similar pattern still seems to have prevailed during the Warring States period, and indeed through much of later Chinese history.[77]

The administrative procedures within which the tallies had their function served to regularize and intensify the transfer of the surplus of outlying areas to the Chu capital. The use of these precious and visually striking objects contributed to the strengthening of the central political control that was exerted by the king simultaneously through the administrative staff at court and through local satraps answerable to himself. In the last analysis, however, the activities circumscribed in the tally inscriptions perpetuated the age-old concentric pattern of economic activity, predicated in turn on very ancient notions of ritual kingship.

IX

It follows that E Jun Qi's tallies, in validating the ordered circulation of goods, mobilized not only the economic resources but also—and perhaps more crucially—the symbolic resources of the Chu kingdom. We may interpret the trading activities as a carefully scripted performance designed to make manifest the king's power—a ritual in which the tallies took the role of indexical icons.[78] Both conceptually and chronologically, the tally inscriptions are situated at the historical juncture at which legal forms began to emanate from ritual tradition. Their matter-of-fact tone notwithstanding, the texts are embedded in a discourse of rulership that is fundamentally religious in nature, charging the tallies with an awesome, mana-like force. I will here sketch out the implications in the form of five theses. While I would not claim that this line of analysis exhausts the significance of the tallies, it is also plain that no one can fully comprehend them without duly considering their connections to the sphere of ritual.

1. *The material of the tallies and the calligraphic execution of the inscriptions carry religious significance.* Bronze was the status material par excellence during the Shang and Zhou periods; from it were manufactured the sacrificial vessels and musical instruments used in ritual communication with the ancestral spirits.[79] Such activity, along with warfare, was the central obligation of the Shang and Zhou elite and the principal means of legitimation of the social order.[80] Inscriptions placed on the vessels communicated messages to the spirits in the course of the ritual process.[81] It was no accident that ritual vessels with cast inscriptions became, in the late Springs and Autumns period, the vehicle for the promulgation of China's earliest legal codes.[82] The connection between the older, ancestor-centered religious system and the more this-worldly systems of administration current during the Warring States is evident.[83]

Aside from being a palpable reminder of earlier uses of writing in contexts of sacrifice (a usage Warring States period users would still have been conscious of), the gold-inlaid characters visually enhance the authority of the tallies—all the more effectively so in the virtual absence of other decoration. Evenly spaced and carefully balanced, they are notable for their formality, especially when compared to those seen in contemporaneous Chu brush-written documents on bamboo and silk, which display a more fluid and relaxed writing style.[84] Part of the calligraphic difference is, of course, due to the nature of the inscribed medium: incising the clay matrix from which the molds for the tallies were taken does not lend itself to the same spontaneity as wielding a brush.[85] But a fastidious concern with correctness is evident as well from other observations: characters occurring more than once are far more uniform in shape than is common in brush-written manuscripts, and characters are never replaced by easier-to-write phonetic equivalents—a practice that is ubiquitous in most Warring States to Early Han manuscripts, reflecting the as-yet-incomplete standardization of the script at this time.

That each of the nine lines on each tally features the same number of characters testifies to considerable advance planning. The scribes who devised the texts must have spent much time manipulating their formulation so that the characters would exactly fit the space available on the tally surface. It is impossible to know whether there was any special significance to the number 9, or to the odd numbers of spaces per line—nineteen on the boat tallies, seventeen on the wagon tallies; [86] but the parallel with similar efforts taken in preparing the inscriptions on Shang and Zhou ritual vessels is undeniable, strongly suggesting continuity in scribal and manufacturing tradition. Aside from the fact that work habits cultivated over the course of a millennium were hard to shed, at least part of the reason why so much care was lavished on the physical presentation of the writing lay, I would argue, in the long-standing religious connotations of the bronze medium.

2. *The texts inscribed on the tallies are couched in a formalized ritual medium of communication.* Obviously, the tallies were not themselves paraphernalia of ancestral sacrifice; their inscriptions do not explicitly relate to ritual celebrations, nor do they make use of prosodic devices such as rhyme and meter, often found in Zhou bronze inscriptions. Even so, their formulation shows significant continuities with the ritual language of Shang and Zhou bronze inscriptions. [87] Overall similarities include the pervasive use of set formulae, as well as the adoption of a predictable, tripartite textual structure, which progresses from an introduction indicating the time, background, and circumstances of the tally's issuance, to a middle section specifying its validity and the itinerary, and to a final section stipulating the tariff exemption. [88]

In an especially striking grammatical, as well as lexical, parallel to inscriptions on ritual bronzes, the introduction of the tally inscriptions parallels the latter's "Statement of Dedication"—the pivot and core of every Zhou bronze inscription that is couched in grammatically complete phrases. [89] In Eastern Zhou inscriptions, such dedication statements moved from the middle to the beginning of long texts, and the verb *zhu* 鑄, "cast," also used in the E Jun Qi tally inscriptions (as part of the double verb *zhuzao* 鑄造), often replaced the earlier *zuo* 作, "make" (both probably to be understood in the causative sense). With minimal adjustments, the introductory sections of the tally inscriptions could begin the dedicatory inscription of any Warring States period ritual vessel. (The adjustments would include, most obviously, the principal direct object of *zhuzao*, where in place of the term *jinjie*, "metal tally," a vessel name would occur in a "normal" bronze inscription, and the indirect object, "E Jun Qi's treasury," in the place of which one would expect to see, in a ritual-vessel inscription, the name of an aristocratic dedicatee. This replacement of a personal name by that of an administrative institution is telling for how the ritual language was slightly adapted to the needs of bureaucratic realities but by no means fundamentally transformed in the process.) We may be certain that the parallel was perceived as significant by contemporaries.

While the occurrence of a long initial sentence with the main verb *zhu* undoubtedly constitutes a direct, specific parallel to ritual-bronze inscriptions, other similarities between the introduction sections of the tally inscriptions and bronze inscriptions relate to the more general similarity between Zhou ritual language and the evolving bureaucratic language of the Warring States. The habit of indicating the date at the beginning, for instance, is common to ritual-bronze inscriptions, the tally inscriptions, and the recently found Warring States and Qin period legal texts.[90] Its significance is nevertheless profound. Following a common calendrical practice of the time, the tally inscriptions specify the year by reference to an important historical event. This event—not accidentally a glorious one for Chu—has no connection at all with the actual subject of the inscriptions. Instead, the mention of it links the tallies' issuance to an officially sanctioned, standard timeline and to the activities of the chronicle writers at the Chu royal court. Moreover, the fact that the month is given in terms of the Chu calendar is an allusion to the Chu king's prerogative of fixing the standards and units for timekeeping—or, in more abstract terms, to the state's domination, continually exerted through the official ritual schedule, of the chronological parameters of the life of its subjects. The king is brought into the discussion by means of a formulaic sentence (which, again, has direct parallels in Western Zhou ritual-bronze inscriptions) specifying his current place of residence. By explicitly linking the tallies to the Chu king's situation in time and space, the beginning portions of the tally inscriptions bestow ritual sanction on the business activities of E Jun Qi's merchants, thereby making their official character explicit. The avoidance of the king's personal name—he is referred to simply as *wang* 王, "the king"—is consistent with the ubiquitous practice of Shang and Western Zhou documents, oracle bone as well as bronze inscriptions; it reflects an archaic religious taboo observed in many premodern societies.

The text continues with an account of the issuance of the tallies that lists the officials involved in their hierarchical order, evoking the ritualized procedures by which official business was handed down. The political structure is thus indexically replicated through language. In this connection, the use of the term *wangming* 王命, "royal order,"[91] is another self-conscious adaptation of earlier ritual language to Warring States bureaucratic terminology. *Ming* 命 (often translated as "mandate") is one of the core terms of the Classical Chinese ritual vocabulary; it designates, most basically, the orders of the ancestral deities as transmitted by the rulers who are their representatives in the world of the living. (Not accidentally, the word had taken on, by Warring States times, the meaning of "fate," as well as "life span.") Again, the ritual connotation is evident—the reference to the religious aura whence emanated the Chu king's power to rule. Just as in the Shang and Western Zhou ritual polities, the royal mandate here constitutes the explicit basis for the legitimacy of all bureaucratic activity, as well as, further down the line, for E Jun Qi's merchants' trading expeditions.

The remainder of the inscriptions as well—the specifications of the tallies' term of validity, the size of the trading expedition and possible equivalent conveyance units, the itinerary, and the nature of the privilege conveyed—are all couched in standard formulaic phrases using a fixed vocabulary of oft-repeated technical terms that have a precise, official significance. They are part of a restricted code that required special expertise to use effectively. Essentially the same linguistic code was used to codify Warring States legal statutes. It is unclear whether Chu in the late fourth century B.C.E. had statutes governing officially sponsored merchant activity, from which the tally inscriptions might have been derived. In any event, the use of this code endowed the texts—and, through them, the inscribed objects—with legal validity, but also with magical power.

3. *The tallies themselves carried transformative, order-generating force.* Tallies—inscribed or, perhaps more frequently, uninscribed—were pervasively used in religious activity as a physical token of the bond between a mortal and a divinity. Historically, their religious function probably precedes—and is fundamental to—their use in political, administrative, legal, and commercial contexts. As Mark Edward Lewis has pointed out, "Like other elements in the new modes of written administration [in the Warring States period,] the use of tallies had its religious correlate, for the ancient sages were said to 'match tallies' with the spirits as a sign of attaining world rule."[92]

On account of the power inherent in their form, material, calligraphic execution, and formulation, the tallies and their inscribed words initiated rule-determined behavior on the part of those to whom they were shown. Whenever proffered (and, perhaps, read) in an appropriate context, they guaranteed a predictable, formalized treatment of the bearer and his entourage; they made things happen.[93] Of course, this effectiveness was predicated on the acceptance of the rules and conventions that underlay the administrative procedures and linguistic formulations and constituted the basis of ritualized behavior. Familiarity with them was a precondition of one's membership in civilized society.[94]

Although more or less arbitrary, these rules and conventions transformed the haphazard flow of life into a succession of standard situations within which all participants had their prescribed roles to follow. Threatening, ungovernable reality was reduced to a readily readable pattern, upheld through patterned behavior—ritual. Objects like E Jun Qi's tallies constituted a material reminder that could induce and facilitate patterned behavior, thus directly acting upon Warring States period social life. They had their place in a powerful symbolic system that encompassed, and iteratively created, the ordered universe.

4. *The tallies may have been tied in with Warring States period cosmological thinking*. Not only does the calendrical date at the beginning of the inscribed texts furnish a link with the cycles of time, but the bronze material, as well, had its position in the cycle of the Five Phases.[95] In this connection, the act of mimicking a bamboo object in bronze may have been viewed as tantamount to the transformation of elements (and thus ritually charged), and the use of gold to inlay the inscribed characters may have had a profound significance in terms of Five Phases color symbolism. Guo Moruo has, furthermore, asserted a possible connection between the fact that these tallies constituted five-part sets and the theory of the Five Phases.[96]

It is likely that, to the extent that they were realized by the users of E Jun Qi's tallies, such cosmological implications reflected novel conceptions of rulership in the Warring States, aiming to encompass the entirety of the cosmos under one universal ruler.[97] The continuity with the earlier forms of political expression also manifested on these objects is worth noting.

5. *The tallies reflect the ritual nature of governmental activity*. The preceding analysis corroborates that, albeit attenuated vis-à-vis earlier epochs, the conceptualization of government as an extension of the sacrifices offered to the ancestors continued to be fundamental in the Warring States. Such a notion is also reflected in the writings of the era's major political thinkers.[98] Different from the royal hunting inspections of the Shang, which involved the physical displacement of the ruler himself, the tallies were effective also in his absence. They are one instance of the ruler's (or his representatives') exercise of authority through writing—an offshoot of earlier uses of writing as a means of communication with the supernatural sphere.[99] Lewis has observed that, during the Warring States, writing diffused to strata of the population that had not been affected by it

during earlier times; but this does not mean—at least not merely—that writing descended into the profane sphere: documents such as the E Jun Qi tallies may, rather, be interpreted as sacralizing an activity that, like commerce, is easily regarded as profane.[100]

If Warring States and Han tallies were indeed the successors of the *gui* and *zhang* documents of the previous age, as Lao Kan has claimed,[101] one must emphasize the contrast between E Jun Qi's metal tallies and the covenant texts inscribed on jade *gui* during the Late Springs and Autumns and Early Warring States period, caches of which have been excavated at Houma 侯馬 (Shanxi) 山西 and Wen Xian 溫縣 (Henan).[102] The tally texts do not refer to deities, and no superhuman sanctions are threatened in case their stipulations are contravened. The entire tenor of the documents is, thus, seemingly secular. Arguably, however, the persons mentioned—the king and various officials involved in the issuance of the tallies—substitute for the deities. The erstwhile religious medium has here been appropriated in order to enhance the authority of the state, subsuming the formerly sacred Other under the scope of a new type of polity with universal aspirations. The supernatural forces have not thereby been rendered harmless—if anything, their virtual identification with the political powers-that-be has made them ever more threateningly immediate; as a consequence, correct behavior is called for more urgently than ever.

Appendix: Translations and Commentary

The following translations are based on a sifting of about three dozen studies. Those quoted repeatedly in the commentary are abbreviated as follows:

CW1	Chen Wei, "'E Jun Qi jie' zhi 'E' di tantao."
CW2	Chen Wei, "E Jun Qi jie yu Chu guo mianshui wenti."
FA	Funakoshi, "Gaku Kun Kei setsu ni tsuite."
GMR	Guo Moruo, "Guanyu E Jun Qi jie de yanjiu."
HLY	He Linyi, "E Jun Qi jie zhoujie shidi sanze."
HSZ1	Huang Shengzhang, "Guanyu E Jun Qi jie jiaotong luxian de fuyuan wenti."
HSZ2	Huang Shengzhang, "E Jun Qi jie dili wenti ruogan buzheng."
HSZ3	Huang Shengzhang, "Zailun E Jun Qi jie jiaotong luxian fuyuan yu dili wenti."
LBH	Liu Binhui, *Chu xi qingtongqi yanjiu.*
LCM	Luo Changming, "E Jun Qi xintan."
LHH1	[Liu] Hehui, "Chu E Jun Qi jinjie."
LHH2	Liu Hehui, "Chu E Jun Qi jie xintan" and *Chu wenhua de dongjian.*

LJH   Li Jiahao, "E Jun Qi jie mingwen zhong de Gaoqiu."
LL1   Li Ling, "Chu guo tongqi mingwen biannian huishi."
LL2   Li Ling, "Guwenzi zashi (liangpian)."
LL3   Li Ling, personal communication, 2000.
LXet al.   Liu Xiang et al., *Shang Zhou guwenzi duben.*
SCZ1   Shang Chengzuo, "E Jun Qi jie kao."
SCZ2   Shang Chengzuo, "Tan E Jun Qi jie mingwen zhong jige wenzi he jige
           diming deng wenti."
TQX1   Tan Qixiang, "E Jun Qi jie mingwen shidi."
TQX2   . Tan Qixiang, "Zailun E Jun Qi jie dili: Da Huang Shengzhang
           tongzhi."
WH   Wang Hui, "Shi jiu, jiu."
YDF   Yin Difei, "E Jun Qi jie liangge diming jianshuo."
Y&L   Yin Difei and Luo Changming, "Shou Xian chutu de 'E Jun Qi jinjie.'"
YXW   Yu Xingwu, "'E Jun Qi jie' kaoshi."
Z&L   Zhu Dexi and Li Jiahao, "E Jun Qi jie kaoshi (bapian)."

Other works specially concerned with these inscriptions that I consulted
include Naitō Shigenobu, "Gaku Kun Kei setsu"; Sun Jianming, "E Jun Qi jie
xutan"; Xie Yuanzhen, "E Jun Qi jie mingwen bushi"; and Xiong and He, "E Jun
Qi jie zhoujie zhong Jiang Xiang diming xinkao."

Phonetic reconstructions (marked with *) are given according to
Schuessler, *A Dictionary of Early Zhou Chinese*, which renders the pronunciations of the archaic ritual language that is the linguistic point of reference of
these texts; the actual pronunciation during the Warring States period—especially in Chu—is likely to have been somewhat different. Seriously uncertain
readings are marked with question marks.

Generally, indications of geographical locations are given according to
Tan Qixiang et al., *Zhongguo lishi dituji*, vol. 1. In transcribing place-names, I
have opted, wherever possible, to give the modern Mandarin pronunciation of
the corresponding present-day place-names. These sometimes diverge from the
Mandarin pronunciations of the characters actually appearing in the inscriptions, which are supplied by the commentary.

Numbers inserted into the translations refer to the numbered sections of
the commentary, which treat corresponding portions of the two documents
jointly.

Boat Tally Inscription

In the year when the Grand Minister of War Shao Yang had defeated the
armies of Jin at Xiangling (1), in the Xiayi month, day *yi hai* (2), when the king
dwelled in the pleasure palace in suburban Ying (3), the Grand Intendant of
Works Sui took a royal order and commanded the Jiyin official Dao X, the Zhiyin
official Ni, and the Zhiling official Qi (4) to cast [these] metal tallies for E Jun
Qi's treasury (5). [They are valid for] fifty *kua*(?), one *kua*(?) being made up of
three boats combined (6), and they are to be returned once a year (8).

[Depart] from the market at E (11), go downstream on the Yu River, go
upstream on the Han River, stop at Yun, stop at Xunyang (12); go downstream

on the Han River, stop at Xiang(?), go downstream on the Xia River, enter the Yun River (13); go downstream on the Jiang [i.e., the Yangzi River], stop at Pengze, stop at Songyang, enter the Lujiang River, stop at Yuanling (14); go upstream on the Jiang, enter the Xiang River, stop at Shi(?), stop at Taoyang, enter the Lei River, stop at Chen, enter the Zi, Yuan, Li, and You Rivers (15); go upstream on the Jiang, stop at Muguan, stop at Ying (16).

When they show their metal tallies, they will not be assessed tariff, [though] they will not be lodged, equipped(?), or fed. When they do not show their metal tallies, they will be assessed tariff (18). If they transport horses, oxen, and sheep in and out of the tariff-collecting stations, then they will be assessed tariff at the Great Treasury, but not at the tariff-collecting stations (19).

Wagon Tally Inscription

In the year when the Grand Minister of War Shao Yang had defeated the armies of Jin at Xiangling (1), in the Xiayi month, day *yi hai* (2), when the king dwelled in the pleasure palace in suburban Ying (3), the Grand Intendant of Works Sui took a royal order and commanded the Jiyin official Dao Hai(?), the Zhiyin official Ni, and the Zhiling official Qi (4) to cast [these] metal tallies for E Jun Qi's treasury. [They are valid for] fifty wagons (7), and they are to be returned once a year (8).

Do not transport metal, leather, or bamboo-shafted arrows (9). When [using] horses, buffaloes, or oxen, add up ten as the equivalent of one wagon; when [using] carrying-pole runners, add up twenty carrying-pole loads as the equivalent of one wagon, and subtract these [equivalents] from the total of fifty wagons (10).

[Depart] from the market at E (11), stop at Tangqiu, stop at Fangcheng, stop at Xianghe, stop at Youfen, stop at Fanyang, stop at Gaoqiu, stop at Xiacai, stop at Juchao, stop at Ying (17).

When they show their metal tallies, they will not be assessed tariff, [though] they will not be lodged, equipped(?), or fed. When they do not show their metal tallies, they will be assessed tariff (18).

Commentary

(1) 大司馬邵陽敗晉師於襄陵之歲

[BOTH DOCUMENTS] In the year when the Grand Minister of War Shao Yang had defeated the armies of Jin at Xiangling:

The use of *sui* 歲 for "year" (referring to the twelve-year cycle of Jupiter), rather than the agricultural year *nian* 年 or the sacrificial year *si* 祀, reflects Warring States calendrical practice and is seen in bronze inscriptions and manuscripts from that period, though rarely before.

From historical sources (*Shiji* "Liuguo nianbiao" 六國年表 and "Chu shijia" 楚世家 [*Shiji* 15.730 and 40.1721]; *Zhanguo ce* "Qice" 齊策 [*Zhanguo ce*, 355]), the Chu victory over Jin 晉 (actually, Jin's successor state of Wei 魏) at Xiangling 襄陵 (near Sui Xian 睢縣 [Anhui]) is known to have occurred in 323 B.C.E. (the sixth year of King Huai 懷王 of Chu). Possibly, in referring to Wei as Jin, the Chu historiographers indicated their official nonrecognition of its takeover of the Jin core area, which had been finalized with the deposition of Jing Gong of Jin 晉靜公 in 376 B.C.E.

The *Shiji* refers to the victorious general by his honorific title of *zhuguo* 柱國 (Pillar of the State). *Dasima* 大司馬 is his title as the Chu Minister of War (see Zhang Zhengming, *Chu wenhua zhi*, 211); this title also existed in other Zhou states (see *Zhou li* "Xiaguan: Dasima" *Zhou li zhengyi* 55–56.2280–2363). *Sima* 司馬 (lit. "Master of Horses") is amply attested in Western Zhou bronze inscriptions, but *dasima* appears only, rarely, in inscriptions of Eastern Zhou date. The transmitted sources give the general's name as Zhao [*djaw?] Yang 昭陽; *zhao* 昭 is equivalent to *shao* 卲 [*djaw], the character given in the inscription; I retain that pronunciation, rather than following the common practice of emending the inscription based on the received texts.

(2) 夏尿（夷）之月乙亥之日
[BOTH DOCUMENTS] in the Xiayi month, day *yi hai*:

GMR intuited, based on context, that Xiayi 夏尿 must be the name of a month. Recently excavated manuscripts have proved that it was indeed the name of the eighth month in the Chu calendar; in the "Almanac" 日書 manuscripts from Shuihudi, *yi* is alternately written as 尿 [*ghljəj], 尸 [*hljəj], or 夷 [*ljəj] (see Shuihudi Qin mu zhujian zhengli xiaozu, *Shuihudi Qin mu zhujian*; the calendar was first reconstructed in Zhu Dexi, "Jingli Quluan jie"). *Yi hai* 乙亥 is day 12 in the Cycle of Sixty. Xie ("E Jun Qi jie mingwen bushi," 152) has calculated the exact date as March 16, 323 B.C.E. (Julian calendar).

(3) 王處於茷（郊）郢之遊宮
[BOTH DOCUMENTS] when the king dwelled in the pleasure palace in suburban Ying:

Ying 郢 was the generic name for any Chu capital, of which there were several during the Eastern Zhou period. It here refers to the Warring States period capital where remains are still visible 5 km to the north of Jiangling 江陵 in central Hubei (e.g., HSZ2). Instead of *chu* 處 [*khlja?], "dwell (temporarily)" (SCZ, LHH2, LL3), most authors read *ju* 居 [*kja], "dwell (permanently)." *Chu* is preferable because of the transitoriness implicit in the term *yougong* 遊宮 "pleasure [lit. traveling-for-pleasure] palace." This palace does not seem to be mentioned anywhere else, nor has it been identified archaeologically.

Liu Xinfang ("Shi 'Jiaoying'") adduces many loci in newly excavated manuscripts and convincingly glosses the character preceding Ying as *jiao* 郊, "suburb." Among many other readings proposed, one that also has some plausibility is LL1's (369) *ji* 紀; LL1 takes *xi* 兮 [*gi?] as the phonetic component and equates it phonetically with *xi* 系 [*kih], which he glosses as *ji* 紀 [*kjə?]. LL1 explains Jiying 紀郢 as Jinancheng 紀南城 (capital to the south of the Jishan 紀山 mountains), an alternative name for the Chu capital at Jiangling.

(4) 大攻尹脽（睢）以王命= 桼（集）尹恕糈裁（織）尹逆裁（織）令阫

[BOTH DOCUMENTS] the Grand Intendant of Works Sui took a royal order and commanded the Jiyin official Dao Hai(?), the Zhiyin official Ni, and the Zhiling official Qi:

The four names of offices given here in their hierarchical order are specific to Chu. Since many Chu official titles end in *yin* 尹, "Intendant" (the chief minister's title, e.g., was *lingyin* 令尹, "Intendant of Mandates"), one may assume that *dagongyin* 大攻尹 (which some commentators emend to 大工尹) is equivalent to *dasikong* 大司空 (lit. "Grand Master of Works") in other parts of the Zhou culture sphere. *Sikong* 司空 (*sigong* 司工 in some bronze inscriptions) were ministerial-level officials in charge of the court artisans, whose purview comprises manufacture as well as commerce. Like them, the Grand Intendant of Works seems to have reported directly to the king. The other titles are less clear. In the title here transcribed as *jiyin*, the first character corresponds to *ji* 集, "assemble" (LL1); in transcribing the following titles as *zhiyin* 織尹 and *zhiling* 織令, respectively, I follow Yin (in Y&L) and YXW. *Zhi* 織 means "weave." Both *ji* and *zhi* seem semantically appropriate for subordinates of the Grand Intendant of Works.

In each case, the personal name follows the official title. LL1 (369) tentatively identifies the Great Intendant of Works Sui with one Zhao Ju 昭睢, mentioned in *Zhanguo ce* "Chuce" 楚策 (*Zhanguo ce*, 524–542, passim), who lived in Chu at exactly the same period. Unlike the other officials listed (or E Jun Qi), but like the Grand Minister of War Shao Yang, the Jiyin official Dao Hai(?) has a two-character name, presumably comprising his lineage name and his birth name (the tentative transcription of the latter was proposed by LL3); LL1 notes (369) that his lineage name is identical with that of the occupant of tomb 1 at Wangshan 望山, Jiangling, a descendant of Dao Wang 悼王 (r. 401–381 B.C.E.), making this official a member of a junior branch of the Chu royal house. YXW glosses the personal name of the Zhiling official as Qi 耆.

(5) 為鄂君啟之府賦（造）鑄金節
[BOTH DOCUMENTS] to cast [these] metal tallies for E Jun Qi's treasury:

I translate the term *fu* 府 (written with the added "cowrie" signific 貝 in the original inscription, a synonymous variant also encountered on other inscribed objects from Warring States period Chu) as the name of an office, but it might just as well designate the occupant of that office. The keeper(s) of E Jun Qi's treasury would presumably have been higher in status than the *fu*, "Accountants," of the *Zhou li*, who are alleged to have been staff members rather than officials.

Zhu 鑄 is here combined into a double verb (*zaozhu* 造鑄, lit. "manufacture and cast") with a character that should be transcribed as 賦, which is phonetically equivalent to *jiu* 就 [*dzjəwh], corresponding in turn to *zao* 造 [*sgəw] (LL2; WH, 148; LJH, 140 n. 1). Supported by new evidence from the Chu bamboo-strip manuscripts in the Shanghai Museum, this reading should supersede all earlier ones (such as *geng* 賡 [*kəraŋ] [glossed by LL1 as *jing* 經 [*kiŋ]], "continue," implying that the tallies were being "reissued" [GMR and most other early commentators]; or *shang* 賣 [= *shang* 商, "merchants"], which, when linked to the preceding *fu* 府, yields the translation—tempting but wrong—that the tallies were "cast for the merchants of E Jun Qi's treasury" [Z&L, rescinded by LJH]).

(6) 屯（純）三舟為一艖五十艖

[BOAT TALLIES ONLY] [They are valid for] fifty *kua*(?), one *kua*(?) being made up of three boats combined:

The use of *tun* 屯 in the meaning of *tun* 純 , "tie together, wrap up" goes back to Western Zhou bronze inscriptions. In these inscriptions, *tun*, "add," is an arithmetical technical term, corresponding with *hui* 毀 ("demolish"), "subtract"; see (10).

The word here tentatively romanized as *kua*(?) 艖 [*khwəra(?)] is otherwise unattested. It has been tentatively identified as *ke* 舸 [*khəj], "large boat," a rare word recorded in *Fangyan jianshu*, 911 (LHH1,2; LX et al.). On the other hand, LL1 deduces from the grammatical usage of the word as a counter that it was a unit for calculation ("boat triplet") rather than a specific kind of boat. *Yikua*(?) 一 艖, "one *kua*(?)," is written as a combined character (*hewen* 合文), occupying a single character space.

(7) 車五十乘

[WAGON TALLIES ONLY] [They are valid for] fifty wagons:

By contrast to the corresponding passage in the boat tally inscriptions (6), specifications concerning the size of each conveyance unit follow later in (10). Perhaps the greater detail of these specifications made it grammatically impossible to append them as a subordinate clause, but the different formulations may also indicate that *che* and *kua*(?) belong to different word classes. Note that a separate counter, *cheng* 乘, is given for *che* (or *ju*) 車, "wagon," whereas *kua*(?) functions as a counter itself.

(8) 歲罷（一）返

[BOTH DOCUMENTS] and they are to be returned once a year:

As shown conclusively by Li Ling ("Du Guodian Chu jian 'Taiyi shengshui,'" 318–319 n. 1; also LL3) in connection with occurrences in the Warring States Chu manuscripts from Guodian, the second character stands for *yi* 一 "one," here to be taken as an adverb to *fan* 返 "return." Consisting of the components *yu* 羽 [*wja?] and *neng* 能 [*nəŋ /nə?], this character in all likelihood stands for a Chu dialect word semantically corresponding to *yi*, "one" [*?jit], without being etymologically identical with it (Wolfgang Behr, Scott Cook, and Martin Kern, personal communications, 2001; see also chap. 5 in this volume). (The most influential of various now-obsolete readings [YXW, FA, LL1] had identified this character with *ying* 贏 > 盈 [*ljiŋ], "fill," with possible semantic implications ranging from "when the year is full" to "[the fifty boats/chariots] every year are filled up and return.") *Fan* 返, like "return" in

English, can be used either intransitively (implying that it was the wagons that returned—the alternative apparently favored by the majority of commentators) or transitively (in which it would be the tallies that are returned to the Great Treasury at Ying [LHH1,2]). The latter alternative appears more consistent with the grammatical context.

(9) 毋載金革黽（箘）箭
[WAGON TALLIES ONLY] Do not transport metal, leather, or bamboo-shafted arrows:

My rendering of *minjian* 黽箭 follows YXW's gloss of *min* 黽 as *mei* 箘, which LL1 identifies as a kind of bamboo used for making arrow shafts. (CW2 reads the *minjian* as two separate words, "toads [for making arrow poison?] and arrows," which seems semantically less felicitous.)

(10)　如馬如牛如億（特）屯（純）十以壹一車如檐（擔）徒屯（純）二十檐（擔）以壹一車以毀於五十乘之中
[WAGON TALLIES ONLY] When [using] horses, buffaloes, or oxen, add up ten as the equivalent of one wagon; when [using] carrying-pole runners, add up twenty carrying-pole loads as the equivalent of one wagon, and subtract these [equivalents] from the total of fifty wagons:

The occurrence of 億 (*te* 特), "male animal, bull" (SCZ, followed by all later commentators) alongside *niu* 牛, a more general term for bovids, suggests the translation of the latter as "buffalo," still today the preferred transport animal in southern China.

Yiche 一車, "one wagon," is twice written as a combined character. As the character standing for "twenty" features a repetition sign, likewise marking it as a combined character, it should be transcribed as two separate characters, *ershi* 二 十, rather than as *nian* 廿, which did not exist in pre–Han times.

YXW and Zhang Zhenlin ("'Dantu' yu 'yidan sizhi' xinquan") were the first to read the character 檐 as *dan* 擔, "carrying load" (檐 appears once in *Lüshi chunqiu* "Mengdongji: Yibao" 孟冬紀異寶 [*Lüshi chunqiu jiaoshi*, 551] as a counter for official salary payments). SCZ1 specifies that this refers to loads carried on carrying poles. The character occurs twice in this passage, the first time as part of the binome *dantu* 擔徒, "carrying-pole runners," the second time as a counter after "twenty." Li Jiahao ("Chuanlin longjie mingwen kaoshi") reads *dan* in the second context as a volumetric unit of measurement, but since no corresponding counter is used after "ten" for the three kinds of animals, I suspect that it must, rather, be treated as an abbreviation of *dantu*. (Widely followed transcriptions of *dan* as *bei* 棓 [< 桮，捎，偝，背], "backpack" [GMR, LHH1,2], do not correspond to the graph.)

(11) 自鄂市
[BOTH DOCUMENTS] [Depart] from the market at E:

The transcription of the last character as *s h i* 市, "market," was established by Qiu, "Zhanguo wenzi zhong de 'shi.'" Almost all earlier commentators had read it as *wang* 往, "depart," which does not correspond to the graph.

The following translation of the itineraries accepts that E is located near present-day Deng Xian 鄧縣 (Henan) (FA and CW1) rather than at or near present-day Echeng 鄂城 (Hubei) as alleged by the majority of commentators. Aside from considerations of historical geography, such a reading also allows a more consistent rendering of the four "verbs of travel" occurring in the boat itineraries: *yu* 逾, "go downstream," *shang* 迬 (= 上), "go upstream," *ru* 入 [*njəp] (written as 內 = 納 [*nəp]), "enter a river course at its mouth, going upstream," and *jiu* 就, "stop."

(12) 逾油（淯）上漢就屑（鄖）就芭（芸〜郇）陽
[BOAT TALLIES ONLY] go downstream on the Yu River, go upstream on the Han River, stop at Yun, stop at Xunyang:

This passage describes the western trajectory of the boat merchants' itinerary, from E to the Han River and following the Han River upstream.

GMR (followed by HSZ1) realized that *yu* 逾 here means the contrary of *shang* 上; HLY, citing Tang Yuhui (*Zhanguo mingwenxuan*, 46), glosses the character as *jiang* 降, "descend." (This is far preferable to the gloss, derived from the *Shangshu* 尚書 commentaries, of *yu* [*lju] as *yue* 越 [*rwjat], "cross, transgress," which—proposed in connection with the assumption that E was located at Wuchang 武昌 [Hubei]—necessitated the awkward claim that *yu* had several distinct meanings in these inscriptions: "cross" in connection with lakes and mountain passes [see below] and "change direction" in connection with rivers [TQX1, LL1].)

The character *jiu* 就—with twenty occurrences, by far the most frequent in these inscriptions—was first thus transcribed by LL2 on the basis of occurrences in the as-yet-unpublished corpus of fourth-century B.C.E. bamboo-strip manuscripts recently acquired by the Shanghai Museum (see also WH, LJH). LL2 glosses *jiu* as "arrive," WH as *wang* 往, "go"; I prefer its base meaning of "stop," which is consistent with CW2's realization that this verb is always followed by the name of a marketplace (*shi* 市) where the merchants were authorized to conduct trade. The reading as *jiu* must supersede earlier transcriptions such as *geng* 庚 [*kəraŋ] > *geng* 賡, "continue," which was commonly glossed as *jing* 經 [*kiŋ], "pass through," with the place-names following it taken as toll-collecting stations (*guan* 關) (GMR, FA, LHH1,2).

CW1 (followed by Z&L) reads the character *you* 油 [*ljəw] as Yu 淯 [*ljəwk], the name of a tributary of the Han River on the banks of which E is located according to the reconstruction here followed. (This is preferable to earlier readings of *gu* 沽, glossed as *hu* 湖, "lake," and identified either with the Donghu 東湖 [East Lake] on the outskirts of modern-day Wuchang [GMR, HSZ1], or with the lake now known as Wutang 吳塘, located between Echeng and Wuchang [SCZ1, TQX1], or taken in the plural as referring to several lakes downriver from Nanyang [FA, 77].)

The reading of the otherwise-unknown character 屑 as Yun 鄖 follows FA (also Z&L, HSZ2), who identifies its location as present-day Yun Xian 鄖縣

(Hubei), on the Han River upstream from Xiangyang. (Rejected alternative transcriptions include 1. *yan* 厭 [*ʔjiams] [LL1, WH, who cites Hubei sheng Jingsha tielu kaogu dui, *Baoshan Chu jian*, nos. 219, 188], unconvincingly identified with Yang 陽 [*ljaŋ], a place on the east bank of the Han River mentioned in *Shuijing zhu*, near present-day Laohekou 老河口 [Hubei]; 2. 青 > *zhe* 者 [*tjaʔ], glossed as *gu* 谷 [*kluk] and identified with Gucheng 谷城 [Hubei] [Tang Yuhui, *Zhanguo mingwen xuan*, 47]; 3. *yan* 厝, identified as Yun 員 near present-day Qianjiang 潛江 [Hubei] [Y&L, GMR, YXW, TQX1]; 4. Yan 鄢, an erstwhile Chu capital thought to have been located near Yicheng 宜城 [Hubei] [HSZ1, SCZ2, TXQ2, LHH1,2]; 5. 厝, an unknown character with the phonetic *she* 舌 [*mljat] [LL3]; 6. She 灄 [*hnjap], identified with Shekou 灄口, in Huangpi 黃陂 [Hubei] [LCM].)

The reading of 芭 as *yun* 芸 and the identification of Yunyang 芸陽 with Xunyang 郇楊 (modern Xunyang 旬陽, on the Han River in southern Shaanxi) (GMR, Z&L, HLY, LL3) seem plausible in the light of recent archaeological finds, which confirm that this was the northwesternmost Chu outpost in the Middle Warring States period (see Xunyang xian bowuguan, "Shaanxi Xunyang faxian Zhanguo Chu mu"; Zhang Pei, "Xunyang you faxian liangzuo Zhanguo Chu mu"). (Rejected alternatives include 1. Yiyang 芭陽 [YXW], which TQX1 locates near Yicheng 宜城 [Hubei]; 2. Jiyang 芭陽, taken as Jiyang 棘陽, south of Nanyang [Henan] [HSZ1; criticized by TQX2, SCZ2, but still followed by Peng Ke, "Coinage and Commercial Development in Classical China," 255–256]; 3. Xi Xian 錫縣, a place on the south bank of the Han River mentioned in *Shuijing zhu* [FA].)

(13) 逾漢就鄉（襄？）逾夏入邔
[BOAT TALLIES ONLY] go downstream on the Han River, stop at Xiang(?), go downstream on the Xia River, enter the Yun River:

This passage describes the central trajectory of the boat merchants' itinerary, down the Han River toward the Yunmeng 雲夢 Marsh.

The object of *ru* 入, "enter a river course at its mouth, going upstream," seem to be rivers along which E Jun Qi's merchants enjoyed trading privileges (CW2); this word is of a similar order as *jiu* 就, which precedes settlements with markets.

The phonetic element in the unknown character 鄉 is *wang* [*wjaŋ] (HSZ1). HLY gives *xiang* 襄 [*sənjaŋ]; an identification with Xiangyang 襄陽 (Hubei) would be compatible with the itinerary reconstructed here. (Rejected alternative readings include 1. *huang* 鄋 [YXW], tentatively identified with the Chu capital known as Chu Huangcheng 楚皇城, at Yicheng [Hubei]; 2. *wang* 汪, identified with a location somewhere along the Han River [SCZ1, LHH1,2]; 3. *huang* 黃, identified with Huangji 黃棘 in southern Henan [Y&L, SCZ, TQX1].)

Xia 夏 was another name for the lower course of the Han River (GMR, HSZ1, FA). (Necessitated by their identification of the character with the *wang* phonetic as Huangji, TQX1 and SCZ identify Xia, not as a river, but as the Xiaguan 夏關, the main pass over the Funiushan 伏牛山 range into the Yellow River drainage, which the traders would have crossed over [*yu* 逾] by way of a long portage into non-Chu territory. After withering criticism by HSZ1, the authors retracted this idea [YDF2, SCZ2, TQX2].)

Though written with the "town" radical, *yun* 邧 is undoubtedly the name of a river, most likely the Yun 溳 River, a tributary of the lower Han (Y&L, GMR, HSZ1, Z&L, HLY, LL3). (Alternatively, LL1 [370] transcribes the character in question as *si* 汜, the name of a river mentioned in the *Shijing* song "Jiang you si" 江有汜 [Mao 22] and identified by Chen Weisong 陳蔚松, "'Mi qiangda yu nan Si' jie," as the branch of the Yangzi River separated from the river's main course by Hundred-Mile Island [Bailizhou 百里洲] in Zhijiang 枝江 [Hubei]. Misled by the shape of the character, FA believes that it must refer to one or several settlements—perhaps a category of settlements—located in the Yunmeng 雲夢 Marsh, near the confluence of the Han and the Yangzi.)

(14) 逾江就彭射（澤）就松陽入瀘江就爰陵
[BOAT TALLIES ONLY] go downstream on the Jiang, stop at Pengze, stop at Songyang, enter the Lujiang River, stop at Yuanling:

This passage describes the eastward trajectory of the boat merchants' itinerary, in present-day Jiangxi and southern Anhui.

Jiang 江 refers to the Yangzi River 揚子江 (Changjiang 長江).

The second character in the place-name Pengze contains the elements "bow" and "arrow" (the widely followed transcription as *li* 蠡 [SCZ1, FA, LHH1,2] is mistaken); Z&L identify it as *she* 射 [*mljak] (also pronounced *yi* [*ljak]), which they consider phonetically equivalent to *ze* 澤 [*dərak]. In antiquity, Pengze 彭澤 was the name of part of the large lake system now known as Lake Poyang 鄱陽湖. FA correctly insists that the place-name here should refer to a settlement, not to the lake itself. The modern county seat of Pengze (Jiangxi) is on the south bank of the Yangzi some 30 km downstream from the mouth of Lake Poyang, but some commentators insist that the place referred to here must have been on the north bank of the Yangzi River (TQX1 proposes Wangjiang 望江 [Anhui]).

FA quotes a passage from the *Shuijing zhu* relating that "Songyang" 松陽 [*sljuŋ-ljaŋ] was inscribed on the city gate of Yuzhang 豫章, present-day Nanchang 南昌 (Jiangxi). Another possible identification would be with Congyang 樅陽 [*tshjuŋ-ljaŋ] (Anhui) (TQX1, SCZ, HSZ, LL1).

That Lujiang 瀘江—a river name in this text—must have something to do with the modern settlement of the same name (in central Anhui) is uncontroversial, but there has been considerable dispute as to the exact identity of the river referred to. The most likely candidate is the Baitujiang 白兔江, a northern tributary of the Yangzi in the area of present-day Lujiang (TQX1, SCZ1, FA, LHH2). This may have been, in the late fourth century B.C.E., an area without major settlements. (Y&L misread the character *lu* 瀘 [= 瀘] in "Lujiang" as *kuai* 澮; accepting this, HSZ1 boldly identified it as the Huai 淮 River, which E Jun Qi's merchants would have reached by a long detour through hostile Yue 越 territory; this idea is abandoned in HSZ2.)

TQX2 (followed by LL1) identifies Yuanling 爰陵 as the place known during the Han dynasty as Yuanling 宛陵, near modern Xuancheng 宣城 (Anhui).

(Based on this, TQX2 takes the Lujiang to be the river now known as Qingyijiang 青弋江, a southern tributary of the Yangzi on the banks of which Xuancheng is located; but there is no need to posit a connection between a river preceded by the verb *ru* and the place-name following it in the itinerary. Alternative proposed locations of Yuanling are also—in my opinion, quite unnecessarily—connected to each commentator's preferred identification of the Lujiang River.)

(15) 上江入湘就睒（誓？）就郴（洮）陽入耒就郙（郴）入資沅澧繇（油）

[BOAT TALLIES ONLY] go upstream on the Jiang, enter the Xiang River, stop at Shi(?), stop at Taoyang, enter the Lei River, stop at Chen, enter the Zi, Yuan, Li, and You Rivers:

This passage describes the far southern trajectory of the boat merchants' itinerary, in present-day Hunan and down to northern Guangxi.

HLY has found the character here tentatively transcribed as Shi 誓 in the Baoshan bamboo-strip manuscripts (Hubei sheng Jingsha tielu kaogu dui, *Baoshan Chu jian* nos. 138, 164, 174) and identifies the place as Shigang 誓港, northwest of Changsha 長沙 (Hunan), on the east bank of the Xiang River. Alternative transcriptions include 睒 (Y&L, SCZ1, TQX1, Naitō, "Gaku Kun Kei setsu"), 睒 (GMR), 睒 (YXW; Sun Jianming, "E Jun Qi jie xutan"), 睒 (YDF), 睒 (Xiong and He, "E Jun Qi jie zhoujie zhong Jiang Xiang diming xinkao"), and 睒 (Z&L). LL3, while conceding an inability to give a phonetic transcription, confirms that the left-hand portion is 見, not 貝, and the right-hand portion is neither 葉 nor 桑. From context, some commentators have attempted to equate this place with Changsha, but CW2 takes the absence of Changsha from the itinerary as an indication that the place-names mentioned are neither the main settlements nor the major toll-collection stations but specific markets where E Jun Qi's merchants enjoyed a trading privilege.

TQX1 identified 郴陽 as the place known during the Han period as Taoyang 洮陽, on the Xiang River northwest of present-day Quanzhou 全州 (Guangxi).

The identification of the character 潘 (SCZ) as *lei* 耒, and its identification with the homonymous river in southeastern Hunan was first proposed by YXW (followed by SCZ1,2, TQX1, FA; LL1 [370] reads the character as Lai 淶, a minor tributary of the Xiang). In taking the character *lin* 郙 [*brjəm?] as *chen* 郴 [*drjəm(?)], I follow Z&L (see also LHH2); I suspect that this is the rendering of a non-Sinitic word. Modern-day Chenzhou 郴州 is on the Lei River. (Alternative readings proposed include Pin(?) 稟 [Y&L] and Bi 鄙 [GMR, SCZ1, TQX1]; TQX1 equates this with Bian 便, a place mentioned in *Shuijing zhu*, situated on the Lei River near present-day Yongxing 永興 [Hunan].)

Of the four river names at the end of this passage (all in the Lake Dongting 洞庭湖 region of northern Hunan), only the last presents some difficulty. YXW (followed by HSZ1, TQX1, LL2,3, Z&Y) renders it as *yao* 繇 [*ljaw]; this is compatible with the river's earlier identification as the You 油 [*ljəw] (Y&L), which has been adopted even by commentators who read the character differently (e.g., as *dan* 澹 [SCZ1, LHH1,2]).

(16) 上江就木關就郢
[BOAT TALLIES ONLY] go upstream on the Jiang, stop at Muguan, stop at Ying:

This passage describes the final stretch of the boat merchants' itinerary, from the Lake Dongting area to the Chu capital. Ying refers to the Chu capital near Jiangling 江陵. Divergent opinions have been expressed merely on whether the place-name Muguan 木關 (the second character as written in the inscription has *chuan* 串 as its phonetic element) has any ulterior meaning. A translation as "Wood Pass" might suggest that the merchants may have made this part of their journey over land. A translation as "The Toll-Collecting Station of the Trees" would suggest that it was the name of an administrative institution, and only secondarily that of a place. The fact that "wood" is one of the Five Phases might lead one to speculate further that Muguan was one of a set of five toll-collecting stations around the Chu capital (or four, the capital itself occupying the fifth position). Since all these questions are undecidable, I render Muguan as just an ordinary place-name. Various locations have been proposed: GMR suggests Shashi 沙市 (Hubei), the Yangzi port nearest to Jiangling; TQX1 and SCZ1 think that it was one of the entrance gates of the Chu capital. HSZ1 identifies it as the water gate of Mulingguan 穆陵關, a solution to which TQX2 objects by pointing out that Mulingguan was not in Chu but in Qi 齊. (Presumably, HSZ1 understood Mulingguan as a generic place-name.)

(17) 就易（湯）丘就邡城就䍃（象？）禾就酉焚就繁陽就高丘下蔡就居巢就郢
[WAGON TALLIES ONLY] stop at Tangqiu, stop at Fangcheng, stop at Xianghe, stop at Youfen, stop at Fanyang, stop at Gaoqiu, stop at Xiacai, stop at Juchao, stop at Ying:

Since the second character occurs identically in all place-names ending in *yang* 陽 throughout the inscription, almost all commentators have transcribed it as *yang*; my reading as Tang 湯 follows LL1, who suggests that it corresponds to Tang 唐, a small state to the north of Suizhou 隨州 (Hubei). This may, however, be out of the way. TQX1, SCZ1, and HSZ1 place Yangqiu 陽丘 near Fangcheng 方城 (Henan), and FA in the Nanyang 南陽 area (Henan), but none of these commentators can point to an exact location. The place-name Fangcheng 邡城 in the inscription must correspond to a locality somewhere near present-day Fangcheng 方城. TQX1 (followed by LL1 and others) identifies it with Bao'anzhen 保安鎮, Ye Xian 葉縣 (Henan), near a major pass over the Funiushan 伏牛山 range, which the wagons had to cross to reach the localities in the Huai River drainage area mentioned further on.

The first character in the following place-name remains to be convincingly deciphered. I tentatively follow Y&L's reading as *xiang* 象. The locality—like that of the following place-name—must be extrapolated as being somewhere between Fangcheng and Fanyang (Henan); FA suggests that it corresponds to the Xiangheguan 象河關 Pass near Bao'anzhen. (Alternatively, YXW and LHH1,2 read the first character in this place-name as *tu* 菟, hazarding an identification with the Xituheshan 西菟和山 [Shaanxi], which is geographically implausible.)

The place-name here read as Youfen 酉焚 [*ljəw-bjən] (Y&L) was identified by Yao ("E Jun Qi jie shiwen"; followed by HSZ2) as Liufen 柳焚 [*(C)rjəw-bjən], a locality in former Zheng territory mentioned in *Zuo zhuan* (*Chunqiu Zuo zhuan zhengyi* [Xuan 9], 1874), which in turn may be identical to Rufen 汝墳 [*njaʔ-bjən], mentioned in the *Shijing* song "Rufen" 汝墳 (Mao 10). Phonetically, the latter equation appears less certain, though a location in the valley of the Ru 汝 River in south-central Henan would fit the itinerary well. (Alternatively, SCZ1 and TQX1 read the first character in this place-name as *fu*[?] 畐; HSZ1 reads *fu* 富. As a location, TQX1 proposes Suiping 遂平 [Henan]; FA, Bugeng 不羹, north of Wuyang 舞陽 [Henan].)

As to Fanyang 繁陽, the sources mention several localities of that name. I find it impossible to decide between a place near Xincai 新蔡, near the Henan-Anhui border, which occurs several times in the *Zuo zhuan* (GMR, SCZ1, TQX1, HSZ1), and a locality considerably further to the north, present-day Fancheng 繁城, near Xuchang 許昌 (Henan) on the Ying 潁 River (FA, based on *Shuijing zhu*).

On the basis of indications in the Baoshan bamboo-strip manuscripts (Hubei sheng Jingsha tielu kaogu dui, *Baoshan Chu jian*, nos. 236–238 and 239–241), LJH has convincingly identified Gaoqiu 高丘 with Fuliji 符離集, near Su Xian 宿縣 (Anhui).

Xiacai 下蔡 was the final capital of the state of Cai 蔡 at Zhoulai 州來, near present-day Shou Xian 壽縣.

HSZ1 points out that the component *ju* 居 in the place-name Juchao 居鄛 is a prefix that occurs in many place-names (as well as proper names) in the language of the southeastern Wu and Yue peoples. Among the half dozen places of that name mentioned in early sources (TQX1, 2, HSZ1), the most likely one is at Chao Xian 巢縣 (Anhui) (GMR, FA).

(18) 見其金節則毋政毋舍桴（棹？）食不見其金節則政
[BOTH DOCUMENTS] When they show their metal tallies, they will not be assessed tariff, [though] they will not be lodged, equipped(?), or fed. When they do not show their metal tallies, they will be assessed tariff:

The reading of the first character (which reoccurs prefixed by a negative in the final sentence of this passage) as *jian* 見, "see, inspect," follows GMR (see also LL1, LBH). The word may here be intended in its intransitive meaning (modern *xian* 現, "appear"). (An earlier reading as 导 > *de* 得, "obtain" [YXW, FA, CW2], while semantically unobjectionable, is untenable for graphic reasons [LL3].)

The character *zheng* 政 corresponds to the word now written as *zheng* 征, "assess tariff."

The negative particle *wu* 毋 governs the following three characters, which I read as three coordinated transitive verbs—technical terms for dealing with traveling officials—forming a single predicate (for more detail on the syntactics of negative sentences see Van Auken, "Negatives in Warring States Texts"). The character following *she* 舍, "lodge," 桴, is unknown, and no decipherment proposed to date is wholly convincing. Following YXW's transcription as *zhao*

棹 (glossed as *zhao* 朝, "morning"), LL1 interprets that character in its alternative reading of *zhuo*, "wooden plank," suggesting that it might refer to the boat as a *pars pro toto* or perhaps to the boat's equipment—hence my tentative verbal reading as "equip." The following verb, 食, should be read as *si*, "feed," not *shi*, "eat." (This reading seems semantically more consistent than the following proposed alternatives: *wu she xunshi* 毋舍遜食, "Don't give them rotten food" [GMR]; *wu she fushi* 毋舍浮食, "Don't give them excessive [amounts of] food" [Y&L]; *wu she zhaoshi* 毋舍朝食, "Don't give them breakfast" [YXW]; *wu she zi shi* 毋舍梓食, "Don't give them firewood or food" [SCZ1, FA]. The readings *wu she li shi* 毋舍理食, "Don't lodge or arrange food for them" [LHH1,2], and *wu shi chuan si* 毋舍傳食, "Don't lodge them or hand them food" [Z&L], are grammatically problematic.)

(19) 如載馬牛羊以出入關則政於大府毋政於關

[BOAT TALLIES ONLY] If they transport horses, oxen, and sheep in and out of the tariff-collecting stations, then they will be assessed tariff at the Great Treasury, but not at the tariff-collecting stations.

For comments on this passage, see main text, section V.

NOTES

This chapter is an expansion of my entry on one of the boat tallies in Yang Xiaoneng, ed., *The Golden Age of Chinese Archaeology*, 339–344; the translation given here supersedes the earlier one. I am grateful to Li Ling and Lai Guolong for many useful references and corrections.

1. Good illustrations are available in *Shodō zenshū*, vol. 26, cat. no. 16; *Zhongguo lishi bowuguan*, no. 68; *Yin Zhou jinwen jicheng*, vol. 18, nos. 12110–12113; Li Xueqin, *Qingtongqi*, vol. 2, no. 136; Anhui sheng bowuguan, *Anhui Sheng Bowuguan cang qingtongqi*, no. 79.

2. From the first period, there is the tomb of Marquis Zhao of Cai 蔡昭侯 (r. 518–491 B.C.E.) at Ximennei, Shou Xian (Anhui sheng wenwu guanli weiyuanhui and Anhui sheng bowuguan, *Shou Xian Cai Hou mu chutu yiwu*). Chu-related archaeological discoveries in Anhui since 1949 are well summarized in Liu Hehui, *Chu wenhua de dongjian*. For earlier discoveries, see Karlbeck, "Selected Objects from Ancient Shou-chou," and *Treasure Seeker in China*, 158–173; *Anhui sheng tongzhi jinshi guwu kao gao* (not seen; cited in Li Xueqin, *Eastern Zhou and Qin Civilizations*, 167).

3. Yin and Luo, "Shou Xian chutu de 'E Jun Qi jinjie,'" 8. Three wagon tallies and one boat tally had been found by farmers in the course of irrigation work at Qiujiahuayuan, Shou Xian, in 1957. In 1960, an additional boat tally was acquired at Xinji 新集, Mengcheng 蒙城 (Anhui). It, too, was said to have been found in Shou Xian (Anhui sheng bowuguan, *Anhui sheng bowuguan cang qingtongqi*, caption for no. 79), presumably at Qiujiahuayuan (see Li Xueqin, *Eastern Zhou and Qin Civilizations*, 167).

4. Ding, "Shouchun cheng kaogu de zhuyao shouhuo," 161–162; see also Ding, "Chu du Shouchun cheng kaogu diaocha zongshu." At 26.3 km², the size of the walled area of Shouchun exceeds considerably that of the famed Warring States capital of Qi 齊 at Linzi 臨淄 (ca. 20 km²); it is comparable in its time only to that of the Lower Capital of Yan 燕下都 (some 30 km², but apparently not fully settled) and, probably, that of the First Emperor's capital at Xianyang 咸陽 (the exact extent of which is as yet undetermined).

5. Li Xueqin, *Eastern Zhou and Qin Civilizations*, 167. The most spectacular of these is a gold-inlaid bronze buffalo figure inscribed "Item of the Great Treasury" (*dafu zhi qi* 大府之器) (Yin, "Anhui Shou Xian xin faxian de tongniu").

6. Shang ("Tan E Jun Qi jie mingwen zhong jige wenzi he jige diming deng wenti," 155) stresses that the tallies were made for multiple uses. Liu Hehui ("Chu E Jun Qi jie xintan," 60–61) believes that they were buried at the time of Qin's conquest of Chu in 223 B.C.E. The idea that Shouchun might have been a "secondary capital" of Chu (and hence named Ying 郢) even before the court moved there in 241 B.C.E. and could have been the originally intended end point of, at least, the wagon expeditions (Yin and Luo, "Shou Xian chutu de 'E Jun Qi jinjie'"; Tan, "E Jun Qi jie mingwen shidi"; Shang, "E Jun Qi jie kao") was harshly criticized by Huang Shengzhang ("Guanyu E Jun Qi jie jiaotong luxian de fuyuan wenti") and thereupon abandoned (Shang, "Tan E Jun Qi jie mingwen zhong jige wenzi he jige diming deng wenti"; Yin, "E Jun Qi jie liangge diming jianshuo").

7. Cf. Ōba, "Kan no setsu ni tsuite," 28–29; Chen Zhaorong, "Zhanguo zhi Qin de fujie," 306–312; Chen Wei, "E Jun Qi jie yu Chu guo mianshui wenti."

8. *Shuowen jiezi* 説文解字, entry *jie*.

9. *Chunqiu Zuo zhuan zhengyi* (Wen 8), 1846–1847.

10. *Zhou li zhengyi* 28.1111–1120 ("Diguan: Zhangjie" 地官掌節).

11. Ibid. 72.2998–2999 ("Qiuguan: Xiaoxingren" 秋官小行人).

12. E.g., ibid. 19.769 ("Diguan: Dasitu" 地官大司徒), 21.859 ("Xiangdafu" 鄉大夫), 22.889 ("Bizhang" 比長), 26.1023 ("Sijiu" 司救), 27.1068 ("Sishi" 司市), 28.1107 ("Siguan" 司關), 58.2409 ("Xiaguan: Sixian" 夏官司險), 64.2696 ("Huaifangshe" 懷方氏), 70.2896 ("Qiuguan: Yelushi" 秋官野廬氏), 70.2921 ("Xiulüshi" 脩閭氏), 71.2982 ("Daxingren" 大行人), 73.3057 ("Xingfu" 行夫), 73.3059 ("Huanren" 環人).

13. Ibid. 19.769 ("Diguan: Dasitu"), 21.859 ("Xiangdafu"), 58.2409 ("Xiaguan: Sixian"), 70.2921 ("Qiuguan: Xiulüshi").

14. Ibid. 22.889 ("Diguan: Bizhang").

15. Ibid. 27.1068 ("Diguan: Sishi"), 28.1107 ("Siguan").

16. Ibid. 26.1023 ("Diguan: Sijiu"), 26.1030 ("Tiaoren" 調人), 70.2889 ("Qiuguan: Buxian" 布憲), 71.2982 ("Daxingren").

17. Ōba, "Kan no dōkofu to chikushifu."

18. Lao, "The Early Use of the Tally in China," 97. Such objects are frequently depicted on Eastern Han stone reliefs (see Hayashi, *Kandai no bunbutsu*, 480–481, figs. 10.90–91; Sun Ji, *Han dai wuzhiwenhua ziliao tushuo*, 150–152, fig. 38.2).

19. The *Zhou li* only mentions *fu* as part of the binome *fujie*, here translated

118   LOTHAR VON FALKENHAUSEN

as "matching tallies." *Shiming*: "Shi shuqi" 釋名釋書契 (*Shiming shuzheng bu* 6.1076) makes explicit the etymological connection of *fu*, "tally," and *fu*, "to match."

20. *Shiji* 10.424; *Hanshu* 4.118. Discussed by Hayashi, *Kandai no bunbutsu*, 531–534.

21. Zhang Yan 張晏 apud *Hanshu* 4.118.

22. *Lüshi chunqiu jiaoshi*, 1257 ("Lisu lan: Shangde" 離俗覽上德); *trad. auct. adiuv.* Wilhelm, *Frühling und Herbst des Lü Bu We*, 327.

23. Ibid.

24. *Zhanguo ce* 5.193 ("Qince 3" 秦策); translation: Crump, *Chan-kuo ts'e*, 107 (Wade–Giles changed to Pinyin).

25. *Shiji* 10.424; the commentary quotes a statement by Ying Shao 應劭 (ca. 140–before 204) that makes the military connotation of the "bronze tiger tallies" explicit.

26. The only provenienced specimen is the Du-*hufu* 杜虎符 from Beichencun 北沉村, Xi'an 西安 (Shaanxi), found in 1973 (Hei, "Xi'an shijiao faxian Qin guo Du hufu"; *Yin Zhou jinwen jicheng,* vol. 18, no. 12109; Li Xueqin, *Qingtongqi,* vol. 2, no. 170). Unprovenienced specimens with almost identical inscriptions include the Xinqi-*hufu* (see below) and the Yuanling-*hufu* 宛陵虎符 in the Museum of Chinese History in Beijing (Wang Guowei, *Guantang jilin* 18.11b–13b; Li Xueqin, *Eastern Zhou and Qin Civilizations*, 236, fig. 102 [n.b. the captions of figs. 102 and 103 are reversed]). Whereas the right half of the Du-*hufu* was to be kept with the lord (*jun* 君)—presumably a regional commander—the Xinqi-*hufu* inscription substitutes the king (*wang* 王) and the Yuanling-*hufu*, the emperor (*huangdi* 皇帝), indicating that the Yuanling-*hufu* date after 221 B.C.E. Another pre-Qin specimen, the Bi Dafu-*hufu* 辟大夫虎符, is in the Palace Museum, Beijing (*Yin Zhou jinwen jicheng,* vol. 18, no. 12107). Wang Guowei (*Guantang jilin* 18.13b–15b) discusses *hufu* from the Wang Mang and Sui periods.

27. Wang Guowei, *Guantang jilin* 18.11a–b; Guo, *Liang Zhou jinwenci daxi tulu kaoshi, kao* 251b–252a, *lu* 292b; Hou, "Xinqi hufu de zaixian"; Li Xueqin, *Eastern Zhou and Qin Civilizations*, 235–237; Chen Zhi, "Qin bingjia zhi fu kao"; *Yin Zhou jinwen jicheng,* vol. 18, no. 12108.

28. According to a commentary on *Shiji* 10.424, Han dynasty bronze tiger tallies were inlaid in silver; Sun Ji discusses such a specimen (*Han dai wuzhiwenhua ziliao tushuo*, 152, fig. 38.5).

29. Guangzhou shi wenwu guanli weiyuanhui et al., *Xi Han Nanyue Wang mu*, vol. 1, 87–88. This object may have been manufactured in Warring States period Chu. There are several comparable unprovenienced pieces (Tang Lan, "Wangming zhuankao"; Li Jiahao, "Chuanlin longjie mingwen kaoshi"; *Yin Zhou jinwen jicheng,* vol. 18, nos. 12094–12096).

30. *Yin Zhou jinwen jicheng,* vol. 18, nos. 12086–12106. See also Luo Zhenyu, *Sandai jijin wencun*, 18.31a–32a, and transcriptions in Luo Fuyi, *Sandai jijin wencun shiwen*, 18.11a–b.

31. Liu Huo, "Tong longjie." Li Ling ("Chu guo tongqi mingwen biannian huishi," 380–382) discusses four specimens; *Yin Zhou jinwen jicheng* (vol. 18, nos. 12097–12102) illustrates six. They are studied by Li Jiahao, "Chuanlin

longjie mingwen kaoshi."

32. This follows Guo Moruo's interpretation ("Guanyu E Jun Qi jie de yanjiu").

33. Ōba, "Kan no dōkofu to chikushifu." Hayashi (*Kandai no bunbutsu*, 533–534) and Sun Ji (*Han dai wuzhiwenhua ziliao tushuo*, 152) discuss some possible instances of such documents among the Juyan 居延 Han strips.

34. Yan Shigu apud *Hanshu* 4.118.

35. This is not altogether certain; Yan Shigu's use of the word *jian* might indicate that the emissaries' tallies were thin strips; broad pieces of bamboo such as those imitated by the E Jun Qi metal tallies would have normally been termed *du* 牘 (Li Ling, "Qin Yin daobing yuban de yanjiu," 527–528). Ōba ("Kan no dōkofu to chikushifu") believes that each of the tallies was broken in half and matched.

36. Shang, "E Jun Qi jie kao," 55. There are several different marks on each of the two pieces examined by Shang. Rather than numbering each member of the set, they may indicate the order or direction in which they were to be assembled.

37. On Warring States long-distance trade in grain, salt, iron, and livestock, see Peng, "Coinage and Commercial Development in Classical China," 257–300.

38. In the case of the boat expeditions, Li Ling ("Chu guo tongqi mingwen biannian huishi," 370) argues that the fifty *kua*(?) 舿 covered by the tally may have been fictitious units of calculation rather than designating an actually existing kind of boat.

39. Liu Hehui, *Chu wenhua de dongjian*, 138–139.

40. Li Jiahao, "Chuanlin longjie mingwen kaoshi," 5–7.

41. Ōba, "Kandai no setsu ni tsuite," 29; Zhang Zhengming's contention (*Chu wenhua zhi*, 219) that a five-part set of tallies covered two hundred and fifty conveyance units is doubted by Chen Wei ("E Jun Qi jie yu Chu guo mianshui wenti," 53).

42. For bronze inscriptions, see Falkenhausen, "Issues in Western Zhou Studies," 162–163 et passim; for wider discussion, see Falkenhausen, "Thoughts on 'Literacy' in Shang and Zhou China."

43. It may be disputed whether these really were "true" originals; their standardized formulations may well have been derived from reference modules ("form letters") that existed in written form.

44. Guo Moruo, "Guanyu E Jun Qi jie de yanjiu," 3.

45. These numbers reflect Funakoshi's idea ("Gaku Kun Kei setsu ni tsuite," 88) that the places mentioned in the inscriptions are the toll-collecting stations where tallies had to be proffered. If these are, instead, the markets where E Jun Qi's merchants were authorized to conduct trade (as suggested by Chen Wei, "E Jun Qi jie yu Chu guo mianshui wenti"), the inscriptions offer no clue as to the number of copies circulated to local officials.

46. On the complex issue of Warring States to Early Han period literacy, see Poo, *In Search of Personal Welfare*, 179–185; Lewis, *Writing and Authority in Early China*, 5–18; Falkenhausen, "Thoughts on 'Literacy' in Shang and Zhou China."

47. The verb *jian* 見 (perhaps intended in the sense of *xian* 現) indicates that such inspections were visual ones (Liu Hehui, "Chu E Jun Qi jie xintan," 60).

48. Peng ("Coinage and Commercial Development in Classical China," 251–252) argues that the main objective was to avoid overlapping taxation, a concern also manifested in Warring States writings on economic issues (see, e.g., *Guanzi* 9.15b ["Wen" 問]).

49. *Shuiyuan jiaozheng,* 277–279 ("Shanshui" 善說).

50. Funakoshi ("Gaku Kun Kei setsu ni tsuite," 74) proposes that E Jun Qi was a direct descendant of the Chu prince Hong 紅, who was briefly established as "King of E" 鄂王 in the time contemporary with Western Zhou (see *Shiji* 40.1692). This is, however, doubtful. The Marquises of E 鄂侯 mentioned in some Western Zhou bronze inscriptions discussed by Funakoshi had no connection whatsoever with Chu.

51. Yu, "'E Jun Qi jie' kaoshi," 444.

52. Funakoshi, "Gaku Kun Kei setsu ni tsuite," 74–75 et passim; Chen Wei, "'E Jun Qi jie' zhi 'E' di tantao." This is accepted by Zhu and Li ("E Jun Qi jie kaoshi [bapian]," 194) and (less overtly) Li Xueqin (*Eastern Zhou and Qin Civilizations,* 167) (*pace* Huang Shengzhang, "Zailun E Jun Qi jie jiaotong luxian fuyuan yu dili wenti"; and Liu Hehui, *Chu wenhua de dongjian,* 141).

53. See Yamada, "Chūgoku kodai no shō to ko."

54. *Zhou li zhengyi* 2.78 ("Tianguan: Taizai" 天官大宰).

55. There are six offices with attached merchants, involving a total of thirty-four merchants, in the Ministry of Heaven (*Zhou li zhengyi* 1 ["Tianguan zhi shu" 天官之屬]); one (with eight merchants) in the Ministry of Earth (*Zhou li zhengyi* 17 ["Diguan zhi shu]); none in the Ministry of Spring; three (with eight merchants) in the Ministry of Summer (*Zhou li zhengyi* 54 ["Xiaguan zhi shu" 夏官之屬]); and one (with two merchants) in the Ministry of Autumn (*Zhou li zhengyi* 65 ["Qiuguan zhi shu" 秋官之屬]). All these are *gu; shang* merchants, though mentioned variously in the *Zhou li* as objects of administrative measures, seem not to have been entrusted with official duties.

56. *Gu* merchants are rarely explicitly mentioned in the officials' "job descriptions"; see *Zhou li zhengyi* 25.975 ("Diguan: Lüshi" 地官閭師), 27.1054–1076 ("Sishi"), 28.1090–1091 ("Gushi" 賈師), 57.2395 ("Xiaguan: Yangren" 羊人), 62.2626 ("Wuma"); "merchants' fields" are referred to in 24.938 ("Diguan: Zaishi" 載師).

57. As to how the wagons might have traveled from Juchao in Anhui to the Chu capital, it has been proposed either that they retraced the route by which they had come (Shang, "Tan E Jun Qi jie mingwen zhong jige wenzi he jige diming deng wenti"; but note that they were not returning to E, their point of departure) or that they followed the course of the Yangzi River overland (Funakoshi, "Gaku Kun Kei setsu ni tsuite"). The idea that Shouchun, rather than Jiangling, might have been the intended end point of the expeditions has been refuted (see n. 6 above).

58. Liu Hehui ("Chu E Jun Qi jie xintan," 61) asserts that it would have been highly inefficient and unprofitable if the trading expeditions followed the itinerary in the exact order described on the tallies; in his opinion, the holders of

the tallies made repeated short trips along varying formations, and he subdivides the itineraries on the boat tallies as well as on the wagon tallies into four segments that he thinks were undertaken separately (see also Liu Hehui, *Chu wenhua de dongjian*, 139–140).

59. Chen Wei, "E Jun Qi jie yu Chu guo mianshui wenti," 53–55. This would explain why neither the journey to Ying nor the merchants' eventual return to their home base at E is specified on the wagon tallies.

60. Chen Wei ("E Jun Qi jie yu Chu guo mianshui wenti," 52 et passim) notes that part of the route described on the wagon tallies passes close to what must have been the front lines of Chu's protracted war against Yue, which was ongoing in 323 B.C.E. and finally ended with the conquest of Yue in 307 B.C.E. Gathering of intelligence may have been among the tasks of the traders.

61. Keightley, *The Ancestral Landscape*, 109 et passim; Fiskesjö, "The Royal Hunt of the Shang Dynasty."

62. Funakoshi ("Gaku Kun Kei setsu ni tsuite," 89) speculates that E Jun Qi's merchants transmitted Chu products to the northern neighbor states; Liu Hehui makes a similar argument ("Chu E Jun Qi jie xintan," 61, and *Chu wenhua de dongjian*, 147–149).

63. As Funakoshi ("Gaku Kun Kei setsu ni tsuite," 87–88) shows with the help of a lost *Shiji* passage quoted in Xiong Huizhen's 熊會貞 commentary to the *Shuijing zhu* 水經注, E Jun Qi's merchants passed close to the eight districts acquired by Chu in the battle of Xiangling 襄陵, with reference to which the tallies are dated.

64. Cf. Liu Hehui, *Chu wenhua de dongjian*, 140.

65. Peng, "Coinage and Commercial Development in Classical China," 201–226.

66. See Wagner, "The Dating of the Chu Graves of Changsha."

67. Gu Donggao, *Chunqiu dashibiao*, vol. 1, 555–557.

68. See Falkenhausen, "The Use and Significance of Ritual Bronzes in the Lingnan Region during the Eastern Zhou Period."

69. Stumpfeldt, *Staatsverfassung und Territorium im antiken China*; Lewis, "Warring States: Political History."

70. The central government might yet delegate the exploitation of these areas to private entrepreneurs. For a pertinent example—iron production in Qin—see Wagner, *Iron and Steel in Ancient China*, 247–265.

71. Chang, "Ancient Trade as Economy or as Ecology."

72. See Huangshi Shi bowuguan, *Tonglüshan gu kuangye yizhi*. For a summary of other sites, see Liu Shizhong et al., "Changjiang zhongyou diqu de gutongkuang."

73. See Peng and Liu, "Guanyu Ruichang Shang Zhou tongkuang yicun yu gu Yangyue ren."

74. These imports spawned the significant independent bronze-manufacturing traditions of the Yangzi Valley first discussed by Kane, "The Independent Bronze Industries in the South of China."

75. See Bagley, "P'an-lung-ch'eng."

76. Zhang Guangzhi, "Xia Shang Zhou sandai duzhi yu sandai wenhua yitong."

77. See Golas, *Mining*.

78. The following analysis is inspired by Tambiah, *Culture, Thought, and Social Action*, 123–166. "Indexical icons," according to Tambiah (156), "possess two dimensions of meaning—by iconically representing an object according to a conventional semantic rule of likeness, and by being existentially linked to it as well."

79. On this point see Chang, *Art, Myth, and Ritual*, 56–80 et passim; Falkenhausen, *Suspended Music*, 21–55.

80. *Chunqiu Zuo zhuan zhengyi* (Cheng 13), 1911.

81. Falkenhausen, "Issues in Western Zhou Studies," 145–156 et passim; Lewis, *Writing and Authority in Early China*, 14–16.

82. *Chunqiu Zuo zhuan zhengyi* (Zhao 29), 2124.

83. See Lewis, "The Ritual Origins of the Warring States," 76 et passim.

84. For Warring States period Chu examples of writing on bamboo and silk, see Hubei sheng Jingsha tielu kaogu dui, *Baoshan Chu jian* (bamboo); Rao and Zeng, *Chu boshu* (silk).

85. The ductus of the incising tool on the clay matrix can still be perceived on the inscribed surface. Illustrations are insufficient to determine whether the molds for each tally were taken from the same matrix (as would have been normal in Warring States) or whether the text was incised anew for each of the five tallies in a set.

86. The total number of character spaces is consequently 171 for the boat tallies, and 153 for the wagon tallies. The character counts given in most epigraphic works are augmented by (1) one combined character (*hewen* 合文) and one repetition sign on the boat tallies, yielding a total of 173 characters, and (2) three combined characters and four repetition signs in the wagon tallies. Only one of these repetition signs actually necessitates repeating the word in question; the others alert the reader to the need to read the combined characters as two separate words. Hence, the total number of characters on the wagon tallies should be counted as 157.

87. See Falkenhausen, "Issues in Western Zhou Studies," 161–171. A sustained, anthropologically informed linguistic analysis of the language of the bronze inscriptions remains an urgent desideratum (for an admirable descriptive treatment of one aspect of it, rhyme, see Behr, "Reimende Bronzeinschriften und die Entstehung der chinesischen Endreimdichtung"; a sophisticated philological approach to a related class of sources is exemplified by Kern, *The Stele Inscriptions of Ch'in Shih-huang*).

88. This basic tripartite structure was first proposed by Funakoshi, "Gaku Kun Kei setsu ni tsuite," 60.

89. See Falkenhausen, "Issues in Western Zhou Studies," 152–156.

90. On the legal texts, see Hubei sheng Jingsha tielu kaogu dui, *Baoshan Chu jian*; and Shuihudi Qin mu zhujian zhengli xiaozu, *Shuihudi Qin mu zhujian*.

91. The binome *wangming* is etymologically identical with *wangling* seen in the inscriptions of the Chuanlin tallies and the tiger-shaped tally from the tomb of the King of Nanyue.

92. Lewis, *Writing and Authority in Early China*, 30.

93. Austin, *How to Do Things with Words*; Tambiah, *Culture, Thought, and*

Social Action, 17–59.

94. Elias, *Über den Prozeß der Zivilisation*, vol. 2, 312–454; Bourdieu, *La distinction*, pt. 2.

95. On this topic, see Wang, *Cosmology and Political Culture in Early China*; see also Major, *Heaven and Earth in Early Han Thought*, 1–21.

96. Guo, "Guanyu E Jun Qi jie de yanjiu," 3.

97. This idea is compellingly developed in Lewis, *Writing and Authority in Early China*.

98. Vandermeersch, *Wangdao*, vol. 2, 267–497; Lewis, "The Ritual Origins of the Warring States."

99. Cf. Kern, *The Stele Inscriptions of Ch'in Shih-huang*.

100. Lewis, *Writing and Authority in Early China*, 13–42; Falkenhausen, review of *Writing and Authority in Early China*.

101. Lao, "The Early Use of the Tally in China."

102. Weld, "The Covenant Texts from Houma and Wenxian."

Chapter 4

The Ritual Meaning of Textual Form
Evidence from Early Commentaries of the
Historiographic and Ritual Traditions

Joachim Gentz

古之善相馬者，寒風是相口齒，麻朝相頰，子女厲相目，衛忌相
髭，許鄙相尻，投伐褐相胸脅，管青相膪吻，陳悲相股腳，秦牙
相前，贊君相後。凡此十人者皆天下之良工也。其所以相者不同
，見馬之一徵也而知節之高卑，足之滑易，材之堅脆，能之長短
。非獨相馬然也。人亦有徵，事與國皆有徵。聖人上知千歲，下
知千歲，非意之。蓋有自云也。綠圖幡薄從此生矣。

Among those in antiquity who were good at interpreting the
physiognomy of horses, Han Fengshi judged according to the
physiognomy of the mouth and of the teeth, Ma Chao according to the
physiognomy of the cheeks, Zi Nüli according to the physiognomy of
the eyes, Wei Ji according to the physiognomy of the mane, Xu Bi
according to the physiognomy of the tail, Tou Fahe according to the
physiognomy of the chest and ribs, Guan Qing according to the
physiognomy of the lips, Chen Bei according to the physiognomy of
the legs, Qin Ya according to the physiognomy of the front, and Zan
Jun according to the physiognomy of the hind part. Those ten men
were all generally held to be the world's best in their craft. The basis of
their physiognomical judgment was not the same, but if they only saw
one mark of a horse, they would discern whether the joints were high
or low, whether the steps were blundering or nimble, whether its
condition was tough or easily exhausted, and whether its abilities were
strong or weak. Such is not only the case with the interpretation of the
physiognomy of horses. Human beings also have [such] marks. Affairs
and states all [likewise] have [such] marks. That the wise men know a
thousand years of the past and a thousand years of the future is not

because they imagine it. They rather seem to have it from what has been stated above. The divination books *Lütu* and *Fanbo* derive from it.

Lüshi Chunqiu 呂氏春秋, "Guan biao" 觀表

Recently, ritual has attracted considerable attention in different areas of the humanities. In these studies, ritual is mostly treated under its performative and theatrical aspects that are clearly distinguished from the textual realm. In contrast to such an approach, the main hypothesis of this chapter is that the textual sphere in the Chinese cultural context should be taken, not as a realm distinct from that of ritual, but rather as part of it.[1] It operates within the same framework of structural patterns hermeneutical presumptions and practices.

The Threefold Structure of Ritual Action and Its Physiognomical Principle

In the early Chinese discourse on *li* 禮,[2] we find explanations in which ritual functions either (a) to differentiate social and political rank;[3] (b) to support the state;[4] (c) to make human behavior accord to the laws and measures of heaven and earth;[5] (d) to regulate human emotions (*qing* 情);[6] or (e) to serve and to influence divine forces,[7] such as ancestors, to exert their beneficial influence.[8] Common to all these explanations is the notion that ritual has to be understood as a twofold relationship.

First, ritual is an outer formal expression of an invisible ideal order. A central point in all reflections on ritual in early Chinese texts is that an invisible ideal order and the visible ritual form should be brought into accord with each other. Ritual rules help to achieve harmony[9] or, as Assmann puts it, coherence with the invisible ideal order.[10] On the other hand, correct ritual expresses the realization of a correct order. The realization of correct ritual is thus the correct order itself. The underlying principle of this relationship is physiognomical: ritual is taken to be the visible manifestation and expression of an invisible ideal order which, as so often mentioned in *Lunyu* 論語,[11] might be an inner quality of a person or some abstract category of order in any other realm. A passage from the beginning of the *Liji* 禮記 may elucidate this relation:

夫禮者所以定親疏，決嫌疑，別同異，明是非也　。。。　行修言道，禮之質也。。。道德仁義，非禮不成，教訓正俗，非禮不

備。分爭辨訟，非禮不決。君臣上🔲父子兄弟，非禮不定。宦學
事師，非禮不親。班朝治軍，涖官行法，非禮威嚴不行。禱祠祭
祀，供給鬼神，非禮不誠不莊。是以君子恭敬撙節退讓以明禮。

It is ritual through which relationships are defined as intimate or
distanced, through which suspicion and doubt are decided upon, through
which equal or different [classes] are differentiated, and through which
right and wrong are elucidated. . . . If the action is cultivated and the
speech is in accordance with the Way, this is the substance of ritual. . . .
Virtue and a sense of humanity and righteousness cannot be realized
without ritual. Teaching and the rectification of ordinary manners
cannot be achieved without ritual. Clearing up quarrels and discriminating in disputes cannot be decided without ritual. The positions of ruler
and subject, of high and low, of father and son, and of elder and
younger brother cannot be determined without ritual. Servants and
students in serving their master cannot have an intimate relationship
with him without ritual. The distribution of positions at the court
audience, the managing of the army, the engagement of officers, and
the enacting of the law cannot be carried out with awe-inspiring
strictness without ritual. Prayers, sacrifices, and the giving of presents
to the spirits cannot be performed in an upright and dignified manner
without ritual. Therefore, the accomplished man is reverent, respectful,
restrained, moderate, reserved, and yielding in order to elucidate ritual.[12]

Second, ritual action always responds to a given situation. Ritual
action cannot stand for itself because different situations demand different
ways of acting in order to be encountered ritually. Since the ideal order
expressed by ritual pertains to every sphere of human action, ritual, too, is
connected to the entire human realm, including disaster, evil, and disorder.[13]
Ritual is not defined through any particular type of situation (which might
include unavoidable harmful ones like death and decline) but through the
correctness of its formal correspondence to any situation, a correctness
through which the ideal order (which also includes unavoidable harmful
situations) is expressed. The relationship of this formal correspondence is
also a physiognomical one: visible ritual action is the immediate manifestation of the invisible ritual value of the situation encountered. The greatest
part of the "Li qi" 禮器 chapter of the *Liji* 禮記 expounds eight different
formal criteria (large and small quantity, large and small size, high and low
position, ornament and simplicity 多、少、大、小、高、下、文、素)
through which such an evaluation is expressed quantitatively.[14]

In early Chinese reflections on ritual, three constitutive elements of ritual action are depicted: first, a certain situation; second, a certain action that responds to this situation; and third, an invisible ideal to which this action corresponds. Accordingly, an action that does not respond to a certain situation is not a ritual action. An action that responds to a certain situation without according to a certain fixed ideal is also not a ritual action. And without action there is no ritual.

A ritual action is conceptualized as the physiognomical expression of both the invisible ideal and the ritual or moral value of the situation at the same time: by expressing the ritual or moral value of the situation, it also expresses the invisible ideal as the basis of this evaluation. The ritual action is the formal, encoded expression of a confrontation between an ideal and a situation. The ritual act thus becomes the visible judgment of the situation's invisible ideal. The ritually acting person is thus judge and witness at the same time.

For static structures, the ideal is perceived as a state where everything has its proper place or position. For dynamic situations, with their process, beginning and end, the ideal lies in the correct sequential order. Besides the correctness of every single element itself, special attention is here paid to the beginning and concluding moments. [15]

Text and Ritual

In ancient China, the comprehensive ritual perspective on human action also covers the textual realm. Texts are used for ritual purposes and within ritual contexts. In their structure, however, texts are also articulations of ritual correctness. They follow certain ritual rules like the fixed formulaic order of inscriptions, the conventions of taboo, the hierarchical (ritual) order of different sorts of enumerations and topics, or, in later prints, the raising of the emperor's name in the text. Since very little is known about the performative context of early Chinese texts, and since reconstructions in most cases remain rather speculative, I focus on what we may call "textual ritual" within the texts proper, a ritual of which the textual structure itself is seen as the performance. Besides being a transmitter of certain contents, in its formal reflection of these contents the text is also regarded as a ritual expression. The ritual performance of composing a text is then reenacted in the reader's retrieval act of intensive textual study. [16]

Most early Chinese texts seem to have a specific direction. They consist of a sequence of words with a fixed beginning and a fixed end.[17] "Textual ritual," besides the selection of the correct individual words, is thus also concerned with the correct sequence of the words within a text.[18] Since sequence in the ritual realm mostly expresses sociopolitical hierarchy, one important element of textual ritual lies in the correct sequence in enumerations. Textual structure thus follows the same principle of formally expressing ideal order that we also find in other realms of ritual. In this case, the textual form corresponds to a fixed set of general ritual rules. Yet besides the self-evident terminology and conventions of hierarchical order and status we find a further layer of ritual expressions that are not immediately obvious. Here, commentators often feel prompted to help readers recognize those phrases that carry specific ritual meaning. Presumably, such exegetical reading of older texts (like the *Chunqiu* 春秋) was also meant to affect the production of new texts (like ritual and philosophical writings from late Zhanguo and early Han times onward). I therefore propose that some ancient Chinese texts require what I call a "ritual reading," that is, a reading entirely based on textual form where the evolving meaning may either supplement the grammatical surface meaning or serve as a commentary to it.

The two texts that I have found were read ritually by the commentators belong to the traditions of historiography and writing about ritual. This is striking because within the framework of the Five Classics, these are the textual traditions whose ritual context is least understood. We know a little about the ritual context of some ancient texts such as covenants, of some inscriptions on bones, bronze, or stone, and also of some of the canonical texts in the *Yijing* 易經, *Shijing* 詩經, and *Shangshu* 尚書. However, whether the *Chunqiu* records were read out loud in the ancestral temple or were part of any other ritual performance is still open to speculation, as is the question of the early role and function of their scribes (*shi* 史).[19] The ritual context of the texts that speak about ritual is also unknown. We do not know whether the ritual rules and descriptions that are given in these texts reflect actual practice or record past or neglected rituals, whether they are reconstructions of some hazy memory or mere constructions of new ideals, or whether they represent any combination of any of these.

The Gongyang zhuan 公羊傳

Let me first outline the analytical model of *Chunqiu* exegesis used by the *Gongyang zhuan*. Apart from reading the common meaning of the single characters in an entry, the *Gongyang* commentary also reads the *Chunqiu* in a formal way, observing the formal composition and the syntactical rules of the single records. In order to give a systematic and comprehensive exegesis of the *Chunqiu*, a specific historiographic form is induced from the routine of the *Chunqiu* itself. This form is then regarded as valid for the entire text. Consider the following record:

Chunqiu Yin 10.4:
辛未取郜，辛巳取防。
Day *xinwei*. We took Gao. Day *xinsi*. We took Fang.

The *Gongyang zhuan* comments:

取邑不日，此何以日。一月而再取也。何言乎一月而再取。甚之也。內大惡諱，此其言甚之何。春秋錄內而略外。於外大惡書，小惡不書，於內大惡諱，小惡書。

In records of the taking of cities the day is normally not recorded. Why was the day recorded here? Within one month there was another taking. What is meant by "within one month there was another taking?" [The *Chunqiu*] considers it as too much. Since "[in the *Chunqiu*] great evils of the Interior are concealed,"[20] why is it said in this case that it considers it as too much? The *Chunqiu* makes a careful record of [matters pertaining to] the Interior but outlines [matters pertaining to] the Exterior. With regard to the Exterior, great evils are written down and small evils are not written down. With regard to the Interior, great evils are concealed and small evils are written down.

The assumption that the text of the *Chunqiu* is written according to specific formal rules (like the rule that in records of the taking of cities the day is normally not recorded), that is, according to a fixed historiographic form, is supported by the formulaic structure of the text[21] and by similar formulaic structures of many other texts of that time. Hereafter, I refer to this fixed historiographic form as *pattern*.[22] The formulaic structure of each type of entry is defined by the *Gongyang zhuan* and is taken as the basically correct historiographic form. It was probably perceived as traditional; nothing in the *Gongyang zhuan* points to Confucius as the creator of this form. On the contrary, statements in the *Gongyang zhuan* suggest that the core elements of this form were already present in the original *Chunqiu* entries.

A record of a covenant (*meng* 盟), for example, should have a form like that in Min 閔1.4:

秋，八月。公及齊侯盟于洛姑。

Autumn, eighth month. The duke with an earl from Qi made a covenant in Luogu.

The *pattern* would thus have the abstract form:

Season **A**,	month **B**.	**C** with **D**	made a covenant	in **E**.
A,	**B** 月	**C** 及 **D**	盟	于 **E**.

The greatest part of the *Chunqiu* is conceived as written according to such strict rules, which make up the *pattern* of the *Chunqiu*. Yet some entries deviate from the *pattern*. These deviations are taken by the *Gongyang zhuan* as signals that Confucius inserted material into the *Chunqiu* to point to a hidden message ("two takings of a city within one month is too much"). Every deviation is thus attentively noted by the commentator, who uses formulaic exegetical questions such as

x 不日，此何以日？

In records of x, the day is normally not recorded. Why was the day recorded here?[23]

x 不書 y，此何以書？

In records of x, normally y is not written. Why was it written here?[24]

x 不卒，此何以卒？

Deaths of x are normally not recorded. Why was the death recorded here?[25]

x 不言 y，此其言y何？

In the case of x, normally y is not stated. Why was it stated here?[26]

何以不言 y？

Why has [in this record] y not been stated?[27]

何以不 y？

Why has [in this record] y not been recorded?[28]

何以書 ？
Why has this event been recorded?[29]

x 未有言 y 者。
In records of x, y has not been stated yet.[30]

x 未有言 y 者，此言 y 何？
In records of x, y has not been stated yet, why was y stated here?[31]

未有言 y 者，此言 y 何？
Why was x stated first and y stated thereafter?[32]

曷為先言 x ？
Why was x stated first?[33]

All such questions, of which we find more than forty different forms in the *Gongyang zhuan*,[34] are based on a specific expectation regarding the form of the record. The function of these questions is to inform the reader about the historiographic *pattern* so as to provide the rules of correct composition. They belong to what David N. Keightley has called a "nonexploratory interrogation" in which "questions are only asked when the answer is known in advance."[35] To sum up: in a first step, the *Gongyang zhuan* induces a historiographic *pattern* from the *Chunqiu* and thus produces a second, fictional, formally ideal text. In a second step, it compares the fictional *pattern* with the actual text and determines the divergences. In a third step, it explains the divergences as deviations. If we take "abcdefg" to be a typical *pattern* sequence of a certain type of record, possible deviations would be

pattern:	abcdefgh
deviation:	bcdefgh
	abcdefkh
	abcqdefgh, etc.

In such cases, the *Gongyang zhuan* would proceed by explaining the deviation either individually or through a rule of deviation such as "If, in a record x, element a is not mentioned, it means w," or "If, in a record x, element k is written instead of element g, it means z," and so forth. The *Gongyang zhuan* thus establishes a second system of rules—a system of "deviation rules"—as in the following two examples:

Chunqiu Yin 1.7:

公子益師卒。

Gongzi Yishi died.

Gongyang zhuan:

何以不日？遠也。所見異辭，所聞異辭，所傳聞異辭。

Why is the day not recorded? Because it was a distant [event]. There are different expressions for what has been seen with one's own eyes, for what has been heard [from others], and for what has been heard through historical transmissions.

Chunqiu Xi 1.1:

元年春王正月。

First year, spring, first month of the calendar of the king [of Zhou].

Gongyang zhuan:

公何以不言即位？繼弒君，子不言即位。

Why is it not stated that the duke ascended the throne? In the case of a succession of a murdered ruler, his son is not said to have ascended the throne.

In most of the other first records of a duke's reign, the accession to the throne is mentioned with the above *pattern* of the date, resulting in a *pattern* like "First year, spring, first month of the calendar of the king [of Zhou], the duke ascended the throne" (元年春王正月公即位).

Explaining the Deviations:
*The Two-*Pattern *Exegesis of the* Gongyang zhuan

A closer look at the exegetical operations reveals that many of the deviations noted by the *Gongyang* commentary are indeed deviations in the *Chunqiu* text. Yet in order to forestall any suspicion of arbitrary exegesis in *explaining* the deviations systematically according to defined rules, the establishment of a *pattern* alone is insufficient. The *Gongyang zhuan* therefore connects every formal deviation of the historiographic *pattern* of a record to its historical content. Accordingly, the formulaic records report normal historical facts. By contrast, the formulaic deviations reflect historical events which deviate from the norm. Either they reflect natural, political, or social events that are extraordinary, or they reflect a certain behavior that is either extremely good or extremely bad. Yet in order to prove the evaluations of historical actions, they again need a basis to be judged upon. According to the *Gongyang zhuan*, every deviation from the norm is judged by Confucius on the basis of his own righteousness (*yi* 義), which conforms to a code of moral and ritual behavior. We can thus find a reflection of two systems of norm and deviation: first, a fixed and normative historiographic *pattern* of records of historical actions; and, second, a normative code regarding the good and the bad in moral and ritual behavior. If actions correspond to this code, Confucius casts their records in accord with the historiographic *pattern*. If actions deviate, their records deviate, too. The formulaic deviations in the *Chunqiu* thus mirror the historical actors' deviations from the normative *pattern* of moral and ritual behavior.

Thus, the basic exegetical method of the *Gongyang zhuan* includes inducing a historiographic *pattern* ("in records of the taking of cities the day is normally not recorded"), discovering and disclosing formal deviations ("in this record, the day was recorded"), and explaining these deviations as formal reflections of deviations from a *pattern* of moral and ritual behavior ("it is a great evil to take two cities within one month"). Given the complex contents of the *Chunqiu* records, the actual exegetic process is much more complex; the *Gongyang zhuan* does not always succeed in offering a coherent exegesis and is time and again forced to invent new rules, including individual, as well as general, ones and even rules that deviate from deviation rules.

The Shaping of a Textual Physiognomy:
The Ritual Character of the Chunqiu

What idea about Confucius's *Chunqiu* compilation is conveyed through the exegetical method of the *Gongyang zhuan*? According to the *Gongyang zhuan*, Confucius put the historical material of the original *Chunqiu* of Lu into a new form that expresses Confucius's moral and ritual evaluations of the content of the historical material as well as his own righteousness. In this, Confucius reshaped the historiographic form of the historical material to make it the full formal equivalent of its historical content. In other words, he gave the historical records a corresponding historiographic physiognomy. This is a ritually correct behavior in its own right because it produces an adequate formal correspondence to every historical situation that attempts to express an ideal order in which everything has its adequate position and expression.[36] The *Chunqiu* thus becomes the expression and the textual remains of a ritual act undertaken by Confucius. In a ritual action, Confucius treats the historical material as he would meet a guest, encounter an official, offer a sacrifice, handle a covenant, or behave at the death of a person. On the basis of his righteousness, and following a moral and ritual *pattern*, he evaluates the historical situation and then chooses the adequate ritual form to bring about a correct and adequate correspondence to the situation. At the same time, he thereby expresses the moral and ritual *pattern* together with his own righteousness in a historiographic physiognomy.

The Xia xiao zheng zhuan 夏小正傳[37]

Apart from the *Guliang zhuan* 穀梁, which uses the same exegetical method and form as the *Gongyang zhuan*, we can find another text with a similar exegetical strategy. The *Xia xiao zheng zhuan* 夏小正傳 commentary to the *Xia xiao zheng* 夏小正 (which originally circulated as an independent text until it was made a chapter of the *Da Dai liji* 大戴禮記) reads the text in a manner that, on the basis of the above definition, should also be called "ritual." Like the *Gongyang zhuan*, it asks questions about the meaning and significance of using certain words and textual structures. We even see the same questions about the meaning of the specific sequence of words in the text:

其先言 x 而後言 y 者何也？	Why does it first say x and only then y?[38]
先言 x 而後言 y 何也？	Why is x said first and only then y?[39]
先 x 而後 y 何也？	Why is x first and only then y?[40]

In the same way as the *Gongyang zhuan*, this commentary tries to induce a *pattern* from the routine of the text itself, as in the following case where the main text reads:

雁北鄉。
The [wild] geese are [back] in the northern dwelling places.

The inserted commentary then asks:

先言雁而後言鄉者，何也？見雁而後數其鄉也。鄉者，何也？鄉
，其居也，雁以北方為居。何以謂之居？生且長焉爾。九月蔕鴻

雁，先言蔫而後言鴻雁，何也？見蔫而後數之，則鴻雁也。何不
謂南鄉也？曰：非其居也，故不謂南鄉。記鴻雁之蔫也，如不記
其鄉，何也？曰：鴻不必當小正之蔫者也。

Why is "geese" said first and only then "dwelling places"? One sees the
geese and only then attaches them to their dwelling places. What are
"dwelling places"? Dwelling places are where they live. Geese live in
the north. Why is it denoted as "to live"? Just because they are born
and grow up there. In the passage of the ninth month, "Migrating are
the wild geese," why does it first say "migrate" and then "the wild
geese"? One sees something flying and only then classifies it as wild
geese. Why is it not written as "[the (wild) geese are in] the southern
dwelling places"? Answer: That is not where they live; therefore, one
does not write "[the (wild) geese are in] the southern dwelling places."
Why is it that if you note the migration of the wild geese, you do not
note the dwelling place [they migrate to]? Answer: Wild geese do not
necessarily have to serve the [*Xia*] *xiao zheng* in their role as migrants
to [a certain place].[41]

If there is a contradiction in the form of the record (such as two
different sequences regarding the geese in the first and the ninth month), the
commentator highlights it through a question and tries to give an
explanation. Yet out of eleven instances of sequence questions such as those
quoted above, ten are explained through recourse to the sequence of the
natural phenomena described in the text; that is, they are explained as being
without particular ritual meaning. It is even questionable whether the
eleventh one is a ritual explanation or whether it should be read as a
statement regarding a specific social hierarchy.[42] These pragmatic answers,
however, need to be understood against the background of a practice of
highly charged ritual reading; by giving a pragmatic, "naturalistic" answer,
this type of reading is rejected in every case. Thus, the ritual option is
always present in the reading of the commentary, if only as a negative foil.
With the *Xia xiao zheng zhuan* we thus have a second text using the
exegetical method of *pattern* and deviation. Taking a commentary to reflect
reading habits and as an influence upon later text production, we should note
that the *Xia xiao zheng zhuan* directly addresses the reader's habit of reading
every formal deviation.

The Origins of the Exegetical Method
of Pattern and Deviation

The formulaic reading and exegetical method of *pattern* and deviation appear all of a sudden as an integral and complete hermeneutical system. We do not find this sort of exegesis prior to the *Gongyang zhuan*, although its intellectual level suggests some preexisting pattern of thought. Indeed, there is a close analogy that points to such a given pattern.[43] In ancient Chinese astrology, omenology, and medicine, we find the same hermeneutic method of reading a certain "text" against a *pattern* that had first been induced from the norm of the "text" itself and is then taken to prove the "text." The movement of the stars follows certain rules that can be induced from observation. This cosmic *pattern* shows or even performs an ideal order just as correct ritual does. But sometimes, deviations from the established astronomical *pattern* such as eclipses or comets occur. These deviations are read physiognomically by exegetical experts as signals containing certain messages—in most cases judgments about human behavior. Deviations in the *pattern* of the sky or of the earth are interpreted as signs of heavenly expression—they are part of the language of Heaven. Taking a closer look at Confucius's subtle language in the *Chunqiu*, we find that he expresses himself just as Heaven does in the cosmos. We thus may draw up a threefold model of *pattern* and deviation that relates by analogy to the three realms of (a) moral and ritual behavior in the *Chunqiu*; (b) historiographic form of the *Chunqiu*; and (c) natural cycles such as star movements, the four seasons, and others. The deviations of the *patterns* of those three realms would be (a) extremely good or bad behavior in the *Chunqiu*; (b) formal deviations of the actual *Chunqiu* vis-à-vis the regular form; and (c) omens (*zaiyi* 災異) such as eclipses, comets, droughts, and others. Looking at the history of the reading of the language of Heaven, one finds that an exegetic level comparable to the reading of Confucius's "subtle words" in the *Gongyang zhuan* appears in the genre of monthly ordinances ("Yueling" 月令) in the first half of the third century B.C.E. In this genre, reasons for deviations from the defined cosmological *pattern* are given on the basis of a fixed set of correspondence rules:

命有司曰：土事毋作，慎毋發蓋，毋發室屋，及起大眾，以固而閉。地氣沮泄，是謂發天地之房。諸蟄則死，民必疾疫，又隨以喪。

Orders are given to the proper office to the following effect: There should be nothing done in the works of earth; care should be taken not to expose anything that is covered, nor to open apartments and houses; and rouse the masses to action in order to firm [heaven] and shut up [the earth]. [44] If [by not following these ordinances] the earthly force leaks out, this would be called the opening of the house of heaven and earth. All the insects would then die, the people would be sure to fall ill from pestilences, and many more losses for the same reason would ensue. [45]

The observation of the wrong ordinances is likewise given as a reason for cosmological deviations:

孟秋行冬令，則陰氣大勝，介蟲敗穀，戎兵乃來。行春令，則其國乃旱，陽氣復還，五穀無實。行夏令，則國多火災，寒熱不節，民多瘧疾。

If in the first month of autumn the winter regulations are observed, then the cold and gloomy force (yinqi) would greatly prevail, the crustaceans would destroy the grain, and soldiers and armies would then come. If the spring regulations are observed, then the state would have droughts, the hot and bright force (yangqi) would return, and the five grains would not yield their fruit. If the summer regulations are observed, then there would be many fire calamities in the state, cold and hot would not be regulated, and the people would greatly suffer from malaria. [46]

Through recourse to the rational scheme of correlative systems based on abstract principles like yinyang and qi, and by operating with rules of correspondence, [47] omens could be systematically explained. This level of standardized omen interpretation becomes possible in the first half of the third century B.C.E. through the amalgamation of two distinct and independent traditions of cycles of cosmological order which can be traced back to the Shang period, and through archaeological findings perhaps even further. I will call them the "phenomenal cycle" and the "agent cycle," respectively. The phenomenal cycle, connected to the agricultural realm, is the cyclical order of visible continuous changes in the phenomenal realm of heaven (stars) and earth (plants, animals). It defines a fixed *pattern* of empirical data on the basis of which deviations in the natural world can be recognized. Such data are transmitted in early astronomical or agricultural calendars and almanacs that are preserved in texts such as the "Yao Dian" 堯

典 chapter of the *Shangshu*, the *Xia xiao zheng* 夏小正 (which became a chapter of the *Da Dai liji*), the Ode "Qi yue" 七月 (Mao 154) of the *Shijing*, the "Yue ling" 月令 fragments of the *Yi Zhoushu* 逸周書, and others. The data are transmitted as empirical observations correlated with a cosmological concept of time; no reference is made to other circumstances. By contrast, the agent cycle, connected to the sacrificial realm, is a hidden cyclical order that reveals itself only through its efficacy within the visible world. It is composed of abstract, rather than phenomenal, agents such as the sixty cyclical stems (*ganzhi* 干支), the ten ancestors in the routine, cyclical, ten-day divinations (*xun* 旬), *yinyang* 陰陽, the Five Phases, and other types of cyclical classification systems built from abstract, yet very specific, qualities.

The combination, but still distinct representation, of these two traditions is evident for the first time in the Chu Silk Manuscript, where we find an outer frame of twelve cyclical agents [48] and an inner textual field. The inner field comprises two parts, which contain mythical narratives about the origin of the order of the phenomenal world and about deviations from this order (which accordingly are written in the opposite direction). In the first half of the third century B.C.E., we have the first textual witnesses for the merger of the two traditions into one elaborate and complex system of correlations. The results of this amalgamation are seasonal ordinances like the "You guan" 幼官, "Si shi" 四時, "Wu xing" 五行, and "Qing zhong (ji)" 輕重 (己) chapters of the *Guanzi* 管子 and the monthly ordinances that we find as "Shi ji" 時紀 in the *Lüshi Chunqiu*, as "Yue ling" 月令 in the *Liji*, as "Shixun jie" 時訓解 in the *Yi Zhoushu*, and as "Tian wen" 天文 and "Shi ze" 時則 chapters in the *Huainanzi* 准南子. These systems combine the empirical data from the early agricultural almanacs with the invisible efficacious agents of the agent cycle.

This new system had considerable explicative powers. The seasonal and monthly ordinances allowed reasonable explanations of deviations in the regular world. They also provided systematic and reasonable grounds for connecting the occurrence of specific portents with specific (governmental) actions, a practice that was to become a core element of Chinese political culture. Only on the basis of the amalgamation of the two different systems of phenomenal cycle and agent cycle could the well-known, all-embracing correlative systems from late Warring States times onward be established, and with them a systematic omenology. Neither one of them alone would have sufficed to explain deviations: first, in the phenomenal cycle, deviations would have been part of the descriptive empirical data that make up the calendrical *pattern*.[49] Yet in order to obtain information about the specific quality of these data, and to relate them to a specific situation at hand, one has to perform an additional act of divination. Second, in the agent cycle there is not even space for deviations since it represents an ideal abstract order that does not relate to empirical (and thus also possibly deviating) data. Instead, it consists of analytical-classificatory categories through which abstract qualities are related to one another. Deviation would cause the collapse of this system.[50]

In the hermeneutics of this systematic omenology we find a perfect analogy to the *Gongyang zhuan* procedure. The amalgamation of the two systems of *Chunqiu* historiography and ritual code served the same purpose as the amalgamation of the two traditions of phenomenal and agent cycle for astrology and omenology. The occurring deviations from the historiographic *pattern* could thus be explained in terms of ritual judgments which, through their own system of deviations from the *pattern*, allowed readers to identify deviations of the textual *pattern* as evaluations of historical actions.

However, we do not find the same technical terminology in the exegesis of the *Gongyang zhuan* and the new omenology. Furthermore, the two perspectives of presentation are fundamentally different. The *Gongyang zhuan* induces a *pattern* from the text and applies an implied set of ritual rules in order to interpret morally and ritually deviating historical actions. The "Yueling," however, combines calendrical *pattern* and ideal rules of action and then inserts specific cases of deviation into this joint system. Returning to the example of Duke Xi 1.1 above, the *Gongyang* text would have to be written in the following form in order to correspond to the "Yueling" text:

公即位春秋曰：元年春王正月公即位。繼弒君，子不言即位。春秋曰：元年春王正月。

If a duke ascends to the throne, the *Chunqiu* records: "First year, spring, first month of the calendar of the king [of Zhou], the duke ascended the throne." In the case of a succession of a murdered ruler, his son is not said to have ascended the throne. The *Chunqiu* record thus goes: "First year, spring, first month of the calendar of the king [of Zhou].

A corresponding text covering all exegetical operations regarding enthronements within the *Gongyang zhuan* would read like this:

In the case of a ritually correct enthronement, the predecessor has not been assassinated and has already been correctly buried ritually within the ritually correct period of time. The new duke is the legitimate successor and is enthroned at the beginning of the new year of the Zhou calendar of King Wen. The *Chunqiu* records the enthronement as the first record of the period of his rulership with the wording 元年，春，王正月，公即位. The date of the day is not given. If the new duke ascends to the throne as a temporary representative of another legitimate ruler, or if his predecessor has been assassinated, the phrase 公即位 is missing in the record. If, however, the predecessor has been assassinated and the successor has the bad intention of resolutely establishing his own person on the throne, then the phrase 公即位 is recorded. If the enthronement is late, the phrase 正月 is not written in the record. If the enthronement is not legitimate, then 立 is written instead of 公即位. If it is a record for the Interior, the date of the day is given.

We see that this hypothetical text (composed of different passages from the *Gongyang zhuan*) perfectly corresponds to the way the "Yueling" text is written.The other option of a representation of the "Yueling" system in the manner of the *Gongyang zhuan*, which would be the result of an application of this handbook-like system of correspondences to historical phenomenal data of deviations, can be found in later texts like the *Hanshu* 漢書 "Wuxing zhi" 五行志. Despite these formal differences, however, the close structural analogy between the two hermeneutical systems suggests a connection in the sphere of hermeneutical expertise. The institutional relationship of the offices of the astrologer and the historiographer in ancient China further supports this hypothesis. In terms of institutional networks, there seem to be close connections between omenology, astrology, calendar, ritual, and historiography.[51] While the *Gongyang zhuan* does not display interest in omenology,[52] its contents are closely related to the ritual sphere.[53] It is thus not surprising to find the ancient calendar *Xia xiao zheng* as well as a system like the "Yueling" included in the ritual books. It is, however, surprising to find the *Xia xiao zheng* commentary containing striking parallels to the *Gongyang zhuan*, especially in its formal reading strategy. The origin of this exegetical reading of *pattern* and deviation seems to lie within the ritual sphere.

The Threefold Structure of Ritual as Principle of Resonance (gan ying 感應) in Oracle Bone Divination, the "Yueling," and the Chunqiu

In the ritual realms of divination, correlative systems, and *Chunqiu* exegesis, we see how certain situations call for human action. In oracle bone divination, the situation is a concrete problem formulated in a specific charge of the diviner; in the "Yueling," it is the empirical data that are defined by certain points or periods of time; in *Chunqiu* exegesis, it is the historical material that is shaped by single historical records. In each case, the human response is based on a set of ideals that are to be turned into action. In oracle bone divination, the ideal is the authority of the ancestors and what they convey through the bone cracks; in the "Yueling," it is the rules of the correlative system, that is, the rules of Heaven that find their expression in normal or deviating phenomena; in *Chunqiu* exegesis, it is the righteousness of Confucius that corresponds to the Way of Yao and Shun and is expressed in a set of ritual rules inserted in the *Chunqiu*. In each case, the invisible ideal becomes manifest in scriptures (oracle bone inscriptions, "Yueling," *Chunqiu*) that then also prescribe the appropriate human response of ritual action.

Thus, specific situations stimulate (*gan* 感) actions of human responses (*ying* 應). The ideal response is defined through reference to a specific set of ideals that is to be adopted: to the cracks embodying the voice of the ancestors, to the Heavenly rules of correspondence, or to the moral and ritual rules attributed to Confucius. In the "Yueling," the ideal relationship of stimulus and response (*gan ying* 感應) is made explicit as a principle of permanent resonance, upheld by Heaven as the Way (*dao* 道). Because the ruler is ordered to follow this principle on the basis of clearly defined ritual instructions, human actions in accordance with the Way are depicted as ritual actions. These actions mediate between situations and ideals: as the stimulus (*gan*) arises from the specific situation, the response is based on the ideal. Offering models of ritually correct action, ideal relations between situations and responses are fixed in different kinds of scriptures. Table 4.1 summarizes these ideal relations as propounded in the three types of text under discussion.

TABLE 4.1

situation (defined through)	→	gan 感 action ying 應 (scripture)	←	ideal (expression)
Concrete problem		Action that follows the divination		Ancestors and their "sayings"
(Divination charge)		(Oracle bone inscriptions)		(Cracks)
Phenomenal data		"Yueling"-ordered action		Correlative System (Heaven, *dao*)
(time)		("Yueling")		(correlative Rules)
Historical material		*Chunqiu* compilation, actions following *Chunqiu* precedents		Way of Yao and Shun, righteousness of Confucius
(Historical records)		(*Chunqiu*)		(Ritual rules)

The *Mozi* 墨子 shows how indeterminate these different instances are and how easily one could stand for another. In the "Ming gui xia" 明鬼下 chapter we find four narratives that all serve the main purpose of the chapter, namely, to prove the existence of ghosts/spirits/demons:

1. The ghost of Du Bo 杜伯, a minister of King Xuan of Zhou 周宣王, who was falsely sentenced to death, takes revenge on his ruler.

2. The ghost of Zhuang Ziyi 莊子儀, a minister of Duke Jian of Yan 燕簡公, who was falsely sentenced to death, takes revenge on his ruler.

3. A minister, Guangu 觀辜, who served in the ancestral temple of his state as a priest, neglected his sacrifices and is thereupon slain by a sorcerer.

4. After overseeing a lawsuit for three years without reaching a decision, two ministers from the state of Qi 齊 were summoned by the duke to take the oath at the altar of the state. While they take the oath, the sacrificial lamb, already sacrificed, suddenly bounds up and hits one of the two ministers so hard that his leg is broken (whereupon he is slain by a sorcerer).

Each story then ends with the same, only slightly varied formula: "This was written down in the Annals [*Chunqiu*] of state x [Zhou 周, Yan

燕, Song 宋, or Qi 齊]. The feudal lords transmitted it and said: 'Everyone who does x will meet with bad fortune. The punishment of the spirits and demons, it is as fast as that!'"[54]

The fact that "justice" is realized by spirits or spirit mediums is not a cultural peculiarity of ancient China.[55] However, it is relevant for our investigation that these cases were recorded in *Chunqiu* Annals of different states and served as precedents for the actions of later generations. We have a mixture of two of the three different types analyzed above (the oracle bone case and the *Chunqiu* case). The authoritative ideal that determines the correctness of an action rests with the ghosts/spirits/demons or their intermediaries (e.g., sorcerers and sacrificial animals).[56] The medium, however, in which the ideal is written down and which provides the basis to guide later actions is a *Chunqiu* text. The *Mozi* passage thus reveals the continuity in the authority of the ideal connected to the *Chunqiu* genre. The righteousness of Confucius perpetuates what was previously the spirits' apodictic sense of right and wrong.[57]

The commentarial assumptions that ritual is a basic principle of text composition show a certain understanding of the nature of a text. The structure of the text becomes more complex and esoteric as the layers of meaning increase; with all the possible interconnections between the various layers, the full meaning of the text has to be grasped through fairly complicated exegetical procedures. Since exegetical options for determining the meaning of the text are vastly increased through these procedures, they also need to be controlled and restricted by rules. The rules, in turn, require a commonly accepted frame of reference in order to be plausible, and they need to be clear and simple enough to comprehend. While the concurrent desire for both complexity and simplicity poses a dilemma seemingly impossible to solve, in early China the exegetical approach outlined above was generally accepted as an option for text reading. Such exegetical practice and expectations will also have played a role in textual composition. For this reason, when reading early Chinese texts we are not free to ignore the commentarial instructions that focus our attention on the ritual form of some of them. Extending the exegetical instructions to a broader range of texts will allow us to identify additional layers of meaning that we can assume were familiar to both authors and their contemporaneous readers.[58] In other words, because the realms of text and ritual were inseparable in ancient China, we can use one to elucidate the other.

NOTES

I wish to thank Professor David N. Keightley for his helpful advice and corrections of the first draft. For further details regarding the questions dealt with in the present chapter, see my *Das Gongyang zhuan*, 1–240.

1. Jan Assmann and others assume that in general, ancient cultures show a transition from ritual to textual coherence; see Assmann, *Das kulturelle Gedächtnis*, 87ff.

2. For more theoretical reflections on this approach to *li*, see my "Ritus als Physiognomie."

3. See *Lunyu* 論語; *Mengzi* 孟子; *Gongyang zhuan* 公羊傳; *Zuo zhuan* 左傳; *Xunzi* 荀子; *Liji jijie*, 8, 11–12 ("Qu li shang" 曲禮上), 586–594 ("Li yun" 禮運), 1268–1272 ("Zhongni yanju" 仲尼燕居), etc.

4. See mainly *Zuo zhuan*. See also Su Zhihong, *Qin Han li yue jiaohua lun*, 42–52; Pines, "Disputers of the *Li*."

5. See *Zuo zhuan* Wen 15.12, Xiang 28 (*fu* 3), Zhao 25.2; *Mengzi* 5A5; *Xunzi* "Li lun" 禮論; *Liji jijie*, 10 ("Qu li shang" 曲禮上), 1283 ("Fang ji" 坊記), 1373–1374 ("Sannian wen" 三年問), 1468, 1470 ("Sangfu sizhi" 喪服四制), etc.

6. See *Lunyu*; *Mengzi* 2A6, 4B28, 6A6, 7A21; *Gongyang zhuan* Zhuang 32.3, Wen 9.1, Xuan 8.6; *Zuo zhuan* Zhao 25.2; *Xunzi* "Li lun"; *Liji jijie*, 271–272 ("Tang gong xia" 檀弓下), 606, 618 ("Li yun" 禮運), 984 ("Yue ji" 樂記), 1115 ("Za ji xia" 雜記下), 1354 ("Wen sang" 問喪), and all the other chapters on mourning, etc. See also Su Zhihong, *Qin Han li yue jiaohua lun*, 84–111.

7. See *Liji jijie*, 1258 ("Ai gong wen" 哀公問); *Gongyang zhuan* Zhuang 25.3 and Xuan 3.1–3, etc.

8. See *Shijing* 詩經; *Shangshu* 尚書; *Liji jijie*, 586–594 ("Li yun"), etc. In most cases we find certain models connected to certain realms of ritual. In the realm of mourning we always find model (d), never model (a). For the rites in the *Yili*, model (a) would fit. In the context of sacrifice, model (e) would be appropriate, etc. We often also find combinations of different explanatory models; see *Zuo zhuan*; *Lunyu*; *Mengzi*; *Liji jijie*, 606 ("Li yun"), 1258 ("Ai gong wen" 哀公問), 1281–1283 ("Fang ji" 坊記), etc. Sometimes, however, certain models are explicitly excluded; see *Liji jijie*, 272 ("Tan gong xia"), 624 ("Li qi"), 1236 ("Ji tong" 祭統), 1373 ("Sannian wen"), etc.

9. The "Ru xing" 儒行 chapter of the *Liji* gives the expression *he* 和 (which normally is associated with the corresponding function of music) for "harmony"; see *Liji jijie*, 1405.

10. Assmann, *Das kulturelle Gedächtnis*, 87.

11. *Lunyu* 8.2, 12.1, 14.12, 15.33, 17.22, etc.

12. *Liji jijie*, 6–9.

13. In the "Yao dian" and "Gao yao mo" 皋陶謨 chapters of the *Shangshu* as well as in the "Chun guan: Da Zongbo" 春官大宗伯 part of the *Zhou li*, we already find the subdivision into five different rituals. In later texts, like Du You's 杜佑 (735–812) *Tongdian* 通典 or Qin Huitian's 秦蕙田 (1702–1764) *Wuli tongkao* 五禮通考, we have highly differentiated subdivisions of ritual.

14. See *Liji jijie*, 630ff.

15. See *Gongyang and Guliang zhuan* Yin 1.1; *Gongyang zhuan* Ai 14.1; *Xunzi* "Li lun," etc.

16. For the "retrieval" act of reading, see Assmann, *Das kulturelle Gedächtnis*, 22, 283ff.

17. Some early Chinese texts, however, seem to have an internal structure that leads in different directions and should thus be reconstructed in diagram (*tu* 圖) form. Examples include the Chu silk manuscript as well as many of the divinatory texts found in early tombs. A diagram structure has also been suggested for the "You guan" 幼官 chapter in the *Guanzi* 管子 (see Rickett, "An Early Chinese Calendar Chart") and for the "Mingtang wei 明堂位" chapter in the *Liji* (see Blinova, "'Presvetly prestol' kak prostranstvenno-administrativnaya [zemleustroitel'naya] skhema" and "Prostranstvenno-zemleustroitel'nye struktury v tekstakh 'Yu gun' i 'Min tan vei'"; Dorofeeva-Lichtman, "The 'Ming tang wei'"). Other texts, such as *Lunyu* and *Laozi* 老子, seem to be without any beginning and end. They consist of short units and were expected to be learned by heart and to be present *in toto* in a scholar's mind.

18. In order to avoid confusion we have to distinguish between two systems of rules that determine the correct sequence of words in early Chinese texts: a system of grammatical rules and a system of ritual rules. Both carry meaning in their own way. Grammatical rules ensure the basic semantic meaning of a sentence, whereas ritual rules determine word sequences that are not grammatically fixed (like enumerations or technical statements). It is the duty of a commentator to decide whether certain conspicuous constructions in a text are to be explained with reference to grammatical, ritual, or any other rules.

19. For the broad range of different interpretations regarding the function and role of the early historiographic records and their scribes, see my *Das Gongyang zhuan*, 8–9.

20. This rule is established in the *Gongyang* commentary to Yin 2.3: 此滅也，其言入何。內大惡，諱也。 ("This is a case of extinction. Why does it then say 'invade'? [In the *Chunqiu*,] great evils of the Interior are concealed.")

21. Regarding the dukes of Lu, tables of all the formulaic records of their installments (*ji wei* 即位), deaths (*hong* 薨), and burials (*zang* 葬), as well as for solar eclipses (*ri shi* 日食) and deaths of the heavenly king (*tianwang beng* 天王崩), see Noma, "Shunjū sanden nyūmon kōza: dai-isshō," 87–88, 94–96. For a table showing the connection between death records and burial records of the dukes of Lu, see Noma, "Shunjū sanden nyūmon kōza: dai-sanshō," 100–101. For a table of normal death records (*zu* 卒), see Kennedy, "Interpretation of the Ch'un-Ch'iu," 42.

22. "Pattern" here translates the German term *Formular*, which is used as a technical term in paleographic reconstructions of legal or religious inscriptions written according to a strictly defined form: a specific Formular.

23. Yin 10.4, etc.

24. Zhuang 4.5, Zhuang 30.4, Xiang 30.6, etc.

25. Ding 4.9, etc.

26. Zhuang 8.1, etc.

27. Xi 1.1, etc.

28. Yin 1.7, etc.

29. Every record of an anomaly and many other records contain this question.

30. Zhao 20.2, etc.

31. Xiang 30.9, etc.

32. Ai 13.3.

33. Yin 1.1, Zhuang 7.5, Zhuang 28.6, Xi 1.2, Xi 16.1 (twice), Xiang 23.9.

34. For further formulaic questions in *Gongyang* and *Guliang* commentaries see Malmqvist, "Studies on the Gongyang and Guuliang Commentaries II," 38–40.

35. Keightley ("Late Shang Divination," 23) therefore has compared those questions to the questions found on oracle bone inscriptions.

36. The close relation to the ideal of the "rectification of names" (*zheng ming* 正名) as expressed by Confucius in *Lunyu* 13.3 has been noted already in the *Chunqiu fanlu* (chap. 35); see Franke, *Studien zur Geschichte*, 181; Unger, "Das konfuzianische Weltgericht," 70; Gassmann, *Cheng ming*.

37. The date and origin of this commentary are unknown.

38. *Da Dai liji jiegu*, 25, 32, 47.

39. Ibid., 44.

40. Ibid., 34–36, etc.

41. Ibid., 25. The final sentence suggests that geese migration serves this calendar only as an indicator for a specific point of time, not as information about the migration itself (to a specific place).

42. Cf. third month: 妾、子始蠶。 ("Women and lads begin [tending] the silkworms.") 先妾而後子，何也？曰：事有漸也，言事自卑者始。 ("Why is 'women' first and only then 'lads'? Answer: Things have their process. It means that things start with the lowest.")

43. I have dealt with this more extensively in my *Das Gongyang zhuan*, 157–240, of which I give a brief summary here.

44. In the translation of this passage I follow the parallel passage in *Lüshi Chunqiu* "Yin lü 音律": 黃鐘之月。土事無作。慎無發蓋。以固天閉地。陽氣且泄 ; see *Lüshi Chunqiu jiaoshi*, 325.

45. *Liji jijie*, 494. The *Lüshi Chunqiu* has a slightly different version; see *Lüshi Chunqiu jiaoshi*, 567; Legge, *The Li Ki*, 302–303.

46. *Liji jijie*, 470; *Lüshi Chunqiu jiaoshi*, 376. Malaria has the characteristic that conditions of hot and cold alternate out of control.

47. For an analysis of these systems see Granet's study *La pensée chinoise*; Eberhard, *Beiträge zur kosmologischen Spekulation Chinas in der Han-Zeit*; Needham, *Science and Civilisation in China*, vol. 2, 261–265, 279–291; Lévi-Strauss, *La pensée sauvage*; Graham, *Yin Yang and the Nature of Correlative Thinking*.

48. If the plants in the four corners represent the different phases of the plants in the four seasons, it would be the only element in this circle taken from the phenomenal world.

49. For example, we have such descriptive notions of astronomical deviations in *Shiji* 史記 descriptions of the movements of planets; see *Shiji*

27.1313, 1319, 1323, etc.

50. For an analysis of such classificatory systems, see Lévi-Strauss, *La pensée sauvage*.

51. See Watson, *Ssu-Ma Ch'ien*, 74; Gernet, *Die chinesische Welt*, 81. For an early connection between omen experts and historiographers, see Kalinowski, "La rhétorique oraculaire dans les chroniques anciennes de la Chine," 56–58. For the same connection in early Han, see Kern, "Religious Anxiety," 29.

52. See Wang Yinzhi (1766–1834), "Gongyang zaiyi"; Zhu Dongrui, "Gongyang tangu," 171; as well as my *Das Gongyang zhuan*, 225–227. The strong connection between omenology and *Chunqiu* exegesis within the *Gongyang* and *Guliang* traditions is not established until Han times. We first find it in the *Chunqiu* exegesis of Lu Jia 陸賈 (d. 178 B.C.E.) and Dong Zhongshu 董仲舒 (ca. 195–115 B.C.E.) (not, however, in the early *Chunqiu* exegetical chapters of the *Chunqiu fanlu* 1–17); see my "From Casuistic Exegesis to Discursive Guidelines." Later it becomes increasingly prominent in the works of omen experts like Sui Hong 眭弘 (fl. 78 B.C.E.), Xiahou Sheng 夏侯勝 (fl. 70 B.C.E.), Jing Fang 京房 (77–37 B.C.E.), Gu Yong 谷永 (d. 8 B.C.E.), Liu Xiang 劉向 (79–8 B.C.E.), Li Xun 李尋 (fl. 5 B.C.E.), Liu Xin 劉歆 (d. 23 C.E.), etc. (see Kern, "Religious Anxiety," 28–30, from where this list is taken) and reaches its peak with the apocryphal *chenwei* 讖緯 exegesis, which was especially developed in the context of the *Chunqiu*. See Yasui, *Isho no seiritsu to sono tenkai*, 221; Yasui and Nakamura, *Isho no kiso teki kenkyū*, 80. A collection of the *Chunqiu wei* 春秋緯 fragments may be found in Yasui and Nakamura, *Chōshū Isho shūsei*, vols. 4a and 4b; and Ma Guohan, *Yuhan shanfang jiyishu*, vol. 3, 2158–2261. See also Dull, "A Historical Introduction to the Apocryphal (*ch'an-wei*) Texts of the Han Dynasty," 186ff., 481. It is striking that in the apocryphal *Chunqiu wei* 春秋緯, concrete precedents no longer play a role. Instead, we find a concentration on numerological-astronomical correlations in connection with the *wuxing* theory but no relation to *Chunqiu* exegesis. In its methodology it rather resembles the more completely transmitted *Yiwei* 易緯, which, however, relates the tri- or hexagrams to *yin* and *yang* (see, e.g., *Chōshū Isho shūsei*, vol. 1b, 38ff.) and does not refer to the *wuxing* theory except in some general statements.

53. For further details see my *Das Gongyang zhuan*, 251–272 (esp. 265–268), 340–344.

54. See *Mozi jiaozhu*, 336–344.

55. See Gaskill, "Reporting Murder."

56. Wang Chong, *Lunheng*, chap. 52 "Shi ying 是應," refers to the Confucian myth about a one-horned goat that was used by Minister Gao Yao 皋陶 in doubtful lawsuits to strike the guilty. See *Lunheng jiaoshi*, 760; and Forke's note in *Lun-hêng II*, 321. For a study on the ritual and legal function of sheep, see Erkes, "Das Schaf im Alten China." See also Lau, "Vom Schaf zur Gerechtigkeit."

57. We should note that this *Mozi* chapter cites only cases that serve the overall argument. According to Graham, *Disputers of the Tao*, 48, the view that it is the function of Heaven and spirits to strengthen moral action through

rewards and punishments in order to bring justice to the world is typical of Mohist thought. Even if the argument of this chapter is "crude," as Graham writes elsewhere (*Later Mohist Logic, Ethics and Science*, 15), the reported cases should still be regarded as existing cases from *Chunqiu* annals and not as freely constructed ones. While not necessarily representative, they should be taken seriously as authentic annalistic material. Gaskill, "Reporting Murder," thinks that the main function of parallel cases in early modern England was to limit the elasticity of juridical truth and of jurisdiction through such additional evidence.

58. Applying such a reading to the quotation sequences in the two versions of the "Zi yi" from the *Liji* and Guodian yields some unexpected insights; see my "Some Preliminary Observations on the Newly Excavated 'Tzu I 緇衣' from Kuo-tien 郭店."

Chapter 5

The Odes *in* *Excavated Manuscripts*

Martin Kern

子曰：書不盡言，言不盡意。然則聖人之意，其不可見乎。子曰
：聖人立象以盡意，設卦以盡情偽，繫辭焉以盡其言，變而通之
以盡利，鼓而舞之以盡神。

The Master said: "Writing does not fully express the words; words do
not fully express the ideas." As this is so, can the ideas of the sages
not be discerned? The Master said: "The sages established the images to
fully express their ideas, they arranged the hexagrams to fully express
what is genuine and what is fabricated, they appended statements to
these to fully express their words, they let them transform and be
continuous to fully express their benefit, they drummed and danced
them to fully express their spirituality."

Zhou Yi 周易, "Xici zhuan" 繫辭傳

Introduction

The present study is a preliminary step toward a full account of the *Odes*
(Shi 詩) quotations and discussions in the texts from Guodian 郭店 tomb 1
(Jingmen 荊門, Hubei; tomb sealed ca. 300 B.C.E.), Mawangdui 馬王堆
tomb 3 (Changsha 長沙, Hunan; tomb sealed 168 B.C.E.), and Shuanggudui
雙古堆 tomb 1 (Fuyang 阜陽, Anhui; tomb sealed 165 B.C.E.). The exact
identity and status of the Guodian tomb occupant is still unclear; the
Mawangdui tomb belongs to the family of Li Cang 李蒼 (d. 185 B.C.E.),
who was ennobled as Marquis of Dai 軑 and appointed as Chancellor of the
princedom of Changsha in the early years of the Han dynasty. The
Shuanggudui tomb belongs to Xiahou Zao 夏侯竈 (d. 165 B.C.E.), the
Marquis of Ruyin 汝陰. In addition to manuscripts from these known

places, another large corpus of Chu bamboo strips, probably dating from the late fourth century B.C.E., was purchased by the Shanghai Museum on the Hong Kong antique market in 1994. The first volume of their publication contains two manuscripts with quotations from the *Odes*.[1]

Compared to the received Mao 毛 tradition of the *Odes*, the textual fragments and quotations unearthed from these tombs provide us with a host of textual variants that in some instances may challenge the traditional reading of certain songs. In a first analytic step, the variants need to be determined as either graphic or lexical. In another step, the *Odes* quotations—whether or not including any variants—need to be considered as proof texts in the Guodian and Mawangdui manuscripts where they are embedded in a larger argument of expository prose. As Mark Edward Lewis has pointed out, such quotations of the hallowed songs not only sanctioned the truth claims made in their embedding text; their potential ambiguity was in turn "eliminated through the insertion of quotations into arguments that indicated how the verses were to be read."[2]

The present study does not aim at a comprehensive semantic discussion of excavated *Odes* fragments, nor will it pursue the thorough interpretation of individual passages that differ from the received tradition, or even discuss the fascinating issue of early *Odes* interpretation in general, onto which the newly excavated manuscripts have opened new perspectives. As a necessary preliminary to such more ambitious endeavors,[3] I will discuss individual *Odes* variants from Guodian, Mawangdui, and the Shanghai Museum in a merely technical way, comparing them with their transmitted counterparts and with each other. As the fragments from Shuanggudui are far more numerous, and as they have already received scholarly attention,[4] I will draw on their individual variants only occasionally. Nevertheless, their overall statistics will be presented in order to put the phenomenon of *Odes* variants in a broader perspective. Undoubtedly, new manuscript finds will further help to refine the preliminary results I can present here; with the *Odes* being the most frequently invoked text in both the received literature from early China and excavated manuscripts, we can be fully confident of obtaining many more quotations and variants from future text finds.

The broader suggestions that I will derive from the following examination of the *Odes* fragments concern the nature of the anthology, the issue of oral and written transmission, the status of the written text, and—finally and briefly—the relation between text and ritual in early China. They are, needless to say, tentative. At this moment in the history of early China studies, it seems quite unwise to offer sweeping statements on these issues, as any new textual find may substantially alter the picture. This, however, does not mean that we have nothing to say; with the evidence from the *Odes* quotations in the Guodian, Mawangdui, Shuanggudui, and Shanghai Museum manuscripts, certain hypotheses seem more persuasive than others. As I will argue, the *Odes* fragments from these various sites help us to reconsider some assumptions about the transmission of the *Odes*, most notably the idea that by the early second century B.C.E.—not to speak of the late fourth century B.C.E.—there was a more or less standardized written version of the *Odes*, shared among the cultural elite.[5] This widely held assumption itself is related to certain claims concerning the cultural status of writing in early China, claims that deserve to be checked against the mounting evidence from recent manuscript finds.[6]

The problem of *Odes* variants is, of course, well known already from transmitted texts and has been dealt with in both traditional and modern scholarship. While the Mao 毛 recension (*Mao Shi zhuan* 毛詩傳) survives—probably only more or less intact—in Zheng Xuan's 鄭玄 (127–200) *Mao Shi zhuan jian* 毛詩傳箋[7] and has been transmitted in remarkably stable condition, it also has since late Eastern Han times largely eclipsed competing versions of the *Odes*. Only indirectly, through *Odes* quotations in various early texts, do scholars get occasional glimpses at some of the other recensions that were circulating in Western Han times but were mostly lost after the Eastern Han, notably those of the "three scholarly lineages" (*san jia* 三家) of the *Odes*, *Han Shi* 韓詩, *Qi Shi* 齊詩, and *Lu Shi* 魯詩. Nearly thirty titles of Western Han exegetical works associated with one of these three or with the Mao recension are known by their titles, but apart from the Mao version, only Han Ying's 韓嬰 (fl. ca. 150 B.C.E.) *Han Shi waizhuan* 韓詩外傳[8] has survived. Exegetical works associated with the *Qi Shi* and the *Lu Shi*—both named after the regions of their origin—have perished altogether. However, with the *Odes* being the most intensely and widely quoted text of Warring States and Han times, a plethora of citations in received texts is available. These *Odes* fragments show not only a certain number of textual differences but in some instances also significantly different interpretations.[9] Several Qing scholars have collected and studied both the textual variants and the exegetical differences, with the three most comprehensive works being those by Li Fusun 李富孫 (1764–1843),[10] Chen Qiaocong 陳喬樅 (1809–1869),[11] and Wang Xianqian 王先謙 (1842–1918).[12] In addition to *Odes* quotations that can be identified with songs in the received *Mao Shi* corpus, a number of texts, or fragments of them, are quoted as *Odes* in transmitted texts but do not have counterparts in the *Mao Shi*. These are usually labeled "lost odes" (*yi shi* 逸詩), and are assembled in several Ming and Qing compilations and studied mainly in relation to the traditional claim, first advanced by Sima Qian 司馬遷 (145–ca. 85 B.C.E.), that Confucius compiled the *Odes* anthology from a ten-times-larger corpus of songs.

Despite their occasional textual differences, the *Han Shi*, *Qi Shi*, and *Lu Shi* fragments display an overall coherence with one another as well as with the *Mao Shi*. This stands in remarkable contrast to the large number of textual variants in excavated *Odes* fragments. We cannot measure the extent to which the surviving *san jia* fragments represent the original form of the canonical text in these recensions. As the fragments are transmitted only in other texts of a literary tradition that since late Eastern Han times was in its *Odes* exegesis dominated by the Mao version, it seems very likely that, in the majority of instances, they might have undergone later adjustment to adhere more closely to the *Mao Shi*. In this case, the remaining textual variants should be seen as a mere residue of originally far greater differences between the *san jia* and Mao versions. It seems that only the manuscript variants give us a realistic idea of what mutually independent *Odes* transmissions may have looked like in late Warring States and early imperial times.

The distribution of *Odes* passages in the manuscripts from Shuanggudui, Mawangdui, Guodian, and the Shanghai Museum is as follows:

1. The more than 170 bamboo strip fragments from Shuanggudui carry passages of sixty-five songs known from the *guofeng* 國風 section and four songs known from the *xiaoya* 小雅 section of the Mao recension.[13] Songs from all but one of the fifteen *guofeng* subsections are represented (only "Gui feng" 檜風 songs are missing), and the titles given for both songs and sections match those of the received Mao version. However, from their substantial textual variants as well as from an apparently different order of the songs it seems clear that the Shuanggudui version of the *Odes* cannot be related to any of the four known Western Han recensions;[14] it may represent another, hitherto unknown, scholarly lineage in the reception of the *Odes*.[15]

2. In a section that has been labeled "Wu xing" 五行 (Five forms of conduct; sometimes also "De xing" 德行 [Virtuous conduct]), the Mawangdui silk manuscript contains textual fragments of seven *Odes*—four of them known from the *guofeng*, two from the *daya* 大雅, and one from the *Shang song* 商頌 section of the Mao text.[16] Structurally, the Mawangdui "Wu xing" text consists of a short basic text and its much

longer explications. This textual organization is known from some transmitted texts as a division of *jing* 經 (canon) and *shuo* 説 (explanation), and
it accounts for certain repetitions among the *Odes* quotations in the "Wu
xing" silk manuscript. In some cases, the interpretation of the *Odes* in the
shuo passages differs radically from the Mao exegesis.[17] The earlier "Wu
xing" bamboo manuscript from Guodian includes only the *jing* portion of
the text and occasionally has shorter *Odes* quotations; it hence does not
contain the repeated quotes in the *shuo* section, nor does it have a quotation
of "Guan ju" 關雎 (which appears only in the *shuo* part of the Mawangdui
manuscript).[18]

3. The "Zi yi" 緇衣 (Black robes) bamboo manuscript from Guodian, a
different version of the text of this name that forms a chapter in the received
Liji 禮記, contains text fragments of seventeen *Odes*—three from the
guofeng (in altogether four quotations), eight from the *xiaoya* (nine
quotations), five from the *daya* (nine quotations), and one that has no
parallel in the Mao recension and should therefore be regarded as a "lost
ode." Another version of the "Zi yi" is among the Shanghai Museum strips;
as its text matches that of the Guodian "Zi yi," it includes all of the *Odes*
quotations found in the latter.

4. A discussion of the *Odes* appears in a highly fragmentary manuscript
among the Shanghai Museum strips that the editors have labeled "Kongzi
shilun" 孔子詩論 (Confucius's discussion of the *Odes*). A text of slightly
more than one thousand characters on parts of twenty-nine bamboo strips,
this manuscript mentions three pieces from the *Zhou song* 周頌, five from
the *daya*, twenty-one from the *xiaoya*, twenty-three from the *guofeng* (here
called *bangfeng* 邦風),[19] and seven titles not found in the present anthology.
Nine of the known songs and one unknown song are quoted directly.[20]

This distributional picture is related to the different nature of the
manuscripts under consideration: the "Kongzi shilun" is devoted to a
discussion of the *Odes* and suggests the existence of a relatively fixed corpus
not too different from the received anthology. The Shuanggudui manuscript
is undoubtedly a copy of the *Odes* anthology, or of a partial version of it. It
includes notes on the number of characters for individual songs as well as
for the individual sections of the *guofeng*. The textual unit according to
which the songs were written on the bamboo strips was not the whole song
but the single stanza (*zhang* 章).[21] Stanzas of up to eleven lines were
mostly written on one strip, and characters were written in smaller script if a
certain number of them had to be accommodated on a single strip. For

stanzas with up to only six lines in length, the lower part of the strip was left blank; for stanzas with twelve or more lines, the characters were evenly distributed over two strips. It is difficult to draw conclusions from the fact that the Shuanggudui bamboo fragments include only passages from a large number of *guofeng* songs in addition to four *xiaoya* pieces. Considering the very poor condition of these excavated bamboo fragments, one might suspect that the other parts of the anthology have simply vanished over time. Yet as no fragment from the *daya* and *song* 頌 sections is among the surviving fragments, one would then perhaps have to assume either (a) that the different sections *guofeng*, *xiaoya*, *daya*, and *song* were buried somewhat separately from one another and were therefore subject to different environmental conditions, or (b) that the *daya* and *song* corpora were not part of the text buried at Shuanggudui.

By contrast, the *Odes* passages in the "Wu xing" and "Zi yi" manuscripts from Guodian, Mawangdui, and the Shanghai Museum are embedded as quotations into a continuous textual framework. In these manuscripts, the *Odes* do not stand on their own but serve to support—apparently due to the traditional authority with which they were imbued—particular arguments made in the surrounding text. This citation practice is identical to that in transmitted pre-imperial and early imperial texts.

While the *Odes* fragments appear thus in three different types of texts, I believe it is still possible to discuss them together because (a) they belong to the same written context of elite tombs where they represent the same type of traditional learning; (b) in the Shanghai Museum manuscript corpus, two of the three types appear together; and (c) both the *Odes* anthology (as from Shuanggudui) and the texts that include *Odes* quotations are not occasional writings but written instantiations of texts with a history of transmission (received in the case of the "Zi yi," not received in that of the "Wu xing"). I thus assume that these writings were produced under similar circumstances. The philological analysis of the *Odes* quotations in these different types of manuscripts, presented below, seems to confirm this a priori assumption: all manuscripts show the same kind and distribution of textual variation in the writing of the *Odes*.

The Odes *and Their Textual Variants in Tomb* *Manuscripts: Distribution, Patterns, Issues*

The *Odes* texts proper of the Shuanggudui fragments—if we leave the accompanying notes on the respective sections and on the number of their characters aside—include 820 characters; of these, 220, or 26.8%, are with certainty textual variants.[22] The actual number of character variants might be substantially higher since on the badly damaged bamboo strips, 212 of the 820 characters are only partly legible; in 63 of these cases, the character fragments contain clear evidence of variants, and only these I have included among the overall number of 220. Theoretically, all the remaining 149 character fragments could equally contain some variant elements. To be accurate, we should therefore note that the 820 characters, compared to the Mao recension, contain between 220 (26.8%) and 369 (45%) variants. By contrast, the fragments from the Han, Qi, and Lu recensions, as far as they are known from quotations in other transmitted texts, altogether contain no more than 18 variants (2.2%) for the same body of texts.[23]

The *Odes* quotations in the "Wu xing" manuscripts from Mawangdui contain 158 characters, 50 (31.6%) of which are textual variants compared to the Mao version. For the same body of quotations, the *san jia* fragments contain 5 (3.2%) variants. Of the 158 characters from the Mawangdui silk text, 50 also occur on the bamboo strips of the Guodian "Wu xing" chapter, now including 18 (36%) variants; for these 50 characters occurring in the Guodian "Wu xing," the *san jia* texts have 2 (4%) variants. All Guodian variants differ from both the Mao text and the Mawangdui manuscript.

The "Zi yi" manuscript from Guodian contains 193 characters of *Odes* quotations, with 70 (36.3%) differing from their counterparts in the Mao text; in addition it has one complete line of "Du ren shi" 都人士 (Mao 225) not found in the received text. The *san jia* fragments of the same texts contain 12 (6.8%) variants. However, the *san jia* variants are partly included in the "Zi yi" chapter of the *Liji*, which is traditionally considered to belong to a Qi lineage of scholarship and textual production; its *Odes* quotations are therefore taken to represent the *Qi Shi*.

The more fragmentary Shanghai Museum "Zi yi" has only 157 characters of *Odes* quotations, including 67 (42.7%) variants. In addition, one character in "Wen wang" 文王 (Mao 235) is missing, as are particles in two of four lines from "Yi" 抑 (Mao 256), resulting in a trisyllabic—instead of the usual tetrasyllabic—meter. As the bamboo strips are intact in each of these passages, the characters are genuinely missing in the manuscript.

TABLE 5.1

Manuscript text	Number of characters	Number of variants	Variants in %	San jia variants in %
Shuanggudui *Odes*	820	220–369	26.8–45.0	2.2
Mawangdui "Wu xing"	158	50	31.6	3.2
Guodian "Wu xing"	50	18	36.0	4.0
Guodian "Zi yi"	193	70	36.3	6.2
Shanghai Museum "Zi yi"	157	67	42.7	7.6
Shanghai Museum "Kongzi shilun"	64	26	40.6	3.1

The "Kongzi shilun" has *Odes* quotations of 64 characters with 26 (40.6%) variants. In four more cases of "Yuan qiu" 宛丘 (Mao 136) and "Yi jie" 猗嗟 (Mao 106), particles are eliminated, again resulting in a trisyllabic meter. The statistics of the *Odes* manuscript fragments under discussion are summarized in Table 5.1; the reference recension against which variants are defined is the received Mao text.

It is difficult to decide to which extent the fragmentary data from the *san jia* recensions are comparable to those from the manuscripts. In attributing a particular quotation to one of the three recensions, the Qing scholars in many cases were offering but educated guesses, not hard evidence.[24] As we are not always sure that a given variant indeed reflects a distinct Lu, Qi, or Han reading, we also cannot claim that our fragmentary evidence comprises all cases of textual differences in these versions. Moreover, as noted above, earlier editors very likely have already normalized most of the *san jia* quotations according to the text of the dominant Mao recension. Despite these uncertainties and possibly severe distortions of the actual character/variant ratios on the side of the *san jia* texts, some observations are still valid and relevant.

First, while it seems unreasonable to assume that all the characters from Shuanggudui that are only partially legible were indeed textual variants, it would be equally abnormal if all of them were in coherence with the Mao recension. A ratio of variants somewhere in the middle between the two extremes of 26.8% and 45% would fall right into the range of the *Odes* quotations in the Mawangdui, Guodian, and Shanghai Museum manuscripts.

Second, all manuscript fragments, regardless of whether they come from the late fourth or the second century B.C.E., are orthographically by and large equally distant from the Mao recension, from the *san jia*, and—with one important exception[25]—from one another. That, according to Ban Gu 班固 (32–92), "the *Odes* remained complete after encountering the Qin [bibliocaust of 213 B.C.E.] because they were recited [from memory] and not only [written] on bamboo and silk"[26] is of no particular relevance in this context. Later scholars have referred to Ban Gu's account to explain the textual differences among the four known Han recensions as resulting from the oral transmission of the *Odes* in early Western Han times,[27] an argument that Baxter has extended to the Shuanggudui manuscript evidence.[28] I would, however, not be surprised if the next find of a pre-imperial manuscript with *Odes* fragments exhibited versions very different from those of the Guodian and Shanghai Museum manuscripts—meaning that the written text of the *Odes* was as unstable before the bibliocaust as it was immediately thereafter. Since the bibliocaust aimed at collecting and burning the "*Odes, Documents* (Shu 書), and sayings of the hundred lineages (*bai jia yu* 百家語)"[29] that were circulating outside the imperial court,[30] their existence in a plurality of written copies—and perhaps more precisely: written copies of a plurality of teaching traditions—is obviously implied.

Third, the overall factor of textual variants (compared to the Mao recension) in the excavated manuscripts is about ten times higher than the same factor in all three *san jia* recensions taken together. The manuscript evidence from both the late fourth and the mid–second century B.C.E.—that is, before and after the bibliocaust—shows us quite drastically the extent to which the *Odes* could differ in their written form. In light of this evidence, we can no longer uphold the traditional view that the transmitted *san jia* fragments are representing mutually independent oral traditions in their pristine condition. Considering (a) the archaic language of the *Odes* combined with (b) the enormous number of homophonous words in early Chinese, the relatively few variants in the *san jia* fragments cannot represent all the differences that would have resulted from three mutually independent oral traditions. We are therefore left with one of two possible scenarios: the known variants are either mere remnants of originally far more diverging texts, or they reflect the fact that the four recensions were never mutually

independent writings to begin with and may instead have adhered to a
single—presumably the early imperial—standard. In fact, the two
alternatives are not mutually exclusive: even if the traditionally known
Western Han versions of the *Mao shi* and the *san jia* represented a by and
large unified imperial text, the manuscript evidence still forces us to assume
an overall retrospective standardization of the numerous *Odes* quotations
throughout Eastern Zhou and early imperial texts. The only question is
whether we assign this standardization already to Western Han or only to
post–Eastern Han times, after the Mao recension had finally gained its
dominance.[31]

Fourth, the fact that all *Odes* variants in the Guodian "Wu xing"
manuscript differ from their Mawangdui "Wu xing" counterparts, and that
the two cases where the Shuanggudui fragments overlap with Mawangdui
citations are again different, suggests that these quotations do not reflect a
written transmission of the *Odes* common to any two of the three texts.
This point is significant given the relations of proximity in time, space, and
contents: on the one hand, the Mawangdui "Wu xing" text is clearly an
elaborated version of its Guodian counterpart, and the Mawangdui, Guodian,
and Shuanggudui sites belong to the same southern cultural geography of
the old state of Chu. On the other hand, the tombs of Mawangdui and
Shuanggudui are chronologically separated by no more than a few years. As
noted above, it is not clear how the Shanghai Museum strips fit into this
picture. They certainly come from the old region of Chu, and they are
probably contemporaneous with the Guodian strips. As long as we may
suspect that the Guodian and Shanghai Museum "Zi yi" texts are actually
retrieved from the same site and are therefore not mutually independent, we
have to refrain from speculating on what their differences and similarities
actually entail.

The manuscripts under consideration contain different kinds of variants,
compared to one another and to their transmitted counterparts. In recognizing
such variants, it is not significant whether a text is written in a particular
local or regional calligraphic form (e.g., what is summarily called the Chu
楚 script of the manuscripts under discussion) as long as scholars can
confidently identify the various graphic elements and transcribe them into
standard *kaishu* 楷書 forms.[32] In general, we see cases of graphic or lexical
variation that can be rationalized on either phonological or semantic
grounds. There also are what seem to be downright scribal errors as well as
textual differences that resist plausible explanation. Some types of textual
variants are more interesting than others or more elucidating in terms of

THE ODES IN EXCAVATED MANUSCRIPTS

how to understand the respective *Odes* line; but all are the results of textual production and follow the same regularities—and irregularities—of this production in early China.

In the *Odes* quotations under discussion, variants based on homophony or near-homophony are by far the most numerous ones, and among these, graphic variants that differ only with respect to their semantic classifiers are again the majority. However, at this point of the analysis, it is not possible to determine in every single case whether we are dealing with a lexical or a graphic variant. In general, the fact that two characters belong to the same *xiesheng* 諧聲 ("homophonophoric") series means that in the overwhelming majority of cases, the two graphs represent homophonous or near-homophonous words and can therefore be used paronomastically for each other.[33] This does not rule out the possibility that they are in fact lexical variants,[34] but within the confines of the present study, I will provisionally treat variants that occur within a given *xiesheng* series as graphic variants, representing the same or nearly the same sound and writing the same word. This is but a pragmatic way to illustrate the distribution of different variant types in our manuscripts and does not entail claims on their semantic interpretation; indeed, it should be expected that this largest group of variants in our manuscripts also includes some, though not many (see my argument below), cases that ultimately will be better interpreted as lexical variants.

Bearing this basic qualification in mind, the following survey is limited to discussing the Guodian, Mawangdui, and Shanghai Museum *Odes* variants that occur outside *xiesheng* series; I will not list the plethora of variants—indeed the great majority of all variants—that occur within the same *xiesheng* series. Only where they occur in the same line with other variants will they be mentioned in passing. The following example from the Guodian (strip 3) and Shanghai Museum (strip 2) "Zi yi" manuscripts may demonstrate the distinction:

"Xiao ming" 小明 (Mao 207):

Mao:	靖共爾位，好是正直。
Guodian "Zi yi":	情共尔立，好氏貞植。
Shanghai Museum "Zi yi":	靜龏尔立，盯是正植。
Liji "Zi yi":	靖共爾位，好是正直。

Wang Xianqian notes that the Qi version has 靖恭 for Mao 靖共, and in one case 靜共; the Han version has 靜恭 or 靖恭. It is clear that 靖, 靜,

and 情, on the one hand, and 共, 恭, and 龏 (龔), on the other, share the same *xiesheng* series and are therefore homophonous or near-homophonous. The same is true for Guodian and Shanghai Museum 立 as a variant of Mao 位 and for Guodian and Shanghai Museum 植 as a variant of Mao 直. All these variants can be attributed to the simple fact that, by Western Han times, the semantic classifiers were still not yet fixed in the writing system. In addition, Guodian and Shanghai Museum 尔 for 爾 reflects merely a different writing convention, as is Shanghai Museum 㚤 for 好.[35] However, Guodian has two more variants that cannot be explained in this way: 氏 [*gjiʔ] for 是 [*djiʔ] and 貞 [*trjiŋ] for 正 [*tjiŋh]. In both cases, the graphs bear no relation to each other but represent near-homophonous words and therefore can be used paronomastically.[36]

The order in which I discuss the individual *Odes* fragments generally follows their sequence in the manuscripts; I group only different quotations from the same *Ode* together with their first instance. My reconstructions of Old Chinese are based on Li Fang-kuei's 李方桂 system with Schuessler's emendations.[37] To determine whether or not two graphs could be used paronomastically, I take as a basis the principles laid out by Karlgren: the two graphs must normally represent words that (a) belong to the same *Odes* rhyme group and (b) have homorganic initials.[38] As noted by Karlgren and further discussed by Boltz,[39] textual evidence forces us to allow occasional exceptions for both principles, but these can be determined only on a case-by-case basis.

The Textual Variants in Guodian and
Shanghai Museum *"Zi yi"* Odes *Quotations*

"Wen wang" 文王 (Mao 235)

Mao:	萬邦作孚	
Guodian:	萬邦乍孚	(strip 2)
Shanghai:	蠆邦复㠯	(strip 1)
Liji "Zi yi":	萬國作孚	

While 蠆 / 萬 and 作 / 乍 / 复 are *xiesheng* series variants, *Liji* 國 for 邦 may represent a later change due to the tabooed 邦 after 195 B.C.E. (see note 19 above). 孚 [*phju; "to trust"] and 㠯 ([服] *bjək; "to submit"] do not share the same rhyme group and are also quite different graphs in Chu script. Instead, they may represent two different lexical choices.

Mao:	於緝熙敬止

Guodian: 於倡遳敬止   (strip 34)

Shanghai: 於幾義之   (strip 17)

熙 and 遳 are *xiesheng* variants. The Shanghai Museum manuscript genuinely lacks the graph 敬, as the bamboo strip is without physical damage here. While 緝 [*tshjəp] and 倡 are again *xiesheng* variants, 幾 [*kjəj] is neither graphically, phonetically, nor semantically related. Similarly, 義 [*ŋjajh] is unrelated to 熙 [*hjə]. However, 緝熙 [*tshjəp-hjə], also appearing in several other *Odes*, is a near-rhyming binome,[40] while 幾義 [*kjəj-ŋjajh] is an alliterative one. The interchangeability of the particles 止 [*tjəʔ] and 之 [*tjə] is well attested. Karlgren notes that 之 originally was only a variant of 止 and calls the words behind the two graphs homophonous; Schuessler and Baxter note a difference in tone.[41]

"Shi jiu" 鳲鳩 (Mao 152)

Mao: 淑人君子

Guodian: 骨人君子   (strips 4–5)

Shanghai: 骨人君子   (strip 3)

The variant 骨 for 淑 [*djəwk]—appearing twice in the Guodian and Shanghai Museum (see also below) "Zi yi" manuscripts—is phonetically grounded, as is 戻 for 淑 in a quotation from the same song in the Guodian "Wu xing" manuscript (see below). As Karlgren has noted,[42] 弔 [*tiagwh] "is always used in the sense of" 叔 [*hnjəwk]. While the reconstructed pronunciations do not exactly fulfill the principles for loan graphs, textual evidence shows the interchangeability of the two graphs which in turn are the phonetics in 骨 and 淑. In the Shanghai Museum "Zi yi," 君子 is written as one character, that is, as a graphic contraction (*hewen* 合文).

Mao: 其儀一兮

Guodian: 其義戈也   (strip 39)

Shanghai: 其義一也   (strip 20)

Liji "Zi yi":   其儀一也

As also in other lines from the *Odes* (see below), the two particles 兮 [*giʔ] and 也 [*ljajʔ] are interchanged not because of any graphic or phonetic proximity but perhaps because of their function as merely rhythmic particles. 儀 and 義 belong to the same *xiesheng* series, as do 戈 and 一.[43]

"Ban" 板 (Mao 254)

Mao: 下民卒瘅

Guodian: 下民卒担   (strip 7)

Liji "Zi yi":   下民卒癉

The three variants 担, 癉, and 壇 are homophonous [*tan?]. Due to physical damage, the line is missing in the Shanghai Museum "Zi yi."

"Jie nan shan"節南山 (Mao 191)

Mao:	不自為政	
Guodian:	不自為貞	(strip 9)
Shanghai:	正	(strip 5)
Liji "Zi yi":	不自為正	

In the Shanghai Museum manuscript, only the last character of the line is preserved. As in the case of 正 [*tjiŋh] / 貞 [*trjiŋ] above, 政 [*tjiŋh] and 貞 could be used paronomastically, with their words having homorganic initials and belonging to the same *Odes* rhyme group. The *Liji* "Zi yi" variant 正 (also in the Shanghai Museum "Zi yi" [strip 5]) belongs to the same *xiesheng* series as 政.

Mao:	赫赫師尹	
Guodian:	㝓㝓帀尹	(strip 16)
Shanghai:	虩虩帀尹	(strip 9)

The reduplicatives 㝓㝓 and 虩虩 are to be interpreted as 虩虩; 虩 [*hərjak] and 赫 [*hərak] both belong to the rhyme group and have homorganic initials. Another phonetically related variant of the same reduplicative appears in a "Da ming" 大明 quotation in the Guodian and Mawangdui "Wu xing" manuscripts (see below). 師 [*srjəj] and 帀 belong to the same *xiesheng* series.

Mao:	民具爾瞻	
Guodian:	民具尔贍	(strip 16)
Shanghai:	民具尔𥸤	(strip 9)

While 瞻 [*tjam] and 贍 are obvious *xiesheng* variants, 𥸤 may also be phonetically related. According to Duan Yucai's 段玉裁 (1735–1815) commentary in the *Shuowen jiezi*, the phonetic in 詹 is 厃,[44] which would then account for 𥸤 as well.

"Yi" 抑 (Mao 256)

Mao:	有覺德行	
Guodian:	又𰋹惪行	(strip 12)
Shanghai:	又共惪行	(strip 7)
Liji "Zi yi":	有梏德行	

又 for 有 is a mere writing convention, as is 惪 for 德. As for the second character of the line, the Shanghai Museum variant makes it clear that the very similar one in Guodian is to be read as 共. However, it seems impossible to relate this to either the Mao recension or the *Liji* "Zi yi" (presumably representing the *Qi shi*). 覺 [*kərəwk] and 梏 [*kəwk], sharing the same rhyme group and having the same velar initial, are perfectly interchangeable. I assume that 共 [*gjuŋh] is to be taken as 恭 [*kjəwŋ], which then also shares the velar initial, the main vowel, and a related rhyme group. In this case, the Guodian and Shanghai Museum variants may give a new clue to the hitherto difficult interpretation of the second character.[45]

Mao:	四國訓之	
Guodian:	四方忎之	(strip 12)
Shanghai:	四或川之	(strip 7)

While 訓 [*hjuəns] and 忎, as well as *Liji* "Zi yi" 順 [*mljuəns] and Shanghai Museum 川 [*khljuan], belong to the same *xiesheng* series, the relation between 方 [*pjaŋ] and 國 [*kwək] is not phonetic but purely semantic ("regions"/"states"). By contrast, 或 [*gwək] is merely a *xiesheng* variant for 國.

Mao:	慎爾出話	
Guodian:	誓爾出話	(strip 30)

慎 [*djins] and 誓 [*djats] are neither phonetically nor graphically related; the variant 誓 (also as 訢) occurs quite regularly in Chu manuscripts, but its exact explanation is still awaited.[46] It might be to some extent based on semantic grounds ("cautious"/"solemn"). Due to physical damage, the present line is lost in the Shanghai Museum manuscript.

Mao:	敬爾威儀	
Guodian:	敬尔悵義	(strip 30)
Shanghai:	敬尔威義	(strip 16)

While 儀 [*ŋjaj] and 義 [*ŋjajh] belong to the same *xiesheng* series, 威 [*ʔjuəj] and 悵 [畏] [*ʔjuəjh] belong to the same rhyme group and have labio-laryngeal initials. In addition, one notes the semantic proximity of the two words ("to overawe"/"fearful"). In "Ji zui" 既醉 (Mao 247, see below), Guodian (but not Shanghai Museum) has again the variant 悵 for 威.

Mao:	淑慎爾止	
Guodian:	叾誓尔止	(strip 32)
Shanghai:	叾訢尔止	(strip 16)

On 淑 / 叾, see "Shi jiu" above; on 慎 / 誓 / 訢, see above.

Mao:	不愆于儀	
Guodian:	不侃于義	(strip 32)
Shanghai:	不侃	(strip 16)
Liji "Zi yi":	不僭于義	

The Shanghai Museum manuscript is physically fragmentary here. 儀 / 義 is again the usual *xiesheng* series phenomenon. 侃 [*khan] and the *Liji* "Zi yi" variant 謍 belong to the same *xiesheng* series, while 謍 is traditionally glossed as representing the same word ("to transgress") as 愆 [*khərjan]. Therefore, it seems that the Mao text follows a different writing convention, while the *Liji* "Zi yi" text and the Guodian and Shanghai Museum manuscripts differ only within the confines of a single *xiesheng* series. In any case, all three variants belong to the same rhyme group and have velar initials.

Mao: 白圭之玷
Guodian: 白珪之石   (strip 35)
Shanghai: 白珪之砧   (strip 18)

While 圭 [*kwi] and 珪 [*kwi] as well as 玷 [*tiam?] and 砧 [*trjəm] belong to the same respective *xiesheng* series, 砧 and 石 [*djak] are graphically closely related, with the former only containing two more strokes. I suspect the Guodian version shows a scribal lapse here, as two lines later, the text includes the following parallel phrase:

Mao: 斯言之玷
Guodian: 此言之砧   (strip 36)
Shanghai: 此言之砧   (strip 18)

Here, both Shanghai Museum and Guodian have 砧 for 玷, that is, a variant within a single *xiesheng* series; one may therefore suspect that in the earlier line, the Guodian scribe, perhaps accidentally, did not write the full form of the character. Mao 斯 [*sji] and Guodian and Shanghai Museum 此 [*?sji?] belong to the same rhyme group, have affricate initials, and are synonymous particles.

"Du ren shi" 都人士 (Mao 225)
Mao: 其容不改
Guodian: 其頌不改   (strip 17)

Due to physical damage, the line is lost in the Shanghai Museum manuscript. 容 [*ljuŋ] and 頌 [*sljuŋh] share the same rhyme group but do not have homorganic initials (dental vs. affricate). Nevertheless, their interchangeability—based on both semantic and phonetic grounds—is well attested, for example, in the Guodian "Xing zi ming chu" 性自命出 manuscript.[47]

"Zheng yue" 正月 (Mao 192)
Mao: 執我仇仇

Guodian:　　　　執我𫘤𫘤　　　(strips 18–19)
Shanghai:　　　　𫐐我敆敆　　　(strip 10)

It is not clear which word Guodian 𫘤 might represent, but any member of the 考 [*khəwʔ] *xiesheng* series would fulfill the phonetic criteria to serve as a loan character for Mao 仇 [*gjəw]. 𫐐 most likely belongs to the same *xiesheng* series as 執, with 幸 (*GSR* 685) as the phonetic. 敆 is to be interpreted as part of the 各 [*klak] *xiesheng* series. No relation to 仇 is apparent.

"Ju gong" 車攻 (Mao 179)

Mao:　　　　　　允矣君子
Guodian:　　　　躳也君子　　　(strip 36)
Shanghai:　　　　夋也君子　　　(strip 18)
Liji "Zi yi":　　允也君子

The variant sequence 躳 / 允 [*ljuənʔ] / 夋 [*tshjuən] is most likely phonetically related, with 允 and 夋 sharing the same *xiesheng* series. On strip 5 of the Guodian "Zi yi," 躳 is used for 尹; in the parallel passage on strip 3 of the Shanghai Museum "Zi yi," the character is again 夋. 允 and 尹 are listed in the same rhyme group (and may have been homophonous or near-homophonous); as argued by the Guodian editors, the phonetic in 躳 is 吕.[48] Guodian, Shanghai Museum, and the *Liji* "Zi yi" have 也 [*ljajʔ] for Mao 矣 [*ljəʔʔ]; in the language of the *Odes*, the two particles are interchangeable not on a phonetic basis but in (loose) semantic terms.

Mao:　　　　　　展也大成
Guodian:　　　　廛也大成　　　(strip 36)
Shanghai:　　　　垦也大壓　　　(strip 18)

I follow Qiu Xigui's reading for the first graph in the line as 廛 [*dranʔ], which, he argues, is "close in sound [to 展 (*trjanʔs) and therefore] interchangeable."[49] No semantic relation is apparent. The Shanghai editors interpret 垦 as 則 [*tsək], which I find doubtful when comparing other instances of 則 in Chu script manuscripts.[50] 壓 and 成 belong to the same *xiesheng* series.

"Ge tan" 葛覃 (Mao 2)

Mao:　　　　　　服之無斁
Guodian:　　　　備之亡懌　　　(strip 41)
Shanghai:　　　　備之亡臰　　　(strip 21)
Liji "Zi yi":　　服之無射

The variants 亡 / 無 [both *mja] simply reflect different writing

conventions. Guodian and Shanghai Museum 備 [*Gbjəkh; "to complete"]
for 服 [*bjək; "to make"] might be lexical, although the two meanings are
clearly related; however, on phonological grounds, the two graphs can as
well have been used paronomastically. 斁 [*ljak] in Mao and 懌 [*ljak] in
Guodian belong to the same *xiesheng* series; 射 [*ljak] in *Liji* "Zi yi" is
homophonous with either one and well attested as a loan graph for 斁. By
contrast, the Shanghai Museum "Zi yi" has 臭, which the Shanghai
Museum editors declare to be "the same character" as 斁; more strictly, it is
睪 [*ljak] which belongs to the same *xiesheng* series.

"Lu ming" 鹿鳴 (Mao 161)
    Mao: 示我周行
    Guodian: 旨我周行   (strip 42)
    Shanghai: 𥄂我周行   (strip 21)
    示 [*mgjiəj?h; "to show"] and 旨 [指] [*kjiəj?; "to point"] share the
same *Odes* rhyme group, have homorganic initials, and are semantically
related. Shanghai Museum 𥄂 belongs to the same *xiesheng* series as 旨.

"Guan ju" 關雎 (Mao 1)
    Mao: 君子好逑
    Guodian: 君子好㦰   (strip 43)
    Shanghai: 君子𡠥坙   (strip 22)
    Liji "Zi yi":   君子好仇
    逑 [*gjəw] and 仇 [*gjəw] are homophonous and semantically
related.[51] For the phonetically related 㦰, see "Zheng yue" above. Shanghai
Museum 坙 is an unidentified character. 𡠥 is a different writing convention
for 好.

"Ji zui" 既醉 (Mao 247)
    Mao: 朋友攸攝
    Guodian: 倗友卣巽   (strip 45)
    Shanghai: 塱旮卣図   (strip 23)
    The variants 倗 and 塱 for 朋 [*bəŋ] and 巽 for 攝 [*hnjap] both
belong to the same respective *xiesheng* series; 図 [*nərəp] is near-
homophonous[52] and in addition semantically related. 卣 [*ljəw] and 攸
[*ljəw] are semantically unrelated but homophonous.
    Mao: 攝以威儀
    Guodian: 巽以悓義   (strip 45)
    Shanghai: 図以威義   (strip 23)

On the variant 慏義 for 威儀, see "Yi" above. The variants 攝 / 奧 / 図 are as in the preceding line.

The evidence from the two "Zi yi" manuscripts can be briefly summarized as follows: the Guodian "Zi yi" manuscript contains twenty-six character variants[53] that do not occur in the same *xiesheng* series as their counterparts in the received tradition. Nineteen of these variants are unambiguously phonetically related and can be used paronomastically. Of the seven remaining cases, 國 / 方 are clearly semantically related, and 慎 / 誓 (twice) probably so; 矣 / 也 and 兮 / 也 are particles that might be primarily rhythmically motivated; 躬 / 允 awaits further clarification but is most likely phonetically based. Only 玷 / 石 can be interpreted as a scribal error; but 石 undoubtedly represents 砧 here, which in turn is in the same *xiesheng* series as 玷. There is no instance where a variant must be interpreted as an error that occurred in the process of copying the text from another written version. The Shanghai Museum "Zi yi" contains twenty-three variants outside the *xiesheng* series,[54] fifteen of which are phonetically related. The remaining cases are the binome 幾義 for 緝熙 (counted as two variants), the particle variants 也 / 兮 and 也 / 矣, the probably semantically related 訢 / 慎, the reduplicative 夅夅 / 仇仇, as well as the instances of 壆 / 展 and 埜 / 逑 where I consider the respective Shanghai Museum graph as unidentified.

The Textual Variants in Shanghai Museum "Kongzi shilun" Odes Quotations

The non-*xiesheng* variants in the *Odes* quotations of the "Kongzi shilun" are relatively few.

"Lie wen" 烈文 (Mao 269)

Mao:	無競維人
Shanghai:	乍競隹人 (strip 6)

While 維 / 隹 belong to the same *xiesheng* series, 乍 [作] [*tsak] and 無 [*mja] are phonetically unrelated. Traditional commentators have always interpreted 無 only as a rhetorical negative ("is he not . . . !"), that is, as an emphatic copula. This corresponds well with 乍 [作], and the Shanghai editors argue that because the two graphs 乍 [作] and 亡 [無] are similar, Mao 無 goes back to a copyist's error.[55]

"Huang yi" 皇矣 (Mao 241)

Mao: 予懷明德

Shanghai: 懷尔㬎㥁   (strip 7)

In the received text of this line, the god addresses King Wen 文 of Zhou 周 in direct speech. This understanding probably also underlies the Shanghai Museum line, yet the personal pronouns are exchanged: instead of "I cherish [your] shining virtuous power," the line now reads "[I] cherish your shining virtuous power." 㬎 for 明 is a *xiesheng* variant; 㥁 is a mere writing convention for 德.

"Yuan qiu" 宛丘 (Mao 136)

Mao: 洵有情兮

Shanghai: 訇有情   (strip 22)

As in the following line (not further discussed here), the Shanghai Museum manuscript does not include the final particle 兮, offering a trisyllabic line instead of the usual tetrasyllabic verse form. 訇 [*gwin] and 洵 [*səwjin] share the same rhyme group and have initial clusters that are to some extent related (labiovelar vs. labialized dental sibilant); I therefore interpret them as phonetically related.

"Yi jie" 猗嗟 (Mao 106)

Mao: 四矢反兮

Shanghai: 四矢夏   (strip 22)

For this line, the Han recension has 四矢變;[56] 反 [*mpjanʔ] and 變 [*pərjuans] belong to the same rhyme group and both have labial initials. As pointed out by the Shanghai Museum editors,[57] a bell inscription from the southern tomb of Marquis Yi of Zeng 曾侯乙 (Leigudun 擂鼓墩, Suizhou 隨州, Hubei), dated ca. 433 B.C.E., has 頧 for 變, apparently with 夏 as the phonetic. This suggests that 反 / 夏 are interchangeable on phonological grounds. Here as in the following line, the Shanghai Museum version does not include the final particle 兮, giving the line as trisyllabic.

"Shi jiu" 鳲鳩 (Mao 152)

Mao: 其儀一兮

Shanghai: 其義一氏   (strip 22)

The line appears also in the "Zi yi" and "Wu xing" manuscripts (see above and below). While 儀 [*ŋjaj] and 義 [*ŋjajh] are common *xiesheng* variants, 氏 [*gjiʔ] is interchangeable with 兮 [*giʔ] phonetically. In the following line of the same quotation, we see another variant:

Mao: 心如結兮
Shanghai: 心女結也   (strip 22)

Here, as in quotations in the "Zi yi" and "Wu xing" manuscripts, 兮 [*giʔ] is also interchangeable with the phonetically and graphically unrelated 也 [*ljajʔ]. This indicates a relatively loose use of these particles, perhaps mainly for rhythmic purposes.

Altogether, the *Odes* quotations in the Shanghai Museum "Kongzi shilun" include six non-*xiesheng* variants. Three of them can be analyzed phonologically. In addition, we see the particle variant 兮 / 也, the pronoun change from 予 to 尔, and the variant 無 / 乍, where the 無 of the received text may be regarded as a graphic error.

The Textual Variants in Guodian and Mawangdui *"Wu xing"* Odes *Quotations*

As above, I will discuss only those variants that are not simply deviations within the same *xiesheng* series.

"Cao chong" 草蟲 (Mao 14)
    Mao: 亦既覯止
    Guodian: 亦既詢止   (strip 10)
    Mawangdui: 亦既鉤之   (§ 5A)

On the variant 止 / 之, see "Wen wang" in the "Zi yi" manuscripts discussed above. The same variant occurs in another line of this *Odes* quotation in the Mawangdui manuscript, with 亦既見之 for 亦既見止. Wang Xianqian notes that 覯 [*kuh] in the Mao version should be read as the homophonous 遘 [*kuh; "to meet with"],[58] as it appears in the Lu version of the *Odes*. The Guodian and Mawangdui variants 詢 [*guʔ] and 鉤 [*ku], which belong to one *xiesheng* series, are semantically unrelated, but phonetically interchangeable, with 遘.
    Mao: 憂心惙惙
    Mawangdui: 憂心祋祋   (§ 5A)

The reduplicatives 惙惙 [*trjuat-trjuat] and 祋祋 [*tuats-tuats] are semantically unrelated but have homorganic initials and belong to the same *Odes* rhyme group. In addition to quoting directly from "Cao chong," the two manuscripts also paraphrase other lines of the same song. Here, the reduplicative 忡忡 [*thrjəwŋ-thrjəwŋ] of the Mao line 憂心忡忡 appears as

忡忡 [*tjəwŋ-tjəwŋ] in the Guodian texts (strip 12); as Wang Xianqian has
noted, the Lu version had 懂懂 [*tjəwŋ-tjəwŋ], while the Qi version had 冲
冲 [*drjəwŋ-drjəwŋ].[59] All these variants share the same rhyme group and
have homorganic initials.

"Shi jiu" 鳲鳩 (Mao 152)

Mao:	淑人君子	
Guodian:	婯人君子	(strip 16)
Mawangdui:	叔人君子	(§ 7A)

叔 [*hnjəwk] and 淑 [*djəwk] belong to the same *xiesheng* series. For
the phonologically acceptable variant 婯, see the note on the "Shi jiu"
quotation in the "Zi yi" manuscripts above.

Mao:	其儀一兮	
Guodian:	其義罷也	(strip 16)
Mawangdui:	其宜一氏	(§ 7A)

For other quotations of this line, see above. The rarely used character
罷 is known only from excavated texts, beginning with an instance in a
Shang oracle bone inscription.[60] In the Guodian corpus, it also appears
twice on strip 8 of the "Taiyi sheng shui" 大一生水 manuscript, once on
strip 18 of the "Cheng zhi wen zhi" 成之聞之 manuscript, and once on
strip 25 of the "Yu cong 4" 語叢四 manuscript.[61] The graph has further
been identified on strip 200 of the "Bushi jidao jilu" 卜筮祭禱記錄
divination manuscript from Baoshan 包山 tomb 2. This tomb is located less
than ten kilometers away from the Guodian site and dated between 323 and
316 B.C.E.; its similarity to Guodian tomb 1 has in fact been used to date
the latter in the same period or only a few years later.[62] In the "Bushi jidao
jilu," the Chinese editors of the bamboo strips have interpreted 罷 through a
vague parallel from a *Guoyu* passage as 嗣 ("successor")—a meaning that
does not fit the present line of "Shi jiu."[63] Another occurrence of 罷 is in
the text of the E Jun Qi 鄂君啟 tallies, found in Shou Xian 壽縣 (Anhui)
and dated 323 B.C.E.; here, a considerable variety of interpretations of the
graph has been offered.[64] However, in the E Jun Qi, "Taiyi sheng shui," and
"Yu cong 4" texts, the reading of 罷 as 一 is probably the most persuasive
choice. By contrast, the graph seems to be used as a loan for 能 in the
Guodian "Cheng zhi wen zhi" manuscript. Most likely, the phonetic in 罷
is 能 [*nəŋ].[65] In the *Odes*, 能 rhymes with words of the rhyme category
之 (with final *-ə); 能 may thus also be reconstructed as *nəʔ.[66] However,
this still cannot phonologically explain the use of 罷 for 一 [*ʔjit].

儀 [*ŋjaj] and 義 [*ŋjajh] belong to the same *xiesheng* series; 宜
[*ŋjaj] is homophonous with and semantically closely related to 儀. For the
discussion of the final particles 氏 [*gjiʔ] / 兮 [*giʔ] / 也 [*ljajʔ], see the
discussion of the line in the "Zi yi" and "Kongzi shilun" manuscripts above.
The variant 氏 for 兮 occurs also in the following line from the same song:

Mao:	其子七兮	
Mawangdui:	其子七氏	(§ 7A)

"Yan yan" 燕燕 (Mao 28)

Mao:	燕燕于飛	
Mawangdui:	□□于蜚	(§ 7A)
Mawangdui:	嬰嬰于罪	(§ 7B)
Shuanggudui:	匽匽于非	(strips 21, 23)

The line is quoted twice in the Mawangdui manuscript. 蜚 [*pjəjʔ], 飛
[*mpjəj], and 非 [*pjəj] are homophonous; 罪 [*bjəjh] is near-homophonous, being within the same *Odes* rhyme group and sharing the labial
initial. The different words are also semantically related. The reduplicatives
燕燕 [*ʔians-ʔians] and 嬰嬰 (perhaps representing 嚶嚶 [*ʔiŋ-ʔiŋ]?) do not
share the same *Odes* rhyme group but might be sufficiently close in sound
to be interchangeable. The variant 匽匽 [*ʔians-ʔians] in the Shuanggudui
manuscript is homophonous with 燕燕. In the Shanghai Museum "Kongzi
shilun" manuscript (strip 10), the song "Yan yan" is also mentioned, here
written as 躴躴. As a member of the 晏 [*ʔjanʔ] *xiesheng* series, 躴 is perfectly interchangeable with 燕.

Mao:	泣涕女雨	
Guodian:	深涕女雨	(strip 17)
Mawangdui:	汲沸女雨	(§ 7A)

The Mawangdui variant 沸 [*mpjət] for Mao and Guodian 涕
[*thiəjʔ(h)] seems to be a scribal error, confusing two very similar graphs;
in another quotation of the same line in the Mawangdui "Wu xing"
manuscript, the text has, correctly, 涕. The variants 汲 [*kjəp] and 泣
[*khərjəp] are perfectly interchangeable; for the identification of the
respective character in the Guodian manuscript, Qiu Xigui suggests 深 (cf.
罙 *gləp],[67] which would seem again interchangeable with the Mao and
Mawangdui characters.

"Da ming" 大明 (Mao 236)

Mao:	赫赫在上	
Guodian:	虩虩才上	(strips 25–26)

| Mawangdui: | 堅堅在上 | (§ 17A) |
| Mawangdui: | 赤赤在嘗 | (§ 17B) |

The line appears twice in the Mawangdui manuscript. 在 [*dzəʔ] and 才 [*dzə] belong to the same *xiesheng* series. 上 [*djaŋ] and 嘗 [*djaŋ] are homophonous. The reduplicatives 赫赫 [*hərak-hərak], 虩虩 [虩虩] *hərjak-hərjak], 堅堅 [*hak-hak], and 赤赤 [*khljak] are all in the same rhyme group, with 赫 and 赤 also being in the same *xiesheng* series; the *k- in 赤 is velar, while the *h- in the other three cases is laryngeal. As velars and laryngeals are almost homorganic, their coincidence is generally accepted in loan characters.

| Mao: | 上帝臨女 | |
| Guodian: | 上帝賢女 | (strip 48) |

There is no phonetic or semantic relation between 臨 [*brjəm] and 賢 [*gin]. Qiu Xigui suspects that the latter is a scribal error for the former; comparing other occurrences of the two graphs in Chu manuscripts, I find this doubtful.[68] It is also possible to think of a genuine lexical variant: instead of the received "God on High is looking upon you," the Guodian text would read "God on High regards you as worthies." The second line of the couplet is the following:

Mao:	無貳爾心	
Guodian:	毌貳尔心	(strip 48)
Mawangdui:	毌膩爾心	(§ 26A)
Mawangdui:	毌澄壐心	(§ 26B)

While the homophonous negatives 無 [*mja] and 毌 [*mjə] are often interchanged, and 爾 / 尔 [*njajʔ] and 壐 belong to the same *xiesheng* series, I have no conclusive explanation for the variant 澄 instead of 貳 [*njəjh; 膩 is in the same *xiesheng* series with 貳]. Note that the *jing* section of the Mawangdui text has 膩 where the *shuo* section has 澄.[69]

"Wen wang" 文王 (Mao 235)

| Mao: | 於昭于天 | |
| Guodian: | □□于而 | (strip 30) |

There is no phonetic relation between 天 [*thin] and 而 [*njə]. However, paleographically, 天 and 而 are so extremely similar in Chu script that they occasionally have been confused by modern scholars.[70] If in the present case we accept the transcription of the graph as 而, we perhaps have to blame the scribe for his carelessness. The same problem is apparent in two other instances in the Guodian "Wu xing" text.[71] The present and following line are also quoted in the Shanghai Museum "Kongzi shilun."

Mao: 文王在上

Mawangdui: 文王在尚   (§ 18B)

上 [*djaŋh] and 尚 [*djaŋh] are homophonous and also semantically closely related.

"Chang fa" 長發 (Mao 304)

Mao: 不競不絿

Guodian: 不彊不㭫   (strip 41)

Mawangdui: 不勮不救   (§ 20A)

絿 [*gjəw], 㭫 [*gjəw], and 救 [*kjəwh] belong to the same *xiesheng* series. 競 [*gərjaŋh] and 彊 [彊] [*gjaŋ] are in the same *Odes* rhyme group, and both have the same velar initial. 勮 [*kjah or *gja(h)] also has a velar initial and the same main vowel as 競 and 彊 but not the *-ŋ final; in the Mawangdui manuscript, it is glossed as 彊 ("strong").

Mao: 不剛不柔

Guodian: 不彊不矛   (strip 41)

剛 [*kaŋ] and 彊 [彊] [*gjaŋ] are in the same rhyme group and both have a velar initial. While 柔 [*njəw; "flexible"] and 矛 [*mjəw; "lance"] are usually not considered to belong to the same *xiesheng* series and have no homorganic initials, the Guodian text obviously employs a simplified version of the graph 柔. In the present case, 矛 is to be taken not in its usual meaning ("lance") but as a character belonging to the 柔 *xiesheng* series. Not only in this *Odes* quotation but also in the sentence preceding it, the Guodian manuscript has 矛 where the Mawangdui manuscript has 柔.[72]

"Guan ju" 關雎 (Mao 1)

Mao: 窈窕淑女

Mawangdui: 苃芍□□   (§ 25B)

The assonating binome 窈窕 [*ʔiəwʔ-gliawʔ], in the variant 窈糾 [*ʔiəwʔ-kjawʔ] also attested in "Yue chu" 月出 (Mao 143), must be seen as interchangeable with 苃芍 [*kəraw-tiawk] despite the phonetic differences between 窈 and 苃.

Mao: 寤寐思服

Mawangdui: 唔眛思伏   (§ 25B)

寤 [*ŋah] and 唔 [*ŋah], as well as 寐 [*mjəs] and 眛 [*məs], belong to the same *xiesheng* series. 服 [*bjək] and 伏 [*bjək] are homophonous.

Mao: 悠哉悠哉

Mawangdui: 繇才繇才   (§ 25B)

悠 [*ljəw] and 繇 [*ljaw] differ in their rhyme groups. Nevertheless,

悠 and 遙 [*ljaw] have been proposed as interchangeable,[73] which would justify the paronomastic use of 繇 in the present case. The particles 哉 [*tsə] and 才 [*dzə] are near-homophonous.

Mao:	輾轉反側
Mawangdui:	婘槫反廁　　(§ 25B)

側 [*tsrjək] and 廁 [*tshrjə?h] belong to the same *xiesheng* series, as do 轉 [*mtrjuan?] and 槫 (it is not clear which word of the series the graph might represent). 輾 [*trjan?] and 婘 [*gərjuan; probably to be interpreted as 卷 (*-kjuan?)] share the same *Odes* rhyme group but differ in their initials (dental vs. velar). However, both 輾轉 and 婘槫 represent rhyming binomes and as such are likely to have written the same word.

In sum, the *Odes* quotations in the Guodian "Wu xing" manuscripts include eleven variants that are not in the same *xiesheng* series as their counterparts in the Mao recension. Eight of these variants represent paronomastic usages based on homophony or near-homophony. In one of these cases—虪虪 in "Da ming" 大明 (Mao 236)—a reduplicative is involved; the same reduplicative, corresponding to 赫赫 in the received *Odes*, also occurs in the "Jie nan shan" 節南山 (Mao 191) quotation of the Guodian "Zi yi" manuscript; in the Shanghai Museum "Zi yi," it is written as 虢虢. Apart from graphic variants that are phonetically related, the Guodian "Wu xing" manuscript contains three other cases: 而 for 天 is most likely either a writing mistake or has not been accurately identified in the modern transcription; 賢 for 臨 might be either a scribal error or a lexical variant; and 也 for 兮 represents a change of the final particle that cannot be explained phonologically.

The *Odes* quotations in the Mawangdui "Wu xing" include twenty-four variants outside the *xiesheng* series. Twenty-one of these are paronomastic, in three cases involving reduplicatives and in two cases occurring twice (繇才繇才). Three variants cannot be explained on phonological grounds: 沸 for 涕 is most likely a scribal error; 澄 for 貳 might represent a lexical variant; and 勴 for 競 is semantically but not phonetically or graphically related.

The Presence of the Oral in the Written:
Reflections on the Early History of the Odes

In their overwhelming majority, the Guodian, Shanghai Museum, and Mawangdui *Odes* variants can be regarded as graphic: they represent different characters that in any given case very likely write one and the same word. It should be noted that this assumption applies even more conclusively to variants within *xiesheng* series, some of which I have only mentioned in passing but which in fact far outnumber all other cases. Only in very few cases are we unable to determine the kind of phonetic relation that most likely suggests a paronomastic character use instead of a scribal error or a lexical variant. While allowing for the possibility that in some exceptional cases, a lexical variant might be hidden behind what appears to be merely a loan character, there is good reason to believe that most of these cases indeed represent paronomastic usages. Lexical variants do not need to be homophonous or near-homophonous. If they occurred with some frequency, we would hence expect a recognizable number of phonological distinctions. As this is not the case, we have no particular reason to engage in what would mostly amount to mere speculation.

On closer examination, it appears that especially with two types of words the relation between word and character was relatively loose: particles and rhyming or reduplicative binomes. The reduplicative 赫赫 [*hərak-hərak], for example, appears in the Guodian, Shanghai Museum, and Mawangdui quotations from "Jie nan shan" (Mao 191) and "Da ming" (Mao 236) as either 虩虩, 𧶠𧶠, 虎虎, 虖虖, 壑壑, or 赤赤. The reduplicative 仇仇 [*gjəw-gjəw] from "Zheng yue" (Mao 192) appears as 㤩㤩 in the Guodian and as 㑙㑙 in the Shanghai Museum "Zi yi." Similarly, 燕燕 [*ʔians-ʔians; in "Yan yan," Mao 28) is written 嬰嬰 (Mawangdui), 匽匽 (Shuanggudui), or 躬躬 (Shanghai Museum). In the quotations from "Cao chong" (Mao 14), 惙惙 [*trjuat-trjuat] appears as 役役, while 忡忡 [*thrjəwŋ-thrjəwŋ] is written 忪忪, 憧憧, or 沖沖; and the famous assonating binome in "Guan ju," 窈窕 [*ʔiəwʔ-gliawʔ], in the variant 窈糾 also attested in "Yue chu" 月出 (Mao 143), is written 茭芍 in Mawangdui. In the Shanghai Museum "Zi yi," the near-rhyming binome 緝熙 [*tshjəp-hjə] of the received text is written 幾義 [*kjəj-ŋjajh]. These and a string of other examples from our manuscripts show precisely the picture we get from other early texts with strong performative elements, like the Western Han *fu* 賦.[74] The unusual graphic instability of rhyming, alliterative, and reduplicative binomes suggests that their written form was by and large irrelevant, as long as they represented certain—and only approximate—aural values. Moreover, they disprove any straightforward interpretation of such binomes on the basis of the written form of their characters.[75]

The second group of words that appear with particular frequency as written in different ways are grammatical particles. They mostly, but not always, are phonetically related: 氏 and 是, 斯 and 此, 也 and 矣, 止 and 之, 氏 and 兮 or 也, 在 and 才, and 哉 and 才 are examples occurring in our manuscripts. These are usually unstressed syllables in their poetic lines, and even in the final position they often are not part of the rhyme scheme.[76] In many cases they seem to have contributed to poetic euphony primarily in rhythmic terms. That particles could be interchanged without being phonetically related shows furthermore that their characters were not necessarily aimed at the same word; this seems to indicate that particles in the *Odes* are employed in less strict a fashion than in the classical Chinese prose of the Warring States period. Moreover, in several cases of the Shanghai Museum "Zi yi" and "Kongzi shilun" manuscripts, the final 兮 is simply absent, resulting in a trisyllabic, and not the usual tetrasyllabic, meter.

Interchanged particles and binomes in the *Odes* did not rigorously adhere to the phonological principles seen in the paronomastic use of other words because the specific word behind a character, that is, a specific semantic value, is not in the same way at stake as in other words. In the case of an onomatopoeic reduplicative or euphonic rhyming binome, the sheer presence of sound overrules narrow semantic distinctions that would be considered important in other paronomastic usages of graphs where the crucial question was whether different written forms would still represent the very same word. Similarly, particles could have very different sounds, as long as they served to structure speech in rhythmic patterns.

Before moving to some suggestions on the transmission and reception of the *Odes* in late Warring States and early imperial times, it is useful to consider more specifically the transmission of the "Wu xing" text for the same period, as we can judge it from the two independent manuscript versions. (As noted above, I am reluctant to consider the Guodian and Shanghai Museum "Zi yi" manuscripts as mutually independent and therefore will not discuss them under this paradigm.) At present, I will not concern myself with the question of whether or not the additional *shuo* part from Mawangdui was composed only after the date of the Guodian tomb, that is, some time in the third or early second century B.C.E., and how this might tally with other philosophical and exegetical developments during this period. Instead, I am first of all interested in how the *jing* portion from

Mawangdui is related to that from Guodian. What is the evidence from the *Odes* quotations, and how is this evidence related to that of the embedding philosophical "Wu xing" texts proper?

Comparing the *Odes* variants in both manuscripts, one recognizes that, in all cases, the manuscripts differ not only from the Mao version but also from each other. Apart from these graphic differences, there are two other ways in which the two "Wu xing" versions differ in their treatment of the *Odes*. First, the Mawangdui text in four instances introduces a quotation with *shi yue* 詩曰 ("an *Ode* says").[77] This never occurs in the Guodian "Wu xing" version, although the Guodian "Zi yi" manuscript does include such introductory formulae, showing that they are not altogether a later phenomenon in referring to the *Odes*. Second, the Mawangdui quotations are in three instances significantly longer: for "Cao chong," the Mawangdui text has five lines (of which Guodian has only the last three), for "Shi jiu," it has four lines (Guodian only the last two), and for "Yan yan," it has six lines (Guodian only the very last). These three quotations are from the *guofeng*; from the *ya* and *song* sections, both "Wu xing" manuscripts quote only couplets.[78] The differences in the length of the quotations as well as in the introductory formulae provide some auxiliary, though weaker, evidence that the two manuscripts are independent instances of writing down a verbally highly coherent "Wu xing" text.[79]

Turning to the two "Wu xing" manuscripts as a whole and comparing their degree of graphic difference to that between their two sets of embedded *Odes* quotations, one finds a somewhat lower, yet still substantial, ratio of non-*xiesheng* variants. Most likely, this results from the different nature of archaic poetic diction versus late Warring States/early imperial philosophical discourse; the latter includes many of the most basic words of the Chinese language that certainly were less prone to be written in many different ways. Yet apart from their graphic variants, the two manuscripts differ occasionally (a) in the presence or absence of particles, (b) in some additional passages, mostly in the Mawangdui manuscript, that have no counterpart in the other text,[80] and (c) in the overall textual order. In the first of the altogether twenty-eight paragraphs distinguished by Ikeda and others, only a slight change in internal order can be discerned; but later on, whole paragraphs are arranged in a different sequence. In the Guodian manuscript, the twenty-eight Mawangdui *jing* paragraphs are arranged as follows: 1–9, 13, 10–12, 17–19, 14–16, 20–23, 25, 24, 26–28. The different order of the two manuscripts has been interpreted as a reflection of two different philosophical arguments; at least one of the two manuscript sponsors chose to change the order of whatever the original sequence—possibly yet another one—may have been. [81] Be this as it may, and despite their geographical proximity, the two manuscripts represent two written versions of the "Wu xing" text that distinctly differ from each other in orthography and in textual order. In its philosophical orientation as well as in its way of using the *Odes*, the "Wu xing" essay is obviously connected with the fourth- and third-century B.C.E. Ru 儒 philosophical discourse and may itself have exerted a certain influence on it. [82] We should therefore not be surprised if more versions of the text were to surface in future excavations.

Similarly, comparing the Guodian and Shanghai Museum "Zi yi" manuscripts with their *Liji* counterpart, we see substantial graphic differences as well as a very different textual order. This is perfectly in line with other known manuscripts that have transmitted counterparts, like the three Guodian manuscripts containing passages known from the *Laozi* 老子, the *Yi* 易 manuscript from Mawangdui, [83] or the *Odes* from Shuanggudui.

How can we best explain the actual relation between the two "Wu xing" versions? Obviously, the Mawangdui scribe could not have looked at the very Guodian text we see today, as it had already been buried for about a century. But is the Mawangdui text copied from a written text closely resembling the Guodian version? What did the Mawangdui scribe look at? Did he look at anything at all? There are at least three possible scenarios under which such manuscripts could have been produced: (a) a scribe copied from another written version; (b) somebody used a written version to read the text aloud to the scribe; or (c) a scribe wrote the text from memory or oral recitation. [84]

The first scenario would ideally lead to a text with very few, if any, differences between the earlier and the new version. This, clearly, is not the case here. The textual differences between the two "Wu xing" manuscripts, between the Guodian and Shanghai Museum "Zi yi" and their *Liji* counterpart, and between the manuscript *Odes* quotations and their received text are in all cases both numerous and substantial. But what if the copyists were just careless or even somewhat lacking in competence? Given the nature of the Chinese script, we would expect graphically similar characters, but these would represent not merely different words but *words of very different sounds*. In the manuscripts under discussion, we see the opposite: *very different graphs* representing words of identical or near-identical sounds that mostly fulfill the rigid criteria of paronomastic use. There is no way in which a Mawangdui copyist following a written model related to the Guodian texts could consistently arrive at this type of textual variant.

Moreover, even the variants in our manuscripts that are not phonetically related are in most cases graphically so different that they still cannot be interpreted as cursory misreadings of a hurried copyist, while even those exceptional cases where this would be possible can still be taken as scribal errors that would occur under any circumstances, with or without a written model. Scribal errors are not necessarily copyist's errors.

The second scenario would account better for the actual evidence. In this case, however, we would still conclude that no particular attention was given to graphic consistency between the earlier and the later version, because these two, as a quality control measure, could have been compared instantaneously. As a result, we would expect a certain number of corrections in the later text—but they are not there.[85] Thus, although an earlier written model may have served to contain the text, it cannot have provided a standard to write it. Yet graphically independent as they are from their possible earlier models,[86] the manuscripts still betray a definite attention to the aesthetics of their outward appearance: expensive silk in the case of Mawangdui, beautifully balanced calligraphy in those of Guodian and the Shanghai Museum. This attention, however, is devoted not to graphic "correctness" (if there was any such concept at all) but to the texts as exquisite items of display.

The third scenario would tally equally well with the evidence: a text was written down from memory or as it was heard. There was no written model at hand to begin with and to which the new version had to, or possibly could, adhere. Instead, this version represented a singular local act of writing, independent of any other such act.

On the basis of our texts, it seems impossible to decide between the second and the third alternative. It perhaps is not even necessary, as both scenarios share the same basic implication: with or without a written model at hand, we cannot identify an attempt at orthographic consistency. Instead, the written text—in addition to being a display item—served its most elementary function: to represent the sounds of the language. The problem is the very substantial number of early Chinese homophonous words written not only with partly different graphs (as in the case of members of the same *xiesheng* series) but with entirely unrelated ones. Paronomastic variants of a caliber as discussed above or as in 州 for 舟 [both *tjəw], 居 [*kjah, *kja] for 車 [*khlja, *kəlja], and 騷 [*səw] for 埽 [*səwʔ]—to mention just some examples from the Shuanggudui *Odes*[87]—illustrate the challenge: even an educated reader who would know that these graphs represented the same (or nearly the same) sounds was confronted with a written textual surface that was not self-evident with respect to the specific words behind it. In order to decide on the right word, the reader indeed would have to already know the text or would need somebody to explain it to him or her. [88] Where did this knowledge come from? How did one master a text that on its written surface alone could be quite opaque? The best answer to such questions is perhaps a traditional one: we know from Warring States and early imperial sources that textual learning was conducted in teacher-disciple lineages, that is, through direct instruction. Indeed, the vast number of possible loan characters in the writing system—as we now see them in the manuscripts—made teaching and memorization not only a priority in the reception and transmission of texts but a plain sine qua non. This is true for contemporaneous prose compositions like the "Wu xing" text; it applies all the more to poetic texts like the *Odes*, characterized by an archaic diction, difficult words, and the general absence of particles. Judging from the manuscript evidence, the dialogical master-disciple exchange that provides the structure for many early Chinese philosophical texts is more than a rhetorical gesture; it is a reflection of how things were done.

Han historical texts are replete with remarks that in the early empire, the works of the traditional canon were orally "discussed" (*lun* 論), "expounded" (*yan* 言), "practiced" (*xi* 習), "explained" (*shuo* 説, *jiang* 講), and, as expression of their "mastery" (*zhi* 治), "recited" (*song* 誦). [89] Such practices of instruction and performance were directly inherited from earlier times, if one recalls the frequent instances of ritual *Odes* recitation in the *Zuo zhuan*, of Confucius speaking of "reciting the three hundred *Odes*," [90] or of *Mozi* mentioning those who "recite the three hundred, play the three hundred with strings, sing the three hundred, dance the three hundred." [91]

The oral use of texts is further reflected in the fact that the works of the Six Arts (Liu yi 六藝, including *yue* 樂, music, which may or may not have been a written canon) [92] and Five Canons (Wu jing 五經) were not transmitted as isolated scriptures but always embedded in an exegetical tradition deemed necessary to transform an archaic and hermeneutically open text into a repertoire of historical paradigms of continual relevance. [93] As the canonical works provided ultimate standards to measure and guide contemporary social practice, exegetical teaching both reaffirmed their elevated status and constructed the necessary bridge by which they could be approached. This is definitely true for the archaic works of the *Odes*, the *Documents*, and the *Changes* but might as well have been extended to contemporaneous texts of a certain status, namely, texts to be transmitted. The strong oral element in the practice of teaching and passing on the canon, reflected in the use of the verbs listed above, does not preclude the use of written versions. But if our sources do not mislead us, these written versions were considered neither the primary goal nor the principal vehicle of this practice. The evidence from the manuscripts may thus illustrate both: the existence of written texts and their integration into practices of oral instruction.[94]

By placing the *Odes* into such a context of early canonical teaching and transmission, the large number of textual variants in their manuscript quotations becomes less disturbing. Moreover, these variants—whether between two manuscripts or a manuscript and the received anthology—are in their vast majority paronomastic, a fact aptly mirrored in the host of paronomastic glosses delivered by the early imperial commentators. Whatever the originally intended words behind such graphic variants may be, we can safely conclude that the received transmission of the *Odes* through the Mao recension is astoundingly faithful in its representation of the original sounds of the text. We should also note that the manuscripts limit their *Odes* quotations almost entirely to songs that appear in the received text, and that they quote them as proof texts to support specific philosophical arguments. In sum, by the late fourth century B.C.E., the *Odes* were the most prestigious Chinese text, they had reached a high degree of canonization, and they were largely fixed in their wording.

At the same time, it seems impossible to argue for a standard written version of the *Odes* in Warring States times. We tend to acknowledge this in some general sense, based on what we know from the literary tradition;[95] yet only the manuscript evidence shows us the true extent to which early written versions of the *Odes* could actually differ. Furthermore, they are a helpful reminder of the fact that *all* received pre–Qin texts went through the hands of Han and later editors. For none of these texts that quote more or less extensively from the *Odes*—*Zuo zhuan* 左傳, *Xunzi* 荀子, *Liji* 禮記, *Guoyu* 國語, *Lunyu* 論語, *Mengzi* 孟子, *Mozi* 墨子, *Yanzi chunqiu* 晏子春秋, *Zhanguo ce* 戰國策, *Lüshi chunqiu* 呂氏春秋, *Guanzi* 管子, *Han Feizi* 韓非子, *Xiaojing* 孝經[96]—can our received version be traced back beyond the first printed editions. These date from the Song period—twelve or more centuries after the original composition of their texts. Similar to the low percentage of known *san jia* variants, the overall graphic coherence of *Odes* quotations in these texts suggests a pervasive Han or post–Han standardization according to the Mao recension.

There are also more particular reasons for questioning the orthographic uniformity of early *Odes* quotations in received texts as being original. Due to their archaic diction, the *Odes* were perhaps more, not less, prone to be written in widely diverging ways than other texts endowed with a history of transmission. Yet because of their canonical status and thus relatively stable framework of learning, their actual written form may also have mattered less than that of contemporary prose. Scribal casualness—something that has been recognized in certain early manuscripts[97]—did not ruin the text as long as the graphs represented words of the right sound. On the other hand, this seems to open the view on a much more diverse world of writing than the one suggested by the uniformity of *Odes* quotations across the broad range of received ancient texts. Even where two manuscripts come from the same old region of Chu and contain largely the same materials, as in the case of the two "Wu xing" manuscripts from Guodian and Mawangdui (and to a significantly lesser degree in that of the Guodian and Shanghai Museum "Zi yi"), their *Odes* quotations are written in such different fashion that it is hard to imagine how they could possibly reflect a unified written *Odes* corpus as their basis. In sum, for the late pre-imperial and early imperial period, we witness the double phenomenon of a canonical text that is as stable in its wording as it is unstable in its writing.

From the use of writing in administrative, economic, legal, divinatory, hemerological, medical, and a number of other practical matters, all of them documented in excavated manuscripts,[98] it is clear that writing was widely employed as an important technology. The earliest testimony to this technology is supplied by the Shang oracle bone and plastron inscriptions, from which we already know the existence of a group of writing specialists.[99] For Western Zhou times, it has been compellingly argued that bronze inscriptions were composed on the basis of archives that were kept on perishable materials, and there is every reason to assume the presence of specialized scribes in charge of both archival records and inscriptions.[100]

On the other hand, it seems to me that, for early China, the later Chinese tradition as well as modern scholarship in its wake has sometimes exaggerated the status of writing at the expense of all other forms of human cultural practice, notably among them the performance of texts.[101] If the early Chinese had any desire to mass-produce those early texts that were manifestly recognized as canonical by the late fourth century B.C.E., they certainly had the means to accomplish such an endeavor in the same way as they were able to locally mass-produce all kinds of weapons, tools, ritual objects, and also administrative writings.[102] We are still looking for some more suggestive traces of such textual mass production than we have glanced so far from both the literary tradition and the archaeological record.

Indeed, before the empire, early Chinese authors rarely cared to emphasize the cultural status of written texts. We find an occasional note here and there:[103] in *Mozi* 墨子, Master Mo is once seen carrying "very many writings" (*zai shu shen duo* 載書甚多) while traveling;[104] in several other places, the same text reiterates the importance of writing to preserve and transmit knowledge.[105] In a *Zhuangzi* 莊子 passage of possibly early Han times, it is noted (and despised) that important words are generally put into writing, and that writings are therefore held in esteem.[106] And in *Han Feizi*, Master Han Fei argues that when families "store" (*cang* 藏) legalist and military writings, they spend their time talking about these matters instead of engaging in them; by contrast, in the land of an enlightened ruler there are no writings on bamboo (*wu shujian zhi wen* 無書簡之文).[107] But there are no reports about the practice of copying texts, about presenting texts (in the way bronze vessels, weapons, clothing, or *Odes* performances were presented), about forging, stealing, losing, buying, exchanging, or arguing over written texts, or about whatever else one may imagine. Even as late as in Eastern Han times, pictorial representations of reading books are exceedingly rare.[108] There is no question about the canonical status and wide circulation of particular texts, about a certain degree of elite literacy, or about the use of writing in numerous local contexts. That canonical and other texts were written down is attested by our manuscripts; that writing was used as a form of cultural display is evident from Shang oracle bones as well as from sometimes quite spectacular bronze inscriptions (one may just think of the beautiful characters, inlaid in gold, on the mid–fifth-century B.C.E. bells buried with Marquis Yi of Zeng 曾侯乙). That prior to the Han writing was indeed *the primary and most prestigious form* of representing and transmitting the canonical texts has yet to be shown. Whenever Warring States texts of the Ru 儒 tradition wish to present cultural mastery, they describe it as the mastery of ritual propriety and as the use of texts as one aspect in the expression of ritual propriety.[109] The kings, nobles, scholars, and philosophers who in our early sources are shown as memorizing, performing, and teaching the canon in general, and the *Odes* in particular, are masters of texts as they are masters of ritual. As Confucius reminds us, to know the *Odes* without being able to apply them in diplomatic exchange is but an idle exercise.[110] Did any of the nobles mentioned in *Zuo zhuan*, when prompted for an *Odes* recitation, excuse himself for a moment to nervously rush through his piles of bamboo strips? Did Confucius need to look things up in order to be left neither with "nothing to use in speech" nor "standing with the face straight to the wall"?[111]

Trusting the sources, I believe it is this sure mastery of the text, internalized through memorization and externalized in performance, that guaranteed the stable tradition of the canon and that allowed scholars and nobles alike to make sense of *Odes* quotations (Guodian, Shanghai Museum, Mawangdui), *Odes* discussions (Shanghai Museum), or the whole anthology (Shuanggudui) in whatever idiosyncratic and local fashion of writing they came. While a good portion of these written versions may have looked aberrant and opaque to the uninitiated, they were perfectly coherent and transparent to those who knew. Written versions of the anthology like the one found at Shuanggudui, and perhaps written discussions of the *Odes* like the one obtained by the Shanghai Museum, will have played their role in the transmission of the *Odes*. At the same time, it is hard to imagine how this transmission could have worked without being embedded in adequate oral instruction.

But why were texts related to the *Odes* and other (philosophical, technical, etc.) writings buried in tombs, alongside a host of ritual paraphernalia? We do not really know. Let me venture a suggestion: the deceased was a sponsor and custodian of learning, and the usually eclectic selection of texts reflects to some extent this person's sponsorship or even mastery of certain philosophical, religious, and technical matters. In their exquisite calligraphy (Guodian, Shanghai Museum) and materiality (the silk in Mawangdui), the entombed texts were perhaps ritual commodities of representational value. In the dark splendor of the grave chamber, and entirely beyond the notion of orthographic "correctness," these manuscripts pleased the eyes of the spirits, contributing to the material splendor that surrounded the dead. In life, true mastery of poetry and philosophical discourse found its ultimate expression in oral performance. The elegant manuscript, perhaps, was its adequate visual form. In death, it was the only one.

NOTES

I am grateful to Wolfgang Behr, William G. Boltz, Michael Nylan, Andrew H. Plaks, and Nathan Sivin for their very helpful comments on earlier versions of this chapter.

1. Volume two, published only after the present study was completed, contains several additional *Odes* quotations in the manuscript "Min zhi fumu" 民之父母. They do not contradict the present conclusions.
2. Lewis, *Writing and Authority in Early China*, 168.
3. Important studies on *Odes* interpretation in the Mawangdui "Wu xing" 五

行 silk manuscript include Riegel, "Eros, Introversion, and the Beginnings of
Shijing Commentary," and Cook, "Consummate Artistry and Moral Virtuosity."
Following the Princeton conference, I have extended my findings from the
present study to issues of early *Odes* exegesis; see Kern, "Early Chinese Poetics
in the Light of Recently Excavated Manuscripts," where I relate some
fundamental interpretative differences to the only-gradual development of a
standardized written version of the anthology.

   4. A full discussion of the Shuanggudui variants can be found in Hu and Han,
Fuyang Han jian Shijing yanjiu.

   5. For the same conclusion, see O Man-jong, *Cong shi dao jing*, 132–137.

   6. For a survey of early archaeological sites with manuscripts, see Giele,
Database of Early Chinese Manuscripts. For my various arguments regarding the
status of the written text and its relation to oral performance in early China, see
my *The Stele Inscriptions of Ch'in Shih huang*, 94–104, 143–144; "Feature:
Mark Edward Lewis, *Writing and Authority in Early China*"; "*Shi jing* Songs as
Performance Texts"; "Ritual, Text, and the Formation of the Canon"; and
"Western Han Aesthetics and the Genesis of the *Fu.*"

   7. For some succinct comments on the philological problems in dealing
with the Mao recension, see Knechtges, "Questions about the Language of *Sheng
Min.*"

   8. On this work, see Hightower, *Han Shih Wai Chuan*; on the relation
between the *Han Odes* and those of the other lineages, see Hightower, "The *Han
shih wai chuan* and the *San chia shih*," and Lin, *Xi Han sanjia shixue yanjiu.*

   9. For an exemplary study of *Lu Shi* exegesis, see Asselin, "The Lu–School
Reading of 'Guanju.'"

   10. *Shijing yiwen shi.* The work was later complemented by Zhang Shenyi
張慎儀 (Guangxu [1875–1908] period) in *Shijing yiwen bushi.*

   11. *Shijing si jia yiwen kao.* The work was later complemented by Jiang
Han 江瀚 (fl. ca. 1875) in his *Shijing si jia yiwen kao bu.*

   12. *Shi san jia yi jishu.*

   13. For the Shuanggudui fragments, I base myself on Hu and Han, *Fuyang
Han jian Shijing yanjiu*; for references to individual passages, I give the number
of the respective bamboo strip fragment.

   14. Hightower, "The *Han shih wai chuan* and the *San chia shih*," 245, also
notes differences in sequence between the Mao recension and the *Han Shi
waizhuan.*

   15. As argued by Hu and Han, *Fuyang Han jian Shijing yanjiu*, 28–35. The
evidence Hu and Han cite for the different order of the songs in the Shuanggudui
recension is one of the marvelous details of archaeological finds: because the
cords that originally linked the bamboo strips are all rotten, and because each
strip, or pair of two strips, never contained text from more than one stanza, it is
now impossible to determine the overall sequence of individual stanzas, let alone
of songs or whole *guofeng* sections. However, because adjacent strips pressed
against one another in the tomb, there are ten cases (in six groups of strips)
where one strip carries on its back traces of the text from the front of another
strip, establishing the direct sequence of these strips and showing that the
internal order of the Shuanggudui *Odes* differed from that of the Mao recension.

16. For the Mawangdui "Wu xing" text, I base myself on Ikeda, *Maōtai Kanbo hakusho gogyōhen kenkyū*. For another transcription of the Guodian and the Mawangdui "Wu xing" manuscripts, as well as for their comparison, see also Pang, *Zhu bo "Wu xing" pian jiaozhu ji yanjiu*, 1–87, and Liu Xinfang, *Jianbo Wu xing jiegu*. For the quotations, I give the paragraph (*zhang* 章 [= §]) numbers according to Ikeda, with "A" denoting the *jing* 經 and "B" denoting the *shuo* 説 sections; thus, "§ 5A" denotes *zhang* 5, *jing* section.

17. See Riegel, "Eros, Introversion, and the Beginnings of *Shijing* Commentary"; Cook, "Consummate Artistry and Moral Virtuosity."

18. For the Guodian manuscripts, I base myself on Jingmen shi bowuguan, *Guodian Chu mu zhujian*; for the "Zi yi" text, see 129–137, for the "Wu xing" text, 149–154. For the quotations, I give the number of the respective bamboo strips.

19. *Bangfeng* is likely the original name, changed to *guofeng* only after 195 B.C.E., when *bang* became tabooed as the late Han founding emperor's (Liu Bang 劉邦, posthumously Han Gaozu 漢高祖, r. 202–195 B.C.E.) given name.

20. For the "Zi yi" and "Kongzi shilun" manuscripts, I base myself on Ma Chengyuan, *Shanghai bowuguan cang Zhanguo Chu zhushu (yi)*.

21. By contrast, the Shanghai Museum "Kongzi shilun" seems to discuss whole songs, while occasionally referring to one of their stanzas; see Ma Chengyuan, *Shanghai bowuguan cang Zhanguo Chu zhushu (yi)*, 143 (strip 14), 155 (strip 25).

22. I am counting reduplicatives as two characters; on the other hand, I do not count the frequent writing convention 亓 for 其 as a variant.

23. For the *san jia* recensions, I base myself on the notes provided in Wang Xianqian, *Shi san jia yi jishu*.

24. For a critique of the rather arbitrary methods employed by Chen Qiaocong, see Hightower, "The *Han shih wai chuan* and the *San chia shih*," 252–253 n. 26.

25. The exception is the relation between the Guodian and the Shanghai Museum "Zi yi" texts: twenty-eight of the sixty-seven variants in the Shanghai Museum manuscript coincide with their counterparts in the Guodian text. This coherence corresponds with the overall appearance of the two "Zi yi" manuscripts: in addition to sharing many of their graphic peculiarities, they are of precisely the same length, contents, and internal textual order (and exhibit the same differences from the received "Zi yi" in the *Liji*). Furthermore, all of this applies to the relation between the Guodian "Xing zi ming chu" 性自命出 and the Shanghai Museum "Xing qing lun" 性情論 manuscripts—and all of it is entirely unprecedented among independently found manuscripts or a manuscript and its received counterpart. The evidence thus corroborates the suspicion (Ma Chengyuan, *Shanghai bowuguan cang Zhanguo Chu zhushu (yi)*, 2) that the Shanghai Museum strips—which began to appear on the Hong Kong market just a few months after the Guodian manuscript excavation of late 1993—may indeed have come from the Guodian area (or even site?) we are already familiar with.

26. *Hanshu* 30.1708.

27. E.g., Hightower, "The *Han shih wai chuan* and the *San chia shih*," 265: "From citations referred to each of the schools it is clear that there were minor

textual variants, frequently only alternative graphs for the same word. This is precisely the situation one would expect to obtain with a text written from memory by different hands."

28. Baxter, *A Handbook of Old Chinese Phonology*, 355–366.

29. *Shiji* 6.254–255, 87.2546.

30. The versions studied by the imperial erudites were exempted from the ban. On the historicity and meaning of the bibliocaust, see my *The Stele Inscriptions of Ch'in Shih huang*, 183–196, with further references given there.

31. These considerations, of course, speak directly against Hightower's conclusion quoted in n. 27 above.

32. With regard to the Chu script, Teng, *Chu xi jianbo wenzi bian*, and the corrections of this work given by Li Ling, "Du 'Chu xi jianbo wenzi bian,'" provide ample assurance.

33. For a discussion of the phenomenon of the *xiesheng* series, see Boltz, *The Origin and Early Development of the Chinese Writing System*, 90–126. In *Loan Characters in Pre-Han Texts*, 1–9, Bernhard Karlgren explicitly excludes characters belonging to the same *xiesheng* series from his analysis of possible loan characters (*jiajie zi* 假借字) since they are by their very nature "authorized" to be used paronomastically for one another. However, there are instances where characters in the same *xiesheng* series show distinct phonetic differences and are not mutually interchangeable as loan characters. Yet these instances are rare enough to not disqualify the general assumption about the overwhelming majority of *xiesheng* variants, and leaving them aside here does not disqualify the particular analysis and argument put forward in the present chapter. I am grateful to Wolfgang Behr for alerting me to the complexity of the issue; see also his "'Homosomatic Juxtaposition' and the Problem of 'Syssemantic (*Huiyi*) Characters."

34. See Boltz, "Manuscripts with Transmitted Counterparts," 258–262.

35. On the latter, see Ma Chengyuan, *Shanghai bowuguan cang Zhanguo Chu zhushu (yi)*, 174. The same variant occurs also in other *Odes* quotations in the Shanghai Museum "Zi yi" (strips 21, 22); below, I will not treat this form as a genuine variant.

36. The 氏 / 是 example seems not to follow the principle of homorganicity (see below) as *g- is a velar and *d- is a dental initial. However, as Boltz has argued, paleographic evidence from pre-imperial texts suggests reconstructing 是 also with the *g- initial; see Boltz, *The Origin and Early Development of the Chinese Writing System*, 169.

37. Schuessler, *A Dictionary of Early Zhou Chinese*.

38. See Karlgren, *Loan Characters in Pre-Han Texts*, 1–18.

39. See Boltz, *The Origin and Early Development of the Chinese Writing System*, 90–101.

40. See Karlgren, "Glosses on the Siao ya Odes," 116–118 (no. 618).

41. Karlgren, *Grammata Serica Recensa*, nos. 961, 962 (hereafter cited in the pattern "*GSR* 961, 962"]; Schuessler, *A Dictionary of Early Zhou Chinese*, 829–831, 835–836; Baxter, *A Handbook of Old Chinese Phonology*, 809.

42. *GSR* 1165a–c.

43. Here and elsewhere, the editors of the Guodian strips mistakenly

transcribe as 弌 what should be 戈; see Jingmen shi bowuguan, *Guodian Chu mu zhujian*, 18, 20, 130–131. (I am grateful to Wolfgang Behr for alerting me to the problem.) This, however, does not affect the interpretation as 一; see He Linyi, *Zhanguo guwen zidian*, 1080, who argues that the element 戈 in the numerals "one," "two," and "three" goes back to 戌. Xu Shen 許慎 (ca. 55–ca. 149) in his *Shuowen jiezi* 說文解字 explains 弌 as an old form of 一 [*?jit]; see *Shuowen jiezi zhu* 1A.1b. That 戈 is indeed used for 一 in both instances is clear from the transmitted parallels: in the above line from "Shi jiu," the *Mao Shi* parallel is 一; in the text on strip 17, the parallel is 壹 (the usual long form of 一 in transmitted texts) in the received *Liji* chapter; see Jingmen shi bowuguan, *Guodian Chu mu zhujian*, 130, and *Liji zhengyi* 55.420b. Also, the Shanghai Museum "Zi yi" (strip 20) has 一 in this very quotation; see Ma Chengyuan, *Shanghai bowuguan cang Zhanguo Chu zhushu (yi)*, 64, 195. In the Guodian manuscripts, 戈 appears in the same way further on strip 14 of the "Qiong da yi shi" 窮達以時 manuscript, on strip 9 of the "Xing zi ming chu" 性自命出 manuscript, and on strips 39, 40, and 43 of the "Liu de" 六德 manuscript, in all cases transcribed as 弌 by the Guodian editors. See Jingmen shi bowuguan, *Guodian Chu mu zhujian*, 28, 61, 72, 145, 179, 188.

44. *Shuowen jiezi zhu* 2A.49a–b.

45. For the traditional discussion of 覺 / 梏, see Karlgren, "Glosses on the Siao ya Odes," 69 (no. 503).

46. For the same variant, see also below in another quotation from "Yi." The variant 誓 occurs in several other places in the Guodian corpus, e.g., on strip 11 of the "Laozi" 老子 "A" manuscript; see Jingmen shi bowuguan, *Guodian Chu mu zhujian*, 111, and Qiu Xigui's comment (115 n. 30).

47. See Jingmen shi bowuguan, *Guodian Chu mu zhujian*, 179, 181. Qiu Xigui (182 n. 17) notes that 頌 is the original character for 容. See also Zheng Xuan's paronomastic gloss in his *Zhou li* 周禮 commentary that "the meaning of 頌 is 誦, or 容" (*Zhou li zhushu* 23.158a).

48. The reconstruction for 尹 is unclear. For Karlgren, 允 and 尹 were homophonous; see *GSR* 468a and 1251. Dong, *Shanggu yinyun biaogao*, 220, lists the two characters in the same rhyme group and tone but with different initials. For the appearance of these variants earlier in the "Zi yi," see Jingmen shi bowuguan, *Guodian Chu mu zhujian*, 129 (with discussion at 132 n. 15 and 135 n. 90); and Ma Chengyuan, *Shanghai bowuguan cang Zhanguo Chu zhushu (yi)*, 177.

49. Jingmen shi bowuguan, *Guodian Chu mu zhujian*, 135 n. 91.

50. See Teng, *Chu xi jianbo wenzi bian*, 350; Zhang Shouzhong et al., *Guodian Chu jian wenzi bian*, 77–78.

51. For a discussion, see Karlgren, "Glosses on the Kuo Feng Odes," 86 (no. 2).

52. While the reconstruction shows a difference in vowel between 囡 and 攝, the Shanghai Museum editors cite a "du ruo" 讀若 ("read as") gloss from the *Shuowen jiezi* that equates 囡 phonetically with 聶 [*njap]; see Ma Chengyuan, *Shanghai bowuguan cang Zhanguo Chu zhushu (yi)*, 198–199.

53. Here, I count reduplicatives as only a single variant. On the other hand, I count each individual case of the same variant. In addition to the variants

discussed here, the *Odes* quotations in the Guodian "Zi yi" manuscript have one instance of character displacement in "Qiao yan" 巧言 (Mao 198), one completely different line in "Du ren shi" 都人士 (Mao 225), and one passage unattested in the received *Odes* text. All these are textual variants, but not on the level of the single graph. Finally, there is also one unintelligible graph in "Du ren shi," not counted here.

54. I do not include the missing character in "Wen wang" in this number. Also, I do not count the two missing particles in "Yi" that result in a change from tetrasyllabic to trisyllabic meter.

55. See Ma Chengyuan, *Shanghai bowuguan cang Zhanguo Chu zhushu (yi)*, 133.

56. See Wang Xianqian, *Shi san jia yi jishu*, 396.

57. Ma Chengyuan, *Shanghai bowuguan cang Zhanguo Chu zhushu (yi)*, 152.

58. See Wang Xianqian, *Shi san jia yi jishu*, 76.

59. Ibid., 75.

60. See He, *Zhanguo guwen zidian*, 77.

61. See Jingmen shi bowuguan, *Guodian Chu mu zhujian*, 125, 167, 218.

62. See Allan and Williams, *The Guodian Laozi*, 119.

63. Hubei sheng Jingsha tielu kaogu dui, *Baoshan Chu jian*, 32 and 53 n. 359.

64. See the translation and annotation by Lothar von Falkenhausen in chapter 3.

65. In agreement with He, *Zhanguo guwen zidian*, 77.

66. See *GSR* 885; Schuessler, *A Dictionary of Early Zhou Chinese*, 438; Baxter, *A Handbook of Old Chinese Phonology*, 687 ("Bin zhi chu yan" 賓之初筵; Mao 220) and 717 ("Sang rou" 桑柔; Mao 257).

67. See Jingmen shi bowuguan, *Guodian Chu mu zhujian*, 152 n. 19.

68. See Teng, *Chu xi jianbo wenzi bian*, 515, 678–679.

69. As Ikeda, *Maōtai Kanbo hakusho gogyōhen kenkyū*, 554–555, notes, none of the editors of, or commentators on, the Mawangdui "Wu xing" manuscript has been able to explain the variant 澄. This remains true for those who wrote after him, like Pang Pu and Liu Xinfang.

70. See Zeng, *Changsha Chu boshu wenzi bian*, nos. 30 and 75.

71. Namely, on strips 20 and 26; see Jingmen shi bowuguan, *Guodian Chu mu zhujian*, 150. The problem also appears in the Mawangdui "Wu xing" manuscript; see Ikeda, *Maōtai Kanbo hakusho gogyōhen kenkyū*, 364.

72. See Jingmen shi bowuguan, *Guodian Chu mu zhujian*, 151 (strip 41); Ikeda, *Maōtai Kanbo hakusho gogyōhen kenkyū*, 419.

73. See Karlgren, *Loan Characters in Pre-Han Texts*, no. 1994.

74. See Kamatani, "Fu ni nankai na ji ga ōi no wa naze ka"; Kern, "Western Han Aesthetics and the Genesis of the *Fu*."

75. This conclusion supports earlier findings made in transmitted texts; see Kennedy, "A Note on Ode 220"; Knechtges, *Wen xuan, or Selections of Refined Literature*, vol. 2, 3–12.

76. The manuscript quotations include the following variants in the final position of a line: 之 / 止 (in "Cao chong"), 兮 / 也 / 氏 ("Shi jiu"), and 才 / 哉

("Guan ju"). In all cases, they do not seem to belong to the rhyme pattern; see Baxter, *A Handbook of Old Chinese Phonology*, 583, 587, 641. There are, however, other instances in the *Odes* where such particles do rhyme; see Baxter, *A Handbook of Old Chinese Phonology*, 809; Takashima, "The So-called 'Third'-Person Possessive Pronoun *Jue* 氒 (= 厥) in Classical Chinese," 418.

77. See Ikeda, *Maōtai Kanbo hakusho gogyōhen kenkyū*, 187, 364, 419, 546 (here in the form 設曰).

78. In its *shuo* part, the Mawangdui manuscript also quotes three couplets from "Guan ju" but separates them from one another by brief comments; see Ikeda, *Maōtai Kanbo hakusho gogyōhen kenkyū*, 533.

79. The evidence from the latter two differences seems weaker because the Mawangdui version could simply include some additions to the preceding one from Guodian. But this is excluded by the evidence from the graphic variants.

80. The Mawangdui text contains four passages of forty-two, five, eight, and twelve characters that are not in the Guodian version; on the other hand, the latter has one passage of ten characters not included in the former.

81. See Xing, "Chu jian 'Wu xing' shi lun"; Pang, *Zhu bo "Wu xing" pian jiaozhu ji yanjiu*, 92.

82. The importance of the "Wu xing" text can be measured on two accounts: on the one hand, the text appears in two versions that are separated by about a century. This means it was transmitted over an extended period of time. On the other hand, the second version contains a commentary, signaling the importance of the base text. The vast majority of the hundreds of Chinese articles and book chapters that have appeared on the Guodian manuscripts since their publication in 1998 is devoted to relating these texts to the contemporaneous philosophical literature.

83. See Shaughnessy, *I Ching*. Despite Ban Gu's claim (*Hanshu* 30.1704) that the *Yi* survived the bibliocaust intact because works on divination were exempted from destruction (*Shiji* 6.255, 87.2546–2547), the textual differences between an early imperial *Yi* manuscript version and its transmitted counterpart are exactly the same as in the cases of those texts that purportedly had suffered from the bibliocaust.

84. I am grateful to Christoph Harbsmeier and Nathan Sivin, who independently from each other have alerted me to scenario b; see also Sivin, "Text and Experience in Classical Chinese Medicine." The practice of having one person read out loud a text to have it written down by one or more scribes is of course nothing new for scholars of Greek and Roman classical literature; see, e.g., Nagy, *Poetry as Performance*, 149–150.

85. For the very few instances of corrections in the Guodian and Shanghai Museum manuscripts, see Kern, "Methodological Reflections."

86. This is probably true already for the Guodian and Shanghai Museum manuscripts, assuming that they are not the very first versions of their texts.

87. Strips 35, 45, 49, 50, 53, 114, 142; see Hu and Han, *Fuyang Han jian Shijing yanjiu*, 5–7, 14, 18.

88. Similarly, Andrew Ford has noted for ancient Greece that manuscripts of archaic songs lacked, among other things, "conveniences for reading, including a standard orthography. Altogether, a lyric song-text of the archaic period was

fairly useless to anyone who had not already heard the song"; see Ford, "From Letters to Literature," 21.

89. Famous references to the recitation (*song*) of canonical texts include comments that Jia Yi 賈誼 (200–168 B.C.E.) became known for his ability to recite the *Odes* and the *Documents* (*Shiji* 84.2491; *Hanshu* 48.2221). When Gongsun Hong 公孫弘 (200–121 B.C.E.) memorialized to promote scholars learned in the traditional canon, he suggested that one should first employ for state service those men who were "able to recite many [canonical works]" (*Shiji* 121.3119; *Hanshu* 88.3594). The *Documents* erudite Fu Sheng 伏勝 (born 260 B.C.E.) is said to have carried canonical books (*jing* 經) with him when traveling and to have recited and memorized them whenever he stopped to rest (*Shiji* 121.3125); we hear the same about Ni Kuan 兒寬 (d. 102 B.C.E.). The *Chunqiu* 春秋 expert Dong Zhongshu 董仲舒 (ca. 195–115 B.C.E.?) reportedly lectured and recited behind a curtain, and because the number of his students was so large, many of them never got to see him at all (*Shiji* 121.3127; *Hanshu* 56.2495). In his rhapsody known as "Da ke nan" 答客難, Dongfang Shuo 東方朔 (ca. 161–86 B.C.E.) presents his discussion with other scholars, who wondered about his lack of an official career, despite his claim of broad learning and the fact that he could recite countless texts from the *Odes*, the *Documents*, and the "speeches of the hundred scholarly lineages" (*bai jia yu* 百家語; *Shiji* 126.3206; *Hanshu* 65.2864); according to a certainly suspicious account in *Hanshu* 65.2841, he was able to recite 220,000 words of the *Odes* and the *Documents* (exegetical traditions, since the two canons are nowhere close to these numbers?) at the age of sixteen *sui*. (At nineteen *sui*, he is said to have recited the same amount from works on military strategy; see *Hanshu* 65.2841). Sima Qian says in his autobiography that he recited "old texts" at the age of ten (*Shiji* 130.3293; *Hanshu* 62.2714). In 9 B.C.E., Emperor Cheng 成 (r. 32–7 B.C.E.) ordered the Prince of Dingtao 定陶 and future Emperor Ai 哀 (r. 7–1 B.C.E.) to recite the *Odes*, and the Prince of Zhongshan 中山 to recite the *Documents* (*Hanshu* 11.333). Liu Xiang 劉向 (79–8 B.C.E.) "during the day recited [canonical] books and their exegetical traditions, and during the night observed the stars and lunar mansions" (*Hanshu* 36.1963). Chao Cuo 鼂錯 (d. 154 B.C.E.), when memorializing his worries about the heir apparent's education, noted that one could "recite many [canonical works] but not understand their explanations" (*Hanshu* 49.2277). When Wang Shi 王式, the teacher of Liu He 劉賀 (ca. 92–59 B.C.E.), Prince of Changyi 昌邑, was accused of not having reproached the prince (and deposed emperor after only 27 days of rule) for his excesses, he insisted that he had instructed the prince from morning to night through the *Odes* and that when they reached the pieces of loyal ministers and filial sons, the prince never failed to repeatedly recite them (*Hanshu* 88.3610). Gong Sui 龔遂 (d. 62 B.C.E.), another classicist in Liu He's entourage, tried to persuade the prince to live with selected men of classical learning and superior morality and, "when sitting, to recite the *Odes* and the *Documents* and, when standing, to practice ritual demeanor" (*Hanshu* 89.3638). In Yang Xiong's 揚雄 (53 B.C.E.–18 C.E.) "Admonition on Ale" (Jiu zhen 酒箴), a witty text intended to reprimand Emperor Cheng, "reciting the canonical texts" is a mark of serious character (*Hanshu* 92.3713). Ban Jieyu 班倢伃 (d. ca. 6 C.E.), one of Emperor Cheng's concubines,

is noted for having recited *Odes* of moral contents (*Hanshu* 97B.3984). In his evaluation (*zan* 贊) of Wang Mang 王莽 (45 B.C.E.–23 C.E.), Ban Gu states that Wang "recited the Six Arts [i.e., the canonical works] to embellish his deceitful speech" (*Hanshu* 99B.4194).

90. *Lunyu zhushu* 13.51a (13/5).

91. See *Mozi jiangu*, 418.

92. There are two definitions of the "Six Arts" (*liu yi* 六藝) known in Western Han times: one that included the arts of ritual, music, archery, charioteering, writing, and computing (*Zhou li zhushu* 14.93b) and another that—perhaps first noted in the *Shiji*—referred to the canonical disciplines or books of the *Yi* 易, *Shu* 書, *Shi* 詩, *Li* 禮, *Yue* 樂, and *Chunqiu* 春秋. I am referring to the second set, as its list of titles appears already in the Guodian manuscripts (which, however, do not include the term *liu yi*).

93. I am indebted to Michael Nylan for bringing this aspect of canonical transmission to my attention. See also Sivin, "Text and Experience in Classical Chinese Medicine," 182, with reference to the transmission of medical texts in the early empire: "When a text is 'received' (*shou*) it is not simply handed over, but ritually transmitted and taught." For further elaboration on this issue, see my "Early Chinese Poetics in the Light of Recently Excavated Manuscripts."

94. See also Baxter, *A Handbook of Old Chinese Phonology*, 355–366.

95. On the development of the *Odes* as a canonical text through the course of its early hermeneutical history, see Van Zoeren, *Poetry and Personality*, 1–115. A succinct account may be found in Allen, "Postface: A Literary History of the *Shi jing*."

96. I take this preliminary list from Goldin, "The Reception of the *Canon of Odes* in Zhou Times," appendix.

97. In a variety of texts, scribes have shown either poor understanding or cavalier handling of the texts they were writing. This has been noted for the Guodian corpus in general as well as for the Western Han administrative bamboo strips from Juyan 居延. See the discussion in Allan and Williams, *The Guodian Laozi*, 134; Loewe, *Records of Han Administration*, vol. 1, 16.

98. See Giele, *Database of Early Chinese Manuscripts*.

99. See Keightley, *The Ancestral Landscape*, 37–39.

100. See Falkenhausen, "Issues in Western Zhou Studies," 161–167. Shaughnessy (*Sources of Western Zhou History*, 169; "Western Zhou History," 298–299, 326) and others have repeatedly emphasized the important role and high status of scribes at the Western Zhou court; see also Bagley, "Anyang Writing and the Origin of the Chinese Writing System." However, it seems to me that some of Shaughnessy's claims go too far (occasionally based on translations that I find questionable); see Kern, "The Performance of Writing in Western Zhou China."

101. Kern, "The Performance of Writing in Western Zhou China." For a healthy dose of skepticism with regard to the status of writing in early China, see also Nylan, "Textual Authority in Pre–Han and Han."

102. See Ledderose, *Ten Thousand Things*; Barbieri-Low, "The Organization of Imperial Workshops"; and Nylan, chapter 1 in this volume. In its summaries of officials in the six ministries, the *Zhou li* 周禮, probably dating

from the fourth or third century B.C.E., lists more than one thousand low-level (unranked) clerks. Excavated manuscripts from Shuihudi 睡虎地 (Yunmeng 雲夢, Hubei) tomb 11 (sealed 217 B.C.E.) and Zhangjiashan 張家山 (Jingzhou 荊州, Hubei 湖北) tomb 247 (sealed 186 B.C.E.) show that the position of administrative clerk was an entry position into local government; see Zhangjiashan ersiqi hao Han mu zhujian zhengli xiaozu, *Zhangjiashan Han mu zhujian*, 203–204; Xu, *Shuihudi Qin jian yanjiu*, 378–382; Kern, "Offices of Writing and Reading in the *Zhouli*."

103. I thank Paul Goldin for several of these references.

104. *Mozi jiangu* 12.407-408.

105. See *Mozi jiangu* 2.62, 4.111, 5.119, 7.185-186, 7.196, 8.214-215, 9.250, 9.254, 12.407, 13.431.

106. See *Zhuangzi jishi* 13.488.

107. *Han Feizi jijie* 19.451–452.

108. For example, among some 450 (mostly Eastern) Han pictorial representations from Sichuan assembled in Gong et al., *Ba Shu Handai huaxiang ji*, only two (nos. 61 and 63) show scholars (?) discussing (?) books.

109. As David Schaberg has shown in his masterful *A Patterned Past*, the entire *Zuo zhuan* is built around the idea of ritual propriety.

110. See *Lunyu zhushu* 13.51a (13/5).

111. Ibid. 16.66c, 17.69b (16/13, 17/10).

Chapter 6

Playing at Critique
Indirect Remonstrance and the Formation
of *Shi* Identity

David Schaberg

In mixtures of fact and fiction, the latter often prevails: accounts that are useful for one reason or another, though not strictly accurate, can carry more weight than inconvenient truths. Such is the case in representations of early Chinese critical speech. Ordinary remonstrance (*jian* 諫)—a subject's open objection to his ruler's policies or behavior, presented in the form of a speech delivered in court—appears to have existed as a political institution and a recognized genre of speech as early as the Eastern Zhou period. Designers of bureaucratic structures in the Han and later dynasties wrote remonstrance into the job descriptions for such officers as the "Grandee Remonstrant and Consultant" (*jianyi dafu* 諫議大夫), and the dynastic histories record numerous remonstrances, many of them submitted to the emperor in writing as part of an administration's ongoing internal correspondence.[1]

In contrast to this patently historical phenomenon, with its solid pre-imperial foundation, a related type of critical speech, the indirect remonstrance (usually called *fengjian* 諷諫), seems to have existed primarily, or exclusively, in legend. Indirect remonstrance had no history as a political practice; it came into being as a literary phenomenon, as part of the lore transmitted by educated elites of the late Warring States and early imperial era. Nonetheless, in visions of critical discourse, and more generally in visions of the literary and aesthetic behavior of educated men, the model of indirect remonstrance has had a more pervasive and lasting influence than any other single model of communication. Tales of indirect remonstrance, I will argue, were the fictional invention of the *shi* 士 (men of service) and reflect the development within that group of a self-conscious conception

194

of its identity and its relation to imperial power.[2] That the fiction was so successful in later eras, and the model of indirect critique so influential, suggests that the conceptions of *shi* identity worked out during the Han continued to be relevant despite changing political and social circumstances.

Because a few of the most famous indirect remonstrances are attributed to *you* 優, "jesters" or "entertainers," theater historians have sometimes seen in these tales the beginnings of Chinese drama.[3] Quite apart from the question of whether the events recounted actually took place, the problem with such an approach is that it treats episodes of clever criticism as if they belonged among the regular duties of the *you* and gives the impression that Chinese theatrical entertainment grew out of institutions of critique.[4] But nothing in the tales of indirect remonstrances suggests that presenting coded rebukes was the *you*'s normal occupation; less fanciful depictions of *you* activities indicate that these jugglers, musicians, and acrobats did not enjoy the sort of status that would have permitted them—or required them—to offer opinions on policy.[5] Further, even in the exceptional cases when their acts might have included the impersonation of mythical or historical entities, the *you* very rarely performed drama in the strict sense of the word, with scripted dialogue and the reenactment of a set plot.[6]

Still, there is a place for tales of indirect remonstrance in the genealogy of Chinese drama. Long before anything like theater existed in China, certain kinds of historical anecdotes were informed by assumptions that we would recognize as theatrical: the court and its environs functioned like a stage, and the deeds and words of the actors there were interpretable as tokens of their character and destiny. Tales of indirect remonstrance simply brought these narrative assumptions into the open by depicting acts calculated to have a specific effect on an interpreting observer, the ruler. Sometimes the signifying act was the sort of thing an entertainer might perform, sometimes not; if riddling, singing, or imitating an individual could be used in presenting an indirect critique, so could many other sorts of expression not immediately associated with *you*.[7] What matters in these tales, besides the early, probably fictional, depiction of something that resembles acting, is the claim that any critic, even one of noble birth, might behave like a *you* and that indirect remonstrance was in some instances a respectable alternative to direct critique. This association of acting with high-minded critique, by which true theatrical representation was linked to the early historiographical tradition, was an important step in the conceptual preparation for Chinese theater and helped to bolster the status of entertainers in later ages.

Of greater consequence for Chinese political and cultural history is the other side of the equation. By depicting the critical subject as a canny entertainer, if only in the imaginary space of anecdotal lore, the tellers of remonstrance tales registered a change in the status of court officials. Older tales of direct remonstrance had presumed near parity between the ruler and the ministers who help to formulate his policies. Episodes of indirect remonstrance, on the other hand, took it as a given that the ruler might, with little fuss, put to death the men who presumed to criticize his actions. While the first set of narratives reflects conceptions of hierarchy that prevailed before the middle Warring States period, the second reflects, probably in an exaggerated form, the concentration of power that took place thereafter.[8] Direct remonstrance did not disappear because of the new power differential, but it underwent a marked change, becoming a formal and often ineffectual act that rulers tolerated but did not necessarily take seriously. The bureaucratic structures that made a place for remonstrance could not ensure that the remonstrant would have the status or practical power to change the imperial circle's ways.[9] Remonstrants in early tales shared the ruler's aristocratic status; those in later tales belonged, with entertainers, to a lower stratum.

In this later historical context, legendary acts of remonstrance, both direct and indirect, were the medium in which educated men formulated and idealized ways of talking back to imperial power. The large bodies of anecdotal material that grew up around Yanzi 晏子, Wu Zixu 伍子胥, and Qu Yuan 屈原, characters who were known primarily for their direct remonstrances, represented one ideal: a brave or suicidal commitment to frank communication with the ruler. By contrast, tales of indirect remonstrance, featuring entertainers or ministers pretending to entertain, held up an ideal of tact, rhetorical cunning, and self-preservation. Neither ideal could qualify as an accurate depiction of the realities of political communication in the late Warring States and Han, but together they neatly frame the self-perception of the class of *shi*, whose advancement (unlike that of other servants to the emperor) depended upon speaking and writing effectively.[10] Too bold an effort to impose one's views, however honorable these were, could lead to demotion, exile, or, rarely, death. Too compliant an attitude in one's relations with the ruler and his circle, however, signified a different sort of degradation, as one joined the ranks of the sycophants and lackeys. Heroes of indirect remonstrance stood for *shi* hopes in that they risked degradation in order to achieve honor, and in so doing translated wit into real power.

The Invention of Indirect Remonstrance

If indirect methods of critique themselves have no recoverable history, interest in them does. Texts commonly dated to the early and middle Warring States period rarely depicted indirect critique and attributed it only to inferior members of the court establishment, including entertainers. By Liu Xiang's 劉向 (79–8 B.C.E.) time, however, indirect critique had a place within an established formal typology of remonstrance, and several well-known anecdotes featured highborn ministers in the role of artful critic. The new narratives that exemplified changed concepts of critique were, I will show, the product of free fictional elaboration on the part of educated men. Most tales of indirect remonstrance have to do with Spring and Autumn period rulers and ministers, yet they proliferated in much later texts, especially those dating to the Western Han. Many contain blatant anachronisms, and almost all turn up in multiple versions, with different settings and different casts of characters. They did not result from any individual's effort to falsify the past or to expand ideas of remonstrance but emerged as a reflection of and consolation for a whole group's changed circumstances.

Narratives of indirect remonstrance share a common morphology. Although this morphology underlies a wide range of early Chinese anecdotes, I have defined indirect remonstrance narrowly for the purposes of this discussion, considering only instances in which the anecdote itself or the material that frames it includes some explicit association with remonstrance proper (*jian*). At the beginning of each of these narratives, the ruler is indulging a pleasure or has adopted a policy that violates accepted norms, frequently sumptuary norms linked to ritual propriety. He forbids remonstrance on pain of death. The prospective remonstrant secures a court audience by promising an innocuous entertainment, then performs an act that in one way or another engages the ruler in a game of decoding: he poses a riddle, sings an obscure song, or wordlessly—as with a sigh or a gesture—defies expectations for court behavior. In his efforts to make sense of this performance, the ruler himself uncovers a latent critique, which often takes the form of some striking analogy for the ruler's unwise behavior. At the moment of identification, when the ruler draws the connection between the analogy and its target, entertainment is revealed as remonstrance and the ruler is transformed. This pattern, with variations in particular anecdotes, appears to have been a constant in the material we are about to examine and served as one guide for the Han authors who made compilations of such scenes from the earlier works that had come down to them.

The *Zuo zhuan* includes only two anecdotes that anticipate the conventions of later indirect remonstrance scenes, and only one of these draws a clear link with the established practice of direct remonstrance. Two household retainers of the Wei 魏 family are urged to remonstrate with their master, Wei Shu 魏舒, as he prepares to accept a bribe of female musicians. They sigh three times as they dine with him, then explain their sighs in terms that refer unambiguously to his greed. He refuses the bribe.[11] In a similar performance not explicitly associated with remonstrance, the provisioner or cook (*shanzai* 膳宰) Tu Kuai 屠蒯 convinces the Jin duke not to feast during a period of mourning: entering the hall, the cook pours punitive toasts to the musicians, to the duke's favorite, and to himself, in each case blaming the drinker for leading the duke astray. The duke is pleased with this approach and calls off the banquet.[12] That both episodes are set in the banquet hall is significant. Later narratives often adopt the same setting, and when they do not, they seem to import these anecdotes' convivial atmosphere into other, more formal settings, including court itself. For both political and literary reasons, a version of the *Zuo zhuan*'s model of the feast, with its characteristic personnel, entertainments, and modes of critique, came to dominate in representations of all sorts of court interactions.

In late Warring States texts, performances like the *Zuo zhuan*'s three sighs and three toasts become more common and are regularly identified as remonstrances. Both the *Han Feizi* 韓非子 and the *Zhanguo ce* 戰國策 record how the Jingguo lord 靖郭君 Tian Ying 田嬰 (fl. ca. 315 B.C.E.) forbade remonstrances against the walling of his city at Xue 薛, then yielded in response to a riddle about a fish.[13] In an episode that Han Fei frames as a remonstrance that went too far, Duke Ping 平 of Jin (r. 557–532 B.C.E.) brags about his own power, and the blind master musician Kuang hurls a zither at him, claiming to have heard a petty man speaking; Kuang is forgiven.[14] The contributors to the *Lüshi chunqiu* 呂氏春秋 recounted several more scenes of indirect remonstrance. King Zhuang 莊 of Chu (r. 613–591 B.C.E.) devotes himself, in the first three years of his reign, to riddling rather than to ruling; the Cheng governor Gu 成公賈 transforms him with a riddle about the great bird that for three years neither flew nor sang.[15] A Lu duke appoints Mi Zijian 宓子賤, a disciple of Confucius, to govern Danfu 亶父 but interferes with his work. Requesting two clerks from the duke's court, Mi dictates a letter to the duke. As they write he jogs their arms, then scolds them for their bad calligraphy. The duke gets the message and desists.[16] King Xuan 宣 of Qi (r. 319–301 B.C.E.) undertakes the construction of an extravagant palace. His courtier Chun Ju 春居 stops him with a series of questions about the duties of rulers and courtiers, culminating in the observation that he himself, having failed to remonstrate about the palace, is no true courtier.[17] The chapter "Direct Remonstrance" (Zhi jian 直諫) contains two more episodes, both of them closely related to indirect remonstrance in that they involve intentional violations of ritual expectations.[18]

The trend continues in works commonly dated to the second century B.C.E. Although Guanzi 管子 has little use for subtlety in the many anecdotes told about him, an early Han chapter in the *Guanzi* attributes to him a rebuke that, like many indirect remonstrances, is set among the trappings of elite entertainment and exploits these for the purposes of critique.[19] In a *Han Shi waizhuan* 韓詩外傳 anecdote that we will consider in greater detail in the following section, Sunshu Ao 孫叔敖 uses the familiar figure of the oblivious cicada to dissuade King Zhuang of Chu from a planned attack on Jin.[20] A dying minister, Scribe Yu 史魚, arranges to turn his own funeral into an indirect remonstrance for a Wey 衛 duke: by having his corpse laid out in a small chamber, contrary to ritual specifications, he denounces his own failure to help the duke—and, indirectly, the duke's failure to accept help.[21] Another anecdote, which features a direct remonstrance from a commoner, alludes to the conventions of indirect remonstrance anecdotes by setting the episode at a banquet and employing the theatrics of the toast.[22] The *Huananzi* 准南子 repeats the tale of master musician Kuang's zither attack on Duke Ping of Jin and adds an anecdote in which the steward Zhesui 折睢, tutor to Duke Ai 哀 of Lu (r. 494–477 B.C.E.), uses a simple riddle about inauspicious behavior to convince the duke not to add a western annex to his palace.[23]

Perhaps inspired by chapters of the *Han Feizi* and *Lüshi chunqiu* devoted to the problem of effective speech, Sima Qian 司馬遷 (ca. 145–ca. 85 B.C.E.) commemorated the deeds of three artful persuaders in his "Biographies of the Slick Reminders" (Guji liezhuan 滑稽列傳).[24] These were men whose words, according to the historian, deserved to be associated with the classics, since by "subtly hitting their mark" (*wei zhong* 微中) they too could solve problems. Chunyu Kun 淳于髡, serving under King Wei 威 of Qi (r. 334–320 B.C.E.), jolts the king out of indolence with a version of the great bird riddle, elsewhere attributed to remonstrants under King Zhuang of Chu. On another occasion, Chunyu laughs out loud in court, claiming to have recalled a scene in which a farmer offered a tiny sacrifice and prayed for a rich harvest; the target of the joke is the king, who has offered the state of Zhao an absurdly small bribe in return for help against an invading Chu force. Finally, asked about his capacity for liquor, Chunyu claims to get drunk on two liters (*dou* 斗) or twenty (*shi* 石), depending on circumstances; the more dissolute the gathering, the more he drinks. The king gives up his nocturnal revels.[25] The remonstrances of Jester Meng 優孟 before King Zhuang of Chu are discussed in the next section; here it should be noted, as a sign of the uncertain historical status of the materials the historian collected in this chapter, that Sima puts Meng "more than a hundred years after" Chunyu Kun, even though King Zhuang ruled in the middle Spring and Autumn period.[26] Sima's final example is Jester Zhan 優旃, who served the First Emperor of Qin (r. 221–210 B.C.E.) and his successor (r. 209–207 B.C.E.) "more than two hundred years after" Meng. With a flagrant insult to the imperial bodyguards, Zhan goads the emperor into inviting them in out of the rain. Later he discourages his rulers' outrageous construction projects by offering sarcastic endorsements.[27]

Sometime during the first century B.C.E., in one of his longer signed supplements to the *Shiji* 史記, Chu Shaosun 褚少孫 (ca. 104–ca. 30 B.C.E.) added anecdotes about six figures: the Member of the Suite (*sheren* 舍人) Guo 郭, Dongfang Shuo 東方朔, the Dongguo Master 東郭先生, Chunyu Kun, Master Wang 王先生, and Ximen Bao 西門豹. All lived under Emperor Wu 武 (r. 140–87 B.C.E.), with the exception of Chunyu Kun, mentioned above, and Ximen Bao, an appointee of Marquis Wen 文 of Wei (r. 445–396 B.C.E.).[28] Commentators were to complain, with good reason, that in the material he chose Chu overstepped the narrow limits Sima Qian had implied for the chapter.[29] In fact, few of his anecdotes fit the pattern of indirect remonstrance outlined above. Instead, they have more generally to do with clever or amusing uses of speech, not necessarily for critical ends. Yet Chu justified himself on terms different from Sima Qian's. Serving the court as a scholar, Chu had had access to the archives and had indulged his passion for "anecdotes passed on in the lineages outside court" (*waijia chuanyu* 外家傳語).[30] In adding to Sima Qian's chapter, he claimed only to cater to the same passion in later readers.[31] The loosening of Sima Qian's original category, paired with the appeal to entertainment as the new reason for collecting and reading, suggests that Chu thought of clever speech first as a source of literary pleasure and only second as an effective mode of political action.

It was not for lack of standard anecdotes of indirect remonstrance that Chu left them out of his addendum to the "Guji liezhuan." His younger contemporary Liu Xiang gathered many such episodes for the collections he edited. The *Lienü zhuan* 列女傳 attributes a pair of indirect remonstrances to Fan Ji 樊姬, queen to King Zhuang of Chu. In the first, when he gives himself over to hunting in the first years of his reign, she reforms him by refusing to eat the flesh of his prey. In the second, he treats a fawning minister as a worthy, and she laughs at him, then explains herself. [32] The *Xinxu* 新序 repeats the *Hanshi waizhuan's* tale of a funereal remonstrance, this time identifying the dying minister as Scribe Qiu 史鰌 and his ruler as Duke Ling 靈 of Wey (r. 534–493 B.C.E.). [33] It also repeats the great bird riddle before King Zhuang of Chu, naming Shi Qing 士慶 as the remonstrant, and the riddle of the fish, pronounced before the Jingguo lord. [34] In an otherwise-unattested episode, after the king of Wei forbids remonstrances about his construction of a huge terrace, the nobleman Xu Wan 許綰 appears in court with hod and hoe and offers to help; it turns out that the real help Xu is prepared to give is a condemnation of the whole project, a critique that he protects by cloaking it in apparent submissiveness. [35]

The culminating point in the early development of indirect remonstrance legends, and the greatest collection of such narratives, is the ninth *juan* of Liu Xiang's *Shuoyuan* 說苑, "Zhengjian" 正諫. Although the title implies a focus on older examples of direct remonstrance, fully half of Liu's twenty-five anecdotes feature clever and heroic acts of indirection. Besides anecdotes relating to King Zhuang, some of which are examined below, there are the indirect remonstrances of Yan Chu 顏斶 before Duke Jing 景 of Qi (r. 547–490 B.C.E.), of Jiu Fan 咎犯 before Duke Ping of Jin, of an unnamed guest of the Mengchang lord, of a Shao Ruzi 少孺子 (literally "young child," but used as a name) before the king of Wu, of Mao Jiao 茅焦 before the First Emperor of Qin, of Chief Minister Zixi 令尹子西 before King Zhao (r. 515–489 B.C.E.) of Chu, and of Gong Lu 公盧 before Zhao Jianzi 趙簡子 (fl. ca. 495–475 B.C.E.). All of these tales are also found in other texts, often attributed to different remonstrants in the courts of different rulers, and it is clear that certain figures of speech—like the fable of the wood figurine and the clay figurine, used by Mengchang's guest—made for such good stories that they were frequently recycled. [36]

By contrast, the direct remonstrances Liu collects here, most of them attributed to Yanzi and Wu Zixu, are very rarely associated with other characters. Because direct remonstrances are typically built on the analysis of particular well-known incidents (e.g., events during the reign of Duke Jing of Qi or Wu's interactions with Yue) they are tightly bound to specific characters. In indirect remonstrance, the striking figure of critique matters more than the historical particulars that are supposed to have triggered it. As the example of King Zhuang will show, the same legendary critique is in some cases recounted for several different sets of individuals and historical settings, and relatively reliable historical accounts are frequently adjusted to make a suitable frame for a good tale of critique. What accounts for the recycling of indirect remonstrance anecdotes, and for their unreliability as history, is the cleverness of specific devices for critique; but this cleverness also makes them the most memorable and pedagogically effective depictions of critical speech and may explain why Liu included so many of them in the *Shuoyuan* and other collections. Partly because he represented his own editorial work as a variety of remonstrance, Liu was able to claim a didactic value for material that Chu Shaosun had seen as mere entertainment. [37]

As legends of indirect remonstrance developed, so did schematic conceptions of remonstrance. In early works, remonstrance is linked to other types of verbal performance, but there is no attempt to rationalize differences among them, and no distinctions are drawn between types of remonstrance. [38] In later texts' depictions of early bureaucratic arrangements, remonstrants steadily grow in importance, as political thinkers come to imagine the Western Zhou court and certain others as places where the free circulation of critical speech was encouraged and even institutionalized. [39] Ritual texts proposed a place for remonstrants in the court hierarchy and prescribed ceremonial preparations for the delivery and reception of remonstrance. [40] By the time Liu Xiang compiled the *Shuoyuan*, five types of remonstrance could be discerned:

是故諫有五：一曰正諫，二曰降諫，三曰忠諫，四曰戇諫，五曰
諷諫。孔子曰：吾其從諷諫乎。

Thus there are five types of remonstrance: first is correct remonstrance; second is humble remonstrance; third is loyal remonstrance; fourth is simpleminded remonstrance; and fifth is indirect remonstrance. Confucius said, "I will follow the path of indirect remonstrance!" [41]

There is a curious inconsistency here. The drawing up of lists like this one attests to the growing importance attributed to remonstrance as an official act; it also accords with Han writers' tendency toward schematization, particularly of bureaucratic institutions and functions. [42] Yet the only type of remonstrance found in all of the lists, and the type given clear priority in all of them, is indirect remonstrance, an act not provided for in institutional or ritual writings. The imperial courts took over the old practice of direct criticism, but on terms that implied its subordination to an imaginary ideal of tact and self-preservation.

Behind indirect remonstrance's changing status lay more than the history of literary developments discussed above. One finds in late Warring States and Western Han texts traces of a philosophical debate over the value of direct remonstrance and a gradual limiting of directness in favor of indirectness or silence. Older texts had had relatively little to say about what the remonstrant was to do if the ruler ignored him, although some of these texts' tales of remonstrant characters who were already becoming exemplary—Zhao Dun 趙盾 of Jin, Wu Zixu, Yan Ying—imply that one must continue to criticize even at the risk of death.[43] Confucius was rarely said to have remonstrated; in most versions of his legend he was not qualified to do so. But his supposed departures from states where he and his views were neglected pointed in the direction of Han solutions.[44] Many Han texts advised aspiring remonstrants to try three times and then, like Confucius, to depart.[45] Starting with the *Han Feizi*, certain other texts, including one normally identified as "Confucian," rejected the very practice of direct remonstrance.[46] Or, again departing from early texts, they held up examples of rulers and individuals, King Zhuang of Chu and Confucius among them, who had had the wisdom to refute wrongheaded remonstrances.[47] In the *Kongzi jiayu* 孔子家語, Confucius is made to distinguish the achievements of the late Shang hero Bigan 比干 and the Spring and Autumn period minister Xie Ye 洩冶. Both remonstrated until their rulers put them to death, but only Bigan had the requisite rank and proximity to the sovereign; the meaner Xie Ye was merely presumptuous and died uselessly.[48] Given constraints of this sort, which accord well with a general recognition that criticism of the ruler and his circle might always bring violent reprisal, it is little wonder that, in the new typologies, the real tradition of remonstrance was placed after imaginary feats of tact.

The Afterlife of King Zhuang of Chu

The meaning of indirect remonstrance tales lies not in their proliferation alone but in the way they embody early Chinese notions of criticism, allegoresis, and literary pleasure. As the examples mentioned above suggest, accuracy and even plausibility seem to have mattered little in this part of the anecdotal lore: the gesture toward history served mainly to frame the more

important business of the narrative. After what was in some cases centuries
of retelling, anecdotes began to cluster around certain rulers, whose images
finally bore little resemblance to depictions given in older historical texts.
The most prominent of these fictionalized figures was King Zhuang of
Chu. [49] Although the earliest accounts already present him as an admirable
ruler, and one who is quite unique in his ability to deliver an uplifting
moralizing speech, it is in the later accounts that he becomes the perfect
audience for indirect remonstrance, both by provoking it and by yielding to
it. Tales of indirect remonstrance told about other figures often ended up
being retold about him, and his persona seems to have inspired some of the
most delightful experiments with the motif. It is perhaps surprising, given
the number of times he was supposed to have threatened his critics with
death, that King Zhuang should have represented one ideal of royal behavior
for Han thinkers. But he clearly did.

The *Zuo zhuan* characterizes King Zhuang as a man made powerful by
his implementation of standards of ritual propriety, his self-restraint, and his
ability to take advantage of opportunities. The most famous anecdote about
him, in which he asks about the weight and size of the cauldrons Zhou has
inherited from previous dynastic houses, may suggest overreaching, but it
also resonates with Warring States notions that a Chu dynasty was destined
to succeed Zhou. [50] Elsewhere, having occupied Chen after the assassination
of Duke Ling 靈 (r. 613–599 B.C.E.), the king heeds the advice of a minister
and gives up plans to annex the state. This decision won the explicit
endorsement of the *Zuo zhuan* authors, of Sima Qian, and, purportedly, of
Confucius himself. [51] The long narrative of Chu's victory over Jin at Bi 邲
in 597 B.C.E. depicts King Zhuang in glowing terms, imputing invin-
cibility to his armies on account of his orderly administration and painting
him finally as a reciter of the *Shi* 詩 (Odes) and an opponent of military
solutions. [52] During the bitter Chu siege of Song, a captured Jin envoy
insists, against the king's orders, on proclaiming a message of encouragement to the defenders. The king is prepared to put him to death but
desists when the envoy explains the principles behind obeying one's own
ruler's commands. [53] In a *Guoyu* passage that some scholars have read as a
source for the history of education, King Zhuang solicits advice on the
training of his heir and learns of the proper use of inherited texts and
practices. [54] Although he was not yet known as a target of indirect critiques,
the king appears to have been an idealized figure even before the Han.

By the late Warring States period, the king had begun to figure
prominently in tales of indirect remonstrance. The *Han Feizi*, *Lüshi*

chunqiu, Shiji, Xinxu, and *Wu Yue chunqiu* 吳越春秋 all associate the following remonstrance with King Zhuang; in a typical inconsistency, the *Shiji* also sets it in the court of King Wei of Qi.[55] This is the *Lüshi chunqiu* version:

荊莊王立三年，不聽而好讔。成公賈入諫。王曰：不穀禁諫者，今子諫，何故？對曰：臣非敢諫也，願與君王讔也。王曰：胡不設不穀矣。對曰：有鳥止於南方之阜，三年不動不飛不鳴，是何鳥也？王射之曰：有鳥止於南方之阜，其三年不動，將以定志意也；其不飛，將以長羽翼也；其不鳴，將以覽民則也。是鳥雖無飛，飛將沖天；雖無鳴，鳴將駭人。賈出矣，不穀知之矣。明日朝，所進者五人，所退者十人。群臣大說，荊國之眾相賀也。故詩曰：何其久也，必有以也，何其處也，必有與也。其莊王之謂邪？

For three years after his accession, King Zhuang of Jing (Chu) would not attend to court matters, but he did enjoy guessing games. The Cheng governor Gu entered to present a remonstrance. The king said, "I have barred remonstrants. What is your reason for remonstrating now?" He replied, "I would not dare to remonstrate. I want to play a guessing game with Your Highness." The king said, "Why don't you try me?" He replied, "There is a bird perched on a hillock in the south. For three years it has neither moved nor taken flight nor uttered a cry. What bird is it?"

The king guessed and said, "There is a bird perched on a hillock in the south. That it has not moved in three years is so that it can confirm its ambitions (*zhiyi*). That it has not taken flight is so that it can grow its wings (*yuyi*). That it has not uttered a cry is so that it can observe the people's principles (*ze*). Although this bird has yet to take flight, when it does fly it will soar into the heavens (*tian*). Although it has not yet uttered a cry, when it does it will amaze people (*ren*). Go now: I know what it is."

The next day he attended court, promoting five men and demoting ten. The assembled ministers were overjoyed, and the common people of Jing congratulated one another. Thus the poem says, "Why has he been so long? He must have a reason. Why does he stay there? He must have companions."[56] Might this not refer to King Zhuang?

Other versions give different conclusions for the anecdote, but the core is the same in all cases.[57]

The great bird remonstrance, simple as it is, is a primer in the art of indirect critique. King Zhuang of the *Zuo zhuan* and *Guoyu* is transformed into a bloodthirsty profligate: only explicit interdictions against remonstrance provide a pretext for an indirect approach. The critic flirts with death, presenting himself for the sake of remonstrating, then claiming to offer a riddle instead, which turns out to be a thinly veiled caricature of the inert king. The critic's defense against death is his wit: not only his verbal skill but also his calculation of the effects of his performance. The king must "get" the joke in precisely the right way; to borrow another term for criticism, he must be "stung" (*ci* 刺) by recognition, and this recognition must entirely dominate his interpretation of the performance and kill his desire for vengeance. As displayed in these anecdotes, allegoresis is a finite art, and its meaning is entirely exhausted by one act of royal interpretation. The laugh that recognition sometimes brings is, for everyone involved, a moment of relief, when all obscurities are dispelled.

King Zhuang understands immediately, as is usually the case in such anecdotes, and even accepts the terms of the critique to the extent of adopting them in his response. As Chen Qiyou points out, the king's response to the riddle is rhymed: *yi* 意, *yi* 翼, and *ze* 則 in a combined rhyme in the *zhi* 之 and *zhi* 職 categories, and *tian* 天 and *min* 民 in the *zhen* 真 category.[58] Although the words of the ruler's response differ, sometimes markedly, in the various versions of the anecdote, all versions are rhymed. Further, all versions, including the one set in Qi, use one or both of the same rhyme categories and many of the same rhyme words as the *Lüshi chunqiu* version.[59] Rhyming language in the central figure was clearly one of the most stable features of this anecdote throughout its transmission. It is generally true of indirect remonstrance anecdotes that features of verbal patterning—whether rhyme or notable rhetorical figures—stay the same where other features, like frame stories, change. The point of the indirect remonstrance was the confrontation of a courtier's resourcefulness with a ruler's deadly will, and the tradition seems always to have been interested more in the nature of the performance itself than in the actors' identities.

As another King Zhuang anecdote suggests, the verbal figure that converts the king may also be useful in other contexts:

楚莊王將興師伐晉，告士大夫曰：敢諫者死無赦。孫叔敖曰：臣聞：畏鞭箠之嚴，而不敢諫其父，非孝子也；懼斧鉞之誅，而不敢諫其君，非忠臣也。於是遂進諫曰：臣園中有榆，其上有蟬，

蟬方奮翼悲鳴，欲飲清露，不知螳螂之在後，曲其頸，欲攫而食
之也；螳螂方欲食蟬，而不知黃雀在後，舉其頸，欲啄而食之也
；黃雀方欲食螳螂，不知童挾彈丸在下迎而欲彈之。童子方欲彈
黃雀，不知前有深坑，後有窟也。此皆言前之利而不顧後害者也
。非獨昆蟲眾庶若此也。人主亦然。君今知貪彼之土而樂其士卒
。國不怠而晉國以寧，孫叔敖之力也。

King Zhuang of Chu was about to muster the army for an attack on
Jin. He told his retainers and ministers, "Whosoever dares to
remonstrate will die without hope of pardon." Sunshu Ao said, "I have
heard that one who fears the severity of the lash and dares not
remonstrate with his father is not a filial son, and that one who is
terrified of punishment by the axe and dares not remonstrate with his
ruler is not a loyal minister."

So he entered and remonstrated, saying, "In my garden there is an
elm. In it there was a cicada, which was just stirring its wings and
buzzing mournfully and was about to sip the clear dew, but did not
know that there was a mantis behind it bending its neck and preparing
to seize and eat it. The mantis, about to eat the cicada, did not know
that there was a titmouse behind it stretching its neck and preparing to
snap it up and eat it. The titmouse, about to eat the mantis, did not
know that there was a boy grasping a pellet-bow below, creeping up
and preparing to shoot it. The boy, about to shoot the titmouse, did
not know that there was a deep trench in front of him and a pit behind.
All these considered the gain in front of them without giving a thought
to the harm behind them. It is not only insects and commoners who are
like this. The people's ruler is also like this. Now my lord knows
about lusting after his land and delighting in his fighting men."

That the state did not face peril and Jin had peace was due to the
force of Sunshu Ao.60

Elsewhere the same remonstrance is attributed to other ministers under
other rulers. Set in the court of King Zhuang, it is appropriate that it should
be credited to Sunshu Ao and that he should present it as a verbal riddle. In
other versions, remonstrants of humbler station appear before the king with
pellet-bow in hand, wearing dew-damp robes, and by this bit of theatrical
business force the king to ask after the figure himself.61

The most interesting use of this trope is also the most familiar. In the
"Mountain Timber" (Shan mu 山木) chapter of the *Zhuangzi* 莊子, the
figure of hunted hunters serves, not to enlighten a warlike king, but to

reveal to Zhuang Zhou 莊周 his own entanglement (*lei* 累) in ties of exploitation.[62] It is neither necessary nor possible to determine whether the philosophical or the remonstrative use of the figure came first. Like *Zhuangzi*'s other famous fables, this one encapsulates a set of relations and serves to expose analogous relations in whatever framing circumstances are provided for it. If the author of this *Zhuangzi* chapter was concerned with liberation from relations of dependence, other users of the figure were more interested in the spectacle of a ruler forced to recognize his dependence upon other states and—more important still—his dependence upon discerning critics.

In another anecdote, a farmer-recluse succeeds in presenting a direct remonstrance despite overt interdiction:

> 楚莊王築層台,延石千重,延壤百里,士有三月之糧者,大臣諫者七十二人皆死矣;有諸御己者,違楚百里而耕,謂其耦曰:吾將入見於王。其耦曰:以身乎?吾聞之,説人主者,皆閒暇之人也,然且至而死矣;今子特草茅之人耳。諸御己曰:若與子同耕則比力也,至於説人主不與子比智矣。委其耕而入見莊王・莊王謂之曰:諸御己來,汝將諫邪?諸御己曰:君有義之用,有法之行。且己聞之,土負水者平,木負繩者正,君受諫者聖;君築層台,延石千重,延壤百里;民之䨻咎血成於通塗,然且未敢諫也,己何敢諫乎?顧臣愚,竊聞昔者虞不用宮之奇而晉并之,陳不用子家羈而楚并之,曹不用僖負羈而宋并之,萊不用子猛而齊并之,吳不用子胥而越并之,秦人不用蹇叔之言而秦國危,桀殺關龍逢而湯得之,紂殺王子比干而武王得之,宣王殺杜伯而周室卑;此三天子,六諸侯,皆不能尊賢用辯士之言,故身死而國亡。遂趨而出,楚王遽而追之曰:己子反矣,吾將用子之諫;先日説寡人者,其説也不足以動寡人之心,又危加諸寡人,故皆至而死;今子之説,足以動寡人之心,又不危加諸寡人,故吾將用子之諫。明日令曰:有能入諫者,吾將與為兄弟。遂解層台而罷民,楚人歌之曰:薪乎萊乎?無諸御己訖無子乎?萊乎薪乎?無諸御己訖無人乎!

King Zhuang of Chu was building a terraced pavilion which extended to a thousand courses of stone and across a hundred *li* of land. Among the retainers were some who had grain rations to last three months before their return.[63] Seventy-two high ministers had remonstrated, and all had died. There was a certain Zhuyu Ji who, while plowing a hundred *li* from the Chu capital, said to his plowing partner, "I am going to go for an audience with the king." His partner said, "In person? I have heard that those who offered persuasion before the ruler of men are all men of leisure, and yet they died after reaching him. And now you are just a hayseed!" Zhuyu Ji said, "If I'm plowing with you, then we are of comparable strength; but when it comes to persuading the ruler of men, I don't compare my cleverness with yours."

He laid down the plow and went for an audience with King Zhuang. King Zhuang said to him, "Come, Zhuyu Ji! Are you going to remonstrate?" Zhuyu Ji said, "A ruler controls the implementation of what is right and the execution of his laws. And I have heard that land that has borne the weight of water is flat (*ping*), wood that has been subjected to the plumb line is straight (*zheng*), and the ruler who accepts remonstrances is a sage (*sheng*). My lord is building a terraced pavilion that extends to a thousand courses of stone and across a hundred *li* of land; with all the slaughter and incrimination of people, blood flows across the paths, but none dares remonstrate. How should I dare to remonstrate? Still, though I am simple, I have heard that, in former times, Yu did not heed Gong zhi Qi and was annexed by Jin; Chen did not heed Zijia Ji and was annexed by Chu; Cao did not heed Xifu Ji and was annexed by Song; Lai did not heed Zimeng and was annexed by Qi; Wu did not heed Zixu and was annexed by Yue; when Qin did not heed the words of Jian Shu, the state of Qin was endangered; Jie killed Guanlong Feng and was taken by Tang; Zhòu killed Prince Bigan and was taken by King Wu; and when King Xuan killed Du Bo, the Zhou house declined. These three kings and six feudal lords were all unable to revere and heed the words of their worthies and debaters, and therefore they died and their states perished." And then he hurried out.

The king of Chu rushed to pursue him, saying, "Ji! Come back! I will heed your remonstrance! The people who tried to convince me before—their persuasions did not serve to move my heart, and they imposed them on me haughtily. Now your persuasion does serve to move my heart, and you don't impose it on me haughtily, so I will heed your remonstrance."

The next day he issued orders saying, "Whosoever can present remonstrances, I shall treat him as a brother." He gave up the terraced pavilion and sent the people home.

The people of Chu sang about it, saying, "Brush and wild weeds (*lai*)—if not for Zhuyu Ji, there would have been no sons (*zi*)! Wild weeds and brush (*xin*)—if not for Zhuyu Ji, there would have been no one at all (*ren*)!"[64]

Although the tale was apparently not told about other rulers and is not found in any texts other than the *Shuoyuan*, it does appear to borrow language from the *Xunzi* 荀子.[65] Like many of the examples considered here, it incorporates rhymed speech.[66] The anachronism in Zhuyu Ji's speech—his reference to the fall of Wu in a speech supposed to have been delivered about a century before that event—underlines the likelihood that this anecdote was a Western Han fiction.

On one level, Zhuyu Ji's speech is an exemplary direct remonstrance and therefore out of place with the other Western Han legends about King Zhuang. This simple address, with its citation of many of the most clichéd examples of spurned critics, becomes a successful remonstrance because of Zhuyu Ji's—and the storyteller's—savvy exploitation of the theatrics of political status. The trope, such as it is, is the bold rejection of any tropic language and the staging of an archaic directness. Like earlier tales of wise commoners (especially the tale of Cao Gui's 曹劌 military advice to the duke of Lu), this one emphasizes a disparity between social status and clear-headedness.[67] In contrast to those earlier tales, however, here the threat of death hovers around the commoner's approach to the center of power. His companion asks him if he will go "in person" (*yi shen* 以身), that is, if he will risk physical harm. The king asks him, as if to warn him, if he really intends to remonstrate. But the absurdity of the social gulf that divides speaker and audience, combined with the daring and perfect orthodoxy of his words, makes for an act of such earnest bravado that it finally convinces the king. Zhuyu Ji, who implies his admiration for "worthies and debaters," knows that his success is the result of intelligence; but the king yields, he says, for aesthetic reasons, because the spectacle of humble devotion has "moved his heart." The emphasis on hierarchical difference and danger turns direct remonstrance into a performance of loyalty and in so doing subordinates this older form of critique to newer models of tact. As I will show, the transformation explains much that is said about literary and critical discourse under the Han.

Sima Qian thought of King Zhuang as a keeper of entertainers, men who in ordinary times contributed to the luxury of the king's court but who under certain circumstances might correct the king with a joke. With a sarcasm that still amuses, Jester Meng 優孟 talks the king out of treating his horse as a minister (*dafu* 大夫):

優孟，故楚之樂人也。長八尺，多辯，常以談笑諷諫。楚莊王之時，有所愛馬，衣以文繡，置之華屋之下，席以露床，啗以棗脯。

馬病肥死，使群臣喪之，欲以棺槨大夫禮葬之。左右爭之，以為
不可。王下令曰：有敢以馬諫者，罪至死。優孟聞之，入殿門。
仰天大哭。王驚而問其故。優孟曰：馬者王之所愛也，以楚國堂
堂之大，何求不得，而以大夫禮葬之，薄，請以人君禮葬之。王
曰：何如？對曰：臣請以彫玉為棺，文梓為槨，梗楓豫章為題湊
，發甲卒為穿壙，老弱負土，齊趙陪位於前，韓魏翼衛其後，廟
食太牢，奉以萬戶之邑。諸侯聞之，皆知大王賤人而貴馬也。王
曰：寡人之過一至此乎！為之柰何？優孟曰：請為大王六畜葬之
。以壠竈為槨，銅歷為棺，齎以薑棗，薦以木蘭，祭以糧稻，衣
以火光，葬之於人腹腸。於是王乃使以馬屬太官，無令天下久聞
也。

Jester Meng was a musician in Chu in former times. He was eight *chi*
tall and had a lot of clever arguments, which he frequently used in jokes
and indirect remonstrance. During the reign of King Zhuang of Chu,
there was a horse that the king especially cherished: he dressed it in
patterned embroidery, lodged it in a highly decorated room, bedded it on
an open platform, and fed it date confections. When the horse grew ill
and died of obesity, the king had the assembled courtiers mourn for it
and wished to bury it with outer and inner coffins and the rites
appropriate to a minister. The men of court contested the matter,
considering it inadmissible. The king issued an order saying, "Those
who dare remonstrate about the horse will be guilty of a crime
punishable by death." Hearing of it, Jester Meng entered the door of the
hall, threw back his head, and cried aloud. Taken aback, the king asked
the reason for his behavior. Jester Meng said, "The horse is something
Your Highness cherishes. To bury it with the rites appropriate to a
minister in a state as grand as Chu, where you can get whatever you
desire, is stingy. Please bury it with the rites appropriate to a ruler."

"How?" said the king.

He replied, "Please grant permission to have the inner coffin
made of carved jade and the outer coffin of patterned catalpa wood, with
decorative fittings made of maple and cedar. Have picked troops dig the
pit for it; have the elderly and the weak carry earth; have Qi and Zhao
take their places at the front while Han and Wei guard the rear;
consume a great sacrifice in the temple and dedicate a city of ten
thousand households. When the feudal lords hear of it, all of them will
know how Your Highness despises men and esteems horses."

The king said, "So my error has come to this! What should I do?"

Jester Meng said, "Permit me to bury it with the rites appropriate to the six domestic animals, Your Highness. Use a stove mound for the outer coffin and a bronze cauldron for the inner coffin; present ginger and dates, give gifts of magnolia wood, and make offerings of grain and rice; clothe it in firelight and bury it in the bellies of men."

With this the king had the horse turned over to the Grand Provisioner, preventing the matter from being famous in the world for a long time. [68]

Again, anachronism mars the tale's historical credibility: Zhao, Han, and Wei did not exist as independent entities in King Zhuang's time.

The king's indulgence in a luxury and his banning of criticism are predictable elements of the tale. The shout of sorrow with which the jester first focuses the king's attention is also in keeping with similar theatrical gestures elsewhere. Everything serves to frame the tale's invention, the jester's mocking exaggeration of the king's intentions, and then, more novel still, his adaptation of the terms of burial to describe a feast. The literary pleasures of the jester's remarks lie both in these cunning turns—horse as lord, feast as funeral—and in his elevated diction, which is at points reminiscent of *fu* 賦. Here and elsewhere it matters that the lowliest of court creatures, the jester, speaks for the voiceless and impotent courtiers and that he succeeds by a brilliant subversion of burial rites and of ruler-subject relations. What keeps the king from going the path of Gaius Caligula, who appointed his horse consul, is the certainty, in imagination at least, that the perfect act of communication could undo the usual constraints of hierarchy and power, allow an inoffensive but effective criticism, and thereby restore good order. But what brings the jester onstage and keeps the courtiers silent is the suspicion that the perfect act of communication sometimes requires a clownish playfulness.

Later in his life, in an act of impersonation that allows him literally to stand in for a social superior, the jester uses all the accoutrements of theater to remind the king of his debts:

楚相孫叔敖知其賢人也，善待之。病且死，屬其子曰：我死，汝
必貧困。若往見優孟，言我孫叔敖之子也。居數年，其子窮困負
薪，逢優孟，與言曰：我，孫叔敖子也。父且死時，屬我貧困往
見優孟。優孟曰：若無遠有所之，即為孫叔敖衣冠，抵掌談語。
歲餘，像孫叔敖，楚王及左右不能別也。莊王置酒，優孟前為壽
。莊王大驚，以為孫叔敖復生也，欲以為相。優孟曰：請歸與婦
計之，三日而為相。莊王許之。三日後，優孟復來。王曰：婦言

謂何？孟曰：婦言慎無為，楚相不足為也。如孫叔敖之為楚相，
盡忠為廉以治楚，楚王得以霸。今死，其子無立錐之地，貧困負
薪以自飲食。必如孫叔敖，不如自殺。因歌曰：山居耕田苦，難
以得食。起而為吏，身貪鄙者餘財，不顧恥辱。身死家室富，又
恐受賕枉法，為姦觸大罪，身死而家滅。貪吏安可為也！念為廉
吏，奉法守職，竟死不敢為非。廉吏安可為也！楚相孫叔敖持廉
至死，方今妻子窮困負薪而食，不足為也！於是莊王謝優孟，乃
召孫叔敖子，封之寢丘四百戶，以奉其祀。後十世不絕。此知可
以言時矣。

The Chu prime minister Sunshu Ao knew that [Jester Meng] was a
worthy and treated him well. When he was sick and about to die, he
gave his son an order: "When I die, you will certainly be poor. Go and
see Jester Meng and tell him that you are the son of Sunshu Ao."

Several years later, his son, poverty-stricken, was gathering
firewood when he ran into Jester Meng and said to him, "I am the son
of Sunshu Ao. When my father was about to die, he ordered me to go
to see Jester Meng when I became poor."

Jester Meng said, "Don't make any long journeys." He made up
the clothing and cap of Sunshu Ao and put his palms together as he
spoke. After more than a year he so resembled Sunshu Ao that the king
of Chu and his men could not tell them apart. When King Zhuang had
a drinking gathering, Jester Meng stepped forward to make a toast.
King Zhuang was flabbergasted; he thought that Sunshu Ao had come
back to life and wanted to make him prime minister. Jester Meng said,
"Permit me to go home and consider it with my wife. Three days from
now I will become prime minister." King Zhuang granted him
permission.

Three days later Jester Meng came back. The king said, "What did
your wife say?"

Meng said, "My wife told me to take every precaution not to do
it, since it's not worth it to be the prime minister of Chu. For
example, when Sunshu Ao was prime minister of Chu, he governed
Chu with the utmost loyalty and fastidiousness, and the king of Chu
therefore managed to become hegemon. Now he is dead, and his son
doesn't have even enough land to stick an awl in; in his poverty he
gathers firewood to feed himself. If I'd have to be like Sunshu Ao, it
would be better to kill myself."

So he sang a song: "Living in the mountains and plowing fields
was bitter; it was hard to get a meal. I might set out and become a

clerk, lusting after the extra wealth of the lowly and knowing no shame. When I die my family might be rich, but I fear that in taking bribes and breaking the law, I might commit some perversion and be convicted of a great crime; I might die and my family might be annihilated. What good is it to become a greedy clerk? I think of being a fastidious clerk, upholding the law and doing my duties, even unto death never daring to do wrong. But what good is it to become a fastidious clerk? The Chu prime minister Sunshu Ao maintained his fastidiousness to the moment of his death, and now his wife and son live in poverty, feeding themselves by gathering firewood. It's not worth it!"

With that, King Zhuang made his apologies to Jester Meng, summoned the son of Sunshu Ao, and gave him a fief of four hundred households in Qinqiu 寢丘 so that he could supply his ancestral sacrifices. Ten generations later the line had not been cut off. This was a matter of knowing the right time for speaking.[69]

Like the first story about Jester Meng, this one is otherwise unattested. Several texts do indicate that Sunshu Ao was famous for his cleverness in securing lasting enfeoffment for his son.[70] This anecdote grew up in the interstices of a well-known legend and made the jester jointly responsible for an act of wit originally ascribed to Sunshu Ao alone.

As observed above, this anecdote has been cited, probably erroneously, as a starting point of Chinese theater. Although it does not grow out of existing traditions of theatrical impersonation, it does go beyond any other early text in making concrete the theatrical assumptions that operated in many narratives. Here, in place of a gesture, a cry, or a minor deviation from ritual propriety that will draw attention to his figure of speech, the jester presents himself as the figure of speech. As a resurrected Sunshu Ao, he restages the implicit covenant by which that minister was first employed. Then, finding the terms unsatisfactory, he rejects them with a joking reference to his own impersonation of the dead: "If I'd have to be like Sunshu Ao, it would be better to kill myself." His peculiar unrhymed song, so ill suited to the terms of the anecdote, nevertheless suggests some of the interests that motivated the telling of this tale.[71] What the jester repairs is not a breach in the impersonal system of ritual propriety that was once thought to order political relations but a lapse in remuneration. If this servant to the king could die unrewarded, then what hope was there for the ordinary functionary, hemmed in as he was between poverty and harsh strictures against corruption? In Sunshu Ao and his proxy, readers who identified with the clerks (*li* 吏) of the song could envision a fantastic solution to the perennial problem of official misprision and stinginess. For all his flamboyance, the jester was a bureaucrat's hero.

Indirect Remonstrance and Shi 士 *Identity*

The shift in King Zhuang's reputation epitomizes larger developments in the anecdotal lore and in the social circumstances that influenced it. Both the philosophical debate about remonstrance and the proliferation of indirect remonstrance legends took place against the background of epochal changes in the Chinese science of government. During the Warring States, regional sovereigns and their immediate subordinates worked out administrative techniques for ruling large territories and populations. The Qin and Han showed that such techniques could be adapted to allow an unprecedented degree of control over the whole of China. As beneficiaries of these developments, the emperors were vastly more powerful than earlier rulers. But, for the maintenance of their power, they were also more dependent than their predecessors had been on clearly defined groups of supporters with competing interests and distinct claims to influence. Some emperors amounted to little more than ciphers in whose names the various groups—eunuchs, in-laws, officials—waged their battles. Others, like Emperor Wu, attempted to wield the power that came with their position. Yet the real disposition of the reigning emperor did little to alter official perceptions of his power or the tone of official communications with him. A simplifying fiction held sway: the emperor's power was absolute.

In much the same way as Zhuyu Ji's direct remonstrance was transformed into a dramatic act by the dizzying hierarchical distance separating him and King Zhuang, the words of functionaries in the Han government were transformed by absolutist assumptions. On the level of ideals, the relation between a "man of service" (*shi*) and the government he served was now defined not by entitlement but by wit, which alone could ensure successful negotiation of the dangers he faced. These dangers were real, in the sense that policy recommendations did sometimes bring reprisals from superiors, including the emperor and his circle. But it was the general climate of danger that had deeper implications for literary and intellectual history. Educated men now saw their words and deeds as command performances, as if the increase in the emperor's power had turned the world into his stage. Under these circumstances, legends of indirect remonstrance held a considerable attraction for them. Nowhere in their experience was there a more effective rhetorical act, a more momentous exploitation of the potential of literary tropes, than in these legends. Other texts might give voice to resentment or celebration, but none confronted deadly force so directly and so deftly or showed how a master of verbal tact might rebuff violence and restore reason with a calculated act of playfulness. The indirect remonstrance was a fantastic realization of intellectual and literary potential as real power.[72]

It was in the heyday of these legends, during the Han, that indirect remonstrance became the premier imaginary justification for literary activity of all sorts. Herein lies the importance of the legends for literary history. Indirect remonstrance always takes the form of an address to a ruler in which a figurative representation exposes the flaws in a policy or a situation. Even though allegoresis in any given indirect remonstrance anecdote is supposed to be finite, in that it is exhausted once the ruler gets the point, allegoresis itself is less easily domesticated. With the possible exception of overt praise, almost no literary representation of the human world is immune to the sort of recontextualization that turns it into a remonstrant's figure, a veiled caricature of the times.[73] Since such second-guessing adds a layer of value to the work, supplementing purely literary pleasures with a putative moral purpose, it is often irresistible. And for Han intellectuals, who sought to explain the historical occasions that had produced their literary canon, the model of indirect remonstrance was indispensable. Not only in *Shi* (Odes) hermeneutics but throughout Han literary and classical scholarship, received texts were read as veiled critiques, whether or not they contained any overt political content or originated in any particular political setting.[74] This way of reading was convenient and was in keeping with the encyclopedic tendencies of Han scholarship, but it also had the effect of imposing the imperial scene of literary production on the whole textual tradition. To put the matter in figurative terms, it was as if the imperial audience exercised such power that it controlled even the staging of pre-imperial works.

All tales of successful remonstrance raise a question about moral transformation. In tales of heroic critiques and, for that matter, in the expectations of readers of the *Mengzi* 孟子 and similar texts, is the king who errs the same man as the king who listens and the king who finally yields? On the one hand, the underlying model appears to be one of recognition and return: through an uplifting anamnesis, the king shakes off his wooziness and dissolution and becomes mindful again of propriety. In this model, the figure of speech is a mirror. On the other hand, the delight that composers and consumers took in these anecdotes was, properly speaking, literary in nature, in the sense that it quite clearly focused on the verbal and formal beauty of the remonstrance text, including the subtlety of its critique and the cunning of its veiled parallels. These turns of phrase might not be as passive a tool as a mirror but might be imagined in a more active role, as the machine that rolls and stamps out a new subject. In this model, the "king" is a subject whose very possibility—to extend a line of thinking advanced by Judith Butler—is produced within the trope, as the listener, confronted with a coded condemnation, "turns" against himself.[75] After all, the true king, in many accounts, is the single individual most prepared to solicit from others speech that he can use in passing judgment on himself and to discover in the world phenomena that will serve the same purpose. Whether he is a king or a *shi*, the achieved moral individual, in early "Confucian" texts and in the more diffuse ideology behind the remonstrance tales, is imagined as continually turning the world against himself, producing himself by finding and interpreting figures for his own failure. The tales of indirect remonstrance were therefore not merely part of the *shi*'s way of defining himself in relation to powerful superiors but may also have expressed and perpetuated a way of thinking in which literary sensitivity was a prop of self-cultivation, a tool for eliciting monitory tropes in the world around oneself.

As the model of indirect remonstrance gained ground, and as legends about the feats of Jester Meng and others multiplied, the gap between imagination and reality began to close, and Han intellectuals found heroic entertainers closer to their own times. Dongfang Shuo 東方朔 (fl. 130 B.C.E.), never mentioned by Sima Qian, was the subject of several anecdotes in Chu Shaosun's supplement to the "Guji liezhuan." By the first century C.E., when Ban Gu 班固 (32–92) wrote, so much lore had accumulated around Dongfang that he merited a lengthy biography of his own, in which the Confucian-minded historian depicted him as a hero of indirect critique (*guji zhi xiong* 滑稽之雄).[76] The *Shiji* biography of Sima Xiangru 司馬相如 (ca. 179-117 B.C.E.)—quite possibly an Eastern Han addition to the text—insists that the entertainer was secretly a remonstrant.[77] Similar but lesser heroes were Mei Gao 枚皋, who with Dongfang Shuo was thought to have been treated as an "entertainer" (*paiyou* 俳優) by Emperor Wu, and Guo, Member of the Suite.[78] Like common jugglers and acrobats, these men occasionally performed before the emperor at the Pingle 平樂 Lodge, where *juedi* 角抵 entertainments were given.[79] Yet they were also, quite clearly, regarded as exemplars of a certain easy familiarity with the emperor,

men who were held up as consummate courtiers because, in their madcap
behavior and inspired verbal performances, they seemed both to "flee the
world in the midst of court" (*bishi yu chaoting* 避世於朝廷) and to gesture
continually at remonstrance. [80] These were the real *yin chen* 隱臣: riddling
officials but also officials hidden away and awaiting discovery. [81] They were
figures of speech embodied.

* * *

Much of the writing that has come down to us from the Warring States and
Western Han periods is of questionable historical value and has been treated
accordingly by historians. Tales of indirect remonstrance are typical in that
they show stereotyped features, contradictions, and anachronisms and are
rarely corroborated in the more reliable historical texts. One might well
suspect that none of the tales of indirect remonstrance discussed here has the
slightest basis in fact; if a pre-imperial entertainer ever did change his ruler's
ways with an amusing hint, we will probably never learn of it. Yet the facts
of literary history have a definite value, and one that is rooted in fictionality
itself. Even in texts whose contents cannot be dated with any great
precision, it is possible to discern the emergence and popularization of a
new type scene, the indirect remonstrance. The tales told about confrontations between King Zhuang and his critics, and between other rulers and
remonstrants, are traces of an imaginary solution—at first tentative, later
irreplaceable—to some of the problems educated men faced with the onset of
the imperial system. They acknowledged the unprecedented concentration of
power in the central court as well as their own relegation to a position of
dependence. They accepted, at least in some contexts, identification with
entertainers, whose low status seemed to make possible an unconventional
intimacy with the ruler. And in imagining their own class in the guise of
entertainers, they idealized the moment when a literary education, projected
as wit, would redeem all the sacrifices that service required. Their fiction
would prove to be very powerful.

NOTES

This chapter is a sequel to Schaberg, "Remonstrance in Eastern Zhou
Historiography." I am grateful to my colleague Richard Strassberg, to graduate
students in the Department of East Asian Languages and Cultures at the
University of California at Los Angeles, and to Haun Saussy for criticism and

encouragement.

1. For overviews of the institution of remonstrance, see Su Zhipi, "Zhongguo gudai yushi, jianguan zhidu di tedian ji zuoyong"; Vandermeersch, "L'institution chinoise de remontrance." For the official title, see Bielenstein, *The Bureaucracy of Han Times*, 209. Despite some pages devoted to remonstrance in his fascinating general study *Detour and Access* (see 125–129), François Jullien is interested less in early narratives of indirect speech than in the ways that notions of indirection characterized other cultural features, including the reception of the *Shijing*. I would argue that late Warring States and early imperial developments in lore and in poetics were closely coordinated.

2. In some ways my discussion parallels that of Zheng Yuyu, who focuses on literati uses of the Qu Yuan character in their conceptualizations of critical speech. See "Zhijian xingshi yu zhishi fenzi," esp. 172–181.

3. See Zhang and Guo, *Zhongguo xiqu tongshi*, vol. 1, 9–15; and the measured remarks of Dolby, "Early Chinese Plays and Theater," 10–11. Yi Junjie collects a number of early and later entertainers' remonstrances; see "Zhongguo gudai shanyu fengjian di youling."

4. This impression, surely a false one, is strengthened by idealized depictions of court communication in which every official, even the lowliest, is expected to correct the ruler. See the examples discussed in my "Remonstrance in Eastern Zhou Historiography."

5. See Zbikowski, "On Early Chinese Theatrical Performances"; Boltz, "Divertissement in Western Han."

6. See Zbikowski, "On Early Chinese Theatrical Performances," 67, 74–75. On the basis of art historical evidence, A. Bulling argued for a wider range of strictly dramatic performances, but was forced at several points into weak speculation; see "Historical Plays in the Art of the Han Period." Some of the weaknesses in her method were pointed out by Soper ("All the World's a Stage: A Note"); in her response ("'All the World's a Stage: A Note': A Rebuttal"), Bulling exposed flaws in Soper's critique without strengthening her own case. Han stone reliefs do not convincingly demonstrate the existence of historical drama in that era.

7. See the examples collected in Li Bingjian, "Xingshi qite di jian."

8. Lewis, "Warring States," 597–603.

9. It is a curious fact, and one not addressed in Vandermeersch's brief account of the institution of remonstrance, that, in the Han histories, officers whose titles make reference to remonstrance very rarely remonstrate. In *Shiji* no "remonstrant" (*jianyi dafu* or *jian dafu* 諫大夫) offers a remonstrance; among dozens of remonstrances in *Hanshu*, I find only two (74.3134–3136 and 77.3243–3246) attributed to titled remonstrants. The ability to present an overt critique and to have it heeded was largely independent of bureaucratic provisions for checking imperial power.

10. As Lewis, "Warring States," 604, writes, starting in the Warring States period, "[a]s royal power increased, the character of office holding changed completely. From being a hereditary element of a government in which power was distributed among the nobility, office became an extension of royal power. . . . The career pattern of these cadres entailed a new ideal type, the 'man of

service' (*shi* 士), who through powers of mind and tongue won for himself the position of guide to the ruler."

11. *Chunqiu Zuo zhuan zhu* (Zhao 28), 1496–1497; cf. *Guoyu*, "Jin yu 9" 晉 語九, 488–489. See discussion in Schaberg, "Remonstrance in Eastern Zhou Historiography," 175–177.

12. *Chunqiu Zuo zhuan zhu* (Zhao 9.5), 1311–1312. Cf. *Liji jijie*, vol. 1, 274–276, where the famous master musician Shi Kuang 師曠 has taken the place of the *Zuo zhuan*'s unnamed performers, the name of the chef is written Du Kui 杜 蕢, and the whole exchange is reframed as a rougher, more striking spectacle.

13. *Han Feizi jishi* 23.476 ("Shuilin xia" 說林下); *Zhanguo ce* 8.304–305 ("Qi yi" 齊一); *Huainanzi jiaoshi* 18.1861–1862 ("Renjian xun" 人間訓); *Xinxu shuzheng* 2.54 ("Zashi" 雜事). The *Han Feizi* version is translated and discussed in Knechtges, "Wit, Humor, and Satire in Early Chinese Literature," 85–86.

14. *Han Feizi jishi* 36.806–807 ("Nan yi" 難一).

15. *Lüshi chunqiu jiaoshi*, 1156 ("Zhong yan" 重言). See translation and discussion below.

16. Ibid., 1225–1226 ("Ju bei" 具備). This is one of several exemplary stories about Mi Zijian's accomplishments in Danfu; several more are collected in *Shuoyuan jiaozheng* 7.158–161 ("Zhengli" 政理).

17. *Lüshi chunqiu jiaoshi*, 1405 ("Jiao zi" 驕恣).

18. Ibid., 1544–1551 ("Zhi jian" 直諫). In one case a minister to Duke Huan 桓 of Qi (r. 685–643 B.C.E.) makes a blunt and ungracious toast; in the other, a tutor to King Wen 文 of Chu (r. 689–677 B.C.E.) punishes the king's profligacy with a symbolic whipping. Also relevant as examples of indirection are remonstrances before "King Zhuang'ai" 莊哀 (an error for King Zhuang) of Chu and the heir of King Hui of Wei (r. 344/334–319 B.C.E.); see 577–578 ("Zhi zhong" 至忠) and 580 n. 10; and 1425 ("Kai chun" 開春).

19. *Guanzi jiaoshi* 22.211 ("Ba xing" 霸形). For dating, see Rickett, *Guanzi*, 348.

20. *Hanshi waizhuan jianshu* 10.870.

21. Ibid. 7.649.

22. Ibid., 10.817–818.

23. *Huainanzi jiaoshi* 11.1174 ("Qisu xun"), 18.1911 ("Renjian xun").

24. The meaning of *guji* is discussed in Pokora, "Ironical Critics at Ancient Chinese Courts (*Shih chi*, 126)," 53; Knechtges, "Wit, Humor, and Satire in Early Chinese Literature," 83, 94; and in commentaries on *Shiji* in Takigawa, *Shiki kaichū kōshō* 126.1. I depart from earlier interpretations in taking *ji* 稽 in its common meaning of "refer to," "test against precedent"; what Sima Qian's examples have in common is their ability to insinuate assertions of precedent without seeming to do so.

25. *Shiji* 126.3197–3199. See translation and discussion in Knechtges, "Wit, Humor, and Satire in Early Chinese Literature," 84–85.

26. *Shiji* 126.3200–3202. Wang Shumin suggests that the text originally had "two hundred years before." But Sima Qian never proceeds backward chronologically in his group biographies, and there are other problems with dating in the chapter. See Wang Shumin, *Shiji jiaozheng*, vol. 10, 3367, 3372.

27. *Shiji* 126.3202–3203.

28. I have related the Ximen Bao anecdote to larger notions of communication in Schaberg, "Travel, Geography, and the Imperial Imagination," 173–175.

29. Takigawa, *Shiki kaichū kōshō* 126.12.

30. The term *waijia* usually refers to imperial in-laws like the family of Empress Lü. Here it appears to apply more broadly to families and/or other groups powerful enough to support their own textual transmissions. Chu claims that Dongfang Shuo was devoted to precisely the same sorts of materials; see *Shiji* 126.3205.

31. Ibid. 126.3203.

32. *Lienü zhuan buzhu* 2.117–118 ("Xianming" 賢明). Cf. *Hanshi waizhuan jianshu* 2.121–122; *Xinxu shuzheng* 1.4 ("Zashi"). The anecdote was apparently still being retold in the second century C.E. as a frame for a zither song attributed to Fan Ji herself; see Lu Qinli, *Xian Qin Han Wei Jin nanbeichao shi*, 305.

33. *Xinxu shuzheng* 1.6 ("Zashi").

34. Ibid. 2.51–52, 54 ("Zashi").

35. Ibid. 6.166 ("Ci she" 刺奢).

36. For Yan Chu and Duke Jing, see *Shuoyuan jiaozheng* 9, "Zhengjian," 207–208; and cf. *Han Feizi jishi* 10.192 ("Shiguo" 十過) (Yan Zhuoju 顏涿聚 and Tian Chengzi 田成子). For Jiu Fan and Duke Ping, see *Shuoyuan jiaozheng* 9.209–210 ("Zhengjian"); and cf. *Lienü zhuan buzhu* 6.119–120 ("Bian tong" 辨通) and *Hou Hanshu* 78.2530. For Mengchang and his guest, see *Shuoyuan jiaozheng* 9.210–212 ("Zhengjian"); and cf. *Shiji* 75.2354 (Su Dai 蘇代 and Mengchang), *Zhanguo ce* 10.374 ("Qi san" 齊三) (Su Qin 蘇秦 and Mengchang), *Zhanguo ce* 18.603 ("Zhao yi" 趙一) (Su Qin and Li Dui 李兌). For parallels to Shao Ruzi's remonstrance, which uses the figure of the cicada, see *Shuoyuan jiaozheng* 9.212–214 ("Zhengjian") and discussion below. For Mao Jiao and the First Emperor, see *Shuoyuan jiaozheng* 9.215–217 ("Zhengjian"); and cf. the abbreviated accounts given at *Shiji* 6.227 and 85.2512–2513. For Zixi and King Zhao, see *Shuoyuan jiaozheng* 9.220–221 ("Zhengjian"); and cf. *Kongzi jiayu shuzheng* 14.89–90 ("Bian zheng" 辯政) (Zixi and unnamed Chu king). For Gong Lu and Zhao Jianzi, see *Shuoyuan jiaozheng* 9.223–224 ("Zhengjian"); and cf. *Liezi jishi* 8.246–247 ("Shuo fu" 説符) (Gongzi Chu 公子鉏 and Duke Wen 文 of Jin [r. 636–628 B.C.E.]) and *Shuoyuan jiaozheng* 13.341–342 ("Quanmou" 權謀) (Gongzi Lü 公子慮 and Duke Wen).

37. Liu's justifications of his editorial work are discussed in Schaberg, "Fictions of History in Liu Xiang's *Shuoyuan*."

38. See the passages translated and discussed in Schaberg, "Remonstrance in Eastern Zhou Historiography," 142–150.

39. The development of notions of institutionalized remonstrance through late Warring States and Western Han works is a case study in early Chinese intertextuality. A passage in the *Xunzi* lays out parallel definitions of remonstrance, insistence (*zheng* 爭), aid (*fu* 輔), and loyal opposition (*bi* 拂) and declares all of these desirable in the minister. Both *Xinshu* 新書 and *Da Dai liji* 大戴禮記 turn two of these functions—aiding and opposing—into the names of official titles, identifying them with the Duke of Zhou and the Duke of Shao 召 respectively and situating these officials with others in the Bright Hall (*ming tang* 明堂). A passage in *Hanshi waizhuan* further historicizes the structure by

claiming that during his regency, the Duke of Zhou employed, among others, five remonstrants (*jian chen* 諫臣), five aides (*fu chen* 輔臣), and five gadflies (*bi chen* 拂臣). Finally, the *Shuoyuan* repeats the *Xunzi* passage almost verbatim, attributing it to Chiyi Zipi 鴟夷子皮 in conversation with Chen Chengzi 陳成子. See *Xunzi xinzhu* 13.213 ("Chen dao" 臣道); *Xinshu*, 52–53 ("Baofu" 保傅); *Da Dai liji jiegu* 48.54–55 ("Baofu" 保傅); *Hanshi waizhuan jianshu* 8.742–743; *Shuoyuan jiaozheng* 2.50-52 ("Chen shu" 臣術). Other texts that project the office of remonstrant (*jian chen*) backward in time from the Han include *Han Feizi jishi* 33.697–698 ("Waichushuo zuo xia" 外儲説左下); *Guanzi jiaoshi* 20.197 ("Xiaokuang" 小匡) (*da jian* 大諫); *Xiaojing zhushu*, 2558 (*zheng chen* 爭臣, a common synonym for *jian chen*); *Lienü zhuan buzhu* 1.10–13 ("Muyi" 母儀). Parallel with this development, new legends emerged concerning sage rulers' devices for soliciting and rewarding remonstrance, especially drums and clappers that prospective remonstrants were to sound to announce their intentions; see *Lüshi chunqiu jiaoshi*, 1601 ("Zizhi" 自知); *Huainanzi jiaoshi* 9.1009 ("Zhushu xun" 主術訓); *Da Dai liji jiegu*, 52–53 ("Baofu"); *Xinshu*, 51–52 ("Baofu"). The inscribed metal statue that Confucius is supposed to have seen in the Zhou court belongs to the same category of objects; see *Shuoyuan jiaozheng* 10.258–259 ("Jing shen" 敬慎). By the Eastern Han, a song inviting remonstrance had been attributed to the Shang king Wu Ding 武丁; see *Qianfulun jianjiaozheng* 34.399 ("Wude zhi" 五德志).

40. See *Zhou li zhushu* 2.731 ("Diguan: Situ" 地官司徒); note the connection implied between the remonstrative and educational duties of the king's tutor (*baoshi* 保氏) and the more public duties of the *sijian* 司諫, "overseer of remonstrance." The *Liji* prescribes ritual measures for the king's reception of remonstrance; see *Liji jijie* 5.376 ("Wang zhi" 王制), 11.691 ("Jiaote sheng" 郊特牲).

41. *Shuoyuan jiaozheng* 9.206 ("Zhengjian").

42. For other such lists, see He Xiu's 何休 (129–182) commentary on the *Gongyang zhuan* 公羊傳, *Gongyang zhuan zhushu* (Zhuang 24), 2238; *Baihu tong shuzheng* 5.279 ("Jianzheng" 諫諍); *Kongzi jiayu shuzheng* 14.89 ("Bianzheng" 辯政).

43. For Zhao Dun, see *Chunqiu Zuo zhuan zhu* (Xuan 2), 656–658. For Wu Zixu, see *Chunqiu Zuo zhuan zhu* (Ai 11), 1664–1665. Although Yan Ying's reputation as a frank remonstrant, best captured in *Yanzi chunqiu* 晏子春秋, developed after the middle Warring States period, he is already a bold critic in earlier accounts: see *Chunqiu Zuo zhuan zhu* (Xiang 25), 1097–1098.

44. See esp. *Lunyu* 18.2, 18.3. It is probably significant that these passages come from what is generally thought to be the very latest portion of the text and may already reflect shifts in notions about proper modes of critique.

45. See *Liji jijie*, vol. 1, 147; *Gongyang zhuan zhushu*, Zhuang 24, 2238; *Shuoyuan jiaozheng* 9.206 ("Zhengjian"); *Baihu tong shuzheng* 5.228–232 ("Jianzheng").

46. The position against remonstrance is represented in *Han Feizi jishi* 6.87 ("Youdu" 有度), 44.918 ("Shuoyi" 説疑). In a discussion related to the actions of Zifan 子反, a general under King Zhuang of Chu, *Chunqiu fanlu* rules out open criticism in favor of less direct means; see *Chunqiu fanlu yizheng* 3.53

("Zhulin" 竹林). It should be observed that the *Han Feizi* also includes apparently admiring tales of indirect remonstrance, as well as some pro-remonstrance sentiments (e.g., *Han Feizi jishi* 10.164, 200–201 ["Shiguo"]).

47. For King Zhuang, see below. Confucius rejects a remonstrance while trapped between Chen and Cai: *Han Shi waizhuan jianshu* 7.599–601; *Shuoyuan jiaozheng* 17.422–424 ("Zayan" 雜言). King Wu 武 of Zhou (r. 1049/45–1043 B.C.E.) also wisely rejects a remonstrance: *Shuoyuan jiaozheng* 13.329–330 ("Quanmou").

48. *Kongzi jiayu shuzheng* 19.132 ("Zilu chu jian" 子路初見), where Xie Ye's name is written 泄冶. The earliest account of Xie Ye's death includes a criticism attributed to Confucius but makes no reference to the remonstrant's class status; see *Chunqiu Zuo zhuan zhu* (Xuan 9), 702.

49. A less familiar example is Zhao Jianzi, who like King Zhuang was renowned for his responses to criticism. Nothing in *Zuo zhuan* prefigures this development in Zhao's image except perhaps his attitude toward divination and one long strategic discussion he is made to engage in: see *Chunqiu Zuo zhuan zhu* (Ai 9), 1652–1654; (Ai 10), 1656; (Ai 20), 1617–1618. Several episodes in *Guoyu* emphasize his willingness to accept critique: see *Guoyu*, 491–492, 496–498 ("Jin yu 9"). For the legendary Zhao, who is both open to critique and singularly qualified to reject faulty advice, see *Lüshi chunqiu jiaoshi*, 792 ("Chang gong" 長攻), 1374–1375 ("Dayu" 達鬱), 1446–1447 ("Qi xian" 期賢), 1636 ("Si shun" 似順); *Shuoyuan jiaozheng* 1.26–27 ("Jun dao" 君道), 2.45–46, 52 ("Chen shu"), 8.200–201, 204 ("Zun xian" 尊賢), 223–224 ("Zheng jian"), 525–526 ("Fan zhi" 反質).

50. *Chunqiu Zuo zhuan zhu* (Xuan 3), 669–672. Cf. *Guoyu*, 511 ("Zheng yu").

51. *Chunqiu Zuo zhuan zhu* (Xuan 11), 713–716; *Shiji* 36.1580; *Kongzi jiayu shuzheng* 10.61 ("Hao sheng" 好生).

52. *Chunqiu Zuo zhuan zhu* (Xuan 12), 718–747, esp. 744–747.

53. *Chunqiu Zuo zhuan zhu* (Xuan 15), 759–760.

54. *Guoyu*, 527–531 ("Chu yu shang" 楚語上).

55. See *Han Feizi jishi* 21.412–413 ("Yu Lao" 喻老) (King Zhuang and an unnamed Right Supervisor of the Horse 右司馬); *Lüshi chunqiu jiaoshi*, 1156 ("Zhong yan"); *Shiji* 40.1700 (King Zhuang and Wu Ju 伍舉); *Shiji* 126. 3197–3198 (King Wei of Qi and Chunyu Kun); *Xinxu shuzheng* 2.51–52 ("Zashi") (King Zhuang and Shi Qing 士慶); *Wu Yue chunqiu* 3.14–15 ("Wang Liao shi Gongzi Guang zhuan" 王僚使公子光傳) (King Zhuang and Wu Ju 伍舉).

56. *Shijing*, "Mao Qiu" 旄丘 (Mao 37).

57. The "Chu shijia" version is exceptional in that this one remonstrance does not change the king's ways, and it is not until several months later, when Su Cong 蘇從 risks a direct remonstrance, that the king finally undertakes reforms. For a rhymed version of Su Cong's remonstrance, see *Shuoyuan jiaozheng* 9.208 ("Zheng jian").

58. *Lüshi chunqiu jiaoshi*, 1161.

59. *Han Feizi*: yi 翼—ze 則, tian 天—ren 人; "Chu shijia": *tian—ren*; "Guji liezhuan": *tian—ren*; *Xinxu*: yi—te 慝, *tian—ren*; *Wu Yue chunqiu*: *tian—ren*.

60. *Han Shi waizhuan jianshu* 10.870.

61. See *Shuoyuan jiaozheng* 9.212–214 ("Zheng jian") (Shao Ruzi and unidentified Wu king planning attack on Qi); *Wu Yue chunqiu* 5.78–80 ("Fuchai neizhuan" 夫差內傳) (the heir You 友 and King Fuchai of Wu [r. 495–473 B.C.E.] planning attack on Qi). Another remonstrance, attributed to Zhuang Xin 莊辛 speaking before King Xiang 襄 of Chu (r. 298–263 B.C.E.), works on the same principles but with different creatures; see *Zhanguo ce* 17.555–561 ("Chu si" 楚 四); *Xinxu shuzheng* 2.47–49 ("Zashi").

62. *Zhuangzi jishi* 20.695 ("Shan mu").

63. 士有反三月之糧者. I find the sentence obscure. In the *Zuo zhuan*, Duke Wen of Jin shows his good faith by employing his army for only three days, having provided them with exactly three days' provisions; King Zhuang does something similar in *Han Shi waizhuan*. See *Chunqiu Zuo zhuan zhu* (Xi 25), 435–436; *Hanshi waizhuan jianshu* 2.105. The *Shuoyuan* line may imply that King Zhuang is using his retainers in excessively long shifts.

64. *Shuoyuan jiaozheng* 9.217–219 ("Zheng jian").

65. See Xiang Zonglu's note, *Shuoyuan jiaozheng*, 219. The parallels are between a paragraph in *Xunzi*, "Yao wen" 堯問, and Zhuyu Ji's examples and conclusion. See *Xunzi xinzhu* 32.510.

66. The saying Zhuyu Ji cites near the beginning of his speech rhymes in the *geng* 耕 rhyme group. The rhymes in the song are *lai* 萊 and *zi* 子 in the *zhi* 之 rhyme group, and *xin* 薪 and *ren* 人 in the *zhen* 真 rhyme group.

67. See *Chunqiu Zuo zhuan zhu* (Zhuang 10), 182–183.

68. *Shiji* 126.3200.

69. Ibid. 126.3201–3202.

70. See *Han Feizi jishi* 21.390 ("Yu Lao"); *Lüshi chunqiu jiaoshi*, 551 ("Yi bao" 異寶); *Huainanzi jiaoshi* 18.1837 ("Renjian xun"); *Liezi jishi* 8.259–260 ("Shuo fu").

71. On the jester's "song" and an Eastern Han epigraphic echo, see Schaberg, "Song and the Historical Imagination in Early China," 333.

72. I thank Martin Kern for bringing to my attention a genre that in some respects resembles the indirect remonstrance anecdotes, the *shelun* 設論, or "hypothetical discourse," in which an author voices dissatisfaction with present political circumstances in a series of responses to an imaginary critic. Both types of composition clearly relate to the status of the *shi* in their confrontations with imperial power; both employ techniques of indirection and copious reference to stock exempla; and in some cases (notably that of Dongfang Shuo), single individuals were thought to have mastered both forms. See the magisterial treatment by Declercq, *Writing against the State*. Among the virtues of the book is its excellent glossary (341–412) of the "emblematic heroes" regularly cited as examples in political arguments (including both remonstrance and *shelun*) during the early medieval period.

73. Allegoresis behaves like irony, which in its most virulent forms is unstable, irrepressible, despotic. To adapt Wayne Booth's terms (*A Rhetoric of Irony*), a "stable" allegory, like the ones demonstrated in the indirect remonstrance anecdotes, is a stalking horse for an "unstable" allegory, the impossibility of speaking in such a way as to mean one and only one thing.

74. Typical are Sima Qian's explanation of the origins of the *Zuo zhuan* and

Wang Yi's 王逸 (second century C.E.) reductive treatment of *Chuci* 楚辭 pieces. See *Shiji* 14.509–510 and *Chuci buzhu*, esp. 99. Instances of the application of the model to works of other genres are collected in Yenna Wu, "In Search of Satire in Classical Chinese Poetry and Prose." One might argue that many Western Han *fu*, including those of Sima Xiangru, have undergone a similar process and now appear as lowly entertainers' bold remonstrative utterances only because later scholars have had good reasons to frame them thus. See note 77 below. Alternatively, one might suggest that mild gestures at critique (and toward Confucian terms of propriety) were gradually being adopted even in certain types of entertainment literature and that in this respect a *fu* performance differed from an indirect remonstrance anecdote mainly in lacking a historical frame and an explicit interpretation of the critical message.

75. See Butler, *The Psychic Life of Power*, 168–169.

76. *Shiji* 117.3002, 3048, 3053, and 3073. The final passage, which cites the views of Yang Xiong 揚雄 (53 B.C.E.-18 C.E.), must have been added by a later hand.

77. In his article "The 'Biography of Sima Xiangru,'" Kern has shown that the *Shiji* biography of Sima Xiangru is almost certainly based on the *Hanshu* biography.

78. *Hanshu* 64A.2775, 51.2366, 65.2844; *Shiji* 126.3204.

79. *Hanshu* 51.2366, 65.2873. For uses of the Pingle Lodge, see Loewe, "The *Juedi* Games," 141.

80. Dongfang Shuo speaks of himself as a court recluse at *Shiji* 126.3205. It is appropriate to recall here the peculiar "song" of Jester Meng, which foregrounds the dilemmas of the lowly official torn between greed and reclusion.

81. On reclusion as a response to the new imperial configuration of power, see Vervoorn, *Men of the Cliffs and Caves*, esp. 88–95.

Chapter 7

Reimagining the Yellow Emperor's Four Faces

Mark Csikszentmihalyi

子貢曰：古者黃帝四面信乎。孔子曰：黃帝取合己者四人使治四
方。。。此之謂四面。

Zigong said: "Should we give credence to the idea that in the past the
Yellow Emperor had four faces?" Confucius said: "The Yellow
Emperor took four people who were in accord with him and sent them
to govern the four directions. . . . This is why they say 'four faces.'"

Taiping yulan 太平御覽, "Huangdi Xuanyuan Shi" 黃帝軒轅氏

This fragment of the *Shizi* 尸子 preserved in a Tang collection recounts a
conversation between Confucius and his disciple Zigong about the legend
that the mythical Yellow Emperor (Huangdi) had four faces. It is
characteristic of the portrayals of Confucius in Warring States and Qin-Han
texts that he offers a historical explanation of lore and curiosities brought to
him by his disciples. Derk Bodde comments on this story: "What is meant
is that the Yellow Lord used four officials to govern the four quarters. . . .
So he was 'four faced' in the sense that the four 'faces' or 'sides' of his
empire were controlled by these officials on his behalf."[1] Zigong's question
indicates familiarity with other, less figurative, readings of the "four faces."
While Confucius was solely concerned with explaining the symbolism of
Huangdi's four faces in a historically reductive fashion, from the viewpoint
of a contemporary reader of early Chinese literature, it is possible that a
more literal answer to Zigong's question may be found.

This chapter has two aims, one specific to the issue of the four faces of
Huangdi and a more general one concerning how epigraphic or pseudepi-
graphic writings became decontextualized as texts were transmitted in early
China. In the first section, I will argue that while Confucius might

226

have correctly identified one meaning of the symbolism surrounding the Yellow Emperor, there are other answers to the riddle of the four faces. It is possible to identify a passage in an inscription-style silk text—"Liming" 立命 (Establishing the mandate), an early Han manuscript excavated at Mawangdui 馬王堆 in the 1970s—that was composed to evoke a vessel that literally depicted the Yellow Emperor as having four faces. The text's evocation of the medium of a vessel with four faces coincides with a message that told of his sending ministers to govern the four directions. The "Liming" is not alone, because for many texts of the period, the assertion of a link between a text and a ritually privileged medium served to valorize or sanctify the text.

The more general argument applies this observation about an excavated text to transmitted texts that do not at first appear to have connections to inscriptions at all. As in the case of the "Liming" inscriptional passage, the connection between ritual medium and text can break down, and the resulting decontextualization is an important phase in the development of some early texts. Reimagining the original medium of inscriptional passages in texts such as the *Laozi* 老子 may provide important information about the genesis of such passages.

This assertion of a link between a text and a ritually privileged medium is related to the phenomenon of the actual shift from bamboo and silk to a ritually privileged medium already described by Falkenhausen and Kern (see chapters 3 and 5). In the case of the "Liming," the sacrality of the text derives not from its message but from the link, either historical or imagined, to a ritually significant medium.

Literary Inscriptions

In order to examine the conventions of Warring States and Qin-Han inscriptions associated with former rulers and sages such as the Yellow Emperor, I will begin with a survey of some inscriptions listed in the bibliographical chapter of the *Hanshu* 漢書. By examining their titles and assembling fragments of these now lost texts, I will develop a list of attributes that describe a subgenre of the political-philosophical writing of the period (*zhuzi baijia* 諸子百家, "the many masters and hundred experts") that I will label "literary inscriptions." Turning to the matter of the four faces of the Yellow Emperor, it will become clear that the Mawangdui silk text "Liming" shares a number of attributes with these and other texts.

Since the "Liming" is written in the voice of the Yellow Emperor and describes the gathering of four ministers to, in the words of Confucius, "govern the four directions," I will hypothesize that this inscription is the key to understanding the claim that the Yellow Emperor had four faces. Specifically, I argue that the claim was not just symbolic but actually describes a four-faced vessel on which the "Liming" text purported to be inscribed. Reimagining this vessel allows us to recontextualize the "Liming" and better understand both this text and other early texts which display the attributes of this subgenre.

During the late fourth through second centuries B.C.E., China produced several genres that claimed authority based on their historical pedigree. Testimony to this development is the elaborate reconstruction of the ritual offices and procedures of the Zhou dynasty that make up the *Three Ritual Compendia* (San li 三禮). Another set of developments that speaks to this phenomenon is treated in Gu Jiegang's 顧頡剛 (1893–1980) analysis of the origins of the doctrine of Huang Lao 黃老 (i.e., the Yellow Emperor and Laozi). Gu asserts that the promotion of the myth that Laozi was Confucius's teacher was a step in a deliberate propaganda campaign on the part of Warring States Daoists. He argues that the Daoists' next step was to find a sage-king who preceded the Confucian exemplars Yao 堯 and Shun 舜:

Using material from their own scholarly faction, they fashioned it into clothing to dress the Yellow Emperor, and as a result the Yellow Emperor came to resemble Laozi. Those in the Daoist faction then took Laozi to be the "great ancestor high emperor," and the Yellow Emperor to be the "original ancestor founding emperor." Their formative period then extended back directly to the start of written history. Even Yang Zhu 楊朱, the one who had begun this trend, had long since been swept aside. The scholarly order was thrown into disarray. The arrangement of Daoist texts in the *Hanshu* "Yiwen zhi" 藝文志 contains the *Four Classics of the Yellow Emperor* (Huangdi sijing 黃帝四經), *Yellow Emperor Inscriptions* (Huangdi ming 黃帝銘), and other works. The comment reads: "They arose during the period of the six states and are similar to the *Laozi*." Joining together the Yellow Emperor and Laozi was a success, and the term "Huang Lao" could never again be separated into its two parts.[2]

Whether or not Gu's explanations of the source of Yellow Emperor-related texts and the origins of Huang Lao doctrine are ultimately correct, he is certainly right that age and association with the doctrines of prior sage-kings gave texts value. His use of the particular example of the *Hanshu*'s description of the *Huangdi ming* is particularly telling, as Han sources attest that pseudepigraphy was a primary means of conferring on texts an aura of age.[3]

Huangdi ming is one of two titles in the "Yiwen zhi" section of the *Hanshu* that are associated with the Yellow Emperor and that claim to have originally been inscribed. The first is the *Huangdi ming*, in six *pian* 篇, listed among the works of the subcategory "Way" (*Dao* 道). The other is associated with the Yellow Emperor's disciple Kong Jia 孔甲, the *Pan and Yu Vessel Warnings* (Panyu jie 盤盂戒), in 26 *pian*, that is listed in the subcategory "Eclectic" (*Za* 雜).[4] The character *ming* 銘, "engravings" or "inscriptions," refers to the process of engraving on bronze and more generally refers to writing that uses a hard object that incises rather than a brush that applies ink. The entries in the "Yiwen zhi" section, however, are explicit that these texts were written on strips of bamboo. Rather than creating a neologism such as "uninscribed inscriptions" to distinguish this type of text from the general class of inscriptions, I will simply refer to texts that purport to be inscriptions, even though they are written on bamboo and silk, as "literary inscriptions." The two examples above share some characteristics that we will see are not unusual for other Han period literary inscriptions. First, they are associated with past rulers, sages, or their ministers or disciples. Below, other examples of literary inscriptions associated with King Wu 武 and the Yellow Emperor will be examined. Second, they are admonitory or instructive in tone. In the *Wen xuan* 文選, *ming* and *zhen* 箴, "admonitions," form most of fascicle 56.[5] While these two characteristics are not present in all writing that purported to have originally been inscribed on vessels and objects and later to have been transmitted separately on bamboo and silk, they are present in a significant subset of those texts.

The *Huangdi ming* and the *Panyu jie* were studied in the Han, and such inscriptions have even had influence in modern times.[6] The didactic use of literary words associated with revered figures from the past is found in several early sources that explain how the placement of the inscription associated with a sage or ruler allows it to be used in situations that are relevant to the inscription's content. The importance of placement of the words of a sage is attested in a passage from the *Analects* that concerns the disciple Zizhang's 子張 sash. Zizhang asks Confucius about taking action, and the Master replies that success is born of "being trustworthy and loyal

in one's words, as well as sincere and reverent in one's actions" (言忠信行
篤敬). The passage concludes:

〔子曰：〕立則見其參於前也。在輿則見其倚於衡也。 夫然後行
。子張書諸紳。

[Confucius continued:] "When you are standing, then you see them
assembled in front of you.[7] When you are riding in a carriage, then you
see them leaning against the horizontal beam [attached to the collars of
the horses]. Only then should you act." Zizhang wrote this on his
sash.[8]

By writing the master's words on his sash, Zizhang is *literally* putting
his master's words where they will always be "assembled in front of him."
Using a similar rationale, Han literati circulated texts suitable for staffs,
carriage tables, and clothing using the same rationale found in the
Analects—one should strive to keep the words of the sages literally in front
of one's eyes at all times. Central to this genre is the connection between
medium and message. The content of the texts under discussion here is a
development of the political-philosophical writing of "the hundred
approaches of the masters." Yet unlike the majority of the extant works in
that genre, part of the text self-referentially identifies a medium with which
the text is connected. Some of these inscriptions were associated with
ordinary objects, and their content was tied to the use of the object. For
example, when the Han historian Sima Qian 司馬遷 (ca. 145–c.86 B.C.E.),
in his *Records of the Grand Historian* (Shiji 史記), recounts the closing
words of the inscription of a *ding* 鼎 vessel of Confucius's deceased ancestor
Zheng 正—"With the thin gruel in this, with the thick gruel in this, I filled
my mouth" (饘於是 粥於是 以餬余口)[9]—the vessel's use for food storage
is intimately connected to the message. The same text records that the
personal effects of Confucius were preserved as relics by his followers.[10]
Han inscriptions with titles such as the *Panyu jie* mentioned above, the
Handkerchief Table Prototypes (Jinji fa 巾机法), the *Bronze Table
Inscriptions* (Jinji ming 金机銘), and the *Carriage Table Admonitions* (Yuji
jian 輿机緘) are mentioned in various sources.[11] These inscriptions
provided constant reminders to their owners, the type of reminder that could
not be avoided, because they were attached to an object used every day.
     Other inscriptions were not on objects of the sages or rulers but on
images of them. The use of this medium can be explained by the perceived
link between human beings and their images. This link is the basis for the

perceived efficacy of the statue double (*ouren* 偶人), which may have derived from the carvings used as stand-ins for the dead or substitutes for the living in tombs. The wider use of statue doubles is provided a historical basis in the "Basic Annals of the Three Sovereigns" (Sanhuang benji 三皇本紀) in Sima Qian's *Shiji*, a chapter partly devoted to reconstructing the circumstances of the composition of the different sections of the *Shangshu* 尚書. In it, the decadent Shang king Wu Yi 武乙 takes various measures to show his superiority to Heaven, one of which is the creation of a statue double, which he nicknames Tianshen 天神 (Heavenly Spirit). The king often gambled against the statue double, having others animate it, and when it lost they would collectively humiliate it. [12] Wu Yi was, of course, killed— hit by lightning on a hunting expedition. During the Han, statue doubles of human beings served multiple functions, one of which was as a tool to adversely affect living people by burying the doubles or shooting them with arrows. [13] Another function of statues was to bring good fortune to the owner. An example of this function is a second-century B.C.E. apotropaic jade figurine bearing an inscription guaranteeing the bearer a nineteen-year extension of life, identified by Jeffrey Riegel as an image of the "King Duke of the East," the consort of the more celebrated Queen Mother of the West. [14] Because of their use of first-person testimony, these examples indicate that there was perceived to be a quasi-magical link between the statue and the individual whose likeness the statue bore. Inscriptions on such statues may be seen as an early form of fictional autobiography.

The genre of inscriptions on everyday objects and on depictions of the speakers of the words was popular in the third and second centuries B.C.E. Yet while these inscriptions were associated with such objects, this does not imply that they were always actually inscribed on such objects. Just as words allegedly uttered in a living room or a supermarket in a modern advertisement may actually have first been spoken in a Madison Avenue ad agency, so too the purported source or antiquity of these literary inscriptions may simply be an attempt to lend them authority. Indeed, among the sources of the texts that will be examined in more detail in the next three sections are some of the more important classical authorities of China of the fourth through second centuries B.C.E. Without going as far as Gu Jiegang does in detecting a conspiracy to create a fictitious and authoritative past, it is nevertheless likely that some of these inscriptions were indeed composed in the fourth century B.C.E. or later and attributed to a figure from the early Zhou or before. Each of the next three sections deals with a separate example of the literary inscription.

The King Wu Inscriptions

In the late Warring States period, one of the earliest figures associated with literary inscriptions is King Wu 武王, the founder of the Zhou dynasty and a major icon of the Ru 儒 tradition. A fragment of Cai Yong's 蔡邕 (132–192) *Discussion of Inscriptions* (Ming lun 銘論) preserved in the Li Shan 李善 (ca. 630–689) commentary to the *Wen xuan* contains the following summary of the relevant lore: "When King Wu ascended to the throne, he sought advice from his Grand Master and created the *Mat, Table, Pillar, Staff*, and various other inscriptions" (武王踐阼咨于太師而作席机楹杖雜銘).[15] Cai's statement refers to the tradition that King Wu created a series of inscriptions on objects to remind himself about appropriate behavior in the context of the situations in which each object was to be used. A more elaborate version of this story appears in the *Elder Dai's Record of Ritual* (Da Dai liji 大戴禮記), traditionally thought to be a Han collection. However, the chapter from which it comes, "King Wu Ascends the Throne" (Wuwang jianzuo 武王踐阼), is part of the set of late Warring States bamboo texts in Chu script now at the Shanghai Museum.[16] These texts show indications of preserving a very early stratum of the disciple tradition of Confucius and perhaps provide a *locus classicus* for this inscription tradition. In the *Da Dai liji*, the narrative begins:

> 武王踐阼三日，召士大夫而問焉曰：惡有藏之約行之，行萬世可以為子孫常者乎。諸大夫對曰：未得聞也。然後召師尚父而問焉曰：昔黃帝顓頊之道存乎。意亦忽不可得見與。師尚父曰：在丹書。王欲聞之則齊矣。

> Three days after King Wu ascended the throne, he summoned his officials and asked of them: "Is there a set of treasured essentials that will work when put into practice, so that myriad future generations will practice them, and they can become a benchmark for my sons and grandsons?" His officials replied: "We have not heard of any." Afterward, [the king] summoned [Grand] Master Shangfu and asked him: "Does the Way of the Yellow Emperor and Zhuan Xu from ancient times still exist? Or is it the case that their intentions have also been lost and can no longer be known?" [Grand] Master Shangfu said: "It is in the cinnabar writings. If your majesty desires to hear them, then you will become their equal."[17]

King Wu, the Confucian paragon, turns to Lü Wang 呂望 (here,

Shangfu 商父), his advisor who is enfeoffed in the state of Qi.[18] Lü Wang is apparently the recipient of an esoteric transmission written in cinnabar ink (*danshu* 丹書) that he is willing to share with King Wu. It is worth noting that while the *Da Dai liji* tells us that King Wu based his governance on the principles of the Yellow Emperor and his grandson Zhuan Xu 顓頊, the Shanghai Museum strip version of this text reads: "the Yellow Emperor, Zhuan Xu, Yao 堯, and Shun 舜."[19]

King Wu was so impressed with the contents of these cinnabar books that he created a number of inscriptions to presumably serve in the same way as Zizhang's sash. In the *Da Dai liji*, examples of the inscriptions are given. Once Lü Wang relates the "treasured essentials" of the Yellow Emperor and Zhuan Xu concerning valuing reverence over idleness and righteousness over desire, King Wu made inscriptions to admonish himself:

王聞書之言惕若恐懼 。退而為戒書於，席之四端為銘焉，於機為銘焉，於鑑為銘焉，於盥盤為銘焉，於楹為銘焉，於杖為銘焉，於帶為銘焉，於履屨為銘焉，於觴豆為銘焉，於戶為銘焉，於牖為銘焉，於劍為銘焉，於弓為銘焉，於矛為銘焉。席前左端之銘曰：安樂必敬。 前右端之銘曰：無行可悔。 後左端之銘曰：一反一側亦不可以忘。 後右端之銘曰：所監不遠視邇所代。

When King Wu heard the words of the books, he was impressed to the point of abject terror. He immediately withdrew and began to inscribe "admonitory writings" on the four corners of his mat, his table, his mirror, his washbasin, the pillar, his staff, his sash, his shoes, his cups and food vessels, the door, the southern windowsill, his sword, his bow, and his halberd. The inscription on the front left corner of his mat reads: "In peace and joy there must be reverence." On the front right corner it reads: "No action should cause remorse." On the back left corner it reads: "Even when turning restlessly, one cannot forget it." On the back right corner it reads: "What one cannot see is what is distant; instead, look at what is near."[20]

Each of the four "inscriptions" (here, a broader sense of the term than "engraving" is clearly intended) on his mat contains an aphorism to think about when sitting. A similar connection is apparent in King Wu's staff inscription. It reads:

惡乎危。於忿疐。惡乎失道。於嗜慾。惡乎相忘。於富貴。

Why does danger arise? From becoming angry. Why does one lose the

Way? From having appetites. Why does one forget this? From wealth and status.[21]

The mid–sixth-century C.E. commentator Lu Bian 盧辯 noted that a staff was an appropriate medium for a message about traveling the Way,[22] and the admonitions of King Wu were adapted to the situations in which each object was used. These admonitions, condemning the forgetfulness of the Way that arises from wealth and status, were designed to arouse fear and awe. The next example, an inscription on a metal statuette, is designed to inspire a similar reaction.

The "Bronze Man Inscription"

The category of inscriptions on images of sages or rulers includes a set of admonitions that the Qing scholar Yan Kejun 嚴可均 (1762–1843) identified as part of the Yellow Emperor's "Bronze Man Inscription" (Jinren ming 金人銘). The admonitions appear in Liu Xiang's 劉向 (79–8 B.C.E.) *Shuiyuan* 説苑 as part of a passage that relates Confucius's inspection of a Zhou ancestral temple. In the preamble, Confucius finds a "bronze man" with a covered mouth and an inscription on its back.[23] The inscription generally urges the bearer to be cautious in speaking[24] and concludes as follows:

> 盜怨主人，民害其貴。君子知天下之不可蓋也。故後之下之，使人慕之。執雌持下，莫能與之爭者。人皆趨彼，我獨守此。眾人惑惑，我獨不從。內藏我知。不與人論技。我雖尊高，人莫害我。夫江河長百谷者以其卑下也。天道無親常與善人。戒之哉。戒之哉。

Robbers resent the rulers; common people regard the nobility as harmful.[25] The gentleman understands that it is best not to be at the top of the empire, so he follows behind and stays underneath.[26] This causes others to admire him. He grasps the female [tally] and holds the inferior [position], so no one is his match.[27] Others all hasten over there, but I alone remain here.[28] The masses are deluded. I alone do not follow.[29] I store my knowledge inside myself; I do not discuss my art with others.[30] Although I am respected and exalted, no one regards me as harmful. This is the reason that the Yangzi and Yellow Rivers are at the head of a hundred valleys, because they always occupy the lowest place.[31] "The Way of Heaven is impartial; it always rewards good people."[32] Take warning! Take warning!

Despite the references and direct quotations in this passage from several chapters of the *Laozi* 老子, this argument for being cautious in one's speech receives Confucius's endorsement. In the *Shuiyuan*, after reading the inscription, Confucius recalls a passage from the *Classic of Poetry* (Shijing 詩經) to convey the sense of fear and awe the message imparts, and he tells his disciples: "If one were to deport oneself like this, how could one court disaster by opening one's mouth?" (行身如此豈以口遇禍哉).[33] Both the cautionary content of the message and the fear it imparts are similar to the earlier example of King Wu. The reverence described by Confucius is certainly the correct attitude in religious matters, and so the inscription is an appropriate one for an object with potential religious significance such as a "bronze man."[34]

"Establishing the Mandate" *and the* Yellow Emperor Inscriptions

As seen above, the *Hanshu* reports the existence of the text *Huangdi ming* in six *pian* during the Han dynasty. In the thirteenth century, Wang Yinglin 王應麟 (1223–1296) argued that the "Jinren ming" was one of the six parts of the lost *Huangdi ming*. Wang based his conclusion on a fragment of the lost Three Kingdoms period text *Huanglan* 皇覽:

> 武王問尚父：五帝之誡可得聞歟。尚父曰：黃帝之誡曰：吾之居
> 民上也。搖搖恐夕不至朝。故為金人，三封其口曰：古之慎言。
> King Wu asked Shangfu: "Can the admonitions of the Five Emperors be accessed and understood?" Shangfu said: "The Yellow Emperor's admonition reads: 'When I lived above the common people, I was unsettled and feared that no dawn would follow the night. Therefore I made a bronze man and bound his mouth thrice, saying, "the ancients guard their words!"'"[35]

This fascinating passage combines the speakers from the King Wu inscriptions with the content of the "Jinren ming." The use of the term "five emperors" (*wudi* 五帝) is worth noting here, since there are several different enumerations of the five emperors. The Shanghai version of the "Wuwang

jianzuo" 武王踐阼 passage discussed above as part of the examination of
the King Wu inscriptions has the names of four of the five emperors as
enumerated in various versions of "The Virtue of the Five Emperors" (Wudi
de 五帝德). This parallel shows a connection between the two texts that
was not available to Wang Yinglin and that supports his inference that there
was a connection between the "Jinren ming" and the lost *Huangdi ming*.[36]
One reason this fragment is so interesting is that it combines the narrative
framework of "Wuwang jianzuo" with the content of the "Jinren ming,"
which it attributes to the Yellow Emperor. It is possible that, as Wang
Yinglin suggested, this shows that the "Jinren ming" was part of the lost
Huangdi ming. It is also possible that the composer of this fragment sought
to reconstruct the *Huangdi ming* and understood that the King Wu
inscriptions were their model. The idea of such modeling of Yellow
Emperor texts on "Confucian" counterparts is consistent with Gu Jiegang's
theory about the origin of the Han Yellow Emperor stories.

   This is not the only extant text that may be connected to the *Huangdi
ming*. The Mawangdui silk text "Liming" is also likely related to it. The
"Liming" is part of the so-called *Sixteen Classics* (Shiliu jing 十六經) or
Ten Great Classics (Shi da jing 十大經) preceding the *Laozi* B 老子乙 text,
discovered at Mawangdui in 1973, on the same piece of silk. This find has
been called by some the *Four Classics of the Yellow Emperor* (Huangdi
sijing 黃帝四經).[37] The "Liming" contains a literary treatment of an
inscription apparently from a four-faced image of the Yellow Emperor.

   Since having four faces is not an ordinary happenstance, it is worth
asking in what sense the Yellow Emperor had four faces. The image of the
Yellow Emperor served as a stand-in for the deified ruler and perhaps also as
a guide for the new Emperor Zhuan Xu. It had four sides, and on each side
there was a face. Symbolically, the four faces were a metaphor for the
Yellow Emperor's four ministers, as described in the context of a discussion
of worthy ministers in the third-century B.C.E. *Lüshi chunqiu* 呂氏春秋:
"The Yellow Emperor established the four faces (*simian* 四面)."[38] The
Eastern Han commentator Gao You 高誘 (fl. 205 C.E.) provides the
following explanation of the sentence:

黃帝使人四面出求賢人。得之立以為佐。故曰：立四面也。

The Yellow Emperor sent people out in all four directions in order to
find worthies. When they were found, the worthies were established as
aides. Therefore, it is said that he "established the four faces."[39]

Gao You coins an extended meaning of "faces," referring to ministers of the four directions. These early quotations attest to the existence of, at the latest, a third-century B.C.E. tradition that figuratively attributed four faces to the Yellow Emperor. There is also a literal attribution of the four faces. A fragment of the third-century B.C.E. *Bamboo Annals* (Zhushu jinian 竹書記年) narrates the creation of such an image of the Yellow Emperor, after his apotheosis, by his minister Zuo Che 左徹.[40] His four faces represented the faces of his ministers, who served as his eyes and ears in the four directions of the empire.

A similar reference to the four directions is found in the preamble to the Mawangdui passage that I am arguing is a literary inscription. At the beginning of the "Liming" text we find such an image of a vessel with a four-faced Yellow Emperor:

> 昔者，黃宗質始好信作。自為象方四面，傅一心。四達自中，前參，後參，左參，右參。踐位，履參。是以能為天下宗。
>
> In the past, the Yellow Ancestor began his material existence with an affinity for trustworthy endeavors. He himself made an image that faced the four directions, and [all four faces] aided a single mind. All four extended out from one center, and they sought verification in front, behind, to the left, and to the right.[41] When he ascended to his office, he carried out this verification. This is the way he was able to be the ancestor of all under Heaven.[42]

Here, the words *jianwei* 踐位 ("ascended to his office") echo King Wu's preparation for ascending the throne (*jianzuo* 踐阼). The term *xiang* 象 ("image" or "representation") is used, and the image is said to have "faced the four directions." This description is a formal preamble describing the inscribed object. The text of the inscription follows this description of the medium and begins:

> 吾受命於天，定位於地，成名於人。唯余一人，德乃配天。乃立王三公，立國置君三卿。數日，曆月，計歲，以當日月之行。吾允地廣，裕類天大明。
>
> I received the mandate from Heaven, was established in my position on Earth, and developed my fame from the people. It is only I, the One Man, whose virtue matches Heaven, who established the princes and three dukes, established states, set up lords and the three ranks of nobility. I counted the days, sequenced the months, calculated the year,

matching each to the movement of the sun and moon. Following Earth in its wide abundance, I am of a kind with Heaven in its great clarity.[43]

Because of textual deterioration, the remainder of the inscription is more difficult to read, but the entire "Liming" uses at least eleven first-person pronouns (*wu* 吾 and *yu* 余) and reflects the importance of the ruler's correspondence with Heaven and Earth. The three phases of the process of his becoming the "ancestor of all under Heaven" involve a sort of verification by the three components of the triad of Heaven, Earth, and human beings, one of the basic cosmological features of Han thought. The speaker emulates Heaven and Earth and in turn is to be emulated by the ruler who heeds his example. While the rest of the inscriptional section is mostly illegible, the content of the testimony indicates that the speaker was supposed to be the Yellow Emperor, or his image.

The first section of the "Liming," like that of the "Jinren ming," sets the stage for the inscription by describing the vessel or image on which the inscription was carved, and the second section provides the inscription. The "Liming" poses an interesting problem in that the first-person description of the means of uniting the empire does not explicitly harken back to the motif of the four directions. The manner of unification, aligning the human world with the cosmos, recalls the astrocalendrical feats of the ministers of the sage-king Yao in the "Yao dian" 堯典 section of the *Shangshu* 尚書.[44] If we consider once more Gu Jiegang's theory that texts like the *Huangdi ming* were one faction's attempt to establish Huang and Lao chronologically prior to Yao and Shun, this parallel raises the intriguing possibility that the multiple ministers of Yao known as Xi 羲 and He 和 were in some way models for the four ministers of the Yellow Emperor.[45]

The Assumed Medium of the
Yellow Emperor Inscriptions

If there were originally six different inscriptions in the edition of the *Huangdi ming* listed in the *Hanshu*, then it is certainly possible that this passage was one of them. But to fit with the literary inscriptions cited above, the inscription must be associated with an object that was its assumed medium. Further, the medium and the message should be connected.

While the text itself does not explicitly specify a medium, the content points to a vessel or image with four faces. The medium matches the story of the figure carved by Zuo Che and exhibits the neat match of medium and message observed in the other examples: a four-sided figure (like Vairocana Buddha) is ideal for observing each of the four directions. By extension, the four faces corresponded to specific ministers of the Yellow Emperor.

One candidate for such a medium would be a vessel with the *siling* 四靈 or *sishen* 四神 (four luminaries) pattern, an important motif in later imperial iconography. In that context, the traditional names for the four are the Azure Dragon (Qinglong 青龍), White Tiger (Baihu 白虎), Red Sparrow (Zhuque 朱雀), and Dark Warrior (Xuanwu 玄武). In late Warring States and Qin-Han texts, however, the names of the four luminaries are still in flux.[46] A Western Han wine-warming vessel found in Xi'an is decorated with these four animals.[47] It is the earliest known depiction on a vessel of the four luminaries and has a dragon, tiger, bird, and tortoise (the tortoise being Dark Warrior). In his treatment of the Chu silk manuscript (Chu boshu 楚帛書), Li Ling 李零 has convincingly argued that the *sishen* are found in that text.[48] These examples do not definitively show that the motif is connected to the assumed vessel of the "Liming" literary inscription, but they do suggest that the motif was known at the time.

A Han dynasty connection between this motif and the Yellow Emperor may be found on several levels. First of all, the commonly attested status of the Yellow Emperor as the inventor of the calendar and of astronomy is detailed in the "Liming," following the description of a four-faced object. The Mawangdui text claims that the Yellow Emperor "counted the days, sequenced the months, calculated the year, matching each to the movement of the sun and moon."[49]

Second, there is some overlap between the Yellow Emperor's four ministers and the four luminaries. In early texts, the *siling* are associated with the four quadrants of the night sky, each comprising seven of the twenty-eight lunar lodges.[50] This association is seen as early as in the astronomical chapter of the *Huainanzi* (Master of Huainan, ca. 140 B.C.E.), where the Blue Dragon (Canglong 蒼龍) is in the east, the White Tiger in the west, the Red Sparrow in the south, and the Dark Warrior in the north. Even the particular association of the Yellow Emperor's ministers with the directions is made in several early texts. Because the color yellow is associated with the center, the association of the Yellow Emperor in the context of the *wudi* 五帝 has always been with the middle. A clear connection is made in the "Wuxing" 五行 chapter of the *Guanzi* 管子.[51]

This quotation links the *siling* tradition with that of the four ministers of the Yellow Emperor. It reads:

昔者，黃帝。。。得奢龍而辯於東方，得祝融而辯於南方，得大
封而辯於西方，得后土而辯於北方。

In the past, the Yellow Emperor . . . employed She Long and was able to discern the east, employed Zhu Rong and was able to discern the south, employed Da Feng and was able to discern the west, employed Hou Tu and was able to discern the north.

Here, the inclusion of the Uncoiled Dragon (She Long 奢龍) as his eastern minister is a connection to the *siling* tradition. [52] The image of the Yellow Emperor observing through the eyes of his dragon minister recalls both the wine-warming vessel and the language of the literary inscription in the description of the Mawangdui image. Further, the presence of Zhu Rong among the employees of the Yellow Emperor is suggestive because the passage combines elements of some of the four-luminaries lists (i.e., animals) with some of the four-ministers lists (i.e., people), indicating that these were perhaps originally overlapping lists. [53] A very clear Eastern Han indication of this may be found in a fragment of an Eastern Han commentary by Cai Yong. In that text, the Yellow Emperor is placed in the center, with the *siling* in the four directions, representing the star Arcturus (Dajiao 大角) and four of twelve lunar lodges, respectively. [54] These connections all constitute supporting evidence that the motif of four-faced vessels, with semidivine beings associated with the four directions, was connected with the Yellow Emperor's four ministers in the early period. This provides a candidate for the form of the vessel described in the "Liming," although there are of course many other possibilities.

Regardless of how one reimagines the "Liming" vessel, the similarities between the "Liming" and literary inscriptions in general, and those connected with the *Huangdi ming* in particular, have implications for the identification of the Mawangdui text of which the "Liming" inscription is a part. The possible identification of the "Liming" as part of the *Huangdi ming* supports the position of Robin Yates and Li Ling that the text in which it appears had multiple authors and was not part of the *Huangdi sijing* listed in the *Hanshu* 漢書. [55] Instead, if the "Liming" is identified as a section of the *Huangdi ming*, this suggests that the entire Mawangdui text of which it is a part is most likely a composite one. [56] It is probably made up of the *Huangdi ming* and several other Yellow Emperor texts, perhaps including *The Yellow Emperor and His Ministers* (Huangdi junchen 黃帝君臣), listed in the *Hanshu* as having ten *pian*.[57] Since this inscriptional excerpt on "verification" is followed by a passage about one of the Yellow Emperor's minister's ability to observe the empire carefully, there may well have been an attempt to integrate the texts in a topical way so as to assemble a collection of Yellow Emperor texts out of what was on hand in the area of the former southern state of Chu.

Imagining Ritual Media

What this discussion of the "Liming" and texts like it demonstrates is that, even in texts that are not inscribed on vessels, images, everyday objects, or other media, the *claim* of a connection with such media may play an important authorizing role. A new understanding and potential identification of the "Liming" only emerges if one matches it to its original medium and reads its first-person passages as the testimony of the subject of the figure or owner of the object on which it purports to have been inscribed. The history, real or fictive, of the creation of the vessel was probably assumed knowledge for the target audience of the "Liming." In the Mawangdui context, however, the text has shifted media, from inscription to political-philosophical essay on silk. The question is: can we understand the text without reading it back into its original medium? The answer depends on what one is trying to get out of the text. Reading the text without knowledge of its purported connection to a vessel does not necessarily decontextualize it beyond understanding.

The conventions of the inscriptional language can only be taken into account once the text is identified as an inscription. The Yellow Emperor's "taking office" resonates with the King Wu inscriptions and stories, and the meaning of the four faces is much clearer when imagined in the context of the four-sided vessels described above. In the same way, the function (theoretical or actual) of these inscriptions may be understood only if the context of the ritual or other use of the object on which they are inscribed is understood, because in most literary inscriptions, the message and the medium are linked. From the point of view of the modern reader of this decontextualized text, the problem is not misconstruing the intent of the author of the text (whether or not that is ever a problem). Rather, the issue is that the text may not be comprehensible when it has been displaced from its claim to authority.

This should not be surprising, since in early China, placement is often important to understanding the function of inscriptions. As Falkenhausen has argued, bronze inscriptions were used in the context of offerings made at the altars of lineage temples, and as such, "the intended recipients of the texts were the ancestral spirits in heaven."[58] In support of this argument, Falkenhausen notes that the placement of inscriptions on ritual objects such as bells is not optimal for being read by human ritual participants. This is the sense in which the relationship of text to object on which it is inscribed is pivotal: "it was arguably their physical association with the offerings to the spirits that made it possible to convey them to the ancestral sphere."[59] Similarly, the Qin imperial stelae inscriptions were likewise embedded in a complex ritual context. Kern argues that the imperial stelae, in common with descriptions of prior stone texts, may represent the result of a practice in which medium and the placement of the inscription dovetailed with the content and function of the text: "their very meaning and efficacy rests on their physical adhesion to these places, and the subject inscribing the texts needs to cross geographical space to *place* the inscriptions, binding text and locale to one another: the inscriptions are assigned to their proper sites, and these sites, geographically real and cosmologically meaningful, are literally inscribed within the texts." [60] In the literary inscription, meaning rests, not in a site "inscribed within the texts," but rather in a ritually or culturally significant vessel or figure.

While placement of text is central in the case of the literary inscriptions being considered here, there is also an added (or, more accurately, a missing) dimension involved with inscriptions that no longer are attached to their original or imagined objects. On one level, the literary inscriptions examined in this chapter are stylized texts that lay claim to some aspect of the formal connection to inscriptions on ritual objects found in culturally significant sites (e.g., in the lineage temples from the Zhou period), and in this sense they may be read as attempts to borrow the authority of the ancient. This idea is similar to Gu Jiegang's theory mentioned above.

Understanding the provenance and the original significance of texts like the "Liming" raises the possibility of reexamining received texts for signs of the same process of decontextualization. Here, I will give an example that indicates the significance of these observations. The *Laozi* is one of the bedrock texts of Chinese civilization, yet the process of its composition is still the subject of much debate. One of the exemplars of the text, the *Laozi* manuscript from Mawangdui, shares a scroll with the "Liming" and in several places uses language that suggests sources in the inscriptional genre that I have been describing.

The shared use of the first person in "Jinren ming" and the *Laozi* provides an interesting insight into the latter text. There are a number of first-person passages in the *Laozi* that exhibit strong similarities to the inscriptional texts. The *Laozi* uses the first-person pronouns *wu* 吾 and *wo* 我 forty-four times.[61] For example, *wo* is used seven times in chapter 20 of the *Laozi*. That chapter reads in part:

俗人昭昭，我獨若昏。俗人察察，我獨悶悶。
The common people are all enlightened; I alone am obscured. The common people are discerning; I alone am muddled.[62]

This passage echoes the language and incorporates the same cadence as the "Jinren ming" and also speaks to the same sense of a special ability that might have an apotropaic function. Some of the same features are exhibited by the first-person language of the quotation in chapter 57 of the *Laozi*: "I do not have desires, and the people themselves become the uncarved block" (我無欲人自朴).[63] In these claims of special ability, perspective, or achievement, the "Jinren ming" and *Huangdi ming* share formal similarities with the first-person passages in the *Laozi*. If the *Laozi* is, as is increasingly believed, a composite text, it is possible that some of its sections once were connected to an authorizing medium as were the above passages with which they share some formal similarities.

The fact that such texts exist separately from their objects may indicate that the inscription is no longer intended only for an ancestral audience. Nevertheless, the ritual significance of the object and the cultural significance of the sage or ruler with whom it was associated are the elements that once valorized the text. Because of the connection between medium and message in these examples of literary inscriptions, whether or not they were ever really inscribed on vessels, the claim that they had been reflects their attempt to capture the religious dimension of the connection between text and ritual object that held for the Zhou and Qin inscriptions.

NOTES

I would like to thank the participants in the Princeton conference for their suggestions, and Lothar von Falkenhausen, Martin Kern, and Zhang Zhenjun for their comments on a later draft of the chapter.

    1. Bodde, "Myths of Ancient China," 50.

    2. "Huang Lao zhi yan 黃老之言," in Gu, *Qin Han de fangshi yu rusheng,* 35.

    3. See, e.g., *Huainanzi* 19, "Xiuwu xun" 脩務訓, 342: "Those who work out methods must attribute them to Shen Nong 神農 and the Yellow Emperor, and only then will they be admitted into the debate."

    4. *Hanshu* 30.1731, 1740.

    5. A rule of thumb for distinguishing the two types of inscriptions in later periods is provided by Lu Ji 陸機 (261–303) in his "Wen fu" 文賦 (Rhyme-prose on literature): "*Ming* are broad and brief, each possessing warmth and smoothness; admonitions are sudden and harsh but possessed of clarity and strength" (*Lu Shiheng wen ji* 1.3).

    6. In *Shiji* 107.2841–2842 we find that "[Tian] Fen 田蚡 was an able debater and studied the *Pan and Yu Vessel* [*Admonitions*] and other writings. [His sister] the Empress thought him worthy" (蚡辯有口學槃盂諸書王太后賢之). In the *Liji* 禮記, the phrase *ririxin* 日日新 was one such inscription on the back of a *pan* 槃 vessel (*Liji zhengyi* 60.3a ["Daxue" 大學]). That phrase, translated by Ezra Pound as "make it new," became the motto of the Modernist movement in American poetry.

    7. The graph *can* 參, translated here as "assembled," is especially problematic. The Six Dynasties commentary of Huang Kan 皇侃 reads it as *sen* 森 ("thicket") and explains the entire phrase as "once he establishes himself in the world, he imagines seeing trustworthy, loyal, sincere, and respectful deeds as if they were growing thickly, packed together in front of him." During the Tang, it is read as *can* 驂 ("outer horses of a carriage team") by Han Yu 韓愈, who explains: "Standing in one's carriage it should be as apparent as the outer horses of the carriage team," which is parallel to the next line about sitting in one's carriage, when one also sees it. The Qing scholar Yu Yue 俞樾 reads it as *lei* 絫 ("to pile up"). Since some textual variants place the adverb modifier *ran* 然 after *can*, and the Han commentary of Bao Xian 包咸 makes the graph adverbial ("*canran* in front of his eyes"), the basic meaning of *can* as multiple (i.e., *san* 糝) can be accommodated. See *Lunyu jishi*, 1066–1068 ("Wei Ling gong" 衛靈公).

    8. *Analects* 15.6; see *Lunyu jishi*, 1065–1068 ("Wei Ling gong").

    9. *Shiji* 47.1908. This inscription is also found in the *Zuo zhuan*; see *Chunqiu Zuo zhuan zhengyi* (Zhao 7) 44.17a.

    10. The belongings of sages and worthies were of great importance as relics during this time, as can be seen from later descriptions of the grave sites of Confucius and the Yellow Emperor. Sima Qian himself went to visit the Confucian temple at the sage's grave in the old state of Lu, where he saw Confucius's clothing, hat, zither, carriage, and documents. Sima reports that these objects had remained at the temple there continuously over the two hundred and some years since the Master had died. He does not mention whether these objects were inscribed. See *Shiji* 47.1945–1946.

    11. A memorial by Liang Yi 梁冀 begins by talking about the inscriptions on the objects that ancient rulers used to rely on, and Li Xian's 李賢 commentary refers to the inscriptions of King Wu, the Yellow Emperor, and Kong Jia. Li

attributed the *Jinji fa* to the Yellow Emperor (*Hou Hanshu* 43.1468–1469).

12. *Shiji* 3.104.

13. Csikszentmihalyi, "Emulating the Yellow Emperor," 199–200, contains examples of these uses.

14. Riegel, "Kou-mang and Ju-shou," 81.

15. *Wen xuan* 56.20a.

16. Zhang, "Zhanguo zhujian lu zhenrong."

17. *Da Dai liji jiegu* 59.103 ("Wuwang jianzuo"). Note that the last graph, *qi* 齊, may also mean "to equal" or "match" the Yellow Emperor.

18. This is significant in that the state of Qi is the location of the earliest extant inscription mentioning the Yellow Emperor; see Csikszentmihalyi, "Emulating the Yellow Emperor," 71.

19. Cao, "Shanhai Hakubutsukan tenji no Sokan ni tsuite," 136.

20. *Da Dai liji jiegu* 59.104–105 ("Wuwang jianzuo").

21. Ibid.

22. Ibid. 59.106–107 ("Wuwang jianzuo").

23. Who the "bronze man" statue depicted is a difficult question to answer. Since Confucius finds the figure at a Zhou ancestral temple, it is possible the figure was King Wu, already associated with inscriptions in the previous examples. The similarity between the content of the inscription and that of the *Laozi* might suggest that the figure is Laozi. Finally, it is possible that the figure depicted no individual in particular. There is also a tradition that holds that the statue was made by the Yellow Emperor or, read differently, by Shangfu based on the Yellow Emperor's admonition.

24. *Shuiyuan* 10.16b–17b ("Jingshen" 敬慎). A version of this inscription also appears in the "Guan Zhou" 觀周, chapter 11 of the *Kongzi jiayu* 孔子家語, a text that probably postdates the *Shuiyuan*.

25. The *Kongzi jiayu* version reads "Robbers detest the rulers; the people resent their superiors" (盜憎主人民怨其上; *Kongzi jiayu* 11.2b ["Jingshen"]).

26. Parallel to *Laozi* 66: 必以身後之 (*Laozi jiaoshi* 66.267).

27. Similar to *Laozi* 28: 守其雌 (*Laozi jiaoshi* 28.112).

28. The *Kongzi jiayu* version has 取 ("take") instead of 趨 ("hasten") as in "Others take what is there" (*Kongzi jiayu* 11.2b ["Jingshen"]). The trope of alternating between conventional behavior and that of "I alone" is also seen in *Laozi* 20.

29. The *Kongzi jiayu* version reads 人皆惑之 ("Others are all deluded by it") for 眾人惑惑 ("the masses are deluded") and 徙 ("shift") as in "I alone do not move" for 從 ("follow"); see *Kongzi jiayu* 11.2b ("Jingshen").

30. The *Kongzi jiayu* version reads 不示人技 ("I do not display my art to others") for 不與人論技 ("I do not discuss my art with others"); see *Kongzi jiayu* 11.2b ("Jingshen").

31. Parallel to *Laozi* 66: 江海所以能為百谷王 以其善下 (*Laozi jiaoshi* 66.267).

32. Paraphrase of the closing line of *Laozi* 79: 天道無親 常與善人 (*Laozi jiaoshi* 79.306).

33. See *Shuiyuan* 10.17a ("Jing shen"). The quotation is the final lines of "Xiaomin" 小旻 (Mao 195): 戰戰兢兢, 如臨深淵, 如履薄冰 (*Mao shi zhengyi*

12B.19b–20a). Karlgren, *The Book of Odes*, 143, translates this as "Tremble, be cautious, as if approaching a deep abyss, as if treading on thin ice!"

34. At the same time, there are important contrasts to be drawn between the two examples, contrasts that go beyond the difference in medium. King Wu receives the message of the Yellow Emperor from the "cinnabar books" and then makes his own inscription, whereas Confucius receives the message from the inscription itself. The brevity of King Wu's admonitions and the length of the bronze man's imperatives may justify a formal contrast between the two examples. Since reminders to the ruler about personal behavior in certain situations are inscribed on objects that are to be used in those situations, they are often reminders in imperative form, but when they are on statues, they use first-person testimony attributed to the subject of the image.

35. Yang Shuda, *Hanshu kuiguan*, 230–231. Note that it is also conceivable that Shangfu resumes his own voice after the word "night" and thus that he made the statue and bound its mouth; in this case, the inscription would be on the statue.

36. Cf. *Da Dai liji jiegu* 62 ("Wudi de" 五帝德) and *Shiji* 1 ("Wudi benji" 五帝本記). The missing emperor is Di Ku 帝嚳. If the *Huanglan* fragment is closer to the Shanghai version—the oldest extant one—this might indicate that the *Huangdi ming* was indeed originally a set of inscriptions of the words of the Yellow Emperor that King Wu consulted.

37. Yates, *Five Lost Classics*, 32, titles it *Canon* and points out that "it seems unlikely that it was composed by a single author at a single point in time."

38. *Lüshi chunqiu jiaoshi* 14.740 ("Benwei" 本味).

39. Ibid. 14.746, n. 21 ("Benwei").

40. "Once the Yellow Emperor left as an immortal, his minister Zuo Che carved wood in the image of the Yellow Emperor. He led the feudal lords in offerings [to it] at the court." For this apotheosthumous portrayal, see *Huang shi yishu kao*, vol. 46, 1a.

41. Note the use of the term *can* 參 as in *Lunyu* 15.6; see note 8.

42. See Mawangdui Hanmu boshu zhengli xiaozu, *Mawangdui Hanmu boshu*, vol. 1, 61. C.f. Yates, *Five Lost Classics*, 104–105.

43. Mawangdui Hanmu boshu zhengli xiaozu, *Mawangdui Hanmu boshu*, vol. 1, 61.

44. The "Yao dian" 堯典 is part of *Shangshu zhengyi* 2.1a–28a ("Yu shu" 虞書); translated by Legge, "The Shoo King," in *The Chinese Classics*, vol. 3, 15–27.

45. A related instance is found in *Huainanzi* 6.6a, where the Yellow Emperor is assisted by two ministers in calibrating the movements of the heavens.

46. Kern, *Die Hymnen der chinesischen Staatsopfer*, 190–193.

47. The initial report on this vessel may be found in Hu Lingui et al., "Xi'an dongjiao Guomian Wuchang Hanmu fajue jianbao," 4.

48. Li Ling, *Zhongguo fangshu kao*, 184–185.

49. One of the primary myths associated with the Yellow Emperor is the creation of the calendar. For example, the Yellow Emperor acted in accordance

with the seasons in order to mimic Heaven (*Shiji* 1.11).

50. Ni, "Lun Liang Han siling de yuanliu," 85.

51. Although the date of the *Guanzi* is uncertain, references to the *siling* exhibit a diversity that might indicate this passage is earlier than the Eastern Han. Generally, earlier texts (e.g., *Zuo zhuan* [Zhao 29] and *Lüshi chunqiu* 呂氏春秋 1–12 ["Shierji" 十二記]) associate Zhu Rong 祝融 with the direction south, while later texts (e.g., *Hanshu* 漢書 "Jiaosi zhi xia" 郊祀志下; Ma Rong's 馬融 [79–166] commentary to *Liji* 禮記 "Jifa" 祭法; and Zheng Xuan's 鄭玄 [127–200] commentary to *Liji* 禮記 "Quli xia" 曲禮下) have Zhu Yong 祝庸. By this criterion the *Guanzi* passage, which uses "Zhu Rong," is the same as the earlier stratum of texts.

52. Note that in Han "Wuxing" (Five Phases) cosmology, Hou Tu is usually located in the center, serving as an assistant spirit to the Yellow Emperor, who also resides in the center; see Kern, *Die Hymnen der chinesischen Staatsopfer*, 182.

53. This may be seen in the way that in the "Jinyu" 晉語 section of the *Guoyu*, the spirit of the west, Ru Shou 蓐收, is described as a white tiger (the animal of the west) and in the fact that both the spirit and animal of the north are *xuan* 玄, "abstruse"; see *Guoyu Wei Zhao zhu* 8.5a ("Jinyu er" 晉語二). A later example of this phenomenon appears in *Hou Hanshu* "zhi" 志 8.3181–3182; see Kern, *Die Hymnen der chinesischen Staatsopfer*, 45.

54. Cai Yong's "Yueling zhangju" 月令章句 is preserved in *Taiping yulan* 6.7a. To his left is Cang Long.

55. Yates, *Five Lost Classics*; Li Ling, "Shuo Huang Lao."

56. Another fragment of the *Huangdi ming* appears in the Song dynasty *Lushi* 路史, which quotes the *Jinji fa*. The succinct passage reads: "Do not cover up weakness; do not skimp on virtue. / Do not be impudent with equals; do not play at ritual. / Do not plot to do what is not virtuous; do not do what is not righteous" (*Lushi* 5.9a). This fragment shares the same imperative tone as the "Jinren ming," although the message is rather different. The first sentence is paraphrased in an admonition to the crown prince of Yan in *Shiji* 60.2112, but it is impossible to know whether the Song text was copied from the Han text or whether they both derived from the *Jinji fa*. Cai Yong's *Ming lun* mentions two similar inscriptional texts connected with the Yellow Emperor: "As for the Yellow Emperor, there is his *Jinji fa*; as for Kong Jia, there is his *Panyu jie*" (*Wen xuan* 56.20a). This raises the possibility that the *Huangdi ming* included the *Jinji fa*, the "Jinren ming," and the "Liming."

57. What of the other instance of first-person language in the Mawangdui text? The first-person passage in the untitled postscript section makes use of the first-person *wo* 我 five times and reads in part: "The myriad things come in a group; I can respond to every one of them. I do not store up the old and do not embrace what has passed. Once the echo is gone, then what comes is new 萬物群至 我無不能應 我不藏故 鄉者已去 至者乃新" (Mawangdui Hanmu boshu zhengli xiaozu, *Mawangdui Hanmu boshu*, vol. 1, 79). This passage emphasizes the "mind as a mirror" metaphor that is also found in *Zhuangzi* and *Xunzi* and that in the latter is associated with the Warring States thinker Guan Yin 關尹. Whether or not this passage is an inscription originally engraved on the Yellow

Emperor's mirror, it is composed of the same first-person claims of potency seen in the *Huangdi ming* and *Laozi*.

58. Falkenhausen, "Issues in Western Zhou Studies," 147.

59. Ibid.

60. Kern, *The Stele Inscriptions of Ch'in Shih-huang*, 57.

61. For a survey of these uses, see Bauer, "Ich und Nicht-Ich in Laozis *Daode jing*." Bauer's category of the "projected I," which he says represents the identification of the text's author with the ideal ruler, is most similar to the use of the first-person pronoun in literary inscriptions.

62. *Laozi jiaoshi*, 83. Cf. Henricks, *Lao-Tzu Te-Tao Ching*, 226–227.

63. *Laozi jiaoshi*, 232–234.

Chapter 8

Text and Ritual in Early Chinese Stelae

K. E. Brashier

I yesterday passed a whole afternoon in the churchyard, the cloisters, and the church, amusing myself with the tombstones and inscriptions that I met with in those several regions of the dead. Most of them recorded nothing else of the buried person, but that he was born upon one day, and died upon another: the whole history of his life being comprehended in those two circumstances, that are common to all mankind. [1]

The terse tombstones of Westminster Abbey visited by Joseph Addison (1672–1719) serve as a stark contrast to the verbose stelae of Eastern Han China (figure 8.1). Addison seems mystified that a person's identity could devolve to the barest minimum of text, and his confrontation with these markers is merely that of a passive, amused tourist, a confrontation devoid of any active remembrance.

From the perspective of Eastern Han grave stelae, Addison's tombstones would indeed seem lacking. Like Addison, the scholar Mi Heng 禰衡 (fl. ca. 200 C.E.) once passed his free time visiting the "regions of the dead," and the *Hou Hanshu* 後漢書 records the following encounter with a tombstone inscription written by the Eastern Han's most famous author of stele texts:

> 嘗與衡俱遊，共讀蔡邕所作碑文，射愛其辭，還恨不繕寫。衡曰：吾雖一覽，猶能識之，唯其中石缺二字為不明耳。因書出之，射馳使寫碑還校，如衡所書，莫不歎伏。

Once [Huang She 黃射] was wandering about together with [Mi] Heng when they both read a stele text by Cai Yong. [Huang] She was fond of its lyrics[2] and upon return regretted not having copied it out. [Mi]

249

Heng said, "Although I only gave it a single glance, I am still able to remember the lyrics. Yet in the middle of the text, the stone is damaged, and two characters have simply become unclear." He accordingly wrote out the lyrics. [Huang] She hastened an attendant to copy the stele and compare it to [Mi] Heng's text upon return. It was just as he had written. There was no one who did not sigh in awe.[3]

In marked contrast with Addison's experience, Mi Heng's encounter with a Han tombstone raises three related questions on text and ritual that are worthy of investigation.

1. Whereas Addison only records his lament as to the commonplace terseness of English tombstone inscriptions, Mi Heng instead *memorized* the stele text. What is Han memorial culture? That is, what is Han culture in terms of how knowledge and texts were committed to memory?

2. Whereas Addison in his frustration sees only a pair of dates, Mi Heng can draw upon the lyrics to a hymn inscribed on stone. What tradition of textuality is here exemplified?

3. Both Addison and Mi Heng behave as cultural tourists encountering heritage relics. Yet was the Eastern Han stele indeed merely a commemorative monument without other functions, or was it a key component of a larger ritual program?

The answers to these three questions will shed further light upon the relationship between text and ritual at the end of the era known as "early" China.

The Han Dynasty as a "Memorial" Culture

The story of Mi Heng's on-the-spot memorization of a stele inscription is not unique in Han or in later standard histories,[4] and yet his companion Huang She privileged the written word. Before exploring the specific textual tradition that informs Eastern Han stelae, it is necessary to pose a more general question of what textual preservation meant in early China. A millennium after Mi Heng, the Song Dynasty's Zhu Xi 朱熹 (1130–1200)—frequently described as "the most influential figure in Chinese intellectual history after Confucius himself"[5]—recognized this difference between memorial and chirographic cultures, drawing upon the Han when he writes the following:

又云：今緣文字印本多，人不著心讀。漢時諸儒以經相授者，只是暗誦，所以記得牢。

[Zhu Xi] also said, "Because there are now many printed texts, no one engages in mindful reading. [Yet] in Han times when the host of classicists in their exchanges made use of the classics, they did so only through well-versed recitation, which is why their memories were secure."[6]

While Zhu Xi often reiterates this distinction between print and memorial cultures, he unfortunately does not fully explore the implications of the latter. Likewise, modern scholarship has devoted little attention to textual memorization in the Han.

Some of the earliest references to recitation from memory ironically do not vaunt its benefits but deny that it was the be-all and end-all of virtue. Guanzi 管子 lamented that the ability to chant one's book learning would not prevent one from falling into destruction if one were not also filial.[7] In a similar vein, Confucius complained that being able to recite the three hundred poems but failing in government was still failing.[8] Their criticisms imply that the ability to recite was only a first step, albeit an important one. Pre–Qin texts abound with examples of how reciting extracts from the classics, particularly from the *Shijing* 詩經, became a *"lingua franca* for polite exchanges and coded negotiations between members of different states."[9]

Acquiring this first step had to begin early. The *Da Dai liji* depicts developing this talent as prior to the ability to analyze and explain when it offers the following warning:

其少不諷誦，其狀不論議，其老不教誨，亦可謂無業之人矣。

If he does not recite and chant as a child, does not analyze and discuss as a youth, and does not instruct and admonish as an elder, then it can also be said he has become a person without a legacy.[10]

The term *fengsong* 諷誦 is here rendered as "recite and chant." Both characters have a sense of oral reproduction, even intoned reproduction, a characteristic recognized in Han glosses.[11] As in the Western medieval tradition, learning a text by heart required a degree of subvocalization or "murmuring."[12] Xunzi 荀子, who explicitly laments that many of his contemporaries are not good reciters, similarly states that reciting and chanting must commence at youth,[13] and elsewhere he adds that education must begin with reciting the classics and conclude with reading the rituals. It must begin with creating the scholar and end with creating the sage.[14]

It is indeed the lack of this ability that is sometimes highlighted as an oddity in a great person's character, and even the future Qin First Emperor noted this gap in his own early learning. The *Zhanguo ce* 戰國策 relates the following:

王使子誦，子曰：少棄捐在外，嘗無師傅所教學，不習於誦。

The king called upon Zi to recite but Zi said, "While still young I was neglected and sent abroad. I never had teaching from a tutor, and I am not practiced in terms of recitation."[15]

Here textual recitation is akin to performance with, in this case, a royal audience, and there underlies an assumption that young nobility should all be able to recite properly. In a later case, one youth's inability to recite the classics in fact cost him the empire. When Emperor Cheng 成 (r. 33–7 B.C.E.) was considering his heir apparent, he called upon his youngest half brother to recite from the *Shangshu* 尚書, but the young man broke off in the middle of the recitation having forgotten the text. When he called upon his half nephew to recite from the *Shijing*, this second young man had "penetratingly studied and capably explained" (*tongxi nengshuo* 通習能説) the classic. Despite his more distant blood relationship, this half nephew became the heir apparent and the future Emperor Ai 哀 (r. 7–1 B.C.E.).[16]

Such textual memorization was of course not limited to royalty, and many Han biographies in the standard histories and on stelae explicitly list the texts "penetrated" (*tong*) in the dedicatee's childhood—a penetration that, in the above anecdote about Emperor Ai, clearly implied memorization. In scores of these biographies, the dedicatee could recite by early adolescence, and in lieu of personal royal connections, recitation was one of the only means to begin the ascent to a high post. At least by the middle of the Western Han and the reign of Emperor Wu 武 (r. 141–87 B.C.E.), the ability to recite the classics translated into official postings when it was explicitly mandated that "preference is to be given to those who can recite the most" (*xian yong songduo zhe* 先用誦多者).[17] It is to this class of officialdom that the later Eastern Han stelae would be dedicated.

Despite the clear necessity to acquire the ability to recite from memory, Han sources rarely compare memorized and chirographic knowledge. Even so, modern scholarship does have recourse to recent Western work on memorized knowledge, and applying such work to Han texts intended for memorization may yield some useful speculations. As the stele inscription regularly exhorts its reader to memorize and recite the stele hymn, such a hymn can provide a useful starting point for this speculative venture into a few of the reading rules of a memorial culture. What follows is the Eastern Han stele hymn dedicated to Yin Zhou 尹宙 (d. 177 C.E.) located in Henan:

於鑠明德	O shiningly bright virtue –
于我尹君	It lies within our Sir Yin.[18]
龜銀之冑	Descendant of those who possessed silver [seals] with turtle [knobs],
弈世載勳	He bore the merits of accumulated generations.
綱紀本朝	When he served as the control line and net for the regional court,
優劣殊分	The excellent and the vile became demarcated.
守攝百里	Where he guarded and held a hundred *li*,
遺愛在民	Lasting affection for him remained among the people.
佐翼牧伯	As an assistant shepherd,
諸夏肅震	All of China reverently trembled.
當漸鴻羽	He served as the feathers of that gradually advancing wild goose,
為漢輔臣	And acted as a supporting minister to the Han.
位不福德	His position did not reflect his virtue,
壽不隨仁	And his longevity did not accord with his benevolence.
景命不永	One's allotment of brightness does not last a long time,
早即幽昏	And while he was [still] young, it became gloomily dark.
名光來世	His name is radiant to future generations,
萬祀不泯	And ten thousand sacrifices will never let it die out.[19]

Using Yin Zhou's hymn as a springboard, the modern reader can discern several features of memorized texts, namely cliché, exaggeration, "memory place" groupings, and the versified format itself. Yet it must be stressed that each culture has its own conceptions of orality, memorization, and recitation—that each culture shapes and is shaped by its oral traditions. Thus, any reference to Western traditions here can *only* raise speculations and make suggestions as to how one might approach textual recitation in early China.

Cliché as Mnemonic

Cliché in Eastern Han stelae regularly takes the form of oft-cited classical allusions, usually allusions to the *Shijing* but in this case also to the *Yijing* 易經. For example, the wild goose refers to the hexagram *jian* 漸, and according to this divination guide, "The wild goose gradually advances to dry land, and its feathers can be used as an emblem—it is auspicious" (*hong jian yu lu, qi yu ke yong wei yi, ji* 鴻漸于陸，其羽可用為儀，吉).[20] As in many stelae dedicated to someone who died before his or her full span of years, this hymn also draws upon a much-debated phrase in the *Lunyu* 論語 that states, "Those who are benevolent possess longevity" (*renzhe, shou* 仁者，壽).[21]

Yet does unoriginal repetition of such allusions indicate tired, amateurish usage usually associated with cliché? When studying contemporaneous Greek tombstones J. W. Day suggests that it does. After describing how Greek tombstones were not read silently but aloud as if reenacting a funeral dirge—an act that may have parallels in terms of the Eastern Han stelae—he states:

> They had as their model the old tradition of praise poetry with its treasury of ready-made, easily recognizable verbal strategies for presenting a *laudandus* as worthy of praise and emulation. Their command of this material was amateur, their efforts normally very humble and derivative; but what they did was formally parallel to Pindar's conversion of a victor's vital statistics into an epinician ode.[22]

Employment of ready-made cliché may indeed seem amateur to the modern eye, but in a culture with a significant oral performative tradition, such language was not without its uses.

In his oft-cited work *Orality and Literacy*, Walter Ong has also studied the high usage of cliché in early texts, particularly texts within a predominantly memorial, rather than chirographic, culture. He argues that cliché is not only intentional but also necessary, and the Homeric tradition, for example, is full of formulaic phrasing. Cliché is in part used for mnemonic purposes and in part used because memorial-culture thinking itself demands it. He summarizes as follows:

> Fixed, often rhythmically balanced, expressions of this sort and of other sorts can be found occasionally in print, indeed can be "looked

up" in books of sayings, but in oral cultures they are not occasional. They are incessant. They form the substance of thought itself. Thought in any extended form is impossible without them, for it consists in them.[23]

That is, when the modern thinker has extended thoughts, he or she has recourse to paper or now to computer so that the thread is not lost. Paper and computer allow one to reexamine ground already covered. Yet in a memorial culture in which the text primarily exists within the mind, long thoughts cannot be consigned to paper. One then requires a host of ready-made strings of words and ideas to carry out any extended thought.

Exaggeration as Mnemonic

Yet there is more at work than cliché in Yin Zhou's hymn. To be blunt, did all of China really "reverently tremble" when he became an "assistant shepherd"? Both the hymn and its prose preface indicate he did not rise up to a high rank, and he is also not mentioned in the standard histories. This national *tremendum* would seem unlikely, but such exaggerations became a trademark of Eastern Han stelae, a fact that stele writers themselves admitted.

Cai Yong 蔡邕 (133–192), whose stele text Mi Heng and Huang She encountered, once confessed to another stele writer, Lu Zhi 盧植 (d. 192), that when composing his numerous inscriptions, "in every case I felt ashamed in exaggerating virtue" (*jie you cande* 皆有慚德). Only rarely did he not have reason "to blush in shame" (*kuise* 愧色).[24] Pei Songzhi 裴松之 (d. 451), commentator to the *Sanguo zhi* 三國志, took to heart Cai Yong's comment and added the following:

而自時厥後，其流彌多。預有臣吏，必為建立。勒銘寡取信之實，刊石成虛偽之常，真假相蒙，殆使合美者不貴。

From that time forth, such currents [of writing] become extremely numerous. If one had previously possessed a lowly office, then [a stele] had to be erected for him. Engraving a record lacks the substance of seeking the truth; cutting the stone creates a principle of baselessness and falsity. Fact and fiction obscure one another, which is in danger of causing the harmonious and beautiful to be unvalued.[25]

Perhaps because stelae developed this reputation for flamboyance, the earliest works devoted to literary criticism, such as the "Wen fu" 文賦 by Lu Ji 陸機 (261–303) and the *Wenxin diaolong* 文心雕龍 by Liu Xie 劉勰 (ca. 465–522), proclaim adherence to true substance as the necessary guiding principle behind stele writing.[26]

Yet like cliché, flamboyance is not without its mnemonic benefits. In her famous study entitled *The Art of Memory*, Frances Yates frequently returns to one of the earliest surviving discussions on memory, a Roman rhetoric text from the first century B.C.E. known as the *Ad Herennium*. This text notes the necessity as well as the naturalness of exaggeration in the development of memory as follows:

> Now nature herself teaches us what we should do. When we see in every day life things that are petty, ordinary, and banal, we generally fail to remember them, because the mind is not being stirred by anything novel or marvellous. But if we see or hear something exceptionally base, dishonourable, unusual, great, unbelievable, or ridiculous, that we are likely to remember for a long time. . . . We ought, then, to set up images of a kind that can adhere longest in memory. And we shall do so if we establish similitudes as striking as possible; if we set up images that are not many or vague but active (*imagines agentes*); if we assign to them exceptional beauty or singular ugliness. . . .[27]

Modern scholars such as Ong have likewise drawn attention to the need for exaggeration in fostering oral memory.[28] If exaggeration as mnemonic is indeed what "nature herself teaches" and if it can thus be similarly applied to early China, then "all of China reverently trembled" so that Yin Zhou could be remembered.

"Memory Places" as Mnemonic

A third reading device could be called the development of loci or memory places, a term here borrowed from a long Western tradition beginning with Aristotle and extending to Albertus Magnus and Thomas Aquinas. Our minds have hotspots in which like things are gathered, each hotspot exemplified by a tangible person, place, or thing.[29] In this vein, Eastern Han stelae often group the dedicatee with someone more famous. Heng Fang

衡方 (d. 168 C.E.), grand commandant of Beiping 北平, is equated with the famed Li Guang 李廣 (d. 129 B.C.E.), who had marshaled troops against the northern nomads under Emperor Wu.[30] The astronomer Zhang Heng 張衡 (78–139) is grouped with the cultural heroes Chong 重 and Li 黎, the founders of the astronomer lineages whose descendants included Xi 羲 and He 和, sent by Yao 堯 to the ends of the earth to observe the sun's movements.[31] Here the stele hymn's prose preface links Yin Zhou to his supposed ancestor Yin Jifu 尹吉甫, said to have composed some of the most famous *Shijing* verses, and the above hymn reiterates that grouping by identifying Yin Zhou as "descendant of those who possessed silver [seals] with turtle [knobs]."

Mary Carruthers argues that in such a process of ethical valorizing, the rememberer gathers a variety of material into these so-called memory places. The dedicatees ride on the coattails of their more famous associates, thus assuring some degree of remembrance. Carruthers provides a useful example of one person correlating herself with a famous forerunner, an example cited here because it leads to an important ethical facet of memorial culture that is evident in the Han. She cites the example of Heloise, the pupil and lover of Abelard (1079–1142), who just before taking the veil justified her action by reciting the exemplar of Cornelia in Lucan's poem "Pharsalia":

> O noble husband,
> Too great for me to wed, was it my fate
> To bend that lofty head? What prompted me
> To marry you and bring about your fall?
> Now claim your due, and see me gladly pay.[32]

This poem is understood only through its context. Cornelia was about to offer herself in sacrifice to the gods, just as Heloise will sacrifice her life by entering the convent. Carruthers writes that this poem was within Heloise's memory and helped to make up her experience; Heloise did not so much "see herself as" Cornelia, but Cornelia's experience—through the process of memorization—had been made hers as well.[33] Carruthers further comments as follows:

> A modern woman would be very uncomfortable to think that she was facing the world with a "self" constructed out of bits and pieces of great authors of the past, yet I think in large part that is exactly what a medieval self or "character" was. Saying this does not, I think, exclude

a conception of individuality, for every person had domesticated and familiarised these *communes loci*, these pieces of the public memory. It does underscore the profound degree to which memory was considered to be the prerequisite for character itself. . . . Perhaps here as clearly as anywhere else in ancient and medieval culture, the fundamental symbiosis of memorized reading and ethics can be grasped, for each is a matter of stamping the body-soul, of *charaktér*.[34]

Carruthers is here playing with the word "character," the Latin derivation of which is "to stamp" or "impress."[35] This relationship between memorized reading and character is by no means foreign to early China. Mencius famously noted that if one wears the clothing of the sage ruler Yao, behaves as Yao did, and "recites the words of Yao" (*song Yao zhi yan* 誦堯之言), one simply *is* a Yao.[36] Xunzi's assessment is similar:

君子。。。故誦數以貫之，思索以通之，為其人以處之，除其害者以持養之。

The gentleman . . . thus recites and enumerates in order to become familiar with [the classics], ponders and inquires in order to penetrate them, becomes their kind of person in order to situate them,[37] and clears away the harmful in order to support and nourish them.[38]

Here the image is of a gentleman reaching into the past with his mind via the classics and bringing them forward until his own person serves as their shelter and support. Yet the message is the same—one begins with memorization and recitation and ends in ethical transformation. Still more explicit is the Eastern Han thinker Wang Chong 王充 (27–ca.100) when praising the value of scholars in his own time:

儒生之性，非能皆善也，被服聖教，日夜諷詠，得聖人之操矣。

As for a scholar's nature, not every one is good, but by clothing himself in the teachings of sages, reciting and intoning them day and night, he takes on the conduct of the sage.[39]

Carruthers's "symbiosis" aptly describes this relationship between the intoned text and the scholar's nature because Wang Chong also draws an analogy of white silk gauze rubbing against dark silks, and taking on dark colors without having been dyed. In other words, the absorption of literature can subconsciously impress the reader's character and actions.[40]

Verse as Mnemonic

Just as Heloise recites a poem in Carruthers's example, the Eastern Han stele likewise urges its reader to memorize its proffered verse. Early Chinese oral culture, which serves as a backdrop for these stele hymns, was already awash with versification within both the established lineages and the general populace. As to the former, early versification survives, for example, in the form of bronze vessel inscriptions, and as Martin Kern states, "one cannot but conclude that already by mid–Ch'un-ch'iu times, rhymes were a carefully chosen and therefore important textual device—and it should go without saying that they represent a device not of the written but of the oral dimension of ritual language."[41] As to the latter, the *Guanzi* warns that, to avoid catastrophes such as mass migrations, regional peoples should be allowed to sing their diverse ballads in sacrificial reverence.[42] In terms of the Han dynasty itself, popular versification ranged from rhymed medical knowledge as exemplified by the Mawangdui 馬王堆 texts[43] to rhymed primers that sorted out general knowledge such as the *Jijiu pian* 急就篇.[44] They stretched from legends about the court collecting popular poems to observe the customs of the people[45] to would-be emperors in turn circulating propaganda poems throughout the empire to affect those customs.[46] The court even treated the spread of various popular children's ditties as omens.[47] By the time of the Eastern Han grave stele era, an era which is mostly limited to the second half of the second century, a versified oral culture was well entrenched.

Yet why verse? It perhaps goes without saying that verse itself, with its rhythms and rhymes, is a mnemonic device. Simonides, said to be inventor of the principles of the art of memory in the Western tradition, was himself a poet.[48] Rosalind Thomas summarizes verse's role in ancient Greece as follows:

> Ancient writers are acutely aware of the importance of memory. As Plato implies in the *Phaedrus*, verse was particularly useful because it could be easily memorized. In other words if something was worth remembering and passing on, it would be better remembered if it was in verse. Sappho's confidence in the survival of her poetry lay in its continuation in song, not in its existence as a written text. . . . Indeed it is a commonplace in the study of oral tradition that anything passed on in verse has a better chance of accurate transmission.[49]

Yet in this case one need not rely on Western studies as to poetry's role
in a memorial culture. The primary and most authoritative statement on the
"poem" (*shi* 詩) throughout the Chinese traditional period is that of the
Shangshu, which states, "The poem articulates what is intently fixed within
the mind; the song makes language last long" (*shi yan zhi, ge yong yan* 詩
言志，歌永言).[50] Stephen Owen explains the second half of this statement
as follows:

> The statement probably referred originally to "intoning," stretching out
> the words in the act of singing. But commentators play on the meaning
> "lasting long," transferring it to another aspect of song, its capacity to
> be preserved, carried afar, and transmitted. Through the patterning of
> song, a text becomes fixed and repeatable. Unlike speech, which
> disappears as soon as it is uttered, song is one of the earliest examples
> of the fixed text; and that repeatability is a miracle.[51]

The commentators to whom Owen refers include Zheng Xuan 鄭玄
(127–200), and here remembrance of the dead is not far away. The *Shangshu*
then records that these poems and songs "cause spirits and humans to thus
be harmonized" (*shen ren yi he* 神人以和), which Zheng Xuan interpreted as
a description of ancestral sacrifice.[52]

Not surprisingly, the *Shijing* thus figures highly within this memorial
culture. When biographies denote the texts memorized in childhood, the
Shijing is relatively common, and lines from this particular classic are the
most frequent to appear in stele inscriptions and in most other early texts.
Because of its relevance to Eastern Han stele hymns—a relevance that will
be demonstrated below—the memorative nature of this work must be further
explored.

The Shijing *as Epitomizing Memorial Culture*

The "fixed and repeatable" nature of poetry is well demonstrated by the
preservation of the *Shijing* itself. This corpus of musical poems and
ancestral hymns was intended for memorization from an early age. The *Liji*
禮記 prescribes its mental retention at the age of thirteen,[53] and Eastern
Han stelae describe boys who could recite it at the age of twelve.[54]
Furthermore, its recitation is said to have assured its survival. The *Hanshu*
漢書 bibliographical chapter states the following:

遭秦而全者，以其諷誦，不獨在竹帛故也。

The reason [the poems] remained intact when they encountered the Qin [book burning] is because they were recited and chanted and not just confined to bamboo and silk documents.[55]

Whether this claim is true and how to interpret the Qin bibliocaust are matters of dispute,[56] but even so, the Han perception of recitation's saving grace remains.

Because it was memorized, the individual verses and phrases of the *Shijing* functioned like a kind of grand vocabulary in the Han. That is, certain clusters of characters stood together as a single symbol, a single complex referent to a meaning understood by both speaker and listener. Sometimes inscribed hymns are riddled with these interjections, hymns such as the following dedicated to the Spirit Lord of Baishi Mountain (Baishi shenjun 白石神君). In its conclusion, all of the quoted passages are taken from the *Shijing*.

卜云其吉	"Divination announced its auspiciousness,
終然允臧	The end result being truly good."[57]
匪奢匪儉	Neither extravagant nor mean,
率由舊章	It "observed and followed the ancient statutes."[58]
華殿清閑	The decorated hall is immaculate and restful,
蕭雍顯相	"Stern and harmonized its distinguished ministers."[59]
玄圖靈象	The dark plan and efficacious forms
穆穆皇皇	"Are extremely reverent and august."[60]
四時禋祀	As for the sacrifices offered in each of the four seasons,
不愆不忘	"Nothing is excessive and nothing forgotten."[61]
擇其令辰	When an excellent morning is selected,
進其馨香	The fragrant incense is brought forward.
犧牲玉帛	[There are] sacrificial animals, jades and silks,
黍稷稻糧	"Broomcorn millet, foxtail millet, rice and common millet."[62]
神降嘉祉	May the spirit send down excellent blessings,
萬壽無疆	Causing extreme longevity without end.
子子孫孫	May children and grandchildren
永永番昌	Be forever numerous.[63]

Here there are six separate quotations from the *Shijing*, mostly from its "Elegantiae" (*ya* 雅) and "Hymns" (*song* 頌), within only eighteen lines of text. Yet how this superabundance of quotations actually affects the general interpretation of the inscribed hymn is unclear. Like many pre–Qin texts, the quotations may not index any original meanings, the meanings instead deriving from how they interact with the newer text that cites them. [64] Alternatively, over the course of the Han certain fixed readings became entrenched as the *Shijing* became anthologized with prefaces that guided interpretation. [65] Furthermore,· the commentarial tradition became more prevalent, a fact that is evinced by the stelae themselves. Stele inscriptions identify their dedicatees as mastering, not merely the *Shijing* or the *Shangshu*, but specifically the *Shijing* tradition of Han Ying 韓嬰 (ca. 200–120 B.C.E.) or the *Shangshu* tradition of Master Ouyang 歐陽生 (fl. early second century B.C.E.). Such fixed readings and preferred commentaries might limit the earlier freedom of interpreting the *Shijing* citations to suit the newer literary context. A third possibility is simply that no such "deeper" meanings were sought at all, that the individual citations carried only their surface meanings and functioned as a kind of grand vocabulary. Even here the inscription reader could be led to images beyond the phrases, images not from commentaries but from the portions of the *Shijing* poems that follow the extracted text. The list of "broomcorn millet, foxtail millet," and so forth may not be merely a catalogue of grains; it is also an idealized depiction of a prosperous farm where proper sacrifices are offered in their season. Such is that phrase's context in the *Shijing*, and it is possible that these lines each carry a certain amount of unstated baggage due to the memorial tradition. The modern equivalent might be if a person hummed a few bars of a popular song and then stopped, and the song naturally carried on in the minds of the listeners.

To summarize, a memorial culture assumes different rules of reading as well as the process of ethics building. One recites the *Shijing* and gradually shapes the psyche. Yet for the Han dynasty, this premise is only where the story begins. That is, the stele hymns not only quote from the *Shijing*, but these same stele hymns also saw themselves as a *new* version of the *Shijing*.

Stele as Text

Westminster Abbey's tombstones were a disappointment for Joseph Addison; in his opinion, they clearly preserved nothing worth remembering. Their contrast with Eastern Han grave stelae is stark. As seen in Mi Heng and Huang She's cemetery visit, stele texts were written by the great scholars of the age such as Cai Yong, and Huang She explicitly expresses his "fondness" (*ai* 愛) for the "lyrics" (*ci* 辭), lyrics that Mi Heng committed to memory.

Without a doubt, different textual traditions inform these stone inscriptions, but the function of the lyrics is a matter of dispute. Recent scholarship likens the lyrics to the "coda" (*luan* 亂) at the end of *Chu ci* 楚辭-style poetry, or it likens them to what the "grand historian says" (*taishi gong yue* 太史公曰) or to the "appraisal" (*zan* 讚) appended to the historical biographies by Sima Qian 司馬遷 (ca. 145–ca. 86 B.C.E.) and Ban Gu 班固 (32–92).[66] As to the biographical appendages, such appraisals were rarely written in verse during the Han. Furthermore, the received literature hints at a different story, a story that identifies the lyrics as the inscription's focal point, not as its appendage.

In 143 C.E. a fourteen-year-old girl by the name of Cao E 曹娥 threw herself into a river because she could not endure life knowing that her father had drowned and his body had become lost.[67] This act of filial respect drew the attention of the regional authorities, and the prefect of Shangyu 上虞 (in modern Zhejiang) commissioned Wei Lang 魏朗 to write her stele inscription. Wei Lang finished it, but before presenting it, he met the prefect at a drinking banquet. The prefect asked for the text, but Wei Lang modestly declined, apologizing for his lack of ability. At this point, the young poet Handan Chun 邯鄲淳 (fl. late Eastern Han) arrived, and the prefect asked him to write the Cao E inscription on the spot. The poet did so, and his result was so good that Wei Lang dejectedly destroyed his own draft.[68] Thus, a poet at a drinking banquet—an occasion later often associated with writing poetry—composed the Cao E inscription in this story, suggesting that the focus of this text was the poem or hymn and not the biographical preface.

Writing a stele inscription was indeed regarded as writing poetry; the Qing scholar Ye Changchi 葉昌熾 wrote, "As for the host of stelae from the Qin and Han, it is clear that they are the same type of composition as odes and hymns" (*Qin Han zhubei, bingyan yu yasong tongwen* 秦漢諸碑，炳焉與雅頌同文).[69] Sometimes the erection of a stele was described as "erecting the stele hymn" (*li beisong* 立碑頌),[70] and in the lists of surviving literature genres appended to the end of fourteen *Hou Hanshu* biographies, the stele genre is usually grouped with hymns and other types of poetry. Aside from recognized stele writers, close relatives were also sometimes asked to write the hymn. For example, the daughter of Dou

Zhang 竇章 (d. 144 C.E.) found favor with Emperor Shun, and upon occasion of her early death, the emperor "summoned the Astronomy Office to erect a stele and hymn her virtue" (*zhao shiguan shubei songde* 詔史官樹 碑頌德), and Dou Zhang himself was singled out to write the lyrics.[71]

Received literature aside, from the stelae themselves it is clear that the verse is not a mere appendage, as will be demonstrated below. First, the stelae place themselves within a tradition of commemorative verses. For example, an inscription dedicated to the water projects of Sima Deng 司馬 登 marks the completion of an irrigation ditch, and just before the verse, it states:

昔禹修九道，《書》錄其功；后稷躬稼，《詩》列于雅。

In ancient times when Yu repaired the nine water courses, the *Shangshu* recorded his achievement; when Hou Ji personally sowed the grain, the *Shijing* classed [this event] among its odes.[72]

There is here an awareness that the inscription is part of a tradition of completion texts, of closure documents, and marking closure through textual creation is wholly appropriate in the context of grave stelae. For a second example, the segue between prose and verse on a stele dedicated to Heng Fang 衡方 (d. 168 C.E.), commandant of Wei 衛, is as follows:

蓋《雅》《頌》興而《清廟》肅，《中庸》起而祖宗　　[graph missing]。故仲尼既歿，諸子綴《論》，《斯干》作歌，用昭于宣 。謚以旌德，銘以勒勳。於是海內門生故吏，　　[three graphs missing]，采嘉石，樹靈碑。鐫茂伐，祕將來。

In general when the "Elegantiae" and "Hymns" appeared, the "Immaculate Shrine" became austere,[73] and when "On the Central and the Universal" arose, the ancestors [lacuna].[74] And so when Confucius died, his disciples bound together the *Lunyu*; at "This Riverbank" they composed a song to illuminate King Xuan.[75] A posthumous title is to banner virtue, and an inscription is to engrave merit. Therefore, [Heng Fang's] students and former subordinates from everywhere within the seas [lacuna],[76] quarried the excellent stone, erected the numinous stele, and engraved his excellent accomplishments, storing them away for the future.[77]

Again, texts are created to mark the completion of a noteworthy era, whether it be the life of Confucius or the construction of King Xuan's 宣 (r.

827–782 B.C.E.) palace on the riverbank. The text mediates between the past era or distant edifice on the one hand and the reader of the here and now on the other because it can temporally survive Confucius and can spatially circulate beyond the sight of Xuan's walls.

The *locus classicus* of the closure text, particularly the inscribed closure text, seems to be the closing lines of the "Tributes of Yu" (Yu gong 禹貢) in the *Shangshu*, which records that a dark tablet (*xuangui* 玄珪) was erected after China's lands were completely surveyed.[78] It is probably not a coincidence that at least one stele refers to itself as a *xuangui*. Yet placing the stele text within the commemorative text tradition is still not the same as dubbing its verses as a newfangled *Shijing*. To move one step closer to that identification, the stelae must acknowledge an explicit debt to this classic. Fortunately, the stelae repeatedly make this acknowledgment. For example, one stele written by Cai Yong is dedicated to Hu Guang 胡廣 (d. 172), grand tutor and marquis of Anle 安樂, and explicitly takes the *Shijing* poems as its model of this proper remembrance.

故吏司徒許詡等相與欽慕《崧高》《烝民》之作，取言時計功之
則，論集行跡，銘諸琬琰。

His former subordinate Minister over the Masses Xu Xu and others together esteemed the composition of the "Towering Loftiness" and "Multitudinous People" poems, and they took on the dictates of "calculating achievements which were carried out in their proper seasons." They organized and collected the impressions [Hu Guang] left behind and inscribed them on *wan*- and *yan*-tablets.[79]

The two *Shijing* poems "Towering Loftiness" and "Multitudinous People" identify the composer as Jifu 吉甫, which the commentarial tradition in turn identifies as Yin Jifu—noted above as the alleged ancestor to Yin Zhou.[80] As for the reference to "calculating achievements," this passage originates from the *Zuo zhuan* 左傳 and describes proper inscriptions for bronze bells,[81] the significance of which will be explained below. Here it is only necessary to note the debt owed to the *Shijing* as an inspiring model for stele hymns, a debt recognized by many Eastern Han stelae.

Even so, several stelae take this identification still one step further, directly equating the inscription writer with the *Shijing* composer. The inscription writer is carrying out the same act as the *Shijing* composer, creating an everlasting closure text in tetrasyllabic verse. These stelae

authors in fact had a surprisingly specific image of the textual role they were
reenacting. In the following segue of a stele dedicated to Grand Commandant
Liu Kuan 劉寬 (d. 185), the inspiration is narrowed down to a specific set
of *Shijing* pieces:

> 於是故吏季謙等，有感殷魯述德之頌，以為洪懿休榮宜著無窮。
> 故雜論攸行，紀其大略，鐫石立碑。
>
> Thereupon, his former subordinate Ji Qian and others, roused by the
> hymns that narrated the virtue of Yin and Lu, believed that vast virtue
> and excellent splendor ought to be manifested into infinity. Therefore,
> they combined and organized that which he had done and recorded the
> overall gist, chiseling out the stone and erecting the stele.[82]

Thus, the inscribers specifically envisioned the Yin 殷 and Lu 魯
hymns, a selection appropriate given that these were regarded as songs for
the ancestral hall. Yet the specificity does not end there. Not only do stele
inscribers identify the specific odes of the *Shijing*, they then go so far as to
liken themselves to these ode composers by name. For example, that of
Yang Zhen 楊震 (d. 124) concludes as follows:

> 門人汝南陳熾等緣在三義一頌有《清廟》。故敢慕奚斯之追述，
> 樹玄石于墳道。
>
> His student Chen Chi of Runan and others were bound by one of the
> three principles, [that of the allegiances to father, teacher, and ruler,]
> and as a hymn they took the "Immaculate Shrine."[83] Daring to emulate
> the retrospective narrations of Xisi, they therefore planted the dark
> stone along the grave's path.[84]

Thus, the stele inscriber is repeating the labors of Xisi 奚斯, who
flourished in the early seventh century B.C.E. and who is said to have
authored the Lu hymns. What is most surprising is how widely this
identification with Xisi is. At least eight surviving inscriptions credit him
as their source of inspiration, inscriptions widely distributed across the
Eastern Han empire from modern Sichuan to modern Shandong.[85]
Therefore, just as the stele dedicatee was necessarily being transformed into a
cliché-driven stereotype or formulaic representation, the stele author was
likewise writing himself into a set piece of the ideal rememberer.

If the Eastern Han stele hymns are indeed a spin-off from the *Shijing*,
then some of the attributes of the *Shijing* can in turn be extended to the

stelae. First, like poems from the *Shijing* the stele hymns were to be memorized, their segues urging that the hymns be intoned (*yong* 詠), chanted (*song* 誦), or recited and chanted (*fengsong* 諷誦). Several anecdotes in the standard histories suggest that this desire for recitation was heeded. That of Mi Heng has already been noted above, but his case is not unique. For example, the famous poet Wang Can 王粲 (177–217) encountered a stele while walking with friends, turned his back to it, and recited it without missing a word.[86] Like a poem from its classical inspiration, the stele hymn was meant to be a literal bedrock of the memorial tradition.

Second, like poems from the *Shijing*, stele hymns were to be orally performed. If there was no silent reading, then any reading or recitation was to some extent a performance with or without an audience. Furthermore, some of the classical poems may have been lyrics accompanied by music and dance, and while we no longer know how an ancestral hymn was sung, the stelae explicitly and repeatedly allude to a musical remembrance. A Qinghai stele erected in 180 C.E. and dedicated to the thrice-venerable Zhao Kuan 趙寬 (d. 152) specifically links the stele's own hymn with this musical evocation:

深惟皇考，懿德未伸，蓋以為垂聲罔極、音流管弦，非篇訓金石，孰能傳焉？乃刊碑勒銘，昭示來今。

Our most honorable father—his excellent virtue has not yet spread forth. As for passing his reputation down to infinity and causing the tones of pipe and string to flow forth, if we could not record such exemplariness upon metal and stone, how could we transmit it onward? Therefore, we cut the stele and engrave the inscription, brightly manifesting him henceforth.[87]

Thus, Zhao Kuan was remembered via pipe and string but only as long as the stele inscription was there to transmit the lyrics. A vocalized remembrance is also the case in a second example, that from a stele dedicated to Chen Shi 陳寔 (d. 186), prefect of Taiqiu 太丘 in modern northeastern Henan:

宜有銘勒表墳墓，俾後世之歌詠德音者，知丘封之存斯也。

Appropriately we have carved an inscription to mark the grave, causing later generations who will singingly intone the fame of his virtue [lit. "the virtuous musical notes"] to know that the tomb mound is located here.[88]

In this regard, Chinese tombstones were akin to their Greek counterparts, at which, as noted above, the funeral dirge was reenacted with every future reading.[89]

To recapitulate, the Eastern Han stele was part of a memorial culture in two senses. First, its hymn existed against a background culture of memorized knowledge, and it explicitly associated itself with the cornerstone of that memorized knowledge, the *Shijing*.[90] Second, the stele was a memorial in the more traditional sense of the word, the tangible presence of its stone intended to preserve the dedicatee for future generations. The stele demanded active mental effort—memorization and recitation—but it will be argued below that its functionality did not end there. On the surface, it may seem like a paradox that a tangible stone medium vaunting chirographic preservation would then demand intangible preservation within the memories of the living, but this same paradox has been recognized in other cultures in which oral performance continues to be advocated together with a well-established written tradition.[91]

Stele as Ritual

Despite the marked differences in the gravestones they encountered, Addison and Mi Heng do seem to share a common reaction. Both are passive spectators, disinterested day-trippers to their local historical monuments. On the surface, such casual interaction with the inscriptions would seem to support one scholar's recent contention that the Eastern Han grave stele was "a memorial without other functions."[92]

Yet is there here a danger of missing the larger ritual program? Part of that program has already been suggested by the stele's role as a vehicle for ancestral hymns, hymns that were intended to be recited and performed.[93] As the above inscriptions such as that by Cai Yong indicate, these hymns were the Han spin-offs of the *Shijing*, a mimicry that included all of that classic's recitative and performative baggage. Yet the same Cai Yong inscription also claimed guidance from the proper rules governing bronze vessel inscriptions, a claim that may serve as a clue to another related ritual role. Han scholars were well aware that their own age was not producing the ornate vessels of past dynasties. The legendary and actual recovery of ancient bronze vessels in the Han was much vaunted, evincing a strong association between these vessels and a bygone era. Furthermore, writers such as Wang Chong explicitly criticized their own generations for not inscribing virtues upon bronze vessels, warning that future generations would regard the Han as no match for the earlier, vessel-producing dynasties.[94] Yet at the same time that this physical discontinuity was being acknowledged, a different kind of continuity was being maintained. Cai Yong himself more than once identified the stone stele as the descendant of the bronze vessel, and in his "Discussion on Inscriptions" (Ming lun 銘論), he concludes as follows:

鐘鼎禮樂之器，昭德紀功，以示子孫。物不朽者，莫不朽于金石，故也。近世以來，咸銘之于碑。

Bells and cauldrons are the vessels of ritual and music; they shed light upon virtue and record achievements in order to express them to one's descendants. This is because among the indestructible materials, nothing is as indestructible as metal and stone. From recent times, everyone inscribes [virtue and achievements] upon stelae.[95]

Later literary critics such as Liu Xie would affirm this link as well, and much later still, Kern has argued that the stone inscriptions of the Qin First Emperor also derived from bronze inscriptions.[96] Thus, if Cai Yong, Liu Xie, and others are to be believed, stelae evolved from ritual vessels.

Yet how can such an evolutionary association be maintained when the two items are so different in appearance and, at least at first glance, function? As to the appearance, modern Chinese speculations on stele shapes range from mimicking jade tablets to representing phallic symbols, from evocations of round-heaven-square-earth cosmology to models of coffin-lowering posts. The last is most common because they share the same character bei 碑, meaning "upright stone." Most enigmatic of all is the stele hole, regularly positioned roughly one and a half meters above the base. The common speculation on coffin-lowering posts explains these holes as guiding the ropes used to lower the coffin. Even so, these same stone stelae are Eastern Han products associated with stone chambered tombs and not with the earlier shaft tombs that might have required such posts, and these stelae were regularly erected several years after the burial had already been completed. Thus, the stele with its hole would have been symbolic at best. Yet even here there is solid ground to express reservations because in several cases the hole was added later, unfortunately obliterating part of the inscription.

This exploration into stele text and ritual will conclude by adding one more brief speculation as to the stele's function: the stone stele continued *both* functions of bronze vessels, namely the presentation of a long-lasting inscription to venerate the ancestors *as well as* the offering of food—suspended from its hole—to feed them. Cai Yong, Liu Xie, and other early scholars were thereby justified in associating the two traditions. This argument begins by analyzing a rarely discussed funerary tablet called a *chong* 重.

The main received texts on early rituals—the *Yili* 儀禮, the *Liji*, the *Zhou li* 周禮, and the *Xunzi*—all describe the *chong*-tablets that accompanied coffins, tablets that both identified the dead and bore food sacrifices to them. For example, the "Shi sangli" 士喪禮 chapter in the *Yili* states that the invocator (*zhu* 祝) prepared the rice gruel in two cauldrons and suspended them from the *chong*-tablet next to the coffin. An inscription (*ming* 銘) was also made which read "Mr. So-and-so's coffin" (*mou shi mou zhi jiu* 某氏某之柩), and this inscription was then attached to the *chong*-tablet. The inscription furthermore marked the temporary burial within the courtyard while lengthy preparations were made for the eventual burial at the grave mound.[97]

The *Liji* further explains the theory behind this tablet's inscribed banner using a paronomastic gloss:

銘，明旌也。以死者為不可別已，故以其旗識之。愛之斯錄之矣，敬之斯盡其道焉耳。

The inscription (*ming*) is a bright (*ming*) banner. The deceased is considered as having become indistinguishable, and so one uses this flag to identify him. If you love him, you make this record of him, and if you respect him, you simply carry out this general principle to the utmost for him.[98]

The tablet's flag was thus the first line of defense against the loss of identity; it was a visible banner that fended off indistinguishability. The *Liji* then explains that "the *chong*-tablet follows the general principle of the ancestral tablet" (*chong, zhu dao ye* 重，主道也),[99] and in like manner, the *Shi ming* 釋名 states that because there was no tablet prior to the burial, one made use of the gruel-bearing *chong*-tablet to serve as the spirit's tablet.[100]

Xunzi describes funerary goods or "illuminating vessels" (*mingqi* 明器)[101] as unfinished, as all "form" (*xiang* 象) and no function. Zithers were stringed but not tuned, the corpse was clothed but the sashes remained unhooked, and a carriage may have been buried but its fittings were not included. This sentiment of incompleteness extended to the *chong*-tablet's banner as well:

FIGURE 8.1
Han stelae at Qufu, Shandong. Photo by the author.

書其名，置於其重，則名不見而柩獨明矣。

When one writes the [deceased's] name and sets it on his *chong*-tablet, the name is not to be seen and only the inscription is visible.[102]

In Xunzi's ideal, the writing was there, but the function of communication was not. Yet Xunzi's usage of the term *jiu* 柩, here rendered "inscription," requires elucidation because it normally means "coffin" or "encoffined corpse." Zheng Zhong 鄭眾 (d. 83 C.E.), in a surviving fragment of his *Zhou li* commentary, writes, "The inscription is writing the name of the dead on the banner, which we now call *jiu*" (*ming, shu sizhe ming yu jing, jin wei zhi jiu* 銘，書死者名於旌，今謂之柩).[103] Significantly, Zheng Zhong is here glossing the *Zhou li*'s reference to erecting the *chong*-tablet and setting the inscription upon it. Two Qing commentators to the *Zhou li*, Kong Guangsen 孔廣森 and Sun Yirang 孫詒讓, support Zheng Zhong's explanation of the term *jiu* 柩 with a Han example, that of Wang Li 王立, who killed himself to protest his innocence in the face of corruption charges. In official recognition of his innocence, an order was issued that stated, "Let it be that the officers of the prefecture's Bureau of Decisions write the *jiu* for [Wang] Li in order to make his *hun* manifest" (*qi yi fu juecao yuan shu Li zhi jiu, yi xian qi hun* 其以府決曹掾書立之柩，以顯其魂).[104] Sun Yirang also believes that, in the above *Xunzi* statement, *jiu* is not the encoffined corpse but the banner inscription.

This search for the meaning of *jiu* highlights a terminological fluidity within Han funerary discourse in which objects associated with one another come to share their labels. By conceptual contagion, *jiu*, which originally meant "the encoffined corpse," becomes *jiu*, "the banner inscription that labels the corpse." In similar fashion, *ming* 銘 (the banner "inscription") also becomes interchangeable with its cognate *ming* 名 ("the name"), because the former bore the latter.[105] In the same chapter of the *Xunzi*, it records: "His inscription, threnody, and genealogical record reverentially pass down his name" (*qi ming, lei, jishi jing zhuan qi ming ye* 其銘、誄、繫世，敬傳其名也).[106] And perhaps not surprisingly, the dividing line between "inscription" and "threnody" also becomes blurred over the course of the Han. Likewise written on a banner or "plain flag" (*suqi* 素旗),[107] the threnody was called an "inscription" as well. The terms become so mixed that the Tang commentator Li Shan 李善 (d. 689), when glossing a threnody by Cao Zhi 曹植 (192–232), even explains Cao Zhi's allusion to the threnody's plain flag by citing Zheng Zhong's explanation of the *chong*-tablet as well as the *chong*-tablet descriptions from the ritual anthologies.[108]

The stelae themselves further evince this terminological fluidity, as they sometimes identify their hymns as either "inscriptions" or "threnodies."[109] Yet *chong*-tablet, threnody, and stele not only overlapped in terminology but also shared functions. For example, the stele dedicated to Guo Jiu 郭究 (d. 184 C.E.), attendant to the director of retainers, states, "Therefore, we cut the stone and erected the stele in order to serve as a banner to his *hun* 魂 -soul and to cause the future to always possess a mirror in it" (*nai fashi xingbei, yi jing jue hun, bei hou yong you jian yan* 乃伐石興碑，以旌厥魂，俾後永有鑑焉).[110] Like the *chong*-tablet and the threnody, the stele functioned as a banner to identify the dead, and like Wang Li's *jiu*, it was a manifestation of the deceased's *hun*. This image of the banner is common to other stelae as well, such as on one allegedly dedicated to Wu Ban 武班 (d. 145 C.E.), chief clerk of Dunhuang, which similarly records, "Therefore, we [lacuna] the stone and inscribed the stele in order to make a banner of bright virtue with it" (*gu* [graph missing] *shi mingbei, yi jing mingde yan* 故 [graph missing] 石銘碑，以旌明德焉).[111] Here the banner was associated with brightness or visibility, another concept ascribed to the *chong*-tablet above. Thus, it becomes clear that, first, stelae are a later part of a larger discourse that included *chong*-tablets, inscribed banners, and threnodies, and, second, these elements of the early mortuary tradition are not clearly distinct from one another in terminology or function.   ·

As for physical features, a large number of surviving stelae are roughly two meters tall, the same height as an Eastern Han imperial *chong*-tablet.[112] More importantly, the stele's enigmatic hole may have likewise evolved from that of the *chong*-tablet. According to the ritual anthologies and their commentaries, a hole was made in the *chong*-tablet so that cauldrons of rice gruel could be suspended from it, presumably from a rope passing through this hole.[113] The stele's hole may have represented that of the *chong*-tablet, or more likely, the hole was still functional and the stele continued to support such sacrifices in the cemetery. As noted above, in a few early cases, the hole was clearly added after the stele had been inscribed, and the subsequent obliteration of the text implies the hole may have been more than purely symbolic.[114] In other words, in these cases the need for a hole even seems to override the role of the inscription.

If indeed the stele was still used to nourish the spirits, its function was further akin to the earlier bronze vessels that both preserved inscriptions and bore food for the ancestors. In support of this speculation, an early stele dated 154 C.E. and dedicated to Li Mengchu 李孟初 that exhibits a prominent hole within its brief inscription explicitly calls itself a "spirit-sacrifice

stele" (*shenci zhi bei* 神祠之碑), clearly associating the stone with the act
of offerings to the dead.[115] The stele inscription dedicated to Li Yi's 李翊
consort concludes with Li Yi "setting forth the spring sacrifice" (*chen yuesi*
陳礿祀),[116] and another dedicated to Gao Biao 高彪 (d. 184) concludes that,
once the name is recorded, it will be "clarified through ten thousand
sacrifices" (*chanyu wansi* 闡于萬祀).[117] Even Yin Zhou's stele hymn
translated above ends with the couplet "His name is radiant to future
generations, / And ten thousand sacrifices will never let it die out." While
"ten thousand sacrifices" in these last two cases could be merely rendered
"ten thousand years," a more literal translation is probably in order.

Thus, in its simplest terms, the stone stele functioned as an outdoor
bronze vessel; it both bore a prominent inscription to the dead and conveyed
food to them in an ancestral setting.[118]

Conclusion

Much more than a mere record of birth and death dates as found on an
English tombstone, the Eastern Han stele transformed its dedicatee into a
memorable classicist template. Although the most tangible of texts itself,
this stone inscription paradoxically advocated a memorial culture, converting
the dead into a stable stereotype, a streamlined memory. Thus, the Eastern
Han stele is not merely a case study that demonstrates how text and ritual
can function in tandem; it instead demonstrates how text *is* ritual. In a
memorial culture, texts were not silently read books that remained tidily
separate from the reader; they instead existed beyond the physical brushwork
or stone engraving, actually changing the psyche of those who memorized
them, if Carruthers, Wang Chong, Xunzi, and others are to be believed. The
Eastern Han stele itself not only urged the reader to memorize, but expressly
adopted the format of the most memorized of classics, transforming its
dedicatee into rhythmic meters, classicist templates, formal representations.
Yet it still fed him in the process.

This last observation leads to a final caveat that must be addressed.
Within the early elitist discourse characterized by memorized classics and
sanitized rituals, the ancestors at best seem to be depicted as intense yet
formulaic memories. They were merged with known exemplars as well as
molded to fit Confucian prescriptions and classicist cliché. Like Xunzi's
funerary goods or "illuminating vessels" (*mingqi*), the dead were transformed
into *xiang* 象, into "form-only," and indeed the stelae themselves sometimes

describe the ancestors by using this term. The classics explicitly demarcate between the sage who understands cosmological patterns and the benighted masses who only believe in hungry ghosts and spirits; the sage in fact invented ghosts and spirits so that the masses would obey. [119] These stelae, almost always dedicated to Han officialdom, would at first seem to be the product of this elitist view because of their textual origins in the classics and their advocacy of an educated, recitative tradition. Yet these same stelae are offering food to those ancestors as if they were real external agencies, hungry spirits dependent upon their living relations for a meal. How is this contradiction resolved?

To be blunt, it cannot be. These two perspectives belong to separate genres of discourse, *not* separate groups of people. The difference is that the same people can simultaneously maintain separate, even contradictory genres of discourse. Few, if any, cultures possess a logical, contradiction-free vision of afterlife existence because reliable accounts of death's experience are inherently impossible. In her study on death in early Greek art and poetry, Emily Vermeule explains:

> The manifold self-contradictions in Greek ideas and phrasing about death are not errors. They are styles of imagining the unimaginable, and are responsive both to personal needs and to old conventions. The same conflicts surge up in many cultures. They are necessary ambiguities in a realm of thinking where thinking cannot really be done, and where there is no experience. [120]

Such "necessary ambiguities" are easily transferable to Han culture.

As closure texts, the stele hymns are "final words" in a literal sense, and thus it may be appropriate for them to bring this exploration of ritual texts and this series of speculations to a close. The last couplets of the following hymn indeed well demonstrate these necessary ambiguities as food, form, and song mix and combine to create a lasting, text-dependent ritual:

亡而像存	He has perished but his *form* survives,
樂嘉靈兮	His excellent spirit made pleased.
宗子于集	The children of his lineage come to gather,
嗜其鳴兮	Their warbling made sweet.
四祀烝嘗	Because of the seasonal sacrifices,
不廢荒兮	He will not be cast off into desolation. [121]

NOTES

1. Enright, *The Oxford Book of Death*, 318.
2. Stele texts consist of a prose preface followed by a tetrasyllabic hymn that repeats much of the same information. After noting the erection of the stele itself, its segue usually introduces the hymn with the phrase "its lyrics are as follows" (*qi ci yue* 其辭曰).
3. *Hou Hanshu* 80.2657.
4. For a Han example involving the poet Wang Can 王粲 (177–217), see *Sanguo zhi* 21.599; for a later example, see *Jiu Tangshu* 190.5048.
5. Mote, *Imperial China*, 340.
6. *Zhuzi yulei*, 153 ("Dushu fa" 讀書法).
7. *Guanzi jiaoshi*, 235 ("Jie" 戒).
8. *Lunyu jishi*, 900 ("Zilu" 子路).
9. Lewis, *Writing and Authority in Early China*, 158.
10. *Da Dai liji jiegu*, 75 ("Zengzi lishi" 曾子立事).
11. Zheng Xuan 鄭玄 (127–200) defines *feng* as "reciting a text" (*beiwen* 倍[背]文) and *song* as "marking it off with tones" (*yi sheng jie zhi* 以聲節之). The Tang subcommentary by Jia Gongyan 賈公彥 (fl. 650) draws upon other early citations to denote the musicality of *song*. See *Zhou li zhushu*, 787 ("Chunguan: Da sile" 春官大司樂). Whether this distinction was broadly recognized is uncertain, although as will be seen in passages below, *fengsong* seems to be interchangeable with *fengyong* 諷詠, "to recite and intone," and stele inscriptions describe the musical nature of their own recited hymns.
12. Carruthers, *The Book of Memory*, 6–7, 74, 173. The act of murmuring a text transformed a cerebral activity into a physical activity, and so murmuring was a mnemonic tool. Silent reading is a relatively recent innovation.
13. *Xunzi jijie*, 509 ("Dalue" 大略).
14. Ibid., 11 ("Quan xue" 勸學).
15. *Zhanguo ce*, 280 ("Puyang ren Lü Buwei guyu Handan" 濮陽人呂不韋賈於邯鄲). Variations of the text specify that he was asked to recite either the classics or his studies.
16. *Hanshu* 11.333.
17. *Shiji* 121.3119.
18. In addition to the usage of tetrasyllabic verse, this style of laudatory introductory couplet of the stele hymn may also elicit the flavor of *Shijing*-style poetry. For example, the *Shijing* poem "Wu" 武 (Mao 285) begins, "O august King Wu!" (*Yu huang Wu wang* 於皇武王), and the poem "Zhuo" 酌 (Mao 293) begins, "O Shining royal army!" (*Yu shuo wangshi* 於鑠王師). See *Mao shi zhengyi*, 597, 604, respectively.
19. *Han bei jishi*, 437.
20. *Zhou Yi jijie*, 445. Interpreting the goose of the *jian* hexagram can lead to more than one image. Shaughnessy writes, "In the worldview of Zhou China the wild goose seems to have been a natural omen evoking marital separation. . . . [S]ince all too many of the soldiers did not return from their campaigns, the appearance of the geese predicted the disappearance of the men. For wives, in particular, this could not have been an auspicious omen." See Shaughnessy, *I*

Ching, 10–11. Yet in Yin Zhou's stele, the image is more positive and evoked the image of a toiling officer who sacrificed himself for the safety of others. Such an image seems to recur in the *Shijing* poem "Wild Goose" (Hong yan 鴻鴈 [Mao 181]); see *Mao shi zhengyi*, 431.

21. *Lunyu jishi*, 408 ("Yong ye" 雍也).

22. Day, "Rituals in Stone," 17.

23. Ong, *Orality and Literacy*, 35.

24. *Hou Hanshu* 68.2227.

25. *Songshu* 64.1699. Pei Songzhi wanted stele inscriptions to be approved by the court before being inscribed. Such a safeguard was attempted in the Tang, and for a discussion on this process as well as the Tang perspective of stele audacity, see Twitchett, *The Writing of Official History under the T'ang*, 68–76.

26. Lu Ji writes, "Stele inscription unfurls pattern to match substance" (*bei pi wen yi xiang zhi* 碑披文以相質); see Owen, *Readings in Chinese Literary Thought*, 130. Liu Xie began his appraisal of stelae and threnodies by writing, "Stele and threnody are based upon writing the truth and discarding the baseless" (*xieshi chuixu, beilei yi li* 寫實追虛，碑誄以立); see *Wenxin diaolong zhu*, 215.

27. Yates, *The Art of Memory*, 9–10.

28. Ong, *Orality and Literacy*, 70, similarly writes as follows: "Oral memory works effectively with 'heavy' characters, persons whose deeds are monumental, memorable and commonly public. Thus the noetic economy of its nature generates outsize figures, that is, heroic figures, not for romantic reasons or reflectively didactic reasons but for much more basic reasons: to organize experience in some sort of permanently memorable form."

29. For a history of this Western concept of artificial memory, see Carruthers, *The Book of Memory*; and Yates, *The Art of Memory*.

30. *Han bei jishi*, 319.

31. *Zhang Heng shiwen jijiao zhu*, 391.

32. Carruthers, *The Book of Memory*, 179.

33. In like manner, Coleman describes the mastery of a text as explained by William of St. Theirry (twelfth century C.E.): "What he means by mastering a work is the concentration on an author until his very habit of expression becomes so familiar as to become one's own, it having entered into the reader's mind. David's Psalms, he says, must be read so that the experiences out of which they were written are made the personal experiences of the reader." See Coleman, *Ancient and Medieval Memories*, 176. Note that the format of the text to be memorized is, like the "Pharsalia," in verse. Coleman (132–133, 149) cites other examples of medieval scholars mastering the Psalms until they become a part of the reciter's own mental landscape.

34. Carruthers, *The Book of Memory*, 180.

35. This diminution of "self" (a term which Carruthers elsewhere replaces with "the one who remembers") seems applicable to the relationship-oriented ideal of early China long before the advent of Buddhism. Graham argues that a strong concept of ego may be conceivable only in a highly atomized society such as our own and concludes that "we may doubt whether a theoretically pure

egoism would be conceived by individuals so closely cemented by kin relations as the ancient Chinese." See Graham, *Disputers of the Tao*, 63. Fingarette writes, "The metaphor of an inner psychic life, in all its ramifications so familiar to us, simply isn't present in the *Analects*, not even as a rejected possibility." One of Fingarette's goals, much criticized by Schwartz, is also to question our modern Western assumption of "self" when approaching Confucius. He writes, "Man is not an ultimately autonomous being who has an inner and decisive power, intrinsic to him, a power to select among real alternatives and thereby to shape a life for himself." See Fingarette, *Confucius—The Secular as Sacred*, 34, 45; Schwartz, *The World of Thought in Ancient China*, 73–75.

36. *Mengzi zhengyi*, 816. According to the same passage, if one wears the clothes of the bad ruler Jie 桀, behaves as Jie did, and recites Jie's words, one simply becomes a Jie, too.

37. I am here following Wang Xianqian's commentary on this line.

38. *Xunzi jijie*, 18–19 ("Quan xue"). Wang Xianqian identifies the *zhi* 之 throughout this extract as the classics.

39. *Lunheng jiaoshi*, 545 ("Cheng cai" 程材). *Cao* 操 here can imply not only "principles" but also the restraints drilled into and imposed upon oneself.

40. Wang Chong also argued that Emperors Wu and Cheng were subconsciously transformed by the poetic expositions (*fu* 賦) and hymns (*song* 頌) of Sima Xiangru and Yang Xiong, respectively; see *Lunheng jiaoshi*, 641–642 ("Qiangao" 譴告).

41. Kern, *The Stele Inscriptions of Ch'in Shih-huang*, 101–102.

42. *Guanzi jiaoshi*, 303 ("Chimi" 侈靡).

43. There also exists a *Hanshu* anecdote (92.3706) that claims a certain individual could recite several hundred thousand words of medical and pharmacological texts.

44. For a brief discussion of the *Jijiu pian's* mnemotechnic poetry, see Sterckx, *The Animal and the Daemon in Early China*, 30–33.

45. *Liji jijie*, 328 ("Wang zhi" 王制).

46. *Hanshu* 99.4076. The propaganda poems circulated throughout the empire by Wang Mang were said to total an impressive thirty thousand characters.

47. Ibid. 27.1393–1396.

48. Yates, *The Art of Memory*, 29.

49. Thomas, *Literacy and Orality in Ancient Greece*, 114.

50. *Shangshu jinguwen zhushu*, 70 ("Yao dian" 堯典).

51. Owen, *Readings in Chinese Literary Thought*, 28–29.

52. *Shangshu jinguwen zhushu*, 70 ("Yao dian").

53. *Liji jijie*, 770 ("Neize" 內則).

54. In a rare stele dedicated to a child, it is stated that the boy Feng Sheng 逢盛, who died at the age of twelve, was able to recite the *Shijing*; see *Li shi* 10.8a ("Tongzi Feng Sheng bei" 童子逢盛碑).

55. *Hanshu* 30.1708. Mozi depicted a Confucian's life as alternating between mourning periods and reciting, playing, singing, and dancing the *Shi*. See *Mozi jiaozhu*, 705 ("Gong Meng" 公孟).

56. For a summation of the arguments, see Kern, *The Stele Inscriptions of*

Ch'in Shih-huang, 187–196.

57. Citation of the *Shijing* poem "Ding zhi fang zhong" 定之方中 (Mao 50), in which a palace is built in Chu; cf. *Mao shi zhengyi*, 316.

58. Citation of the *Shijing* poem "Jia le" 假樂 (Mao 249), which praises a ruler's proper government; cf. *Mao shi zhengyi*, 540.

59. Possible paraphrase or alternative version of the *Shijing* poem "Qing miao" 清廟 (Mao 266), which praises the manner in which King Wen's sacrifices were executed; cf. *Mao shi zhengyi*, 583. The inscription has *yong* 雍 for the *Shijing*'s *yong* 雝. The usage of homonyms may of course be a further symptom of a predominantly memorial, rather than chirographic, culture.

60. Second citation of "Jia le"; cf. *Mao shi zhengyi*, 540.

61. Third citation of "Jia le"; cf. *Mao shi zhengyi*, 540.

62. Possible paraphrase or alternative version of the *Shijing* poem "Fu tian" 甫田 (Mao 211), a sacrificial song that presents an idealized vision of a prosperous farm; cf. *Mao shi zhengyi*, 475. The inscription has *liang* 糧 for the *Shijing*'s *liang* 粱.

63. *Qin Han bei shu*, 518–519 ("Zengbu 'Jiao bei suibi: Baishi shenjun bei'" 增補「校碑隨筆：白石神君碑」). The last four lines are akin to the auspicious words at the end of bronze inscriptions known as *guci* 嘏辭, suggesting a textual link between these two traditions. For a discussion of *guci* in inscriptions, see Falkenhausen, "Issues in Western Zhou Studies," 151–156; and Kern, *The Stele Inscriptions of Ch'in Shih-huang*, 93–104. For a discussion further linking the bronze vessel tradition and the stone stele tradition, see below.

64. Lewis has studied this phenomenon in depth, a phenomenon not limited to the *Zuo zhuan* but also extending to the *Lunyu*, the *Mencius*, and the *Xunzi*. He writes as follows: "While this practice often distresses modern scholars—but not postmodern ones—who privilege original meanings and an author's intent, the men of the Spring and Autumn and early Warring States period perhaps valued the ability to make the poem say something other than what had originally been intended. To repeat a poem was a simple-minded enterprise, but to actively adapt it to new circumstances required skill and perception. This use of the odes in the Spring and Autumn courts may have set a pattern for the Confucian ideal of adapting teaching—including the meaning given to key terms—to the circumstances and the interlocutor. It also anticipates the later philosophical and commentarial assumption that the *Odes* contain hidden meanings." See Lewis, *Writing and Authority in Early China*, 158. One of the foremost authorities on Eastern Han inscriptions, Gao Wen (*Han bei jishi*, 83), takes a similar position in reference to Eastern Han grave stelae.

65. The most famous example would be the "Great Preface" (Da xu 大序) that identifies the ruler as the origin and theme of all *Shijing* verses.

66. For example, see Weng, "Lun Shandong Han bei," 13.

67. *Hou Hanshu* 84.2794. Her father was a shaman invocator who drowned during a river ritual.

68. This anecdote is from the *Kuaiji dianlu* 會稽典錄 by Yu Yu 虞預 (fl. early fourth century) as recorded in the commentary for *Hou Hanshu* 84.2795. For most of the stories surrounding Cao E and her stelae, see *Shui jing zhu beilu*,

433–436. The existing Cao E stelae in Zhejiang are most likely Song products; see Yang Zhenfang, *Beitie xulu*, 153–154.

69. Ye and Ke, *Yushi yitongping*, 388.

70. *Hou Hanshu* 52.1731.

71. Ibid. 23.822. Note that the Astronomy, or History, Office is here already involved in composing the stele text; government offices would in later dynasties be ordered to write, regulate, or at least approve stele texts. To cite another example of commissioned lyrics, according to *Hou Hanshu* 44.1511 the emperor ordered Cai Yong to compose a hymn (*song* 頌) for Hu Guang, which survives in the form of a stele.

72. *Shui jing zhu beilu*, 47–48 ("Han Rongkou shimen ming" 漢榮口石門銘). The annotator of *Shui jing zhu beilu*, Shi Zhicun 施蟄存, comments that if Li Daoyuan 酈道元 (d. 527) had not recorded this stele, then the achievements of Sima Deng would never have been made manifest and concludes that "this is truly the so-called longevity of metal and stone, which is unlike that of bamboo and silk."

73. The "Immaculate Shrine" (Qing miao 清廟 [Mao 266]) is the first of the *Shijing* "hymns" (*song* 頌); see *Mao shi zhengyi*, 583.

74. Attributed to Confucius's grandson Zisi 子思, "On the Central and the Universal" (Zhong yong 中庸) discusses veneration of ancestors among other things.

75. This *Shijing* poem "Si gan" 斯干 (Mao 189) praises the completion of an elaborate palace, and the Mao preface identifies the palace as that of King Xuan. See *Mao shi zhengyi*, 436.

76. Judging from other, similar inscriptions, the three missing characters probably refer to their traveling through or ascending the "famous mountains" (*mingshan* 名山).

77. *Li shi* 8.2b ("Wei wei Heng Fang bei" 衛尉衡方碑); *Han bei jishi*, 319.

78. *Shangshu jinguwen zhushu*, 207.

79. *Cai zhonglang ji* 4.6a. The jade *wan*-tablets were square on top, and *yan*-tablets were triangular on top, the allusion being to stele shapes.

80. *Mao shi zhengyi*, 565, 568.

81. *Chunqiu Zuo zhuan zhu* (Xiang 19), 1047.

82. *Li shi* 11.2b–3a ("Taiwei Liu Kuan bei" 太尉劉寬碑).

83. Hong Gua 洪适 (1117–1184), the compiler of the *Li shi*, takes the "three principles" as allegiances to father, teacher, and ruler. Alternatively, these three allegiances seem similar to the three means of forming relationships explained by Shangzi; see *Shang jun shu zhuizhi*, 51–52 ("Kaisai" 開塞). According to this text, the three ages of humankind were based on kinship, on the moral guidance of worthies, and on rulership, respectively. As another possibility, Xunzi (*Xunzi jijie*, 374 ["Li lun" 禮論]) depicts the three individuals to whom one owes a duty of mourning as father, mother, and lord (*junzi* 君子), the last of whom feeds, teaches, and serves as both father and mother.

84. *Li shi* 12.2a–b ("Taiwei Yang Zhen bei" 太尉楊震碑).

85. In addition to Yang Zhen, the other seven are *Li shi* 5.12a ("Ba jun taishou Zhang Na bei" 巴郡太守張納碑); 7.11a ("Jingzhou cishi Du Shang bei" 荊州刺史度尚碑); 7.16a–b ("Pei xiang Yang Tong bei" 沛相楊統碑); 11.18b

("Liang xiang Fei Fan bei" 梁相費汎碑); 11.15b ("Suimin jiaowei Xiong jun
bei" 綏民校尉熊君碑); *Han bei wenfan* 2.18a ("Gucheng zhang Tangyin ling
Zhang jun biaosong" 穀城長蕩陰令張君表頌); 2.16b ("Heyang ling Cao jun
bei" 郃陽令曹君碑).

86. *Sanguo zhi* 21.599.

87. *Han bei jishi*, 446. Unfortunately, the stone, discovered in 1943, was
mostly destroyed by a fire in 1950. In 220 C.E., the first year of the Wei dynasty,
a stele dedicated to the reconstruction of the Confucian shrine records that during
the late chaos, the sacrifices stopped, the shrine fell into disrepair, and one
"could not hear the sounds of recitations" (*bu wen jiangsong zhi sheng* 不聞講誦
之聲). To commemorate the repairs, the author of the stele includes a laudatory
"hymn" (*song* 頌) of his own. See *Li shi* 19.12a–13a ("Wei xiu Kongzi miao
bei" 魏脩孔子廟碑).

88. *Cai zhonglang ji* 2.5a. In the *Shijing*'s "Huang yi" 皇矣, the phrase
"the fame of his virtue" (*deyin* 德音) describes the reputation of King Wen's
father, thus marking the ascension of a great lineage; see *Mao shi zhengyi*, 520.
Cai Yong may have intended to play upon this allusion in reference to Chen
Shi's descendants, but even here the phrase *deyin*, literally "the virtuous musical
notes," carries with it an explicit musicality. Citing this "Huang yi" passage,
the *Liji* states that in antiquity when the five notes harmonized and the poems
were accompanied with strings and sung, these harmonies were "the virtuous
musical notes," and the virtuous musical notes were called "music" (*yue* 樂). See
Liji jijie, 1015 ("Yue ji" 樂記).

89. Kern reaches similar conclusions in reference to the Qin First
Emperor's mountain inscriptions, that there is a clear element of recitation and
possibly even musicality manifested in what are essentially performance pieces.
See Kern, *The Stele Inscriptions of Ch'in Shih-huang*, 142–145.

90. While the stelae explicitly and repeatedly link themselves to the
Shijing tradition, it should also be noted, even if just in passing, that the larger
prosimetric form of these Eastern Han inscriptions is similar to that of Buddhist
sutras. Those sutras circulating in the Eastern Han already included *gathas*, the
versified passages that function in tandem with prose passages. Erik Zürcher
notes that some of the *gathas* summarized the essential content of the prose and
that some took "the form of extremely concentrated mnemonic verses." Eastern
Han stele hymns also repeat and essentialize the content of their prose prefaces
in a mnemonic format. However, Zürcher also notes that *gathas* of the first-
generation translators (150–170 C.E.) were rendered in clumsy prose and that
those of the second generation (170–190 C.E.) were translated either as prose or
unrhymed verse. Thus, translators were still struggling with the format of
Buddhist sutras while the stelae were already employing this format. (Later
literary works, such as Tao Qian's famous "Peach Blossom Spring," make use of
a similar format of prose followed by verse that repeats the content.) For *gathas*
in the Han, see Zürcher, "A New Look at the Earliest Chinese Buddhist Texts,"
286–288.

91. Rosalind Thomas also notes that oral transmission overlapped with the
written text in early Greece; see Thomas, *Literacy and Orality in Ancient Greece*,
122–123. In more general terms, Jack Goody explains such an overlap as

follows: "Why should people who could read from the Bible, the Qur'an, the Rig Veda, or Homer commit those works to memory and then produce them as spoken language? Partly because, as I have mentioned, 'knowing' a text often means memorizing it word for word; internalizing the meaning with the words means that those words become part of you, integral to your consciousness, and may be helpful in organizing your experience. Another factor is that being able to quote in this way from, say, *King Lear* is prestigious (showing you are an educated, possibly self-educated, man or woman); also, memorization is often necessary in turning a text into a performance (as with a play onstage) for broadcasting purposes. And to speak the words of the gods is especially charismatic." See Goody, *The Power of the Written Tradition*, 35. His first factor here is akin to Carruthers's comment on "stamping the body-soul" with memorization. Goody also notes that literate societies, not oral societies, develop the most extensive mnemonic devices, an observation that would clearly apply to early China as well.

92. Wu Hung, *Monumentality in Early Chinese Art and Architecture*, 222.

93. The full ritual import of memorization, hymn recitation, and mental concentration in ancestral remembrance will be explored in my forthcoming book on ancestor worship in early imperial China.

94. *Lunheng jiaoshi*, 851 ("Xu song" 須頌). Elsewhere in the same essay (855), he similarly lamented the lack of Han stone inscriptions like those of the Qin First Emperor.

95. *Cai zhonglang waiji* 2.10b. Another Cai Yong inscription that forges this link is his stele text to the grand commandant Li Xian 李咸 (d. 175 C.E.): 名莫隆于不朽，德莫盛于萬世。銘勒顯于鍾鼎，清烈光于來裔。刊石立碑，載德不泯。("As for one's name, nothing is more exalted than indestructibility, and as for one's virtue, nothing is considered more flourishing than its lasting ten thousand generations. When inscriptions are made manifest on bells and vessels, their pure radiance will brighten posterity. We cut the stone and erect the stele so that this recorded virtue is never destroyed.") See *Cai zhonglang ji* 5.5a.

96. Kern, *The Stele Inscriptions of Ch'in Shih-huang*, 68–69, argues that the First Qin Emperor paid serious attention to matters of the ancestral temple and deduces a possible relationship between pre-imperial bronze inscriptions and the emperor's stone inscriptions, the texts for the latter preserved in the *Shiji*. While these inscriptions are not the type of ancestral veneration espoused by the Eastern Han grave stele tradition, they demonstrate that the stele tradition did not suddenly emerge without precursors. For further context specifically on Han mountain inscriptions, see Brashier, "The Spirit Lord of Baishi Mountain."

97. *Yili zhushu*, 1130, 1135 ("Shisang li" 士喪禮). "Inscription" in both Chinese and English is not limited to casting in or engraving upon metal and stone; it more generally refers to the physical application of language, to a chirographic act.

98. *Liji jijie*, 253 ("Tan Gong"檀弓).

99. Ibid., 254 ("Tan Gong").

100. *Shiming shuzheng*, 272–273 ("Sangzhi" 喪制).

101. For a brief account of "illuminating" grave goods, see also *Hou*

Hanshu 81.2690 (including commentary).

102. *Xunzi jijie*, 367 ("Li lun"). It is unclear how the name was not visible; perhaps the banner did not face outward or the suspended cauldrons covered the inscription. Perhaps the hidden written text is parallel to inscriptions inside bronze vessels, which were also not seen when covered with food and drink. (My thanks to Martin Kern for this last suggestion.) Unfortunately, Xunzi does not explain the ritual itself. This banner is in a long list of wares of the living that, in their incomplete state, were taken to the tomb to give the impression that only the abode had changed. The *chong* banner may thus have had a counterpart within the realm of the living.

103. *Zhou li zhengyi*, 2035–2036 ("Chunguan: Xiao zhu" 春官小祝).

104. *Hanshu* 83.3390.

105. *Zhou li zhengyi*, 2035–2036 ("Chunguan: Xiao zhu").

106. *Xunzi jijie*, 371.

107. Cao Zhi often referred to the plain banner in the introductions to his threnodies. For four examples, see *Yiwen leiju*, 241, 243, 282. On this last page, there is also a Han threnody that introduces its verse with "the *chong* says" 重曰, which may further indicate this interchangeability of terms. However, *chong* as an introduction of verse within the middle of a literary piece exists elsewhere without clear reference to mortuary traditions, such as in the plaintive poetic exposition by Emperor Cheng's favorite beauty, surnamed Ban 班 (*Hanshu* 97.3987). Yan Shigu here explains it as a poetic exposition's "recapitulation" that indicates emotional intent had not been fully expressed yet. While this explanation is not wholly satisfying, to claim a mortuary reference here would also be somewhat speculative.

108. *Wen xuan* (Shanghai ed.) 56.2434 ("Wang Zhongxuan lei" 王仲宣誄). Li Shan also cites a threnody by Yang Xiong that refers to its banner, thus dating the practice to before the Eastern Han.

109. For examples, see *Li shi* 6.9b ("Beihai xiang Jing jun ming" 北海相景君銘); *Zhou li zhengyi*, 2036 ("Chun guan: xiao zhu") commentary.

110. *Li shi* 10.21a ("Sili congshi Guo Jiu bei" 司隸從事郭究碑). For other examples of ancestral remembrance manifesting the *hun*, see *Hanshu* 16.529; *Cai zhonglang ji* 3.5b ("Sikong Linjin hou Yang gong bei" 司空臨晉侯楊公碑).

111. *Li shi* 6.12a ("Dunhuang zhangshi Wu Ban bei" 敦煌長史武班碑).

112. *Hou Hanshu, zhi* 志 6.3144.

113. *Yili zhushu*, 1135 ("Shisang li"). *Yili yizhu*, 564 ("Shisang li"), offers an illustration of how its commentators envision the rope passing through the *chong*-tablet to suspend a cauldron on either side. Other sources with interpretive illustrations use more elaborate additions of planks attached to the hole with cauldrons hanging off the ends.

114. Kinseki takuhon kenkyūkai, *Kan hi shūsei*, 13–14, 129.

115. *Han bei jishi*, 181; Kinseki takuhon kenkyūkai, *Kan hi shūsei*, 144.

116. *Li shi* 12.17a ("Li Yi furen bei" 李翊夫人碑).

117. Ibid. 10.25b ("Waihuang ling Gao Biao bei" 外黃令高彪碑).

118. "Cauldron texts" (*dingwen* 鼎文) were even preserved on the back of one stele; see *Shui jing zhu beilu*, 239–242; *Cai zhonglang ji* 1.8b–1.10a.

119. *Liji jijie*, 1204 ("Jifa" 祭法); 1220 ("Jiyi" 祭義).

120. Vermeule, *Aspects of Death in Early Greek Art and Poetry*, 118. For a lengthy discussion on multiple simultaneous interpretations of a single ritual in the Han, see Brashier, "The Spirit Lord of Baishi Mountain."

121. *Li shi* 8.9a ("Xiaolian Liu Min bei" 孝廉柳敏碑); *Sichuan lidai beike*, 69 (italics mine).

Works Cited

Abbreviations

SBBY   *Sibu beiyao* 四部備要
SBCK   *Sibu congkan* 四部叢刊
SSJZS   *Shisan jing zhushu* 十三經注疏
ZZJC   *Zhuzi jicheng* 諸子集成
XBZZJC   *Xinbian Zhuzi jicheng* 新編諸子集成

Allan, Sarah, and Williams, Crispin, eds. *The Guodian Laozi: Proceedings of the International Conference, Dartmouth College, May 1998*. Berkeley: Society for the Study of Early China and Institute for Asian Studies, University of California, 2000.

Allen, Joseph R. "Postface: A Literary History of the *Shi jing*." In *The Book of Songs: The Ancient Chinese Classic of Poetry*, translated by Arthur Waley and edited by Joseph R. Allen, pp. 336–383. New York: Grove Press, 1996.

Anhui sheng bowuguan 安徽省博物館. *Anhui sheng bowuguan cang qingtongqi* 安徽省博物館藏青銅器. Shanghai: Shanghai renmin meishu chubanshe, 1987.

Anhui sheng wenwu guanli weiyuanhui 安徽省文物管理委員會 and Anhui sheng bowuguan 安徽省博物館. *Shou Xian Cai Hou mu chutu yiwu* 壽縣蔡侯墓出土遺物. Kaoguxue zhuankan, ser. II, no. 5. Beijing: Kexue chubanshe, 1956.

Arbuckle, Gary. "The Five Divine Lords or One (Human) Emperor? A Problematic Passage in the Material on Dong Zhongshu." *Journal of the American Oriental Society* 113.2 (1993): 227–280.

Asselin, Mark Laurent. "The Lu-School Reading of 'Guanju' as Preserved in an Eastern Han *fu*." *Journal of the American Oriental Society* 117.3 (1997): 427–443.

Assmann, Jan. *Das kulturelle Gedächtnis: Schrift, Erinnerung und politische*

Identität in frühen Hochkulturen. Munich: C. H. Beck Verlag, 1992.

Austin, John. *How to Do Things with Words*. London: Oxford University Press, 1962.

Bagley, Robert W., ed. *Ancient Sichuan: Treasures from a Lost Civilization*. Seattle: The Seattle Art Museum; Princeton: Princeton University Press, 2000.

———. "Anyang Writing and the Origin of the Chinese Writing System." In *The First Writing*, edited by Stephen D. Houston, chap. 7. Cambridge: Cambridge University Press, 2004.

———. "Meaning and Explanation." In *The Problem of Meaning in Early Chinese Ritual Bronzes*, edited by Roderick Whitfield, pp. 34–55. London: Percival David Foundation, 1993.

———. *Music in the Age of Confucius*. Edited by Jenny F. So. Washington, DC: Smithsonian Institution, 2000.

———. "P'an-lung-ch'eng, a Shang city in Hupei." *Artibus Asiae* 39 (1977): 165–213.

Baihu tong shuzheng 白虎通疏證. Edited by Chen Li 陳立. *XBZZJC* ed.

Balazs, Etienne. *Chinese Civilization and Bureaucracy: Variations on a Theme*. New Haven: Yale University Press, 1984.

Barbieri-Low, Anthony. "The Organization of Imperial Workshops during the Han Dynasty." Ph.D. diss., Princeton University, 2001.

Barr, James. *The Semantics of Biblical Language*. Oxford: Oxford University Press, 1961.

Bauer, Wolfgang. "Ich und Nicht-Ich in Laozis *Daode jing*." *Monumenta Serica* 47 (1999): 25–70.

Baxter, William H. *A Handbook of Old Chinese Phonology*. Berlin: Mouton de Gruyter, 1992.

Behr, Wolfgang. "'Homosomatic Juxtaposition' and the Problem of 'Syssemantic' (*Huiyi*) Characters." In *Langue, parole, écriture: le cas chinois*, edited by Francoise Bottéro & Redouane Djamouri. Paris: Éditions du CNRS, forthcoming.

———. "Reimende Bronzeinschriften und die Entstehung der chinesischen Endreimdichtung." Ph.D. diss., Universität Frankfurt, 1996.

Bell, Catherine. *Ritual Theory, Ritual Practice*. New York: Oxford University Press, 1992.

———. "Ritualization of Texts and the Textualization of Ritual in the Codification of Taoist Liturgy." *History of Religions* 27 (1988): 366–392.

Bi Yuan 畢沅 and Ruan Yuan 阮元. *Shanzuo Jinshizhi* 山左金石志. 1816. Reprint, Beijing: Zhonghua shuju, 1980.

Bielenstein, Hans. *The Bureaucracy of Han Times*. Cambridge: Cambridge University Press, 1980.

Blinova, Ekaterina A. "'Presvetly prestol' kak prostranstvenno-administrativ-naya (zemleustroitel'naya) skhema" [The "Luminous Hall" as a spatioadministrative (earth-ordering) scheme]. In *19th Scientific Conference "Society and State in China,"Abstracts of Papers*, vol. 1, pp. 68–72. Moscow: Nauka—Glavnoe izdatel'stvo Vostochnoi Literatury, 1988.

———. "Prostranstvenno-zemleustroitel'nye struktury v tekstakh 'Yu gun' i 'Min tan vei'" [Spatial earth-ordering structures in the "Yu gong" and the "Ming tang wei"]. In *20th Scientific Conference "Society and State in China," Abstracts of Papers*, vol. 1, pp. 155–160. Moscow: Nauka—Glavnoe izdatel'stvo Vostochnoi Literatury, 1989.

Bodde, Derk. *Festivals in Classical China: New Year and Other Annual Observances during the Han Dynasty, 206 B.C.–A.D. 220*. Princeton: Princeton University Press, 1975.

———. "Myths of Ancient China." In *Essays on Chinese Civilization*, edited by Charles Le Blanc and Dorothy Borei, pp. 45–84. Princeton: Princeton University Press, 1981.

Boltz, Judith Magee. "Divertissement in Western Han." *Early China* 1 (1975): 56–63.

Boltz, William G. "The Fourth–Century B.C. Guodiann Manuscripts from Chuu and the Composition of the *Laotzyy*." *Journal of the American Oriental Society* 119.4 (1999): 590–608.

———. "*Liijih* 'Tzy i' and the Guodiann Manuscript Matches." In *Und folge nun dem, was mein Herz begehrt: Festschrift für Ulrich Unger zum 70. Geburtstag*, edited by Reinhard Emmerich and Hans Stumpfeldt, pp. 209–221. Hamburg: Hamburger Sinologische Gesellschaft, 2002.

———. "Manuscripts with Transmitted Counterparts." In *New Sources of Early Chinese History: An Introduction to the Reading of Inscriptions and Manuscripts*, edited by Edward L. Shaughnessy, pp. 253–283. Berkeley: Society for the Study of Early China and Institute for Asian Studies, University of California, 1997.

———. *The Origin and Early Development of the Chinese Writing System*. New Haven: American Oriental Society, 1994.

Booth, Wayne. *A Rhetoric of Irony*. Chicago: University of Chicago Press, 1974.

Bourdieu, Pierre. *La distinction: Critique sociale du jugement*. Paris: Éditions de Minuit, 1979.

Bowman, Alan K., and Woolf, Greg, eds. *Literacy and Power in the Ancient World*. Cambridge: Cambridge University Press, 1994.

Brashier, K. E. "The Spirit Lord of Baishi Mountain: Feeding the Deities or Heeding the Yinyang?" *Early China* 26–27 (2001–2002): 159–231.

Brooks, E. Bruce, and Brooks, A. Taeko. *The Original Analects: Sayings of Confucius and His Successors*. New York: Columbia University Press, 1998.

Brown, Miranda. "Men in Mourning: Ritual, Politics, and Human Nature in Later Han China, A.D. 25–220." Ph.D. diss., University of California at Berkeley, 2002.

Bulling, A. "'All the World's a Stage': A Note: A Rebuttal." *Artibus Asiae* 31 (1969): 204–209.

———. "Historical Plays in the Art of the Han Period." *Archives of Asian Art* 21 (1967–1968): 20–38.

Butler, Judith. *The Psychic Life of Power: Theories in Subjection.* Stanford: Stanford University Press, 1997.

Cai zhonglang ji 蔡中郎集. *SBBY* ed.

Cai zhonglang waiji 蔡中郎外集. *SBBY* ed.

Cai Zhonglang wenji 蔡中郎文集. By Cai Yong 蔡邕. Changsha: Shangwu yinshuguan, 1938.

Cao Feng 曹峰. "Shanhai Hakubutsukan tenji no Sokan ni tsuite 上海博物館展示の楚簡について." *Kakuten Sokan no shisōshiteki kenkyū* 郭店楚簡の思想史的研究 2 (1999): 122–140.

Carruthers, Mary. *The Book of Memory: A Study of Memory in Medieval Culture.* Cambridge: Cambridge University Press, 1993.

Chang Kwang-chih. "Ancient Trade as Economy or as Ecology." In *Ancient Civilization and Trade,* edited by C. C. Lamberg-Karlovsky and Jeremy Sabloff, pp. 211–224. Albuquerque: University of New Mexico Press, 1975.

———. *Art, Myth, and Ritual: The Path to Political Authority in Ancient China.* Cambridge: Harvard University Press, 1983.

———. "Xia Shang Zhou sandai duzhi yu sandai wenhua yitong 夏商周三代都制與三代文化異同." *Zhongyang yanjiuyuan lishi yuyan yanjiusuo jikan* 中央研究院，歷史語言研究所集刊 55.1 (1984): 51–71.

Chavannes, Édouard. "Les livres chinois avant l'invention du papier." *Journal Asiatique,* ser. 10, vol. 5 (1905): 5–75.

Chen Qiaocong 陳喬樅. *Shijing si jia yiwen kao* 詩經四家異文考. Reprint, *Huang Qing jingjie xubian* 皇清經解續編. Edited by Wang Xianqian. Shanghai: Shanghai shudian, 1988.

Chen Wei 陳偉. "E Jun Qi jie yu Chu guo mianshui wenti 鄂君啟節與楚國免稅問題." *Jiang Han kaogu* 江漢考古 1989.3: 52–58.

———. "'E Jun Qi jie' zhi 'E' di tantao 鄂君啟節之鄂地探討." *Jiang Han kaogu* 江漢考古 1986.2: 88–90.

Chen Weisong 陳蔚松. "'Mi qiangda yu nan Si' jie "芈強大于南巳"解." *Jiang Han luntan* 江漢論壇 1983.2: 70–74.

Chen Zhaorong 陳昭容. "Zhanguo zhi Qin de fujie: Yi shiwu ziliao wei zhu 戰國至秦的符節—以實物資料為主." *Zhongyang yanjiuyuan lishi yuyan yanjiusuo jikan* 中央研究院，歷史語言研究所集刊 66.1 (1995): 305–366.

Chen Zhi 陳直. *Juyan Hanjian yanjiu* 居延漢簡研究. Tianjin: Tianjin guji chubanshe, 1986.

———. "Qin bingjia zhi fu kao 秦兵甲之符考." In *Wenshi kaogu luncong* 文史考古論叢, edited by Chen Zhi, p. 310. Tianjin: Tianjin guji chubanshe, 1988.

Cheng, Anne. Review of *From Chronicle to Canon,* by Sarah Queen. *Early China*

23–24 (1998): 353–366.

Chuci buzhu 楚辭補註. Annotated by Hong Xingzu 洪興祖. Taipei: Yiwen chubanshe, 1981.

Chunqiu fanlu yizheng 春秋繁露義證. By Dong Zhongshu 董仲舒. Annotated by Su Yu 蘇輿. Beijing: Zhonghua shuju, 1992.

Chunqiu Zuo zhuan zhengyi 春秋左傳正義. *SSJZS* ed.

Chunqiu Zuo zhuan zhu 春秋左傳注. Annotated by Yang Bojun 楊伯峻. Rev. ed. Beijing: Zhonghua shuju, 1990.

Coleman, Janet. *Ancient and Medieval Memories: Studies in the Reconstruction of the Past*. Cambridge: Cambridge University Press, 1995.

Connerton, Paul. *How Societies Remember*. Cambridge: Cambridge University Press, 1994.

Cook, Constance A., and Major, John, eds. *Defining Chu: Image and Reality in Ancient China*. Honolulu: University of Hawai'i Press, 1999.

Cook, Scott. "Consummate Artistry and Moral Virtuosity: The 'Wu xing 五行' Essay and Its Aesthetic Implications." *Chinese Literature: Essays, Reviews, Articles* 22 (2000): 113–146.

Crump, J. I. *Chan-kuo ts'e*. 2d rev. ed. San Francisco: Chinese Materials Center, 1979.

Csikszentmihalyi, Mark. "Emulating the Yellow Emperor: The Theory and Practice of HuangLao, 180–141 B.C." Ph.D. diss., Stanford University, 1994.

Csikszentmihalyi, Mark, and Nylan, Michael. "Constructing Lineages and Inventing Traditions through Exemplary Figures in Early China." *T'oung Pao* 89.1–3 (2003): 59–99.

Cui Shi 崔寔. *Simin yueling jishi* 四民月令集釋. Annotated by Miao Qiyu 繆啟愉. Beijing: Nongye chubanshe, 1981.

Da Dai liji jiegu 大戴禮記解詁. Annotated by Wang Pinzhen 王聘珍. Beijing: Zhonghua shuju, 1983.

Day, J. W. "Rituals in Stone: Early Greek Grave Epigrams and Monuments." *Journal of Hellenic Studies* 109 (1989): 16–28.

Declercq, Dominik. *Writing against the State: Political Rhetorics in Third and Fourth Century China*. Leiden: E. J. Brill, 1998.

Demiéville, Paul. "Philosophy and Religion from Han to Sui." In *The Cambridge History of China*, vol. 1, *The Ch'in and Han Empires, 221 B.C.–A.D. 220*, edited by Denis Twichett and Michael Loewe, pp. 808–872. Cambridge: Cambridge University Press, 1986.

DeWoskin, Kenneth. *A Song for One or Two: Music and the Concept of Art in Early China*. Ann Arbor: Center for Chinese Studies, University of Michigan, 1982.

Ding Bangjun 丁邦鈞. "Chu du Shouchun cheng kaogu diaocha zongshu 楚都壽春城考古調查總述." *Dongnan wenhua* 東南文化 1987.1: 25–43.

———. "Shouchun cheng kaogu de zhuyao shouhuo 壽春城考古的主要收獲." *Dongnan wenhua* 東南文化 1991.2: 159–163.

Dolby, William. "Early Chinese Plays and Theater." In *Chinese Theater: From Its Origins to the Present Day*, edited by Colin Mackerras, pp. 7–31. Honolulu: University of Hawai'i Press, 1983.

Dong Tonghe 董同龢. *Shanggu yinyun biaogao* 上古音韻表稿. Taipei: Zhongyang yanjiuyuan lishi yuyan yanjiusuo, 1977.

Dorofeeva-Lichtman, Vera. "The 'Ming tang wei': A Description of a Ritual or a Prescriptive Scheme (*tu*)?" Paper presented at the 9th International Conference on the History of Science in East Asia, National University of Singapore, August 23–27, 1999.

Du You 杜佑. *Tongdian* 通典. Beijing: Zhonghua shuju, 1988.

Dull, Jack. "A Historical Introduction to the Apocryphal (*ch'an-wei*) Texts of the Han Dynasty." Ph.D. diss., University of Washington, 1966.

Eberhard, Wolfram. *Beiträge zur kosmologischen Spekulation Chinas in der Han-Zeit*. 1933. Reprinted in *Sternkunde und Weltbild im Alten China*, pp. 11–110. Taipei: Chinese Material and Research Aids Center, 1970.

Ebrey, Patricia Buckley. *The Aristocratic Families of Early Imperial China: A Case Study of the Po-ling Ts'ui Family*. Cambridge: Cambridge University Press, 1978.

———. *The Cambridge Illustrated History of China*. Cambridge: Cambridge University Press, 1996.

———. "Estate and Family Management in the Later Han as Seen in the *Monthly Instructions for the Four Classes of People*." *Journal of the Economic and Social History of the Orient* 17 (1974): 173–205.

Elias, Norbert. *Über den Prozeß der Zivilisation*. 2d ed. Frankfurt: Suhrkamp, 1981.

Enright, D. J. *The Oxford Book of Death*. Oxford: Oxford University Press, 1987.

Erkes, Eduard. "Das Schaf im Alten China." In *Asiatica: Festschrift Friedrich Weller: Zum 65. Geburtstag gewidmet von seinen Freunden, Kollegen und Schülern*, edited by Johannes Schubert and Ulrich Schneider, pp. 82–92. Leipzig: Harrassowitz, 1954.

Falkenhausen, Lothar von. "Issues in Western Zhou Studies: A Review Article." *Early China* 18 (1993): 139–226.

———. Review of *Writing and Authority in Early China*, by Mark Edward Lewis. *Philosophy East and West* 51.1 (2001): 127–136.

———. "Ritual Music in Bronze Age China: An Archaeological Perspective." Ph.D. diss., Harvard University, 1988.

———. *Suspended Music: Chime Bells in the Culture of Bronze Age China*. Berkeley and Los Angeles: University of California Press, 1993.

———. "Thoughts on 'Literacy' in Shang and Zhou China." Paper presented at the conference "The Sociology of Writing in Ancient China," University of Chicago, November 5–7, 1999.

———. "The Use and Significance of Ritual Bronzes in the Lingnan Region during the Eastern Zhou Period." *Journal of East Asian Archaeology*

(Festschrift in Honor of K. C. Chang, pt. 3, edited by Robert E. Murow-chick et al.) 3.1/2 (2001): 193–236.

————. "The Waning of the Bronze Age: Material Culture and Social Developments, 770–481 B.C." In *The Cambridge History of Ancient China: From the Origins of Civilization to 221 B.C.*, edited by Michael Loewe and Edward L. Shaughnessy, pp. 450–544. Cambridge: Cambridge University Press, 1999.

Fan Shengzhi shu jin shi 范勝之書今釋. Translated with commentary by Shi Shenghan 石聲漢. Beijing: Kexue chubanshe, 1963.

Fan Xiangyong 范祥雍. *Guben zhushu jinian jijiao dingbu* 古本竹書紀年輯校訂補. Shanghai: Xin zhishi, 1956.

Fang Shiming 方詩銘 and Wang Xiuling 王修齡. *Guben zhushu jinian jizheng* 古本竹書紀年輯證. Shanghai: Shanghai guji chubanshe, 1981.

Fangyan jianshu 方言箋疏. In *Erya, Guangya, Fangyan, Shiming Qing shu sizhong hekan* 爾雅廣雅方言釋名清疏四種合刊, pp. 778–1001. Shanghai: Shanghai guji chubanshe, 1989.

Feng su tong yi 風俗通義. By Ying Shao 應邵. Beijing: Zhong Fa Hanxue yanjiusuo, 1943.

Fingarette, Herbert. *Confucius—The Secular as Sacred*. New York: Harper Torchbooks, 1972.

Fiskesjö, Magnus. "The Royal Hunt of the Shang Dynasty: Archaeological and Anthropological Perspectives." M.A. thesis, University of Chicago, 1994.

Ford, Andrew. "From Letters to Literature: Reading the 'Song Culture' of Classical Greece." In *Written Texts and the Rise of Literate Culture in Ancient Greece*, edited by Harvey Yunis, pp. 15–37. Cambridge: Cambridge University Press, 2003.

————. *Homer: The Poetry of the Past*. Ithaca: Cornell University Press, 1992.

Forke, Alfred. *Lun-hêng II: Miscellaneous Essays of Wang Ch'ung*. New York: Paragon, 1962.

Foucault, Michel. *Discipline and Punish: The Birth of the Prison*. Translated by Alan Sheridan. New York: Pantheon Books, 1977.

Franke, Otto. *Studien zur Geschichte des konfuzianischen Dogmas und der chinesischen Staatsreligion: Das Problem des Tsch'un Ts'iu und Tung Tschung-schu's Tsch'un Ts'iu Fan Lu*. Hamburg: L. Friederichsen, 1920.

Freedman, Maurice. *Lineage Organization in Southeastern China*. London: Athlone, 1958.

Fukui Shigemasa 福井重牙. "Rikukei, rikugei to gokei: Kandai ni okeru gokei no seiritsu 六經六藝と五經: 漢代における五經の成立." *Chūgoku shigaku* 中國史學 4 (1994): 139–164.

————."Shin Kan jidai ni okeru hakase seido no tenkai: Gokei hakase nosecchi no meguru gigi sairon 秦漢時代における博士制度の展開: 五經博士の設置めぐる嶷義再論." *Tōyōshi kenkyū* 東洋史研究 53 (1995): 1–31.

————. "Tō Chūjo no taisaku no kisoteki kenkyū 董仲舒の對策の基礎的研究."

Shigaku zasshi 史學雜誌 106 (1997): 157–204.

Funakoshi Akio 船越昭生. "Gaku Kun Kei setsu ni tsuite 鄂君啟節について." *Tōhō gakuhō* 東方學報 43 (1972): 55–95.

Gaskill, Malcolm. "Reporting Murder: Fiction in the Archives in Early Modern England." *Social History* 23.1 (1998): 1–30.

Gassmann, Robert H. *Cheng Ming, Richtigstellung der Bezeichnungen: Zu den Quellen eines Philosophems im antiken China; Ein Beitrag zur Konfuzius-Forschung*. Bern: Peter Lang, 1988.

Gentz, Joachim. *Bibliographie zu Grabtexten von Joachim Gentz*. http:// www.sino.uni-heidelberg.de/staff/gentz/biblio.html (last update: June 17, 1998).

———. "From Casuistic Exegesis to Discursive Guidelines: Early Han *Chunqiu*-Exegesis of Lu Jia (*Guliang*) and Dong Zhongshu (*Gongyang*)." Paper presented at the Second International Convention of Asia Scholars (ICAS2), Berlin, August 9–12, 2001.

———. *Das Gongyang zhuan: Auslegung und Kanonisierung der Frühlings- und Herbstannalen (Chunqiu)*. Wiesbaden: Harrassowitz, 2001.

———. "Ritus als Physiognomie: Frühe chinesische Ritentheorien zwischen Kosmologie und Kunst." In *Ritualdynamik: Kulturübergreifende Studien zur Theorie und Geschichte rituellen Handelns*, edited by Dietrich Harth and Gerrit Schenk, pp. 307–337. Heidelberg: Synchron, 2004.

———. "Some Preliminary Observations on the Newly Excavated 'Tzu I 緇衣' from Kuo-tien 郭店." Paper published on CD-ROM of the XIIIth EACS Proceedings 2000, edited by Stefania Stafutti, 2002.

Gernet, Jaques. *Die chinesische Welt*. Frankfurt: Suhrkamp, 1988.

Giele, Enno. *Database of Early Chinese Manuscripts*. Website of the Society for the Study of Early China. http://www.lib.uchicago.edu/earlychina/res /databases/decm/ (last update: September 1, 2000).

———. *Early Chinese Manuscripts*. Taipei: self-published, 1999.

———. "Early Chinese Manuscripts: Including Addenda and Corrigenda to *New Sources of Early Chinese History: An Introduction to the Reading of Inscriptions and Manuscripts*." *Early China* 23–24 (1998–1999): 247–336.

Golas, Peter J. *Mining*. Vol. 5, pt. 13, *Science and Civilisation in China*, edited by Joseph Needham. Cambridge: Cambridge University Press, 1999.

Goldin, Paul. "The Reception of the *Canon of Odes* in Zhou Times." Paper presented at "Interpretation and Intellectual Change: An International Conference on the History of Chinese Hermeneutics," Rutgers University, October 2001.

Gong Tingwan 龔廷萬, Gong Yu 龔玉, and Dai Jialing 戴嘉陵. *Ba Shu Handai huaxiang ji* 巴蜀漢代畫像集. Beijing: Wenwu chubanshe, 1998.

Gongyang zhuan zhushu 公羊傳注疏. *SSJZS* ed.

Goody, Jack. *The Power of the Written Tradition*. Washington, DC: Smithsonian Institution, 2000.

Graham, Angus C. *Disputers of the Tao: Philosophical Argument in Ancient China*. La Salle, IL: Open Court, 1989.

———. *Later Mohist Logic, Ethics and Science*. Hong Kong: Chinese University Press, 1978.

———. *Yin Yang and the Nature of Correlative Thinking*. Singapore: Institute of East Asian Philosophies, 1986.

Granet, Marcel. *La pensée chinoise*. Paris: La Renaissance du livre, 1934.

Gu Donggao 顧棟高. *Chunqiu dashibiao* 春秋大事表. Rev. ed. Beijing: Zhonghua shuju, 1993.

Gu Jiegang 顧頡剛. *Qin Han de fangshi yu rusheng* 秦漢的方士與儒生. Shanghai: Shanghai guji chubanshe, 1998.

Guanzi 管子. *SSBY* ed.

Guanzi jiaoshi 管子校釋. Annotated by Yan Changyao 顏昌嶢. Changsha: Yuelu shushe, 1996.

Guangzhou shi wenwu guanli weiyuanhui 廣州市文物管理委員會, Zhongguo shehui kexueyuan kaogu yanjiusuo 中國社會科學院考古研究所, and Guangdong sheng bowuguan 廣東省博物館. *Xi Han Nanyue Wang mu* 西漢南越王墓. Zhongguo tianye kaogu baogaoji, Kaoguxue zhuankan, ser. IV, no. 43. Beijing: Wenwu chubanshe, 1991.

Guo Moruo 郭沫若. "Guanyu E Jun Qi jie de yanjiu 關於鄂君啟節的研究." *Wenwu cankao ziliao* 文物參考資料 1958.4: 3–7.

———. *Liang Zhou jinwenci daxi tulu kaoshi* 兩周金文辭大系圖錄考釋. Kaoguxue zhuankan, ser. I, no. 3. Rev. ed. Beijing: Kexue chubanshe, 1957.

Guoyu 國語. Shanghai: Shanghai guji chubanshe, 1978.

Guoyu Wei Zhao zhu 國語韋昭注. *SBBY* ed.

Habermas, Jurgen. *The Structural Transformation of the Public Sphere: An Inquiry into a Category of Bourgeois Society*. Cambridge: MIT Press, 1989.

Hallock, Richard T. "The Use of Seals on the Persepolis Fortification Tablets." In *Seals and Sealing in the Ancient Near East*, edited by McGuire Gibson and Robert D. Biggs, pp. 127–133. Malibu: Undena, 1977.

Han bei jishi 漢碑集釋. Compiled by Gao Wen 高文. Kaifeng: Henan daxue, 1985.

Han bei wenfan 漢碑文範. Compiled by Wu Kaisheng 吳闓生. N.p., 1926.

Han Chang'an cheng Weiyanggong fajue baogao 漢長安城未央宮發掘報告. Beijing: Xinhua shudian, 1996.

Han Feizi jijie 韓非子集解. Annotated by Wang Xianshen 王先慎. *XBZZJC* ed.

Han Feizi jishi 韓非子集釋. Annotated by Chen Qiyou 陳奇猷. Shanghai: Renmin chubanshe, 1974.

Han Jing 韓敬. *Fayan zhu* 法言注. Beijing: Zhonghua shuju, 1992.

Hanshi waizhuan jianshu 韓詩外傳箋疏. Annotated by Qu Shouyuan 屈守元. Chengdu: Ba Shu shushe, 1996.

Hanshi waizhuan zhuzi suoyin 韓氏外傳逐字索引. Chinese University of Hong

Kong, ICS Ancient Chinese Text Concordance Series. Hong Kong: Shangwu yinshuguan, 1992.

Hanshu 漢書. By Ban Gu 班固. Beijing: Zhonghua shuju, 1962.

Harper, Donald. *Chinese Medical Texts: The Mawangdui Medical Manuscripts*. London: Kegan Paul, 1998.

———. "Communication by Design: A Study of a Mawangdui Silk Manuscript of Diagrams (*tu*)." Paper presented at the European and North American Exchanges in East Asian Studies Conference, "From Image to Action: The Dynamics of Visual Representation in Chinese Intellectual and Religious Culture," Paris, September 3–5, 2001.

———. "Wang Yen-shou's Nightmare Poem." *Harvard Journal of Asiatic Studies* 47.1 (1987): 239–283.

Harrist, Robert E. Jr. "Replication and Deception in Calligraphy of the Six Dynasties Period." Draft.

Hayashi Minao 林巳奈夫. "Chūgoku sen Shin jidai no hata 中國先秦時代の旗." *Shirin* 史林 49.2 (1966): 66–94.

———. Concerning the Inscription 'May Sons and Grandsons Eternally Use This [Vessel].'" *Artibus Asiae* 53.1–2 (1993): 51–58.

———. *Kandai no bunbutsu* 漢代の文物. New ed. Kyoto: Hōyū shoten, 1996.

He Linyi 何琳儀. "E Jun Qi jie zhoujie shidi sanze 鄂君啟節舟節釋地三則." *Guwenzi yanjiu* 古文字研究 22 (2000): 141–145.

———. *Zhanguo guwen zidian: Zhanguo wenzi shengxi* 戰國古文字典: 戰國文字聲系. Beijing: Zhonghua shuju, 1998.

Hei Guang 黑光. "Xi'an shijiao faxian Qin guo Du hufu 西安市郊發現秦國杜虎符." *Wenwu* 文物 1979.9: 93–94.

Heng, Chye Kiang. *Cities of Aristocrats and Bureaucrats: The Development of Medieval Chinese Cityscapes*. Honolulu: University of Hawai'i Press, 1999.

Henricks, Robert. *Lao-Tzu Te-Tao Ching*. New York: Ballantine Books, 1989.

Hightower, James Robert. *Han Shih Wai Chuan: Han Ying's Illustrations of the Didactic Application of the Classic of Songs*. Cambridge: Harvard University Press, 1952.

———. "The *Han shih wai chuan* and the *San chia shih*." *Harvard Journal of Asiatic Studies* 11 (1948): 241–310.

Holzman, Donald. *Poetry and Politics of Juan Chi, A.D. 210–263*. Cambridge: Cambridge University Press, 1976.

Hou Hanshu 後漢書. By Fan Ye 范曄. Beijing: Zhonghua shuju, 1973.

Hou Jinglang 侯景郎. "Xinqi hufu de zaixian 新郪虎符的再現." *Gugong jikan* 故宮季刊 10.1 (1975): 35–77.

Hsia Nai. "The Classification, Nomenclature, and Usage of Shang Dynasty Jades." In *Studies of Shang Archaeology: Selected Papers from the International Conference on Shang Civilization*, edited by K. C. Chang, pp. 207–236. New Haven: Yale University Press, 1986.

Hu Lingui 呼林貴 et al. "Xi'an dongjiao Guomian Wuchang Han mu fajue jianbao

西安東郊國棉五廠漢墓發掘簡報." *Wenbo* 文博 1991.4: 3–18.

Hu Pingsheng 胡平生. "Fuyang Hanjian *Shijing* jiance xingzhi ji shuxie geshi zhi lice 阜陽漢簡詩經簡冊形制及書寫格式之蠡測." In *Fuyang Hanjian Shijing yanjiu* 阜陽漢簡詩經研究, edited by Hu Pingsheng 胡平生 and Han Ziqiang 韓自強, pp. 90–97. Shanghai: Shanghai guji chubanshe, 1988.

———. "Fuyang Hanjian 'Zhou yi' gai shu 阜陽漢簡周易概述." *Jianbo yanjiu* 簡帛研究 3 (1998): 255–266.

Hu Pingsheng 胡平生 and Han Ziqiang 韓自強, eds. *Fuyang Han jian Shijing yanjiu* 阜陽漢簡詩經研究. Shanghai: Shanghai guji chubanshe, 1988.

Huainan honglie jijie 淮南鴻烈集解. By Liu Wendian 劉文典. Beijing: Zhonghua shuju, 1989.

Huainanzi 淮南子. Annotated by Gao You 高誘. *XBZZJC* ed.

Huainanzi jiaoshi 淮南子校釋. Annotated by Zhang Shuangti 張雙棣. Beijing: Beijing daxue chubanshe, 1997.

Huang Hui 黃暉. *Lunheng jiaoshi (fu Liu Pansui jijie)* 論衡校釋 (附劉盼遂集解). *XBZZJC* ed.

Huang Shengzhang 黃盛璋. "E Jun Qi jie dili wenti ruogan buzheng 鄂君啟節地理問題若干補正." In *Lishi dili lunji*, pp. 286–288. Beijing: Renmin chubanshe, 1982.

———. "Guanyu E Jun Qi jie jiaotong luxian de fuyuan wenti 關於鄂君啟節交通路線的復原問題." *Zhonghua wenshi luncong* 中華文史論叢 5 (1964): 143–168.

———. "Zailun E Jun Qi jie jiaotong luxian fuyuan yu dili wenti 再論鄂君啟節交通路線復原與地理問題." *Anhui shixue* 安徽史學 1988.2: 16–31.

Huangshi shi bowuguan 黃石市博物館. *Tonglüshan gu kuangye yizhi* 銅綠山古礦業遺址. Beijing: Wenwu chubanshe, 1999.

Huang shi yishu kao 黃氏遺書考. By Huang Shi 黃奭. *Hanxuetang congshu* 漢學堂叢書. Jiangdu, 1934.

Huang Zhanyue 黃展岳. "Handai zhuhou wang mu lunshu 漢代諸侯王墓論." *Kaogu xuebao* 考古學報 1998.1: 11–34.

Hubei sheng bowuguan 湖北省博物管. *Suixian Zenghou Yi mu* 隨縣曾侯乙墓. Beijing: Wenwu chubanshe, 1980.

———. *Zeng Hou Yi mu* 曾侯乙墓. Beijing: Wenwu chubanshe, 1989.

Hubei sheng bowuguan 湖北省博物管, and Hubei sheng wenwu kaogu yanjiusuo 湖北省文物考古研究所. *Zhanguo dixia yuegong: Hubei Suixian Zeng Hou Yi mu* 戰國地下樂宮：湖北隨曾侯乙墓. Beijing: Wenwu chubanshe, 1994.

Hubei sheng Jingsha tielu kaogu dui 湖北省荊沙鐵路考古隊, ed. *Baoshan Chu jian* 包山楚簡. Beijing: Wenwu chubanshe, 1991.

Hubei sheng Jingzhou diqu bowuguan 湖北省荊州地區博物管. *Jiangling Mashan yihao Chu mu* 江陵馬山一號楚墓. Beijing: Wenwu chubanshe, 1985.

Hulsewé, A. F. P. "Fragments of Han Law." *T'oung Pao* 76 (1990): 208–233.

Ikeda Tomohisa 池田知久. *Maōtai Kanbo hakusho gogyōhen kenkyū* 馬王堆漢墓帛書五行篇研究. Tokyo: Kyūko Shoin, 1993.

Jiang Han 江瀚. *Shijing si jia yiwen kao bu* 詩經四家異文考補. *Chenfengge congshu* 晨風閣叢書. Beijing, 1909.

Jiang Yingju 蔣英炬. "Guanyu Han huaxiang shi chansheng beijing yu yishu gongneng de xikao 關於漢畫像石產生背景與藝術功能的細考." *Kaogu* 考古 1998.11: 90–96.

Jingmen shi bowuguan 荊門市博物館. *Guodian Chu mu zhujian* 郭店楚墓竹簡. Beijing: Wenwu chubanshe, 1998.

Jining diqu wenwuzu 濟寧地區文物組 and Jiaxiang xian wenguansuo 嘉祥縣文管所. "Shandong Jiaxiang Songshan 1980 nian chutu de Han huaxiang shi 山東嘉祥宋山1980年出土的漢畫像石." *Wenwu* 文物 1982.5: 60–70.

Jiu Tangshu 舊唐書. Beijing: Zhonghua shuju, 1975.

Jullien, François. *Detour and Access: Strategies of Meaning in China and Greece.* Translated by Sophie Hawkes. New York: Zone Books, 2000.

Juyan Hanjian jiayi bian 居延漢簡: 甲乙編. Beijing: Kaogusuo/Wenwu chubanshe, 1980–1997.

Kalinowski, Marc. "La rhétorique oraculaire dans les chroniques anciennes de la Chine: Une étude des discours prédictifs dans le *Zuozhuan*." *Extrême-Orient, Extrême-Occident* (Divination et rationalité en Chine ancienne) 21 (1999): 37–65.

———. "Les traités de Shuihuidi et l'hémérologie chinoise à la fin des Royaumes-Combattants." *T'oung Pao* 72 (1986): 175–228.

Kamatani Takeshi 釜谷武志. "Fu ni nankai na ji ga ōi no wa naze ka: Zen-Kan ni okeru fu no yomarekata 賦に難解な字が多いのはなぜか: 前漢における賦の讀まれかた." *Nihon Chūgoku gakkai hō* 日本中國學會報 48 (1996): 16–30.

Kamiya Noriko 神矢法子. "Gokan jidai ni okeru 'karei' o megutte iwaguru 'gokanmatsu fuzoku' saikô no kokoromi toshite 後漢時代における「過禮」をめぐって一所謂「後漢末風俗」再考の試みとして." *Kyūshu daigaku Tōyōshi ronshū* 九州大學東洋史論集 7 (1979): 27–40.

Kane, Virginia C. "The Independent Bronze Industries in the South of China Contemporary with the Shang and Western Chou Dynasties." *Archives of Asian Art* 28 (1974–1975): 77–107.

Karlbeck, Orvar. "Selected Objects from Ancient Shou-chou." *Bulletin of the Museum of Far Eastern Antiquities* 27 (1955): 41–130.

———. *Treasure Seeker in China.* Translated by Naomi Walford. London: Cresset, 1957.

Karlgren, Bernhard. *The Book of Odes.* Stockholm: Museum of Far Eastern Antiquities, 1950.

———. "Glosses on the Kuo Feng Odes." *Bulletin of the Museum of Far Eastern Antiquities* 14 (1942): 71–247.

———. "Glosses on the Siao ya Odes." *Bulletin of the Museum of Far Eastern Antiquities* 16 (1944): 25–169.

————. *Grammata Serica Recensa.* Taipei: Southern Materials Center, 1996.

————. *Loan Characters in Pre-Han Texts.* Göteborg: Elanders Boktryckeri Aktiebolag, 1968.

Kawasaki Takaharu 河崎孝治. "*Ryoshi shunjū* 'Setsusōhen' to 'Anshi hen' to ni tsuite 呂氏春秋節喪篇と安死篇とについて." *Nihon Chūgoku gakkai hō* 日本中國學會 31 (1979): 31–42.

Keegan, D. "The *Huang-ti Nei-ching*: The Structure of the Compilations; the Significance of the Structure." Ph.D. diss., University of California at Berkeley, 1988.

Keightley, David N. *The Ancestral Landscape: Time, Space, and Community in Late Shang China (ca. 1200–1045 B.C.).* Berkeley: Institute of East Asian Studies, University of California, 2000.

————. "Late Shang Divination: The Magico-religious Legacy." In *Explorations in Early Chinese Cosmology*, edited by Henry Rosemont Jr., pp. 11–34. Chico: Scholars Press, 1984.

————. *Sources of Shang History: The Oracle-Bone Inscriptions of Bronze Age China.* Berkeley and Los Angeles: University of California Press, 1985.

Kennedy, George A. "Data zur Deutung des Wesens des Tschun Tsiu." *Sinica-Sonderausgabe* 9–10 (1934): 23–34.

————. "Interpretation of the *Ch'un-Ch'iu.*" *Journal of the American Oriental Society* 62 (1942): 40–48.

————. "A Note on Ode 220." In *Studia Serica Bernhard Karlgren Dedicata: Sinological Studies Dedicated to Bernhard Karlgren on His Seventieth Birthday*, edited by Søren Egerod and Else Glahn, pp. 190–198. Copenhagen: E. Munksgaard, 1959.

Kern, Martin. "The 'Biography of Sima Xiangru' and the Question of the *Fu* in Sima Qian's *Shiji.*" *Journal of the American Oriental Society* 123.2 (2003): 303–316.

————. "Early Chinese Poetics in the Light of Recently Excavated Manuscripts." In *Recarving the Dragon: Understanding Chinese Poetics*, edited by Olga Lomová, pp. 27–72. Prague: Charles University—Karolinum Press, 2003.

————. "Feature: Mark Edward Lewis, *Writing and Authority in Early China.*" *China Review International* 7.2 (2000): 336–376.

————. *Die Hymnen der chinesischen Staatsopfer: Literatur und Ritual in der politischen Repräsentation von der Han-Zeit bis zu den Sechs Dynastien.* Stuttgart: Franz Steiner Verlag, 1997.

————. "Methodological Reflections on the Analysis of Textual Variants and the Modes of Manuscript Production in Early China." *Journal of East Asian Archaeology* 4.1–4 (2002): 143–181.

————. "Offices of Writing and Reading in the *Zhouli.*" Paper presented at the Workshop "*Zhouli* and the Codification of Rites in Early China," University of California at Los Angeles, November 8, 2003.

————. "The Performance of Writing in Western Zhou China." In *The Poetics of*

Grammar and the Metaphysics of Sound and Sign, edited by Sergio La Porta. Forthcoming.

———. "The Poetry of Han Historiography." In *Early Medieval China* 10–11.1 (2004): 23–65.

———. "Religious Anxiety and Political Interest in Western Han Omen Interpretation: The Case of the Han Wudi 漢武帝 Period (141–87 B.C.)." *Chūgoku Shigaku* 中國史學 10 (2000): 1–31.

———. "Ritual, Text, and the Formation of the Canon: Historical Transitions of *wen* in Early China." *T'oung Pao* 87.1–3 (2001): 43–91.

———. "*Shi jing* Songs as Performance Texts: A Case Study of 'Chu ci' ('Thorny Caltrop')." *Early China* 25 (2000): 49–111.

———. *The Stele Inscriptions of Ch'in Shih-huang: Text and Ritual in Early Chinese Imperial Representation*. New Haven: American Oriental Society, 2000.

———. "Western Han Aesthetics and the Genesis of the *Fu*." *Harvard Journal of Asiatic Studies* 63.3 (2003): 383–437.

Kertzer, David I. *Ritual, Politics, and Power*. New Haven: Yale University Press, 1988.

Kinseki takuhon kenkyūkai 金石拓本研究會. *Kan hi shūsei* 漢碑集成. Kyoto: Dōbōseki, 1994.

Knechtges, David R. "Questions about the Language of *Sheng Min*." In *Ways with Words: Writing about Reading Texts from Early China*, edited by Pauline Yu, Peter Bol, Stephen Owen, and Willard Peterson, pp. 14–24. Berkeley and Los Angeles: University of California Press, 2000.

———. *Wen xuan, or Selections of Refined Literature*, Vol. 2. Princeton: Princeton University Press, 1987.

———. "Wit, Humor, and Satire in Early Chinese Literature (to A.D. 220)." *Monumenta Serica* 29 (1970–1971): 79–98.

Knechtges, David R., and Swanson, Jerry. "Seven Stimuli for the Prince: the *Ch'i-fa* of Mei Ch'eng." *Monumenta Serica* 27 (1970–1971): 99–116.

Kongzi jiayu shuzheng 孔子家語疏證. Annotated by Chen Shike 陳士珂. *Congshu jicheng* 叢書集成 ed. Shanghai: Shangwu yinshuguan, 1939.

Lao Kan. "The Early Use of the Tally in China." In *Ancient China: Studies in Early Civilization*, edited by David T. Roy and Tsuen-hsuin Tsien, pp. 91–98. Hong Kong: Chinese University of Hong Kong Press, 1978.

Laozi jiaoshi 老子校釋. Beijing: Zhonghua shuju, 1984.

Lau, Ulrich. "Vom Schaf zur Gerechtigkeit—Der sakrale Hintergrund einiger frühchinesischer Rechtstermini." In *Tradition und Moderne—Religion, Philosophie und Literatur in China*, edited by Christiane Hammer and Bernhard Führer, pp. 37–47. Dortmund: Projekt Verlag, 1997.

Ledderose, Lothar. *Ten Thousand Things: Module and Mass Production in Chinese Art*. Princeton: Princeton University Press, 2000.

Legge, James. *The Chinese Classics*. London: Clarendon Press, 1895.

———. *The Li Ki*. In *The Sacred Books of the East*, edited by Max Müller, vols.

27–28. Oxford: Clarendon Press, 1885, multiple reprints.

Leslie, Donald, Colin Mackerras, and Wang Gungwu, eds. 史 *Essays on the Sources for Chinese History*. Canberra: Australian National University Press, 1973.

Lévi-Strauss, Claude. *La pensée sauvage*. Paris: Plon, 1962.

Lewis, Mark Edward. "The Ritual Origins of the Warring States." *Bulletin de l'École française d'Extrême-Orient* 84 (1997): 73–98.

———. "Warring States: Political History." In *The Cambridge History of Ancient China: From the Origins of Civilization to 221 B.C.*, edited by Michael Loewe and Edward L. Shaughnessy, pp. 587–650. Cambridge: Cambridge University Press, 1999.

———. *Writing and Authority in Early China*. Albany: SUNY Press, 1999.

Li Bingjian 李秉鑑. "Xingshi qite di jian 形式奇特的諫." *Huaxia wenhua* 華夏文化 1996.4: 20–21.

Li Fusun 李富孫. *Shijing yiwen shi* 詩經異文釋. Reprinted in *Huang Qing jingjie xubian* 皇清經解續編. Edited by Wang Xianqian. Shanghai: Shanghai shudian, 1988.

Li Jiahao 李家浩. "Chuanlin longjie mingwen kaoshi: Zhanguo fujie mingwen yanjiu zhi san 傳賃龍節銘文考釋：戰國符節銘文研究之三." *Kaogu xuebao* 考古學報 1998.1: 1–10.

———. "E Jun Qi jie mingwen zhong de Gaoqiu 鄂君啟節銘文中的高丘." *Guwenzi yanjiu* 古文字研究 22 (2000): 138–140.

Li Junming 李鈞銘. "Hanjian suojian churufu, chuan yu churu mingji 漢簡所見出入符、傳與出入銘記." *Wenshi* 文史 19 (1983): 27–35.

Li Ling 李零. "Chu guo tongqi mingwen biannian huishi 楚國銅器銘文編年彙釋." *Guwenzi yanjiu* 古文字研究 13 (1983): 353–397.

———. "Du 'Chu xi jianbo wenzi bian' 讀《楚系簡帛文字編》." *Chutu wenxian yanjiu* 出土文獻研究 5 (1999): 139–62.

———. "Du Guodian Chu jian 'Taiyi shengshui' 讀郭店楚簡‘太一生水’." *Daojia wenhua yanjiu* 道家文化研究 17 (1999): 316–331.

———. "Guwenzi zashi (liangpian) 古文字雜釋（兩篇）" In *Yu Xingwu jiaoshou bainian danchen jinianwenji* 于省吾教授百年誕晨紀念文集, pp. 270–274. Changchun: Jilin daxue chubanshe, 1996.

———. "Qin Yin daobing yuban de yanjiu 秦駰禱病玉版的研究." *Guoxue yanjiu* 國學研究 6 (1999): 526–548.

———. "Shuo Huang Lao 説黃老." *Daojia wenhua yanjiu* 道家文化研究 5 (1994): 142–156.

———. *Zhongguo fangshu kao* 中國方術考. Beijing: Renmin chubanshe, 1993.

Li Mingjian 黎明劍. "Handai haozu daxing de yanjiu huigu 漢代豪族大姓的研究回顧." In *Jiegang erbian* 結綱二編, edited by Zhou Liangkai 周梁楷, pp. 92–133. Taipei: Dongda tushu gongsi, 2003.

Li shi 隸釋. By Hong Gua 洪适. In *Shike shiliao xinbian* 石刻史料新編, ser. 1, vol. 9. Taipei: Xinwenfeng chubanshe, 1982.

Li Xueqin 李學勤. *Eastern Zhou and Qin Civilizations*. Translated by K. C.

Chang. New Haven and London: Yale University Press, 1985.

———, ed. *Qingtongqi* 青銅器. Zhongguo meishu quanji: Gongyi meishu bian 中國美術全集工藝美術編, vols. 4–5. Beijing: Wenwu chubanshe, 1986.

Li Yunfu 李運富. *Chuguo jianbo wenzi gouxing xitong yanjiu* 楚國簡帛文子構形系統研究. Shandong: Qi Lu shushe, 1997.

Li Zehou 李澤厚. *The Path of Beauty: A Study of Chinese Aesthetics*. Translated by Gong Lizeng. Hong Kong: Oxford University Press, 1994.

Liji jijie 禮記集解. Annotated by Sun Xidan 孫希旦. Beijing: Zhonghua shuju, 1989.

Liji zhengyi 禮記正義. *SSJZS* ed.

Lian Shaoming 連劭名. "Yunmeng Qin jian 'Jie' pian kaoshu. 雲夢秦簡《詰》篇考述." *Kaogu xuebao* 考古學報 2002.1: 23–38.

Lienüzhuan buzhu 列女傳補注. Annotated by Wang Zhaoyuan 王照圓. Taipei: Taiwan Shangwu, 1976.

Liezi jishi 列子集釋. Annotated by Yang Bojun 楊伯峻. Beijing: Zhonghua shuju, 1979.

Lin Yaolin 林耀潾. *Xi Han sanjia shixue yanjiu* 西漢三家詩學研究. Taipei: Wenjin, 1996.

Lingnan Xi Han wenwu baoku: Guangzhou Nanyuewang mu 嶺南西漢文物寶庫：廣州南越王墓. Beijing: Wenwu chubanshe, 1994.

Liu Binhui 劉彬徽. *Chu xi qingtongqi yanjiu* 楚系青銅器研究. Wuhan: Hubei jiaoyu chubanshe, 1995.

Liu, Cary. "Seeing Double: Copies and Copying in the Arts of China." *Orientations* 32.3 (2001): 154.

Liu Hehui 劉和惠. "Chu E Jun Qi jie xintan 楚鄂君啟節新探." *Kaogu yu wenwu* 考古与文物 1982.5: 60–65.

———. "Chu E Jun Qi jinjie 楚鄂君啟金節." *Anhui wenbo* 安徽文博 2 (1981): 15–17.

———. *Chu wenhua de dongjian* 楚文化的東漸. Wuhan: Hubei jiaoyu chubanshe, 1995.

———. "Guanyu Shou Xian Chu wangmu de jige wenti 關於壽縣楚王墓的幾個問題." *Wenwu yanjiu* 文物研究 5 (1989): 129–134, 177.

Liu Huo 流火. "Tong longjie 銅龍節." *Wenwu* 文物 1960.8–9: 81.

Liu Qing 劉慶. "Qin Han kaoguxue wushi nian 秦漢考古學五十年." *Kaogu* 考古 1999.9: 803–814.

Liu Shizhong 劉詩中, Cao Keping 曹柯平, and Tang Shulong 唐舒龍. "Changjiang zhongyou diqu de gutongkuang 長江中游地區的古銅礦." *Kaogu yu wenwu* 考古与文物 1994.1: 82–88.

Liu Xiang 劉翔, Chen Kang 陳抗, Chen Chusheng 陳初生, and Dong Kun 董琨. *Shang Zhou guwenzi duben* 商周古文字讀本. 2nd ed. Beijing: Yuwen chubanshe, 1996.

Liu Xinfang 劉信芳. *Jianbo Wu xing jiegu* 簡帛五行解詁. Taipei: Yiwen chubanshe, 2000.

———. "Shi 'Jiaoying' 釋荍郢." *Jiang Han kaogu* 江漢考古 1987.1: 78–83.

Loewe, Michael. *Crisis and Conflict in Han China*. London: George Allen and Unwin, 1974.

———. "The Imperial Tombs of the Former Han Dynasty and Their Shrines." In *Divination, Mythology, and Monarchy in Han China*, compiled by Michael Loewe, pp. 267–299. Cambridge: Cambridge University Press, 1994,

———. "The Imperial Way of Death in Han China." In *State and Court Ritual in China*, edited by Joseph P. McDermott, pp. 81–111. Cambridge: Cambridge University Press, 1999.

———. "The *Juedi* Games: A Re-enactment of the Battle between Chiyou and Xianyuan?" In *Thought and Law in Qin and Han China: Studies Presented to Anthony Hulsewé on the Occasion of His Eightieth Birthday*, edited by W. L. Idema and E. Zürcher, pp. 140–157. Leiden: E. J. Brill, 1990.

———. *The Men Who Governed Han China:* Companion to *A Biographical Dictionary of the Qin, Former Han and Xin Periods*. Leiden: E. J. Brill, 2004.

———. *Records of Han Administration*. Cambridge: Cambridge University Press, 1967.

———. "The Wooden and Bamboo Strips Found at Mo-chü-tzu (Kansu)." *Journal of the Royal Asiatic Society* 1965.1–2, 13–26.

———. "State Funerals of the Han Empire." *Bulletin of the Museum of Far Eastern Antiquities* 71 (1999): 5–72.

Loewe, Michael, and Shaughnessy, Edward L., eds. *The Cambridge History of Ancient China: From the Origins of Civilization to 221 B.C.* Cambridge: Cambridge University Press, 1999.

Lu Qinli 逯欽立. *Xian Qin Han Wei Jin nanbeichao shi* 先秦漢魏南北朝詩. Beijing: Zhonghua shuju, 1983.

Lu Shiheng wenji 陸士衡文集. By Lu Ji 陸機. *SBCK* ed.

Lunheng jiaoshi 論衡校釋. Annotated by Huang Hui 黃暉. Beijing: Zhonghua shuju, 1995.

Lunyu jishi 論語集釋. Annotated by Cheng Shude 程樹德. Beijing: Zhonghua shuju, 1990.

Lunyu zhushu 論語注疏. *SSJZS* ed.

Luo Changming 羅長銘. "E Jun Qi xintan 鄂君啟新探." In *Luo Changming ji* 羅長銘集. Hefei: Huangshan shushe, 1994.

Luo Fuyi 羅福頤. *Sandai jijin wencun shiwen* 三代吉金文存釋文. Hong Kong: Wenxueshe, 1983.

Luo Zhenyu 羅振玉. *Sandai jijin wencun* 三代吉金文存. Shanghai: privately published, 1937.

Lushi 路史. By Luo Bi 羅泌. *SBBY* ed.

Lü Simian 呂思勉. *Lü Simian du shi zha ji* 呂思勉讀史札記. Shanghai: Shanghai guji chubanshe, 1982.

Lüshi chunqiu 呂氏春秋. Annotated by Gao Yu 高誘. *XBZZJC* ed.

Lüshi chunqiu jiaoshi 呂氏春秋校釋. Annotated by Chen Qiyou 陳奇猷.

Shanghai: Xuelin chubanshe, 1984.

Ma Chengyuan 馬承源. *Ancient Chinese Bronzes*. Edited by Hsio-yen Shih. Hong Kong: Oxford University Press, 1986.

———, ed. *Shanghai bowuguan cang Zhanguo Chu zhushu (yi)* 上海博物管藏戰國楚竹書（一）. Shanghai: Shanghai guji chubanshe, 2001.

Ma Guohan 馬國翰. *Yuhan shanfang jiyishu* 玉函山房輯佚書. Tokyo: Chūbun shuppansha 中文出版社, 1979.

Major, John S. *Heaven and Earth in Early Han Thought: Chapters Three, Four, and Five of the Huainanzi*. Albany: SUNY Press, 1993.

Makeham, John. *Balanced Discourses*. New Haven: Yale University Press, 2004.

———. Review of *The Original Analects: Sayings of Confucius and His Successors*, by E. Bruce Brooks and A. Taeko Brooks. *China Review International* 6.1 (1999): 1–15.

Malmqvist, Göran. "Studies on the Gongyang and Guuliang Commentaries II." *Bulletin of the Museum of Far Eastern Antiquities* 47 (1975): 19–69.

Mao Han-kuang. "The Evolution in the Nature of the Medieval Genteel Family." In *State and Society in Early Medieval China*, edited by Albert E. Dien, pp. 73–109. Stanford: Stanford University Press, 1990.

Mao shi zhengyi 毛詩正義. *SSJZS* ed.

Mawangdui Hanmu boshu zhengli xiaozu 馬王堆帛書整理小組. *Mawangdui Hanmu boshu* 馬王堆漢墓帛書. Beijing: Wenwu chubanshe, 1985.

Mengzi zhengyi 孟子正義. Annotated by Jiao Xu 焦循. Beijing: Zhonghua shuju, 1996.

Morris, Ian. *Archaeology as Cultural History: Words and Things in Iron Age Greece*. Malden: Blackwall, 2000.

Mote, F. W. *Imperial China: 900–1800*. Cambridge: Harvard University Press, 1999.

Mozi jiangu 墨子閒詁. Annotated by Sun Yirang 孫詒讓. *XBZZJC* ed.

Mozi jiaozhu 墨子校注. Annotated by Wu Yujiang 吳毓江. Beijing: Zhonghua shuju, 1993.

Nagy, Gregory. *Poetry as Performance: Homer and Beyond*. Cambridge: Cambridge University Press, 1996.

Naitō Shigenobu 內藤茂信. "Gaku Kun Kei setsu 鄂君啟節." In *Shodō zenshū* 書道全集, vol. 26, pp. 151–153. Tokyo: Heibonsha, 1967.

Needham, Joseph. *Science and Civilisation in China*. Vol. 2, *History of Scientific Thought*. New York: Cambridge University Press, 1956.

Ni Run'an 倪潤安. "Lun Liang Han siling de yuanliu 論兩漢四靈的源流." *Zhongyuan wenwu* 中原文物 1999.10: 83–91.

Noma Fumichika 野間文史. "Shunjū sanden nyūmon kōza: dai-isshō: Shunjū kyōmon no seikaku 春秋三傳入門講座: 第一章: 春秋經文の性格." *Tōyō kotengaku kenkyū* 東洋古典學研究 1 (1996): 80–97.

———. "Shunjū sanden nyūmon kōza: dai-sanshō: Kuyō den no seiritsu to sono dembun kōzō 春秋三傳入門講座: 第三章: 公羊傳の成立とその傳文構造." *Tōyō kotengaku kenkyū* 東洋古典學研究 2 (1996): 88–111.

Nylan, Michael. "Calligraphy: The Sacred Test and Text of Culture." In *Calligraphy and Context*, edited by Cary Liu, Dora C. Ching, and Judith Smith, pp. 1–42. Princeton: The Art Museum, 1999.

———. *The Five "Confucian" Classics.* New Haven: Yale University Press, 2001.

———. "On the Politics of Pleasure." *Asia Major* 14 (2001): 73–124.

———. "A Problematic Model: The Han 'Orthodox Synthesis,' Then and Now." In *Imagining Boundaries: Changing Confucian Doctrines, Texts, and Hermeneutics*, edited by Kai-wing Chow, On-cho Ng, and John B. Henderson, pp. 17–56. Albany: SUNY Press, 1999.

———. "Sima Qian: A True Historian." *Early China* 24 (1998): 1–44.

———. "Textual Authority in Pre-Han and Han." *Early China* 25 (2000): 205–258.

Nylan, Michael, and Nathan Sivin. "The First Neo-Confucianism: An Introduction to Yang Hsiung's 'Canon of Supreme Mystery' (*Tai hsuan ching*, c. 4 B.C.)." In *Chinese Ideas about Nature and Society: Studies in Honour of Derk Bodde*, edited by Charles le Blanc and Susan Blader, pp. 41–99. Hong Kong: Hong Kong University Press, 1987.

O Man-jong 吳萬鐘. *Cong shi dao jing: Lun Mao Shi jieshi di yuanyuan ji qi tese* 從詩到經：論毛詩解釋的淵源及其特色. Beijing: Zhonghua shuju, 2001.

Ōba Osamu 大廳脩. "Kan no dōkofu to chikushifu 漢の銅虎符と竹使符." In *Kamata hakushi kanreki kinen rekishigaku ronsō* 鎌田博士還曆紀念歷史學論叢, pp. 43–54. Tokyo: Kamata sensei kanreki kinenkai, 1969.

———. "Kan no setsu ni tsuite: Shōgun kasetsu no zentei 漢の節について：將軍假説の前提." *Kansai Daigaku Tōzai gakujutsu kenkyūjo kiyō* 関西大學東西學術研究所紀要 2 (1969): 23–58.

———. "Kandai no kanjo to pasupōto 漢代の関序とパスポート." *Kansai Daigaku Tōzai gakujutsu kenkyūjo ronsō* 関西大學東西學術研究所論叢 16 (1954): 1–30.

Ong, Walter J. *Orality and Literacy: The Technologizing of the Word.* London: Routledge, 1982.

Owen, Stephen. *Readings in Chinese Literary Thought.* Cambridge: Council on East Asian Studies, Harvard University Press, 1992.

Pang Pu 龐樸. *Zhu bo "Wu xing" pian jiaozhu ji yanjiu* 竹帛《五行》篇校注及研究. Taipei: Wanjuan lou, 2000.

Pattison, R. *On Literacy: The Politics of the Word from Homer to the Age of Rock.* Oxford: Oxford University Press, 1982.

Peng, Ke. "Coinage and Commercial Development in Classical China, 550–221 B.C." Ph.D. diss., University of Chicago, 1999.

Peng Shifan 彭適凡 and Liu Shizhong 劉詩中. "Guanyu Ruichang Shang Zhou tongkuang yicun yu gu Yangyue ren 關於瑞昌商周銅礦遺存與古楊越人." *Jiangxi wenwu* 江西文物 1990.3: 25–31, 41.

Pian Yuqian 駢宇騫 and Duan Shu'an 段書安. *Ben shiji yilai chutu jianbo gaishu* 本世紀以來出土簡帛概述. Taipei: Wanjuan lou, 1999.

Pines, Yuri. "Disputers of the *Li* 禮: Breakthroughs in the Concept of Ritual in Preimperial China." *Asia Major*, 3d ser., 13.1 (2000): 1–41.

———. *Foundations of Confucian Thought: Intellectual Life in the Chunqiu Period, 722–453 B.C.E.* Honolulu: University of Hawai'i Press, 2002.

———. "Intellectual Change in the Chunqiu Period: The Reliability of the Speeches in the *Zuo zhuan* as Sources of Chunqiu Intellectual History." *Early China* 22 (1997): 77–132.

Pokora, Timoteus. "Ironical Critics at Ancient Chinese Courts (*Shih chi*, 126)." *Oriens Extremus* 20.1 (1973): 49–64.

Poo, Mu-chou. *In Search of Personal Welfare: A View of Ancient Chinese Religion.* Albany: SUNY Press, 1998.

Qianfulun jian jiaozheng 潛夫論箋校正. Annotated by Wang Jipei 汪繼培. Beijing: Zhonghua shuju, 1985.

Qin Han bei shu 秦漢碑述. Compiled by Yuan Weichun 袁維春. Beijing: Beijing gongyi meishu chubanshe, 1990.

Qin Huitian 秦蕙田. *Wuli tongkao* 五禮通考. 1880. Reprint, Taipei: Xinxing, 1970.

Qiu Xigui 裘錫圭. *Chinese Writing.* Translated by Gilbert Mattos and Jerry Norman. Berkeley: Society for the Study of Early China and Institute for Asian Studies, University of California, 2000.

———. "Zhanguo wenzi zhong de 'shi' 戰國文字中的市." *Kaogu xuebao* 考古學報 1980.1: 285–296.

Rao Zongyi 饒宗頤 and Zeng Xiantong 曾憲通. *Chu boshu* 楚帛書. Hong Kong: Zhonghua shuju, 1985.

Raphals, Lisa. *Sharing the Light: Representations of Women and Virtue in Early China.* Albany: SUNY Press, 1998.

Rawson, Jessica. "Western Zhou Archaeology." In *The Cambridge History of Ancient China: From the Origins of Civilization to 221 B.C.*, edited by Michael Loewe and Edward L. Shaughnessy, pp. 352–449. Cambridge: Cambridge University Press, 1999.

Rickett, W. Allyn. "An Early Chinese Calendar Chart: *Kuan-tzu* III,8 (*Yu kuan* 幼官)." *T'oung Pao* 48 (1960): 195–251.

———. *Guanzi: Political, Economic, and Philosophical Essays from Early China.* Vol. 1. Princeton: Princeton University Press, 1985.

Riegel, Jeffrey. "Do Not Serve the Dead as You Serve the Living: The *Lüshi chunqiu* Treatises on Moderation in Burial." *Early China* 20 (1995): 301–330.

———. "Eros, Introversion, and the Beginnings of *Shijing* Commentary." *Harvard Journal of Asiatic Studies* 57.1 (1997): 143–177.

———. "Kou-mang and Ju-shou." *Cahiers d'Extrême-Asie* 5 (1989–1990): 55–83.

Rong Geng 容庚. *Han Wu Liang ci huaxiang lu* 漢武梁祠畫像錄. Beijing: Beiping kaogu xueshe, 1936.

Rouzer, Paul. *Articulated Ladies: Gender and the Male Community in Early*

Chinese Texts. Cambridge: Harvard University Asia Center, Harvard University Press, 2001.

Sanguozhi 三國志. By Chen Shou 陳壽. Beijing: Zhonghua shuju, 1959.

Satō Taketoshi 佐藤武敏. "Sen Shin jidai no kan to kanzei 先秦時代の關と關税." *Kōkotsugaku* 甲骨學 10 (1964): 158–173.

Schaberg, David. "Fictions of History in Liu Xiang's *Shuoyuan.*" Paper presented at the annual meeting of the Association for Asian Studies, San Diego, March 9–12, 2000.

———. *A Patterned Past: Form and Thought in Early Chinese Historiography.* Cambridge: Harvard University Press, 2001.

———. "Remonstrance in Eastern Zhou Historiography." *Early China* 22 (1997): 133–179.

———. "Song and the Historical Imagination in Early China." *Harvard Journal of Asiatic Studies* 59.2 (1999): 305–361.

———. "Travel, Geography, and the Imperial Imagination in Fifth-Century Athens and Han China." *Comparative Literature* 51.2 (1999): 152–191.

Schuessler, Axel. *A Dictionary of Early Zhou Chinese.* Honolulu: University of Hawai'i Press, 1987.

Schwartz, Benjamin I. *The World of Thought in Ancient China.* Cambridge: Harvard University Press, 1985.

Shang Chengzuo 商承祚. "E Jun Qi jie kao 鄂君啟節考." *Wenwu jinghua* 文物精華 2 (1963): 49–55.

———. "Tan E Jun Qi jie mingwen zhong jige wenzi he jige diming deng wenti 談鄂君啟節銘文中幾個文字和幾個地名等問題." *Zhonghua wenshi luncong* 中華文史論叢 6 (1965): 143–158.

Shang jun shu zhuizhi 商君書錐指. Compiled by Jiang Lihong 蔣禮鴻. Beijing: Zhonghua shuju, 1986.

Shangshu jinguwen zhushu 尚書今古文注疏. Annotated by Sun Xingyan 孫星衍. Beijing: Zhonghua shuju, 1986.

Shangshu zhengyi 尚書正義. *SSJZS* ed.

Shaughnessy, Edward L. *I Ching: The Classic of Changes.* New York: Ballantine Books, 1996.

———, ed. *New Sources of Early Chinese History: An Introduction to the Reading of Inscriptions and Manuscripts.* Berkeley: Society for the Study of Early China and Institute for Asian Studies, University of California, 1997.

———. *Sources of Western Zhou History: Inscribed Bronze Vessels.* Berkeley and Los Angeles: University of California Press, 1991.

———. "Western Zhou History." In *The Cambridge History of Ancient China: From the Origins of Civilization to 221 B.C.,* edited by Michael Loewe and Edward L. Shaughnessy, pp. 292–351. Cambridge: Cambridge University Press, 1999.

———. "The 'Zi Yi': A Case Study in the Comparison of an Archaeologically Discovered Manuscript with a Received Counterpart, together with

Thoughts on the Processes of Textual Transmission and the Production of Definitive Texts in Early China." Paper presented at the conference "Text and Ritual in Early China," Princeton University, October 20–22, 2000.

Shiji 史記. By Sima Qian 司馬遷. Beijing: Zhonghua shuju, 1959.

Shiming shuzheng 釋名疏證. By Bi Yuan 畢沅. *Congshu jicheng* 叢書集成 ed. Shanghai: Shangwu yinshuguan, 1935–1937.

Shiming shuzheng bu 釋名蔬證補. In *Erya, Guangya, Fangyan, Shiming Qing shu sizhong hekan* 爾雅廣雅方言釋名清疏四種合刊, pp. 1005–1019. Shanghai: Shanghai guji chubanshe, 1989.

Shi Quan 石泉. *Gudai Jing Chu dili xintan* 古代荊楚地理新探. Wuhan: Wuhan daxue chubanshe, 1988.

Shodō zenshū 書道全集. Vol 26. Tokyo: Heibonsha, 1967.

Shuihudi Qin mu zhujian zhengli xiaozu 睡虎地秦墓竹簡整理小組, ed. *Shuihudi Qin mu zhujian* 睡虎地秦墓竹簡. Beijing: Wenwu chubanshe, 1990.

Shuijing zhu beilu 水經注碑錄. Compiled by Shi Zhicun 施蟄存. Tianjin: Tianjin guji chubanshe, 1987.

Shuiyuan 說苑. *SBCK* ed.

Shuiyuan jiaozheng. See *Shuoyuan jiaozheng.*

Shuowen jiezi zhu 說文解字注. Annotated by Duan Yucai 段玉裁. Shanghai: Shanghai guji chubanshe, 1988.

Shuoyuan jiaozheng 說苑校證. Annotated by Xiang Zonglu 向宗魯. Beijing: Zhonghua shuju, 1987.

Sichuan lidai beike 四川歷代碑刻. Compiled by Gao Wen 高文 and Gao Chenggang 高成剛. Chengdu: Sichuan daxue chubanshe, 1990.

Sivin, Nathan. "The Myth of the Naturalists." In *Medicine, Philosophy, and Religion in Ancient China: Researches and Reflections*, compiled by Nathan Sivin, chap. 4. Aldershot, UK: Variorium, 1995.

———. "Text and Experience in Classical Chinese Medicine." In *Knowledge and the Scholarly Medical Traditions*, edited by Don Bates, pp. 177–204. Cambridge: Cambridge University Press, 1995.

Sommer, Matthew H. *Sex, Law, and Society in Late Imperial China.* Stanford: Stanford University Press, 2000.

Songshu 宋書. Beijing: Zhonghua shuju, 1974.

Soper, Alexander Coburn. "All the World's a Stage: A Note." *Artibus Asiae* 30 (1968): 249–259.

Spence, Jonathan. *Mao Zedong.* New York: Penguin/Viking, 1999.

Steinhardt, Nancy. "From Koguryo to Gansu and Xinjiang: Funerary and Worship Space in North Asia, 4th–7th Centuries." In *Between Han and Tang: Cultural and Artistic Interaction in a Transformative Period*, edited by Wu Hung, pp. 153–203. Beijing: Wenwu Press, 2001.

Sterckx, Roel. *The Animal and the Daemon in Early China.* Albany: SUNY Press, 2002.

Stumpfeldt, Hans. *Staatsverfassung und Territorium im antiken China: Über die Ausbildung einer territorialen Staatsverfassung.* Düsseldorf: Bertelsmann

Universitätsverlag, 1970.

Su Zhihong 蘇志宏. *Qin Han li yue jiaohua lun* 秦漢禮樂教化論. Chengdu: Sichuan renmin chubanshe, 1990.

Su Zhipi 宿志丕. "Zhongguo gudai yushi, jianguan zhidu di tedian ji zuoyong 中國古代御史、諫官制度的特點及作用." *Qinghua daxue xuebao (zhexue shehui kexue ban)* 清華大學學報（哲學社會科學版） 9.2 (1994): 34–42.

Sun Ji 孫機. *Han dai wuzhiwenhua ziliao tushuo* 漢代物質文化資料圖説. Beijing: Wenwu chubanshe, 1991.

Sun Jianming 孫簡明. "E Jun Qi jie xutan 鄂君啟節續探." *Anhui sheng kaoguxuehui huikan* 安徽省考古學會會刊 6 (1982): 28–34.

Taiping yulan 太平御覽. Beijing: Xinhua shudian, 1963.

Takashima, Ken-ichi. "The So-called 'Third'-Person Possessive Pronoun *Jue* 氒 (= 厥) in Classical Chinese." *Journal of the American Oriental Society* 119.3 (1999): 404–431.

Takigawa Kametarō 瀧川龜太郎. *Shiki kaichū kōshō* 史記會注考證. Taipei: Yiwen chubanshe, 1976.

Tambiah, Stanley J. *Culture, Thought, and Social Action: An Anthropological Perspective*. Cambridge: Harvard University Press, 1985.

Tan Qixiang 譚其驤. "E Jun Qi jie mingwen shidi 鄂君啟節銘文釋地." *Zhonghua wenshi luncong* 中華文史論叢 2 (1962): 169–190.

———. "Zailun E Jun Qi jie dili: Da Huang Shengzhang tongzhi 再論鄂君啟節地理：答黃盛璋同志." *Zhonghua wenshi luncong* 中華文史論叢 5 (1964): 169–193.

Tan Qixiang et al. *Zhongguo lishi dituji* 中國歷史地圖集. Vol. 1. Beijing: Zhongguo dituxueshe, 1975.

Tang Lan 唐蘭. "Wangming zhuankao" 王命傳考. *Guoxue jikan* 國學季刊 6.4 (1946): 61–73.

Tang Yuhui 湯余惠. *Zhanguo mingwen xuan* 戰國銘文選. Changchun: Jilin daxue chubanshe, 1993.

Tao Zhenggang 陶正剛, Hou Yi 侯毅, and Qu Chuangfu 渠川福. *Taiyuan Jin guo Zhaoqing mu* 太原晉國趙卿墓. Beijing: Wenwu chubanshe, 1996.

Teng Rensheng 勝壬生. *Chu xi jianbo wenzi bian* 楚系簡帛文字編. Wuhan: Hubei jiaoyu chubanshe, 1995.

Thomas, Rosalind. *Literacy and Orality in Ancient Greece*. Cambridge: Cambridge University Press, 1999.

Twitchett, Denis. *The Writing of Official History under the T'ang*. Cambridge: Cambridge University Press, 1992.

Unger, Ulrich. "Das konfuzianische Weltgericht." Inaugural lecture at the Philosophische Fakultät der Westfälischen Wilhelms-Universität, July 8, 1967. Sonderdruck Jahresschrift 1969 der Gesellschaft zur Förderung der Westfälischen Wilhelms-Universität zu Münster, pp. 64–77.

Van Auken, Newell Ann. "Negatives in Warring States Texts." M.A. thesis, University of Washington, 1996.

Van Zoeren, Stephen. *Poetry and Personality: Reading, Exegesis, and Hermeneutics in Traditional China*. Stanford: Stanford University Press, 1991.

Vandermeersch, Léon. "L'institution chinoise de remontrance." *Études Chinoises* 13.1–2 (1994): 31–45.

———. *Wangdao ou la voie royale: Recherches sur l'esprit des institutions de la Chine archaïque*. Vol. 2, *Structures politiques; les rites*. Paris: École française d'Extrême-Orient, 1980.

Vermeule, Emily. *Aspects of Death in Early Greek Art and Poetry*. Berkeley and Los Angeles: University of California Press, 1981.

Vervoorn, Aat. *Men of the Cliffs and Caves: The Development of the Chinese Eremitic Tradition to the End of the Han Dynasty*. Hong Kong: Chinese University Press, 1990.

Wagner, Donald B. "The Dating of the Chu Graves of Changsha: The Earliest Iron Artifacts in China?" *Acta Orientalia* (Copenhagen) 48 (1987): 111–156.

———. *Iron and Steel in Ancient China*. Handbuch der Orientalistik, vol. 4.9. Leiden: E. J. Brill, 1993.

Wagner, Rudolf G. "The Impact of Conceptions of Rhetoric and Style Upon the Formation of the Early *Laozi* Editions: Evidence from Guodian, Mawangdui and the Wang Bi *Laozi*." *Transactions of the International Conference of Orientalists* (*Kokusai tōhō gakusha kaigi kiyō* 國際東方學者會議紀要) 44 (1999): 32–56.

Wang Aihe. *Cosmology and Political Culture in Early China*. Cambridge: Cambridge University Press, 2000.

Wang Guowei 王國維. *Guantang jilin* 觀堂集林. Rev. ed. Beijing: Zhonghua shuju, 1959.

Wang Hui 王輝. "Shi jiu, jiu 釋[illegible]、[illegible]." *Guwenzi yanjiu* 古文字研究 22 (2000): 146–149.

Wang Shumin 王叔岷. *Shiji jiaozheng* 史記斠證. *Zhongyang yanjiuyuan lishi yuyan yanjiusuo zhuankan* 中央研究院歷史語言研究所專刊 78. Taipei: Zhongyang yanjiuyuan lishi yuyan yanjiusuo, 1983.

Wang Sili 王思禮. "Cong Ju Xian Dongwan Han huaxiang shi zhong di qi nü tushi Wushi ci shuilu gongzhan tu 從莒縣東莞漢畫像石中的七女圖釋武氏祠水陸攻戰圖." *Ju Xian wenshi* 莒縣文史 1999.10: 201–218.

Wang Xianqian 王先謙. *Shi san jia yi jishu* 詩三家義集疏. Beijing: Zhonghua shuju, 1987.

Wang Yinzhi 王引之. "Gongyang zaiyi 公羊災異." In *Jingyi shuwen* 經義述聞. *SSBY* ed.

Wardy, Robert. *Aristotle in China*. Cambridge: Needham Research Institute, 2001.

Watson, Burton. *Ssu-Ma Ch'ien, Grand Historian of China*. New York: Columbia University Press, 1958.

Weld, Susan R. "The Covenant Texts from Houma and Wenxian." In *New Sources of Early Chinese History: An Introduction to the Reading of Inscriptions and Manuscripts*, edited by Edward L. Shaughnessy, pp. 125–160. Berkeley: Society for the Study of Early China and Institute for Asian Studies, University of California, 1997.

Wenxin diaolong zhu 文心雕龍註. Annotated by Fan Wenlan 范文瀾. Beijing: Renmin wenxue chubanshe, 1978.

Wen xuan 文選. Annotated by Li Shan 李善. Shanghai: Shanghai guji chubanshe, 1986.

Wen xuan 文選. Taipei: Zhengzhong chubanshe, 1971.

Weng Kaiyun 翁闓運. "Lun Shandong Han bei 論山東漢碑." In *Han bei yanjiu* 漢碑研究, edited by Zhongguo shufajia xiehui Shandong fenhui 中國書法家協會山東分會, pp. 12–23. Jinan: Qi Lu shushe, 1990.

Wilhelm, Richard, trans. *Frühling und Herbst des Lü Bu We*. Rev. ed. Düsseldorf: Diederichs, 1979.

Wu Hung. *Monumentality in Early Chinese Art and Architecture*. Stanford: Stanford University Press, 1995.

Wu Wanzhong. See O Man-jong.

Wu Xinghan 吳興漢. "Shou xian Chu wangmu ji qi youguan wenti 壽縣楚王墓及其有關問題." *Anhui wenbo* 安徽文博 3 (1983): 36–43.

Wu, Yenna. "In Search of Satire in Classical Chinese Poetry and Prose." *Tamkang Review* 28.4 (1998): 3–39.

Wu Yue chunqiu 吳越春秋. Edited by Miao Lu 苗麓. Nanjing: Jiangsu guji chubanshe, 1999.

Xia Nai. "Continuity and Change of the Jade Tradition in Han China." In *Jade and Silk of Han China*, by Xia Nai, translated and edited by Chu-tsing Li, pp. 17–49. Franklin D. Murphy Lectures 3. Lawrence: Helen Foresman Spencer Museum of Art, University of Kansas, 1983.

Xiaojing zhushu 孝經注疏. *SSJZS* ed.

Xie Yuanzhen 謝元震. "E Jun Qi jie mingwen bushi 鄂君啟節銘文補釋." *Zhongguo lishi bowuguan guankan* 中國歷史博物館館刊 15–16 (1991): 152–153.

Xinshu 新書. By Jia Yi 賈誼. *SBBY* ed.

Xinshu 新書. By Jia Yi 賈誼. Edited by Lu Wenchao 盧文弨. *Congshu jicheng* 叢書集成 ed. Shanghai: Shangwu yinshuguan, 1937.

Xinxu shuzheng 新序疏證. Annotated by Zhao Shanyi 趙善詒. Shanghai: Huadong shifan daxue chubanshe, 1989.

Xing Wen 邢文. *Boshu Zhou yi yanjiu* 帛書周易研究. Beijing: Renmin chubanshe, 1997.

———. "Chu jian 'Wu xing' shi lun 楚簡《五行》試論." *Wenwu* 文物 1998.10: 57–61.

Xiong Chuanxin 熊傳新 and He Guangyue 何光岳. "E Jun Qi jie zhoujie zhong Jiang Xiang diming xinkao 鄂君啟節舟節中江湘地名考." *Hunan shiyuan xuebao* 湖南師院學報 1982.3: 85–121.

Xu Fuchang 徐富昌. *Shuihudi Qin jian yanjiu* 睡虎地秦簡研究. Taipei:

Wenshizhi chubanshe, 1993.

Xu Zhongshu 徐中舒. "Jinwen guci shili 金文嘏辭釋例." *Zhongyang yanjiuyuan lishi yuyan yanjiusuo jikan* 中央研究院歷史語言研究所季刊 6.1 (1936): 1–44.

Xue Yingqun 薛應群. "Han dai fuxin kaoshu: Juyan Han jian yanjiu 漢代符信考述：居延漢簡研究." *Xibei shidi* 西北史地 1983.3: 72–82; 1983.4: 69–80.

Xunyang xian bowuguan 旬陽縣博物館. "Shaanxi Xunyang faxian Zhanguo Chu mu 陝西旬陽發現戰國楚墓." *Wenwu* 文物 1987.5: 52–54.

Xunzi jijie 荀子集解. Annotated by Wang Xianqian 王先謙. Beijing: Zhonghua shuju, 1988.

Xunzi xinzhu 荀子新注. Annotated by Beijing daxue *Xunzi* zhushi zu 北京大學荀子注釋組. Beijing: Zhonghua shuju, 1979.

Yamada Katsuyoshi 山田勝芳. "Chūgoku kodai no shō to ko 中國古代の商と賈." *Tōyōshi kenkyū* 東洋史研究 47.1 (1988): 1–29.

Yang Jiuxia 楊鳩霞. "Changfeng Zhanguo wanqi Chu mu 長豐戰國晚期楚墓." *Wenwu yanjiu* 文物研究 4 (1988): 89–98.

Yang Lien-sheng. "Great Families of Eastern Han." In *Chinese Social History: Translations of Selected Studies*, edited by E-Tzu Zen Sun and John de Francis, pp. 103–134. Washington, DC: American Council of Learned Societies, 1956.

Yang Shuda 楊樹達. *Hanshu kuiguan* 漢書窺管. Shanghai: Shanghai guji chubanshe, 1984.

Yang Xiaoneng, ed. *The Golden Age of Chinese Archaeology: Celebrated Discoveries from the People's Republic of China*. Washington, DC: National Gallery of Art, 1999.

Yang Zhenfang 楊震方. *Beitie xulu* 碑帖敍錄. Shanghai: Shanghai guji chubanshe, 1984.

Yao Hanyuan 姚漢源. "E Jun Qi jie shiwen 鄂君啟節釋文." *Guwenzi yanjiu* 古文字研究 10 (1983): 199–203.

Yasui Kōzan 安居香山. *Isho no seiritsu to sono tenkai* 緯書の成立とその展開. Tokyo: Kokusho kankōkai 國書刊行會, 1984.

Yasui Kōzan and Nakamura Shōhachi 中村璋八. *Isho no kiso teki kenkyū* 緯書の基礎的研究. Tokyo: Kokusho kankōkai 國書刊行會, 1986.

———, eds. *Chōshū Isho shūsei* 重修緯書集成. Tokyo: Meitoku shuppansha 明德出版社, 1971–1988.

Yates, Frances A. *The Art of Memory*. Chicago: University of Chicago Press, 1974.

Yates, Robin D. S. *Five Lost Classics: Tao, Huang-Lao, and Yin-Yang in Han China*. New York: Ballantine, 1997.

———. "Some Notes on Ch'in Law: A Review Article." *Early China* 11–12 (1985–1987): 243–275.

Ye Changchi 葉昌熾 and Ke Changsi 柯昌泗. *Yushi yitongping* 語石異同評. Beijing: Zhonghua shuju, 1994.

Yi Junjie 易俊傑. "Zhongguo gudai shanyu fengjian di youling 中國古代善於諷諫的優伶." *Lishi yuekan* 歷史月刊 75.4 (1994): 98–103.

Yili yizhu 儀禮譯注. Annotated by Yang Tianyu 楊天宇. Shanghai: Shanghai guji chubanshe, 1994.

Yili zhushu 儀禮注疏. *SSJZS* ed.

Yiwen leiju 藝文類聚. Annotated by Shao Yingjiao 紹楹校. Shanghai: Shanghai guji chubanshe, 1985.

Yin Difei 殷滌非. "Anhui Shou Xian xin faxian de tongniu 安徽壽縣發現的銅牛." *Wenwu* 文物 1959.4: 1–4.

———. "E Jun Qi jie liangge diming jianshuo 鄂君啟節兩個地名簡説." *Zhonghua wenshi luncong* 中華文史論叢 6 (1965): 82.

Yin Difei and Luo Changming 羅長銘. "Shou Xian chutu de 'E Jun Qi jinjie' 壽縣出土的鄂君啟金節." *Wenwu cankao ziliao* 文物參考資料 1958.4: 8–11.

Yin Zhou jinwen jicheng 殷周金文集成. Beijing: Zhonghua shuju, 1986–1996.

Yu Xingwu 于省吾. "'E Jun Qi jie' kaoshi 鄂君啟節考釋." *Kaogu* 考古 1963.8: 442–447.

Zbikowski, Tadeusz. "On Early Chinese Theatrical Performances." *Rocznik Orientalistyczny* 26.1 (1962): 65–83.

Zeng Xiantong 曾憲通. *Changsha Chu boshu wenzi bian* 長沙楚帛書文字編. Beijing: Zhonghua shuju, 1993.

Zhanguo ce 戰國策. Shanghai: Shanghai guji chubanshe, 1985.

Zhang Geng 張庚 and Guo Hancheng 郭漢城. *Zhongguo xiqu tongshi* 中國戲曲通史. Beijing: Xinhua shudian, 1980–1981.

Zhang Guangzhi 張光直. See Chang Kwang-chih.

Zhang Heng shiwen jijiao zhu 張衡詩文集校注. Annotated by Zhang Zhenze 張震澤. Shanghai: Shanghai guji chubanshe, 1986.

Zhangjiashan ersiqi hao Han mu zhujian zhengli xiaozu 張家山二四七號漢墓竹簡整理小組. *Zhangjiashan Han mu zhujian* 張家山漢墓竹簡. Beijing: Wenwu chubanshe, 2001.

Zhang Jiefu 張捷夫. *Zhongguo sangzangshi* 中國喪葬史. Taipei: Wenjin chubanshe, 1995.

Zhang Lixing 張立行. "Zhanguo zhujian lu zhenrong 戰國竹簡露真容." *Wenhuibao* 文匯報 5 (January 1999): 1.

Zhang Pei 張沛. "Xunyang you faxian liangzuo Zhanguo Chu mu 旬陽又發現兩座戰國楚墓." *Wenbo* 文博 1991.5: 82–83.

Zhang Shenyi 張慎儀. *Shijing yiwen bushi* 詩經異文補釋. *Aiguo congshu* 籛國叢書. Guangxu period (1875–1908).

Zhang Shouzhong 張守中, Zhang Xiaocang 張小滄, and Hao Jianwen 郝建文. *Guodian Chu jian wenzi bian* 郭店楚簡文字編. Beijing: Wenwu chubanshe, 2000.

Zhang Zhengming 張正明. *Chu wenhua zhi* 楚文化志. Wuhan: Hubei Renmin chubanshe, 1988.

Zhang Zhenlin 張振林. "'Dantu' yu 'yidan sizhi' xinquan '柟徒' 與 '一柟飤之' 新詮." *Wenwu* 文物 1963.3: 48–49.

Zhao Chao 趙超. *Zhongguo gudai shike gailun* 中國古代石刻概論. Beijing: Wenwu chubanshe, 1994.

Zheng Yuyu 鄭毓瑜. "Zhijian xingshi yu zhishi fenzi 直諫形式與知識分子." *Zhongguo wenzhe yanjiu jikan* 中國文哲研究集刊 16 (2000): 151–212.

Zhongguo kexueyuan kaogu yanjiusuo 中國科學院考古研究所, ed. *X i n Zhongguo de kaogu shouhuo* 新中國的考古收獲. Kaoguxue zhuankan, ser. 1, no. 6. Beijing: Wenwu chubanshe, 1961.

Zhongguo lishi bowuguan 中國歷史博物館. Beijing: Wenwu chubanshe, 1984.

Zhou li zhengyi 周禮正義. Annotated by Sun Yirang 孫詒讓. Rev. ed. Beijing: Zhonghua shuju, 1987.

Zhou li zhushu 周禮注疏. *SSJZS* ed.

Zhou Yi jijie 周易集解. Annotated by Sun Xingyan 孫星衍. Shanghai: Shanghai shudian, 1988.

Zhu Dawei 朱大渭 et al. *Wei Jin nanbeichao shehui kexue shenghuo shi* 魏晉南北朝社會科學生活史. Beijing: Zhongguo shehui kexue chubanshe, 1998.

Zhu Dexi 朱德熙. "Jingli Quluan jie 荊篱屈欒解." In *Zhu Dexi guwenzi lunji* 朱德熙古文字論集, pp. 113–114. Beijing: Zhonghua shuju, 1995.

Zhu Dexi and Li Jiahao 李家浩. "E Jun Qi jie kaoshi (bapian) 鄂君啟節考釋（八篇）." In *Zhu Dexi guwenzi lunji* 朱德熙古文字論集, pp. 189–202. Beijing: Zhonghua shuju, 1995.

Zhu Dongrui 朱東潤. "Gongyang tangu 公羊探故." In *Zhongguo wenxue lunji* 中國文學論集, pp. 169–187. Beijing: Zhonghua shuju, 1983.

Zhuangzi jishi 莊子集釋. Annotated by Guo Qingfan 郭慶藩. Beijing: Zhonghua shuju, 1985.

Zhuangzi yinde 莊子引得. Harvard-Yenching Institute Index, supplement no. 20. Beijing: Yanjing daxue tushuguan yinde biancuanchu, 1947.

Zhuzi yulei 朱子語類. Compiled by Li Jingde 黎靖德. Changsha: Yuelu shushe, 1997.

Zufferey, Nicolas. *To the Origins of Confucianism: The Ru in Pre-Qin Times and during the Early Han Dynasty*. Bern: Peter Lang, 2003.

Zürcher, Erik. "A New Look at the Earliest Chinese Buddhist Texts." In *From Benares to Beijing: Essays on Buddhism and Chinese Religion*, edited by Koichi Shinohara and Gregory Schopen, pp. 277–304. Oakville, Ontario: Mosaic, 1991.

Contributors

William G. Boltz is Professor of Classical Chinese at the University of Washington, Seattle.

K. E. Brashier is Associate Professor of Religion and Humanities at Reed College.

Mark Csikszentmihalyi is Associate Professor of Chinese and Religious Studies at the University of Wisconsin, Madison.

Lothar von Falkenhausen is Professor of Chinese Archaeology and Art History at the University of California, Los Angeles.

Joachim Gentz is Junior Professor of Religious Studies at Göttingen University.

Martin Kern is Associate Professor of Chinese Literature at Princeton University.

Michael Nylan is Professor of History at the University of California, Berkeley.

David Schaberg is Associate Professor of Chinese History at the University of California, Los Angeles.

Index

academicians, 14, 15, 17, 19–20, 43 n. 59. *See also boshi*
"Admonition on Ale" (Jiu zhen), 191 n. 89
almanacs (*rishu*), 106
Analects. See Lunyu
archives, 71, 91, 182, 200. *See also* libraries/collections of texts

bai jia yu, 157, 191 n. 89
Baishi shenjun, hymn to, 261–262
bamboo, xviii, 36; and silk xii, 6, 34, 98, 122 n. 84, 157, 227, 229, 261, 280 n. 72; strips 8, 11, 29–31, 35–36, 44 n. 69, 62–63, 65–66, 68–71, 72 n. 4, 73 n. 5, 74 n. 10, 74 n. 17, 76–77 n. 28, 150, 152–155, 161, 170, 183, 185 n. 13, 185 n. 15, 186 n. 18, 229, 232; tablets, 81. *See also* tallies, bamboo; Baoshan bamboo-strip manuscripts; Guodian, manuscripts; Shanghai Museum bamboo manuscripts; texts, excavated
Ban Gu (32–92), ix, xv, 38 n. 5, 38 n. 6, 44 n. 69, 63, 70, 77 n. 28, 157, 190 n. 83, 191 n. 89, 217, 263. *See also Hanshu*

Ban Jieyu (d. ca. 6 C.E.), 191 n. 89
banquets/feasts, 4, 15, 23, 28-29, 45 n. 102, 198–199, 212, 263
Bao Xian, 42 n. 53, 44 n. 83, 244 n. 7
Baoshan bamboo-strip manuscripts, 113, 115. *See also* "Bushi jidao jilu"
bells. *See* bronze bells
Bi Dafu-*hufu*. *See* tallies, Bi Dafu-*hufu*
Bigan, 203, 209
binomes, 167, 176; alliterative, 175; assonating, 173, 175; reduplicative, 162, 167, 169, 171, 172, 174–176, 186 n. 22, 188 n. 53; rhyming, 174–176
Biyong, 40 n. 25
bone/plastron inscriptions, viii, x–xi, xiii, 62, 72 n. 4, 100, 128, 141–143, 146 n. 36, 170, 182–183
books. *See* texts
boshi, 187 n. 30, 191 n. 89. *See also* academicians
bronze, 34, 36, 39 n. 22, 75 n. 19, 98, 102; bells, xi, xiii, xiv, xxvi n. 6, 5, 9, 36, 51, 168, 183, 242, 265, 269, 282 n. 95; casting, xviii, 75 n. 19, 99–100, 107, 282 n. 97; figures, 117 n. 5

314

Documents (Classic of). *See Shujing*

Dong Zhongshu (ca. 195–115 B.C.E.), 38 n. 5, 43 n. 69, 44 n. 70, 147 n. 53, 191 n. 89

Dongfang Shuo (ca. 161–86 B.C.E.), xxi, 191 n. 89, 200, 217, 221 n. 30, 224 n. 72, 225 n. 80

Dongguo, Master, 200

Dou Zhang, 264

drama. *See* theater/drama

Du-*hufu*. *See* tallies, Du-*hufu*

Du Bo, 142, 209

Du You (735–812), 144 n. 13

Du Yu, 82

Duan Yucai (1735–1815), 82, 162

Duke Ai of Lu (r. 494–477 B.C.E.), 199

Duke Huan of Qi (r. 685–643 B.C.E.), 220 n. 18

Duke Jian of Yan, 142

Duke Jing of Jin, 106

Duke Jing of Qi (r. 547–490 B.C.E.), 201

Duke Ling of Chen (r. 613–599 B.C.E.), 204

Duke Ling of Wei (r. 534–493 B.C.E.), 201

Duke Ping of Jin (r. 557–532 B.C.E.), 198–199, 201

Duke of Shao, 221 n. 39

Duke Wen of Jin, 224 n. 63

Duke Wen of Teng, 40 n. 29

Duke of Zhou, 221–222 n. 39

Dunhuang, 3, 7, 273

E (ancient state), 92–94, 104–105, 109–110, 120 n. 50, 120 n. 57, 121 n. 59

E Jun Qi. *See* Lord Qi of E; tallies, E Jun Qi

E Jun Zi Xi. *See* Lord Zi Xi of E

Eastern Capital. *See* Luoyang

education, 65, 204, 218, 222 n. 40, 251, 275. *See also* teaching/instruction

Emperor Ai (r. 7–1 B.C.E.), 191 n. 89, 252

Emperor An (r. 106–125), 21, 44 n. 84

Emperor Cheng (r. 33–7 B.C.E.), xxvi n. 2, 191 n. 89, 252, 278 n. 40, 283 n. 107

Emperor Gaozu (r. 202–195 B.C.E.), 9, 186 n. 19

Emperor Gengshi period (r. 23–25 C.E.), 15

Emperor Guangwu (r. 25–57), 15

Emperor Huan (r. 146–167), 42 n. 52

Emperor Jing (r. 157–141 B.C.E.), 13

Emperor Ming (r. 57–75), 15

Emperor Shun (r. 125–144), 40 n. 25, 264

Emperor Wen (r. 180–157 B.C.E.), 31, 32, 47 n. 122

Emperor Wu (r. 141–87 B.C.E.), 13–14, 20, 40 n. 23, 200, 215, 217, 252, 257, 278 n. 40

Emperor Zhao (r. 97–74 B.C.E.), 20

Empress Dowager Dou (d. 135 B.C.E.), 13

Empress Dowager Liang, 16

entertainers/jesters, xxi–xxii, 195, 200, 210, 217–218, 219 n. 3, 225 n. 74. *See also* "Guji lie-zhuan"; Jester Meng; Jester Zhan

Er Shi (second emperor of Qin, r. 209–207 B.C.E.), 200

erudites. *See boshi*

eunuchs, 42 n. 52, 48 n. 128

excavated texts. *See* texts, excavated